Authoritarianism

Authoritarianism

Constitutional Perspectives

Günter Frankenberg

Goethe University, Frankfurt am Main, Germany

Edward Elgar
PUBLISHING

Cheltenham, UK • Northampton, MA, USA

Translated from *Autoritarismus: Verfassungstheoretische Perspektiven*

Published by
Edward Elgar Publishing Limited
The Lypiatts
15 Lansdown Road
Cheltenham
Glos GL50 2JA
UK

Edward Elgar Publishing, Inc.
William Pratt House
9 Dewey Court
Northampton
Massachusetts 01060
USA

A catalogue record for this book
is available from the British Library

Library of Congress Control Number: 2020944724

This book is available electronically in the **Elgar**online
Law subject collection
http://dx.doi.org/10.4337/9781800372726

Printed on elemental chlorine free (ECF)
recycled paper containing 30% Post-Consumer Waste

ISBN 978 1 80037 271 9 (cased)
ISBN 978 1 80037 272 6 (eBook)

Printed and bound in the USA

Contents

Figures

Preface

Political authoritarianism is back. Perhaps it never went away, but was merely hiding backstage. Its proliferation – like a pandemic, one is tempted to say – is puzzling. Why do people succumb to the authoritarian temptation? What are the social and economic conditions, and the psychological preconditions or other drivers of its apparent success? Is democracy in crisis – or even dying, as some authors would have it – and playing into the hands of despots? In this book, I will not be able to answer all of these – very troubling – questions in adequate detail, let alone analyse in depth the authoritarianism that has accompanied the coronavirus pandemic. Instead, I will touch on some crucial aspects and concentrate on developing a critical analytics of authoritarianism (what are the main characteristics of autocracies?) and examining why authoritarian regimes invariably have constitutions (what do constitutions 'do' for autocracies?).

Authoritarian constitutionalism was previously discussed, in a collective effort, in a comparative study.[1] I am greatly indebted to the authors who helped me to develop my ideas, especially to co-editor Helena Alviar García, Roberto Gargarella, Duncan Kennedy, Maximilian Pichl, Norman Spaulding, Nimer Sultany and Mike Wilkinson. I must thank Klaus Günther for urging me to turn my article into a book: *Autoritarismus – Verfassungstheoretische Perspektiven*, published by Suhrkamp in 2020.[2] The translated, revised and updated version is presented here. Its production again was not a solitary undertaking, but was supported by another collective effort: thanks are due to Michele Graziadei, David Kennedy, Hans Lindahl, Giuseppe Mastruzzo, Horatia Muir Watt and Fernanda Nicola, who read and commented on some of the chapters. Fernanda Nicola, Alvaro Santos, Mahendra P. Singh, Hans Vorländer and Peer Zumbansen generously invited me to their seminars and workshops, and gave me the invaluable opportunity to 'test run' some of my ideas – and were generous in their helpful comments and criticisms. The

[1] Alviar García, H. and Frankenberg, G. (eds) (2019), *Authoritarian Constitutionalism. Comparative Analysis and Critique* (Cheltenham: Edward Elgar Publishing).

[2] Frankenberg, G. (2020), *Autoritarismus. Verfassungstheoretische Perspektiven* (Frankfurt am Main: Suhrkamp).

translation project was expedited by other colleagues and friends who kindly provided feedback and insights – in particular, Russell Miller, Gary Peller, Maximilian Pichl, Philo Tsoukala, Yvonne Tew and Uwe Volkmann.

As several times before, I am greatly indebted to my Edward Elgar team: Stephen Gutierrez generously opened the door to my manuscript; and Catherine Cumming, Fiona Todd, Katia Williford and Barbara Pretty edited it circumspectly and helped with copyright problems. Carolyn Boyle congenially read and edited the final version. Her close reading was amazing – I am very grateful!

I dedicate this book to two teachers: John Rensenbrink at Bowdoin College, Brunswick/Maine; and Hans Weber at Helmholtz-Gymnasium in Dortmund. They taught me that authority need not be authoritarian.

Introduction

> A government approaches perfection, the more it persuades, by the power of its constitution, the subjects and even the least virtuous ones to voluntarily do what the common weal may demand...[1]

Karl Marx introduced The Eighteenth Brumaire of Louis Bonaparte' with Hegel's remark that 'all great world-historic facts and personages appear, so to speak, twice'. For the sake of precision, Marx added with magisterial authority: 'the first time as tragedy, the second time as farce.'[2] Caution would advise against contradicting two eminent philosophers at the very beginning of a book. Let's settle for a few questions instead. Did the authoritarian-populist marriage of *Cinque Stelle* and *Lega* in Italy[3] (now divorced) provide the farce to the fascist tragedy written by Benito Mussolini and his black-shirt militias? And is the autocracy of Hungary's Viktor Orbán likewise the farce to Mátyás Rákosi's Stalinist tragedy?[4] Has Donald Trump evoked memories of Richard M. Nixon's tragedy of democracy? Or – almost forgotten in the 'Global North', although not in Ethiopia – was Mengistu Haile Mariam's 'Red Terror'[5] a tragedy replaying the imperial farce of Haile Selassie's massacre of peasants and pastoralists? Hardly. The victims who bear indelible scars in their minds and on their bodies would object to that framing. And they would be right.

Sultan Selim I, a devout Sunni, ruled the Osman Empire from 1512 until 1520.[6] During his reign, the cruel and heavy-handed despot disempowered

---

[1] Anonymous author (1789), *Révolutions de Paris, dédiées à la Nation*, Prudhomme, L.M. (ed) (Paris: Imprimerie des Révolutions), No 20, 21–28 November, quoted from Preuß, U.K. (1990), *Revolution, Fortschritt und Verfassung* (Berlin: Wagenbach), 12.

[2] Marx, K. (1852), 'The Eighteenth Brumaire of Louis Bonaparte', *Works of Marx & Engels*, Chapter I, www.marxists.org/archive/marx/works/1852/18th-brumaire/ch01.htm/ (last accessed 25 November 2019).

[3] See Tronconi, F. (ed) (2015), *Beppe Grillo's Five Star Movement. Organisation, Communication and Ideology* (London: Ashgate).

[4] Rákosi, first secretary general of the Communist Party, then also prime minister of Hungary, referred to himself as 'Stalin's best Hungarian student'.

[5] Tegegn, M. (2012), 'Mengistu's "Red Terror"', in: 10 *African Identities*, 249 ff.

[6] See Çıpa, H.E. (2017), *The Making of Selim: Succession, Legitimacy and Memory in the Early Modern Ottoman World* (Bloomington: Indiana University Press).

his father, had his brothers and nephews executed, fought against Shiites and Alawites and waged war against Persia. Would Marx have described this as a tragedy, since replayed as farce by Recep Tayyip Erdoğan's authoritarian sultanate? As likely as not, the Turkish president would not mind being compared to the Osman ruler. After the Turkish society had explored and accepted – or to be precise: had been forced to accept – a new post-Osman collective identity under the anything but liberal Kemal Atatürk,[7] it seems 'the State has returned to its oldest form – the shamelessly simple domination of the sabre and the cowl'.[8]

In short, one harbours scepticism towards the alluring metaphor of tragedy and farce, and has little confidence in their sequence, even if it could be reversed – allowing, for example, for the regime of Nicholas Maduro in Venezuela to be interpreted as the tragedy that has followed Hugo Chávez's farce. Those who suffer in the setting of political farce are likely to object strenuously against a naïve reading of Marx's correction of Hegel.

1. AUTHORITARIANISM: APOCALYPSE NOW?

If the twentieth century is remembered as the epoch of human rights, then it might be hoped that the breakthrough of liberal democracy would in the same way come to characterize the following century. However, both are eclipsed by dark shadows. Mass murder organized by governments, torture, deportations and other macro-crimes must be inscribed on the balance sheet of the past century.[9] Modifying Marx's famous quote, one might say that the victims of past generations weigh like a nightmare on the psyche of the living.

There is ample evidence that authoritarian regimes have been on the rise for some time; unless it is to be assumed that they have been lurking in the shadows of normality for even longer, waiting for their historical moment. The renaissance and globalization[10] of political authoritarianism[11] – indeed, 'the

---

[7] Just a few years back, the world learned about massacres committed against religious minorities in Turkey ordered by the brutal civilizer Atatürk; www.deutschlandfunk.de/minderheiten-unter-atatuerk-der-massenmord-des-tuerkischen.886.de.html?dram:article_id=323714/ (last accessed 4 December 2019).

[8] Marx (n 2), 13.

[9] Arendt, H. (1951), *The Origins of Totalitarianism* (New York: Harcourt, Brace & Co).

[10] See Heitmeyer, W. (2018), *Autoritäre Versuchungen* (Berlin: Suhrkamp), whose empirical analyses of authoritarian attitudes, movements, programmes and temptations have been invaluable for the following considerations and interpretations.

[11] Definitions and characteristics of authoritarianism are discussed in Chapters 2 and 4–7 below. See Frantz, E. (2018), *Authoritarianism: What Everyone Needs to Know* (Oxford: Oxford University Press) with further references; Brown, W., Gordon,

ascendancy of a [ubiquitous] new authoritarian international' – is reflected in the statistics. According to a study by the Bertelsmann-Foundation, the total population of autocracies increased continually from 2.3 billion in 2003 to 3.3 billion in 2017. Currently, 58 out of 128 states are governed by authoritarian regimes.[12] In contrast, democracies registered only a modest demographic increase over the same period, from 4 billion to 4.2 billion. Other research groups count more autocratic than democratic regimes and constitutions;[13] although the majority of studies suggest that most societies still come under democratic rule. A sorry comfort.

No wonder, then, that recently an apocalyptic tone has sounded. Its protagonists deduce from these frightening statistics, as per a zero-sum calculation, a democratic malaise. The discourse abounds with dramatic formulae: the 'reversal of 1989'; dangers to freedom; and the 'collapse', 'decline' or even 'death' of democracy.[14] And the scenario is indeed dramatic.

P.E. and Pensky, M. (2018), *Authoritarianism: Three Inquiries in Critical Theory* (Chicago: University of Chicago Press).

12 See the transformation index of the Bertelsmann-Foundation: www.bertelsmann-stiftung.de/de/unsere-projekte/transformationsindex-bti/ (last accessed 6 November 2018); Lührmann, A. *et al* (2017), 'Regimes in the World (RIW): A Robust Regime Type Measure Based on V-Dem', V-Dem-Institute Working Paper, 4 May 2017: ranking 97 out of 174 countries as democratic, but only 52 as 'liberal democracies; www.v-dem.net/media/filer_public/8bc/c9/8bc9f1c8-0df2-4ea4b46d-81539c791aad/v-dem_working_paper_2017_47.pdf (last accessed 7 December 2019).

13 See Ginsburg, T. and Simpser, A. (eds) (2013), *Constitutions in Authoritarian Regimes* (Cambridge: Cambridge University Press); Alviar Garcia, H. and Frankenberg, G. eds (2019), *Authoritarian Constitutionalism – Comparative Analysis and Critique* (Cheltenham: Edward Elgar Publishing), with further references.

14 See, for example, Mounk, Y. (2018), *The People vs.* Democracy: *Why Our Freedom Is in Danger and How to Save It* (Cambridge: Harvard University Press) (action is urgently needed if democracy is to be rescued); Levitsky, S. and Ziblatt, D. (2019), *How Democracies Die – And What History Reveals About Our Future* (London: Penguin) (democracy can be rescued with 'targeted' defence, if need be on its death-bed); Luce, E. (2017), *The Retreat of Western Liberalism* (New York: Abacus) (the end of Western hegemony); Snyder, T. (2018), *The Road to Unfreedom* (New York: Random House) (democracy is threatened by revolt against established political practices in the United States and the United Kingdom); Deneen, P. (2018), *Why Liberalism Failed* (New Haven: Yale University Press) (liberalism's strengths account for failures); Huq, A.Z. and Ginsburg, T. (2018), 'How to Lose a Constitutional Democracy', in: 65 *UCLA Law Review*, 13 ff and the rescue mission by the same authors: *id* (2018): *How to Save a Constitutional Democracy* (Chicago: University of Chicago Press). See also Choudry, C. (2018), 'Will Democracy Die in Darkness? Calling Autocracy by Its Name', in: Graber, M.A. *et al* (eds) *Constitutional Democracy in Crisis?* (Oxford: Oxford University Press), 571 ff.

The European Union – widely deemed to be plotting a safe course towards wealth, democracy and an almost 'perpetual peace' that Kant[15] would have appreciated – must now cope with phenomena of nationalism and political and constitutional authoritarianism. At the heart of the European Union itself, statespersons and the European Commission demonstrated little resistance to the temptations of authoritarianism during the global financial (or rather, investment banking) crisis.[16] Moreover, the ghosts of a past that it was believed had long been exorcised – nationalism, racism, xenophobia, anti-Semitism – are alive and well in many member states as movements, parties or governments that have already yielded to the authoritarian temptation. Both at Europe's centre and at the peripheries, one witnesses transitions to autocratic forms of participation and decision making, intolerance of minorities, dismantling of the media and independent courts, harassment of opposition movements and parties, and so on. The Bermuda triangle of nation, race and ethnicity[17] has become the site in which resentment organizes under the banner of identity politics, rises up against strangers and elites (in a turn generally referred to as 'populist') and promotes intolerance against all groups of society that come under the term 'minority'.

Autocrats have seized power and hijacked constitutions. Anti-democratic rhetoric and propagated illiberalism reap considerable electoral benefits – even in societies that should know better from the experiences of their own submission and liberation, and that seemed to be well on their way to sustainable democratization, such as Hungary and Poland.

Authoritarian movements and parties continually try to obtain power. In France, piqued by electoral defeat, the nationalist-chauvinist *Rassemblement National* (better known until 2018 as *Front National*) hoped that the protests of the Yellow Jackets (not gloves)[18] might help them to overthrow the Macron government and finally have power placed in their authoritarian laps. In Italy, the *Lega Nord* (then *Lega*) successfully morphed from an extremist xenophobic and nationalist movement to a no less extremist party and coalition

---

[15] Kant, I. (1982), *Perpetual Peace and Other Essays* [1795] (Indianapolis: Hackett Publishing).

[16] Gill, S. (1998), 'European Governance and New Constitutionalism: Economic and Monetary Union and Alternatives to Disciplinary Neoliberalism in Europe', in: 1 *New Political Economy*, 5 ff; Wilkinson, M. (2013), 'The Spectre of Authoritarian Liberalism: Reflections on the Constitutional Crisis of the European Union', in: 14 *German Law Journal*, 527 ff; *id* (2019), 'Authoritarian liberalism and authoritarian constitutionalism', in Alviar Garcia and Frankenberg (n 13), 317 ff.

[17] Hall, S. (2017), *The Fateful Triangle: Race Ethnicity, Nation* (Cambridge: Harvard University Press).

[18] See Marx (n 2), 12 f, referring to the ghost of the old revolution: the '*républicains en gants jaunes*'.

government partner – first Berlusconi IV and finally *Cinque Stelle*.[19] With immigration increasing and Euroscepticism rising, Britain witnessed the rise of first the 'right-wing populist' UK Independence Party and then in 2019 the Brexit Party, shaking up the two-party system at least momentarily.[20] The Sweden Democrats, with their roots in Swedish fascism, began as a white nationalist movement and remained isolated in Parliament; but in 2019, they were invited to commence negotiations with the Christian Democrats to form a coalition.[21] Likewise, other Scandinavian, Central and Eastern European countries must deal with extremist, authoritarian nationalist movements and parties – some of them already in government.

In 2016, courtesy of the country's antiquated election system, the 'majority' of US voters – or certainly the majority of those who believe that being white is important – succumbed to the authoritarian temptation and voted for Donald Trump. As president, he has since demonstrated how fast what had been assumed to be a consolidated democracy can be transformed into a semi-democratic autocracy – in particular, by deploying the rhetorical arsenal of authoritarianism. Since his victory, Trump has demonstrated how a political culture can be officially poisoned by the official normalization of racist, sexist and xenophobic language and practices, and how a president can create an atmosphere of siege.

To better understand the logic of authoritarianism, it might be preferable to disregard particularly egregious versions of despotism – such as Robert Mugabe, until recently the cruel dictator of Zimbabwe; his Sudanese colleague, Omar al-Baschir, or the Ethiopian dictator Mengistu; or the post-Soviet despot from Turkmenistan, Gurbanguly Berdymuhamedov. In the category of the bizarre fall the absolutist centre of Islamic-Wahhabite fundamentalism in Saudi Arabia and the absolutist monarchy of Brunei Darussalam. By avoiding these outlandish specimens, one can gain a better view of regimes and protagonists that mark the often less conspicuous, but no less dangerous standard of authoritarianism – the autocratic middle of the road, so to speak. Here Vladimir Putin (Russia) and Xi Jinping (China) take centre stage as global actors. However, in perusing the register of authoritarianism, one should not overlook Narendra D. Modi in India; the theocratic regime in Iran; the al-Assad clan in

---

19 Bulli, G. and Tronconi, F. (2011), 'The Lega Nord', in: Elias, A. and Tronconi, F. (eds), *From Protest to Power: Autonomist Parties and the Challenges of Representation* (Vienna: Braumüller), 51 ff.

20 See Bale, T. and Wager, A.J. (2015), 'The United Kingdom Independence Party: Insurgency or Splinter?', in: Decker, F. *et al* (eds), *Rechtspopulismus und Rechtsextremismus in Europa. Die Herausforderung der Zivilgesellschaft durch alte Ideologien und neue Medien* (Baden-Baden: Nomos, 217 ff).

21 See Widfeldt, A. (2014), *Extreme Right in Scandinavia* (London: Routledge).

Syria; Paul Kagame, president of Rwanda since 2000; Hun Sen, Cambodian prime minister for more than 30 years; Alexander Lukashenko, well into his fifth term as president of Belarus; and Viktor Orbán, who since 1998 has managed to convert Hungarian democracy into a façade for a despotic, radically nationalist regime with a xenophobic agenda. One may also want to take a look at Thailand, Bangladesh, Burundi, Pakistan, Lebanon, Turkey, Uganda, Mozambique, Malaysia, Egypt, Poland, Morocco, Vietnam and many more.

Not to forget hybrids such as the para-civilian military regime of Myanmar; and the recently elected, far-right extremist president of Brazil, Jair Bolsonaro, who makes no bones about his admiration for the military, torture and other forms of violence – like torching the rainforest, terrorizing the indigenous people and, most recently, the violence of a pandemic. After the orchestrated impeachment of former President Dilma Rousseff – who had long been persecuted by evangelical groups as an enemy of the family – on charges of breaking budgetary laws, and after the protracted lawfare against popular former President Lula, the conservative economic elites finally cleared the decks for Bolsonaro to re-establish in 2019 the dictatorship of 1964–85 as a mix of militarism and electoral democracy.[22] Meanwhile, sharp turns towards authoritarianism were also taken by erstwhile revolutionary, now despot Daniel Ortega in Nicaragua; and by Nicholas Maduro, heir of *Chavismo*, in his struggle to stay in power in Venezuela. They all will be revisited below.

2. THE CONSTITUTIONAL QUESTION

But why draft and adopt a constitution in an autocracy where repression is always an option, in the form of show trials, deportations, arrest of opposition groups, discrimination against minorities, intimidation of political adversaries and even mass murder (albeit that not all of these measures are always available to the same degree)? Do constitutions actually have any impact or are they mere paper tigers? Where constitutions are bestowed with authority, whom do they address and what purposes do they serve in an authoritarian context? Do they come with practical import or are they intended merely as empty rhetoric and window-dressing for authoritarian regimes? Together, these queries – which will be answered in the following chapters – encompass the 'constitutional question'.

---

[22] Sousa, J.J. (2019), 'Subversive, Mother, Killjoy: Sexism against Dilma Rousseff and the Social Imaginary of Brazil's Rightward Turn', in: 44 *Signs*, no 3; Leahy, J. (2015), 'What is Brazil's president Dilma Rousseff accused of?' in: *Financial Times*, 12 May; Hunter, W. and Power, T.J. (2019), 'Bolsonaro and Brazil's Illiberal Backlash', in: 30 *Journal of Democracy*, 68 ff.

Given the deep aversion of autocrats to control by parliaments and courts, by the media and, of course, by the people, as well as their dislike of democratic political risks and actionable legal obligations, one wonders why they would submit to a charter of government – albeit merely symbolical. Why bow to a founding document if constitutional constraints can ultimately be shaken off, flouted or manipulated? Why pay tribute to a constitution that has been established by the constitutive power of a previous generation? Thus, the constitutional question harks back to a theme that has been agonized over for centuries – at least since the times of the Old Testament: why would an almighty God submit to a covenant?

3. HOW TO ANSWER THE CONSTITUTIONAL QUESTION

A tentative answer to the constitutional question in autocratic settings might be that the authoritarian heart of darkness hides a paradox that combines odium and fascination. The discursive hegemony of liberalism suppresses this paradox without solving it. The radiation of liberal constitutionalism does not illuminate ambivalence, but casts a shadow over what can be neither measured nor resolved.

As political authoritarianism proliferates globally, and in some regions runs riot, it may be propitious to suspend the rehearsed perspective of liberal dominance in order to take authoritarianism – and thus authoritarian constitutionalism – seriously. Authoritarian regimes and their constitutional practices should be brought under close scrutiny and assessed from a critical distance. In this way, authoritarianism is not analysed as deviant or distorted liberalism – liberalism in deficit or liberalism's other – and thus cannibalized; but instead is treated as a phenomenon in its own right that should be submitted to analysis and critique on its own terms. The methodological challenge is 'how the deeply different can be deeply known without becoming any less different; the enormously distant enormously close without becoming any less far away'.[23]

This programme of approaching and investigating, critiquing and rejecting political authoritarianism will be embarked on primarily from the perspective of constitutional theory and practice. After this introduction, the constitutional question is posed once again, illustrated by a few historical scenes and projects (Chapter 1), without examining *why* autocrats bother with drafting or revising constitutions. It seems crucial to clarify, first, how even authoritarian

---

[23] Geertz, C. (1983), 'Found in Translation: Social History of Moral Imagination', in: *id*, *Local Knowledge: Further Essays in Interpretive Anthropology* (New York: Basic Books), 48.

regimes work the constitutional narrative as a way to perceive and shape reality. Second, I am interested in uncovering the benefits that autocrats may hope to reap from constitutions and the extent to which (if at all) they obey the grammar of authoritarianism. Third, it strikes me as crucial to explore whether and how authoritarian constitutionalism mobilizes the magical powers accredited to constitutions for instrumental and/or symbolic purposes, as did the charters of the *ancien régime* which incorporated society (as body politic), personalized monarchic rule and transformed constitutional-legal obedience into a duty that subjects owed to their king or, later, leader.[24]

This preliminary treatment of the constitutional question is followed by an attempt to clarify the complex notions and relations of power and authority, of authoritarian and totalitarian regimes (Chapter 2), so that they may inform the further study of authoritarian constitutionalism. Authoritarianism is investigated as a collective singular less for attitudes and psychic dispositions than for concepts of power, forms of governance and communication, and political technologies.

The relationship between power and authority determines the spectrum and the pathologies of political authoritarianism and its constitutional brand. If authoritarian constitutionalism is to be understood and criticized, one must maintain a distance from the liberal orthodoxy which considers authoritarian constitutions to be mere façades or shams, or 'constitutions without constitutionalism' which have nothing to contribute to the understanding of 'authentic constitutionalism' (Chapter 3). This jargon of authenticity will be confronted with the authoritarian moments of liberalism that it denies or camouflages – not to denounce liberalism or democracy, but rather to open the space for a robust analysis of functions of constitutions other than warranting rights, limiting government or separating powers – functions that autocratic systems might avail themselves of.

Chapters 4 to 7 assemble what I consider to be the crucial building blocks or modules of authoritarian constitutionalism. As a whole, they configure the essential elements that determine – in diverse combinations and specificity, depending on historical contexts, political constellations, cultural practices and economic imperatives – how political authoritarianism is moulded and constituted.

Rather common are authoritarian techniques of governing (Chapter 4). Drawing on my earlier work, I define these techniques (or political technology) as the ensemble of practices, norms and principles, forms of knowledge

---

[24] The imagined personal relationship will be discussed in Chapter 7. See also the Nazi-slogan: '*Führer befiehl! Wir folgen.*' ('Leader command! We [the people] follow!')

and skills, calculations, strategies and tactics that actors and institutions of the state bring to bear in their operations and decisions.[25] Autocratic political technology – that is, methods of exercising power – are characterized not only by 'shifting the weights' to the executive branch, but also by their *constitutional opportunism* and preference for *informal governance*. Opportunism connects claims to power with strategies to give authoritarian practices the dignity of law. Informality means that autocrats operate in the shadow of the constitution and institutions, not bound to forms and procedures, between law-rule and arbitrariness, and always shoulder to shoulder with the state of exception.

Furthermore, authoritarianism intimately connects *political power* and *private property* (Chapter 5). Autocrats (single leaders, groups, clans or political parties) tend to see and treat their political-legal powers – whether obtained by election or appointment, manipulation or usurpation – as their personal effects, which they are entitled to dispose of like proprietors. The right to centralize power, determine its termination and select a successor are all co-opted to their private domain and disposition. More often than not, they feel entitled to enrich themselves pursuant to a perverted Hobbesian 'right to everything'.[26]

Whether authoritarian regimes invite or even depend on participation, or avoid it like the plague, is a matter of controversy (Chapter 6). I intervene in these debates with a thesis that does not seek a happy medium, but rather tries to accommodate both autocrats' fear of risk and their desire to be hailed and supported by the people; their affinity for repression and their yearning for acclamation. Autocracies, I argue, permit and encourage forms of participation that are targeted at attuning rather than voting, in order to entrap the citizenry as accomplices of government without actually sharing information or granting an active part in decision making. For *complicity* to come into being, both leader and followers must be present in the public sphere – whether at rallies, parades, referendums or (manipulated) elections – or must communicate through 'authoritarian speech situations', such as national consultations, rulers' monologues or tweets.

Such participation and resulting complicity pave the way for the *cult of immediacy* celebrated by autocrats who occupy the theatrical dimension of politics and bring their charisma and propaganda to bear without institutional or media control (Chapter 7). They deactivate intermediary organizations (associations, guilds, political parties), the media and mediating institutions (parliament, courts). In this way, they replace the distanced, yet potentially

---

25 Frankenberg, G. (2014), *Political Technology and the Erosion of the Rule of Law – Normalizing the State of Exception* (Cheltenham: Edward Elgar Publishing).

26 Hobbes, T. (1958), *Leviathan* [1661] (New York/Indianapolis: Bobbs-Merrill), Chapter 14.

civilizing law-rule and democratic representation with varieties of direct communication with 'their' people aimed at inspiring delusions of *community* between leader and followers.

Chapter 8 translates these elements of authoritarian constitutionalism – the techniques of governing, the concept and practices of power, participation as complicity and the cult of immediacy – into a matrix composed of instrumental and symbolic purposes, as well as internal and external audiences. Since constitutions do not wear their purpose on their sleeves, and the motives of their drafters usually remain unknown, this matrix offers a heuristic that allows for plausible readings and attributions of authoritarian constitutions. It also generates constitutional patterns related to the political manifesto: the constitution as *manual of governance*, *tool for mobilization*, *identity card* in international relations and *showcase*.

After this manuscript had been written, the coronavirus pandemic hit the world and a global drama of human suffering began to unfold – also on the stage of authoritarianism. While a thorough analysis of how the virus spread and the destruction it caused is beyond the scope of this book, it seemed important to refer to authoritarian methods of infection prevention and to add some brief observations on the challenge of coping with a pandemic in a situation of uncertainty. Therefore, Chapter 9 discusses, albeit briefly, aspects of the coronavirus crisis as a driver of authoritarianism.

4. HOW TO READ CONSTITUTIONS

Constitutions are not hermetically closed texts, but rather opaque and porous. Therefore, they are open to interpretation. The constitutions of authoritarian regimes are no different. (Napoleon is said to have wanted them 'short and dark'.) They have interesting stories to tell if one does not dismiss them as mere poetry or façades, but takes them seriously as texts with specific purposes written for specific audiences – competing elites, the opposition, the people, international actors and so on. Very much like liberal constitutions, authoritarian charters of government should not be expected to delineate a reliable map that neatly registers the allocation of power and how it can be controlled, or the use value of rights. But while they may be deceptive,[27] they are not without merit (as the thesis of constitutions as façades or shams would have it). Authoritarian constitutions are difficult to read and interpret. Between naïve constitutional faith (routinely given to liberal constitutions) and cynical disdain (usually implied with regard to authoritarian constitutions), there is a wide area

[27] See Frankenberg, G. (2019), *Comparative Constitutional Studies – Between Magic and Deceit* (Cheltenham: Edward Elgar Publishing).

to be covered by careful differentiated analysis. This looks out for imprudent moments, camouflaged premises or marginal comments that may reveal the purposes to be pursued and the audiences to be reached through a constitution. This is the project that will be undertaken in the following chapters.

1. Constitutions

> Every country has its own constitution … ours is absolutism moderated by assassination.[1]

> Constitutions imagine a world that does not exist, and present it as if it existed.[2]

This book seeks to examine how authoritarian regimes constitute themselves, with reference to several historical projects. The purpose is to further develop the 'constitutional question': why do autocracies need a constitution? What purposes do they serve and which audiences do they aim to address? The possible motives of autocrats and plausible strategies that they may pursue will be considered in Chapter 8.

As an introduction, I outline some authoritarian constitutional moments in history. These will take readers from the horrors of a civil war battleground, through the cradle of socialism and the Soviet Union, to two casualties of colonialism and a site of nationalism, and finally to consider the constitutional question in a fascist setting.

1. SCENES AND PROJECTS[3]

1.1 A Wartime Constitution

In January 2011 the Kingdom of Silence blossomed – albeit briefly – through the 'Arab Spring'. That same year and the next, Syria suffered a 'baptism of horror'.[4] Peaceful protests against poverty, unemployment, nepotism, censor-

---

1 Comment by a Russian contemporary of the nineteenth century, quoted by Hill, C. and Menzel, J. eds. (2008), *Constitutionalism in Southeast Asia* (Singapore: Konrad-Adenauer-Stiftung), 5.

2 Bhatia, G. (2018), 'Review', in: *International Journal of Constitutional Law* 16, 1364 ff.

3 This chapter draws very much on Frankenberg, G. (2018), *Comparative Constitutional Studies – Between Magic and Deceit* (Cheltenham: Edward Elgar Publishing).

4 After 40 years of dictatorship, member of the opposition Riad al Turk saw Syria as a 'Kingdom of Silence'; see Aimee Kligman's interview with al Turk in: *Washington Examiner*, http://exm.nr/LAN26R/ (last accessed 18 July 2018). Concerning the Arab

ship and oppression were met by the despotic regime of Baschar al-Assad with violent repression, which soon escalated into a uniquely cruel war against its own people.[5] Amid bloodshed and state terrorism, the use of heavy artillery against rebel groups, the mass arrest of critics of the regime and members of the opposition, and the deportation of thousands of families, children and opponents, al-Assad indulged in a bizarre 'constitutional moment'. On 26 February 2012 he held a referendum on a new Constitution that had been drafted by a hand-picked committee pursuant to his demands. Ironically, the old Constitution of 1973 had already been superseded by a 1963 emergency law, which was temporarily lifted by al-Assad in April 2011 in an empty gesture to appease protesters. Just two days after the referendum, al-Assad issued Decree 94, publishing his Constitution of the Syrian Arab Republic.

In theory, the new Constitution promised two significant changes: divesting the ruling Ba'ath Party of its leadership role in state and society in favour of political pluralism; and limiting the president's term to two seven-year periods.[6] However, this pluralist rhetoric was undermined by Article 8, Section 4, which declared unconstitutional significant elements of plurality (notably religion) as follows: 'Carrying out any political activity or forming any political parties or groupings on the basis of religious, sectarian, tribal, regional, class-based, professional, or on discrimination based on gender, origin, race or color may not be undertaken…' It also remains to be seen whether al-Assad will indeed step down at the end of the constitutionally allowed two terms.[7]

Spring, see Manhire, T. ed. (2012), *Arab Spring. Rebellion, Revolution and a New World Order* (London: Guardian Books); Ventura, L. (2017), 'The "Arab Spring" and Orientalist Stereotypes: The Role of Orientalism in the Narration of the Revolts in the Arab World', in: 19 *Journal of Postcolonial Studies*, 282 ff.

[5] Yassin-Kassab, R. (2016), *Burning Country: Syrians in Revolution and War* (London: Pluto Press). See also the dramatic report 'from the inside of the revolution' by Samar Yazbek (2016), *The Crossing: My Journey to the Shattered Heart of Syria* (London: Ebury Press); and the relatively sober but not very convincing analysis of International Crisis Group Working to Prevent Conflict Worldwide (2011), 'Popular Protest in North Africa and the Middle East (VII): The Syrian Regime's Slow-Motion Suicide', in: *Middle East/North Africa Report,* Nr 109, 13 July.

[6] 'The leading party in the society and the state is the Socialist Arab Ba'ath Party' (Article 8 of the 1973 Constitution of Syria) now reads: 'The political system is based on the principle of political pluralism.' It takes a great deal of faith and denial to believe that these words mean what they say.

[7] Article 88: 'The President of the Republic is elected for 7 years as of the end of the term of the existing President. The President can be elected for only one more successive term.' al-Assad was elected in 2007 (97 per cent) and 2014 (88.7 per cent). Since there was no other candidate, and hence no choice, the election was strictly speaking nothing but an acclamation.

Apart from the cynical nature of these revisions, the question remains as to what might have driven al-Assad to partly reconstitute his regime – a question that will be answered in Chapter 8. One might assume that the 'useful tyrant'[8] was astute enough to recognise that constitutions were invented not only to limit government and promote unity, but also to serve as instruments of deceit. Hence, the revision might have been intended to disguise an authoritarian move: to conjure the constitutional magic of order, while the country was in fact drowning in chaos.

This strategy links al-Assad with other autocrats cut from similar cloth. They include Recep Tayyip Erdoğan, the president of Turkey, who has pursued a slightly less murderous political agenda – his assaults on the Kurds notwithstanding. Following a conspicuously amateurish attempted coup in 2016, Erdoğan deployed an autocrat's customary tools: the declaration and repeated extension of a state of exception; mass arrests of members of the public services, teachers, prosecutors and judges; intimidation; show trials and imprisonment of journalists; and a revision of the Turkish Constitution to establish a political and normative order to his liking. His plan worked: the majority of the Turkish people[9] supported Erdoğan in establishing a presidential sultanate.

1.2 Constituting Soviets

Amid violent civil war during and in the aftermath of the October Revolution, the Bolshevik cadres opted for a different strategy, following a path of constitution-making distinguished by its revolutionary rhetoric and practices. Instead of projecting a reformist agenda for the exercise and legitimation of power, they established, through their 1918 Russian Constitution, the dictatorship of the proletariat, comprising workers, soldiers and peasants, which had been propagated during the October Revolution. The Preamble sanctioned decisions already made by the revolutionary All-Russian Congress:

> The declaration of rights of the laboring and exploited people (approved by the Third All-Russian Congress of Soviets in January 1918), together with the Constitution of the Soviet Republic, approved by the fifth congress, constitutes a single fundamental law of the Russian Socialist Federated Soviet Republic.

---

[8] See the documentary *Bashar al-Assad – der nützliche Tyrann*, directed by Antoine Vitkine, www.zdf.de/dokumentation/zdfinfo-doku/bashar-al-assad-der-nuetzliche-tyrann-108.html (last accessed 12 June 2018).

[9] Newton, S. (2017), *The Constitutional Systems of the Independent Central Asian States. A Contextual Analysis* (Oxford: Bloomsbury), 55 ff; Frankenberg, G. (n 3), 46 ff.

The drafters introduced two key words – 'development' and 'transition' – and a general principle – 'socialist legality' – to contextualize rights, powers and constitutionalism in general within the overall socialist project: 'Being guided by the interests of the working class as a whole, the Russian Socialist Federated Soviet Republic deprives all individuals and groups of rights which could be utilized by them to the detriment of the socialist revolution.'[10]

While the 1918 Constitution intervened in an ongoing struggle – arguably to prejudice and seal its outcome by legitimizing the authority of the Bolsheviks – the first Constitution of the Soviet Union inaugurated the birth of the Soviet Union, uniting Russia, the Ukraine, White Russia and the Transcaucasian Republics of Armenia, Azerbaijan and Georgia. The document reiterated the official Manichaean narrative by pitting the (good) socialist camp of 'reciprocal confidence and peace, national liberty and equality, the pacific co-existence and fraternal collaboration of peoples' against the (evil) capitalistic camp, marked by 'national hate and inequality, colonial slavery and chauvinism, national oppression and massacres, brutalities and imperialistic wars'.[11]

According to the 'laws' of historical materialism, the authority of the Soviet Union (and subsequently of other socialist states) had to be reconstituted whenever political and socio-economic development reached a new stage, at least ideologically. In 1936, the Stalin Constitution expressed the new correlation of class forces and consolidated the principles of the new socialist state. In 1977, the Brezhnev Constitution documented, in strong constitutional rhetoric, a further step in the transition from socialism to communism. In its preamble, it extolled the 'developed socialist society' and declared triumphantly that the aims of the dictatorship of the proletariat had been fulfilled, and therefore – with a touch of magic – that 'the Soviet state has become the state of the whole people', and not only of the workers and peasants.

One wonders why socialist states – or rather, cadres – pursued this path and adopted the rhetoric of liberal-political constitutionalism, instead of relying on authoritative party programmes and four or five-year plans, or inventing a different vocabulary. As power maps, socialist constitutions remained inconsequential because no political status could be derived from texts that did not adequately describe the power of the people's representatives, the party and the party elites. As charters of rights (if they contained any) modelled on the liberal paradigm, they conveyed a different normative grammar insofar as rights were granted only relative to duties, placed in the shadow of the overriding interests of state and society; and, in the absence of an institutional

---

[10] 1918 Russian Constitution, Number 23; similarly Article 24 of the 1924 Constitution.

[11] 1924 Constitution of the Soviet Union, Part I.

arrangement administering justice, could not in fact be enforced. One also wonders why socialist constitutions, given their basically programmatic and symbolic nature, became obsolete rather than being revised with the political and socio-economic transition to the next historical stage: 'The constitution of a socialist state must change with the transition of society from one historical stage to another… The constitution adopted in 1936 conformed to the period of the consolidation of socialism… Naturally, the chief provisions of this constitution are now obsolete.'[12]

'Naturally'? Neither nature nor the nature of things or the semantic surface explains why socialist constitutional documents are not amenable to amendment; and some of them show that they are, and why socialist regimes tend to be (re)constituted in the first place: to revitalize their miraculous power of transformation or to affirm their authority. It seems that they obey the law of 'planned obsolescence'[13] not because they are treated like commodities, but rather because of their specific role in the context of Marxist-Leninist theory[14] – that is, to ratify a new stage of socio-economic development and a new form of authoritarian government:

> The fundamental problem of the constitution of the Russian Socialist Federated Soviet Republic involves, in view of the present transition period, the establishment of a dictatorship of the urban and rural proletariat and the poorest peasantry in the form of a powerful All-Russian soviet authority, for the purpose of abolishing the exploitation of men by men and introduction of socialism, in which there will be neither a division into classes nor a state of autocracy.[15]

1.3 Two Postcolonial Charters

The 1805 Constitution of the *Empire d'Haiti,* with a forerunner in 1801, deserves to be remembered for documenting the first successful revolt against slavery; yet it was (deliberately?) forgotten until recently.[16] After the suc-

---

[12] See Unger, A.L. (1981), *Constitutional Development in the U.S.S.R.* (London: Methuen), 174 f, quoting the programmatic statement made by Nikita S. Khrushchev, then first secretary of the Communist Party of the Soviet Union.

[13] Bulow, J. (1986), 'An Economic Theory of Planned Obsolescence', in: 101 *Quarterly Journal of Economics*, 729 ff.

[14] Newton (n 9); Frankenberg (n 3), 46 ff.

[15] 1918 Russian Constitution, Number 9.

[16] Liberated from obscurity notably by Sibylle Fischer's insightful analyses of 'postrevolutionary constitutions', Fischer, S. (2004), *Modernity Disavowed: Haiti and the Cultures of Slavery in the Age of Revolution* (Durham NC: Duke University Press), 227 and 260. For a different perspective on the silencing of the Haitian revolution, see Trouillot, M.-R. (1995), *Silencing the Past: Power and the Production of History* (Boston MA: Beacon Press).

cessful revolt against slavery and colonial occupation, the new elite not only declared 'slavery ... forever abolished', but also unmistakably – and with a racial twist – stated their commitment to an egalitarian society:

> The Citizens of Hayti are brothers at home; equality in the eyes of the law is incontestably acknowledged, and there cannot exist any titles, advantages, or privileges, other than those necessarily resulting from the consideration and reward of services rendered to liberty and independence.[17]

On the cusp what would be called 'modernity', Haiti's 'Black Jacobins' went far beyond the French revolutionaries' abolition of privilege when they introduced, under the umbrella of the modern narrative, the concept of racialized citizenship:

> [T]he 1805 Constitution contains what in today's lexicon would be called a set of radical postcolonial aspirations, a community imagined, through a legal narrative, as capable of doing something none of its models had done before: identifying both blackness and humanity as the basic signifiers of citizenship.[18]

One must bear in mind that the constitutional regime of the United States coexisted quite comfortably with slavery until the Thirteenth Amendment was passed in 1865. And even thereafter, the slaveholder logic was confirmed two years later by the infamous *Dred Scott* decision of the US Supreme Court;[19] as well as by the 1896 decision in Plessy v Ferguson,[20] which declared racial segregation constitutional and inaugurated the doctrine of 'separate but equal'. In a similar spirit, the French *Déclaration des Droits de l'Homme et du Citoyen*, in all its philosophical splendour, did not prevent France from establishing colonial regimes, treating colonized populations as a lesser species than *hommes* and attempting, through a colonial war, to undo the liberation of slaves in Haiti. In stark contrast, the authoritarian regime of Haiti dared to confront Anglo-American and in particular French constitutionalism – more

---

[17] 1805 Constitution of the *Empire d'Haiti*, Article 3.

[18] Gulick, A. (2008), 'We Are Not the People: The 1805 Haitian Constitution's Challenge to Political Legibility in the Age of Revolution', in: 78 *American Literature*, 802. See also: Garraway, D.L. (2008), '"Légitime Défense": Universalism and Nationalism in the Discourse of the Haitian Revolution', in: Garraway, D.L. ed., *The Tree of Liberty* (Charlottesville: University of Virginia Press), 63, 80.

[19] *Dred Scott v Sandford*, 60 US. 393 (1857). The majority of the Taney Court held that 'a negro, whose ancestors were imported into [the US], and sold as slaves', whether enslaved or free, could not be an American citizen and therefore had no standing to sue in federal court; and that the federal government had no power to regulate slavery in 'the federal territories acquired after the creation of the United States'.

[20] *Plessy v Ferguson*, 163 US 537 (1896).

bravely, the elites – with a rupture and consistency more radical than the 1776 and 1789 declarations,[21] as well as the 1791 Bill of Rights, by reversing the slave-master relation:

> There cannot exist slaves on this territory, servitude is therein forever abolished. All men are born, live and die free and French.[22]
>
> No whiteman of whatever nation he may be, shall put his foot on this territory with the title of master or proprietor, neither shall he in future acquire any property therein.[23]

Rather than feigning colour blindness and ignorance of the reality of slavery and racism, 'the Haitian constitutions take the opposite direction and infuse distinctions of skin color with political meaning':[24]

> All acception [*sic*] of colour among the children of one and the same family, of whom the chief magistrate is the father, being necessarily to cease, the Haytians shall hence forward be known only by the generic appellation of Blacks.[25]

It is true that the Haitian documents contain diverse accents and provisions that seem contradictory or reflect 'tensions and conflicting desires',[26] such as the combination of liberty and slavery; the affirmation of French sovereignty ('All men are born, live and die free and French'); the declaration of the Haiti Constitution of 1801 as 'part of the French Empire, but ruled under particular laws'; and the sacredness of property (1805). Yet the Haitian post-revolutionary constitutions testify to an enlightened spirit and the courage to address the problems of social reality, rather than sweeping them under the carpet. The results differ sharply from liberal individualism and modernity; but by the same token, critique 'white universalism' and defy it with both a 'black universalism' and the political-constitutional resignification of a racial category:

> Calling all Haitians, regardless of skin color, black is a gesture like calling all people, regardless of the sex, women: it both asserts egalitarian and universalist intuitions and puts them to a test by using the previously subordinated term of the opposition as the universal term.[27]

---

21 Fischer (n 16) 201.

22 Toussaint Louverture's Constitution of 1801, Article 3.

23 Dessaline's Constitution of 1805, Article 12.

24 Fischer (n 16) at 227.

25 Dessaline's Constitution of 1805, Article 14.

26 *Ibid*, at 228.

27 Fischer (n 16) at 233.

Although Haiti fulfilled the promises of the Enlightenment and the 'modern project' – and of the era of democratic revolutions – by abolishing slavery and proclaiming racial equality,[28] the mainstream of constitutional historiography and comparative constitutional law has thus far overlooked the constitutional revolution in Haiti, failing to understand what it means. In fact, it purported to write a constitution for an overwhelmingly illiterate society and to recognize former slaves as actors on the constitutional stage; braver than 'Federalists' and 'Anti-federalists' or members of *the Assemblée Nationale*, the authoritarian Haitian drafters came up with generically 'black' Madisons and Lafayettes.

Haiti's two early modern charters were short-lived, but should not be dismissed as ephemeral documents. They raise the question of why the authorities (an emperor and high-ranking military officers) constituted and reconstituted Haiti. Correcting Hegel's rather foolish ethnocentric remarks about Africa[29] (Haiti would not have been treated much better), Haiti should be taken more seriously.[30] The Constitution of 1805 certainly reflects a spirit of triumph after years of bloodshed and war, defeat and struggle against various colonial powers.[31] The constitution makers must have realized that they would provoke the French colonial power with their black universalism, a stronger stance on equality and a more radical farewell to privilege:

> There shall exist no distinction other than those based on virtue and talent, and other superiority afforded by law in the exercise of a public function. The law is the same for all whether in punishment or in protection.[32]

> The Citizens of Hayti are brothers at home; equality in the eyes of the law is incontestably acknowledged, and there cannot exist any titles, advantages, or privileges, other than those necessarily resulting from the consideration and reward of services rendered to liberty and independence.[33]

---

[28] Nesbitt, N. (2008), *Universal Emancipation: The Haitian Revolution and Radical Enlightenment* (Charlottesville: University of Virginia Press, 2008); Buck-Morss, S. (2009), *Hegel, Haiti, and Universal History* (Pittsburgh: University of Pittsburgh Press); Garraway (n 18), 63.

[29] Hegel writes in his philosophy of history (1837): 'Herewith we leave Africa, only to never mention it again later. For it is no historical part of the world, it has neither movement nor development, and what happened… in its north belongs to the Asian and European world.' Hegel, G.W.F. (2015), *Vorlesungen über die Philosophie der Geschichte*, *Werkausgabe* vol 12 (Berlin: Suhrkamp), 163.

[30] Since 1805 to the present, Haiti has had more than 20 constitutions.

[31] James, C.L.R. (1938), *The Black Jacobins: Toussaint L'Ouverture and the San Domingo Revolution* (London: Secker & Warburg Ltd).

[32] Constitution of 1801, Article 5.

[33] *Ibid*, Article 3.

They were also aware that the abolition of slavery was a thorn in the side of their slave-holding neighbours, notably the United States. Why risk their newly acquired freedom when other autocrats, and even the United States, condoned slavery?[34] One might guess that the Haitian Constitutions aimed to legitimize the new political order, to herald the postcolonial era and to mobilize Haitians – exhausted from war and destitution – to support and defend their state. All of this seemed to justify taking some risk.

1.4 Constituting the 'Burmese Way to Socialism'

Burma suffered for decades under British colonial domination; as did first Burma and then Myanmar under the brutal rule of the military. While the country can compete with Haiti when it comes to the bitter experience of colonial suppression, it is perhaps even more deeply divided along ethnic and religious lines. Ethnicity and religion triggered revolts and wrote the script for a series of coups, as well as the permanent repression of the population – especially its ethnic minorities. Since 1948 – 'released into independence', as its British colonial masters tended to absolve themselves from the atrocities of their rule – Burma has been a battleground of separatist movements, religious struggles between Buddhists and Muslims,[35] military coups and – particularly since 2007 – protests and demonstrations against the military regime.[36] What began in 1962 under General Ne Win as a lie about progress – the 'Burmese way to socialism' – continued as a series of repressive practices of several

---

[34] Napoleon reversed a 1794 decision of the French National Convention and reintroduced slavery in the French colonies. The US Founding Fathers lived quite comfortably with this institution and considered slaves as chattels and private property. Not even the 13th Amendment (1865) put an end to slavery, because the US Supreme Court confronted the Abolitionists with two infamous rulings which asserted the authoritarian and racist internal structure of the country: *Dred Scott* confirmed that slaves were private property, while *Plessy v Ferguson* 163 US 537 (1896) justified segregation through the 'separate but equal' doctrine. The African-American population had to wait until 1954 (*Brown v Board of Education*) and the Civil Rights Legislation ten years later to experience a constitutional Haiti in the United States. See Kluger, R. (1975), *Simple Justice* (New York: A. Knopf); and Plumelle-Uribe, R.A. (2004), *Weiße Barbarei. Vom Kolonialrassismus zur Rassenpolitik der Nazis,* (Zurich: Rotpunktverlag).

[35] See Smith, M. (1991), *Burma. Insurgency and the Politics of Ethnicity* (Ann Arbor: University of Michigan Press).

[36] Holliday, I., Htun Aung, M. and Joelene, D. (2015), 'Institution Building in Myanmar: The Establishment of Regional and State Assemblies', in: 55 *Asian Survey*, 641 ff. Cheesman, N. and Farrelly, N. (2018), *Conflict in Myanmar: War, Politics and Religion* (Singapore: ISEAS – Yusof Ishak Institute); https://diepresse.com/home/politik/aussenpolitik/610133/Burma_Geschichte-eines-leidenden-Landes/ (last accessed 14 June 2018).

juntas and ended in 2015 (for the time being) with the country's first elections, which were gracefully accepted by the commanders of the 'controlled democracy'.[37]

Unsurprisingly, constitutions were but a cameo in the history of military authoritarianism in Burma/Myanmar. By virtue of training and routine, which become second nature, soldiers develop an affinity for rules and standards that directly guide behaviour, like the regulations of military service. Those who are comfortable with command and control are likely to react with suspicion to constitutions that encompass spheres of values and porous principles. This is one reason why, in 1988, the Constitution was suspended by the *de facto* state of exception. Twenty years later, the regime sought to accommodate protest and discontent with a new Constitution. With military discretion and almost politeness, the preamble allocated responsibility for past mistakes and wrongdoings:

> In order to gain independence *speedily*, the Constitution was *hastily* drafted, and it was adopted by the Constituent Assembly on 24th September 1947. After attaining independence, Parliamentary Democracy System was practiced in the State in accord with the Constitution of the Union of Myanmar. However, *as democratic system could not be effectively materialized,* the new Constitution of the Socialist Republic of the Union of Myanmar was drafted based on the single party system, and after holding a National Referendum, a socialist democratic State was set up in 1974. The Constitution came to an end *because of the general situation* occurred in 1988.
>
> Later, due to public aspirations, the State Peace and Development Council made efforts to adopt multi-party democratic system and market economy in accord with the National situation …
>
> Despite *many difficulties and disturbances* encountered the National Convention, it was unwaveringly reconvened in 2004 in accord with the seven-step Roadmap adopted in 2003. As the National Convention was able to adopt the Basic Principles and Detailed Basic Principles for formulating a Constitution, it successfully concluded on 3rd September 2007.[38]

The phrase 'many difficulties and disturbances' refers to the riots across the country that accompanied the debates of the National Convention in 1993. Surprisingly, these debates ended in 2008, when the government decreed to submit the draft to the people of Myanmar in a referendum. Somewhat miraculously, 98.12 per cent of the population reportedly participated in the referendum, with a staggering 92.48 per cent voting in favour – despite the fact that the Constitution was and still is extraordinarily controversial. Critics

---

[37] Zin, M. (2016), 'Burma Votes for Change: The New Configuration of Power', in: 27 *Journal of Democracy*, 116 ff.

[38] Taken from the Preamble of the 2008 Myanmar Constitution – emphasis added.

interpreted the constitution making as a manoeuvre to pacify the nationwide protests and prevent the head of the opposition, Aung San Suu Kyi, from becoming president.[39] *Divide et impera* (divide and rule) appears to have been the strategy with regard to the protest movement.

1.5 Downslide into Authoritarianism

In Hungary, a constitutional transition from Soviet-style socialism to a project of socialism and a subsequent era of post-socialism appeared to be completed when the Hungarian Constitution of 1949 – which had been modelled on the Stalin Constitution of 1936 – was comprehensively and sustainably revised in 1972 and again in 1989. In a first and rather cautious step, the Constitution of 1972 reinvented the 'Hungarian People's Republic' as a 'socialist state', still integrated in the 'socialist world system', in which private property was guaranteed and (agricultural) cooperatives were promoted. After the Iron Curtain came down, the constitutional revision of 1989 aimed to prepare for a 'peaceful political transition to a multi-party system, parliamentary democracy, and law-rule accomplishing the social market economy', and to shed the authoritarian traditions of the past. Parties and elections were positioned as the engines of the transition, while the Constitutional Court and the commissioner for civil rights would function as godfathers. After partially reconstituting itself, Hungary seemed on the path towards stable democratization.

However, this supposed model student of transformation went on to surprise the world with a revamped Constitution in 2011 that invoked the ghosts of the darkest past.[40] The Basic Law – a text informed by the history of salvation and the Book of Revelation – became the centrepiece of the conservative revolution. The originally conservative, then increasingly radically nationalist Orbán government and the governing *Fidesz* Party celebrated the Basic Law as the end of Hungary's transition to democracy.[41] Their opponents criticized the Basic Law as a slide into a new authoritarian rule. The principle that the whole Constitution must be interpreted in accordance with the 'National Avowal' –

---

[39] Because of her marriage to British citizen Michael Aris and her two children's British citizenship, Aung San Suu Kyi was disqualified from the office of the president pursuant to Article 59 of the Constitution.

[40] See the contributions to *Sonderheft Ungarn. Aus Politik und Zeitgeschichte,* H. 29–30 (2009), www.bpb.de/apuz/31841/ungarn/ (last accessed 12 December 2019).

[41] Scheppele, K.L. (2018), 'Autocratic Legalism', in: 85 *The University of Chicago Law Review*, 545 ff, with further references. See also Lendvai, P. (2016), *Orbáns Ungarn* (Vienna: Kremayr & Scheriau).

'we, the Nation' – and the achievements of the 'historical constitution'[42] cast a pall over the allegedly democratic transition. The references to 'our king and founder, Saint Stephen I', to Christianity and to national culture do not follow the rules of a democratic grammar; even less so the restrictions on the freedom of communication for the benefit of 'the dignity of the Hungarian Nation', the freedom to study and conduct research and the independence of the judiciary for the sake of national unity: 'The right to freedom of speech may not be exercised with the aim of violating the dignity of the Hungarian nation ...'[43]

The essence of the fundamental law is captured not by the democratic republic, but by the sacred Crown, which embodies the imaginary continuity of the Hungarian constitutional state and 'the unity of the nation' (see the Preamble). According to this peculiar nationalist understanding of the Constitution, the Crown – not the monarch – functions as the symbolic agency of sovereignty and towers above all worldly powers and the political general will of the people; but not the nation.

Thus far, critiques of Orbán's constitutional package have focused on its flagrant illiberalism – notably the nationalization of the media and the dismantling of the Constitutional Court and the lower courts.[44] However, another aspect of authoritarianism should not be overlooked: the Basic Law also legitimizes repressive measures such as censorship and limitations of freedom of speech and academic freedom. Moreover, flanked by a politics of history, historical martyrdom and apocalypse, the Basic Law contains the ingredients for a new form of imaginary community based on the illusion of a collective identity underpinned by xenophobic paranoia. It is not altogether clear why Orbán committed himself to this constitutional project – which, as he well knew, would antagonize the European Commission, because it strays quite evidently from European values.[45] However, he also knew that the imposition of sanctions pursuant to Article 7 of the Treaty on European Union was unlikely, because the Commission would find it difficult to summon the necessary 'qualified majority' to pursue these cumbersome proceedings.

---

[42] Pichl, M. (2019), 'The Constitution of False Prophecies: The illiberal Transformation of Hungary', in: Alviar and Frankenberg, *Authoritarian Constitutionalism,* 240 ff; Uitz, R. (2015), 'Can you tell when an illiberal democracy is in the making?' in: 13 *I.CON*, 279 ff.

[43] 2011 Constitution, Article 9, Section 5.

[44] Editorial, 'A Test for the European Union', in: *New York Times*, 1 August 2014, www.nytimes/com/2014/08/02/opinion/a-test-for-the-european-union.html/ (last accessed 12 July 2018); for a more elaborate discussion, see Chapter 7.

[45] Treaty on European Union, Article 2.

1.6 Enabling Fascism

The infamous Enabling Act of 23 March 1933 for all intents and purposes ended the constitutional democracy of the Weimar Republic, the first German democracy that was proclaimed (twice) in 1919, and paved the way for the Nazi dictatorship.[46] It followed on the heels of the *Reichstag* Fire Decree, which had already begun to abolish civil and political freedom and transferred state powers to the executive. Technically, the Enabling Act was an amendment to the Weimar Constitution of 1919, which secured the necessary two-thirds majority after the rules of parliamentary procedure were manipulated by the Nazi president of the *Reichstag* and – more importantly – the opposition (Communists and Social-Democrats) were variously arrested, prevented from attending Parliament, intimidated and prevented from voting by the Nazi stormtroopers who illegally monitored the vote in the *Reichstag*.

Under the Act, the government – which is to say the *Führer* – acquired the authority to pass laws without parliamentary consent or control. With certain exceptions, these laws could diverge from the Constitution:

> Laws enacted by the government of the *Reich* may deviate from the constitution as long as they do not affect the institutions of the *Reichstag* and the *Reichsrat*. The rights of the President remain unaffected.[47]
>
> Laws enacted by the *Reich* Government shall be issued by the Chancellor and announced in the *Reich* Gazette.[48]

Thus, the Enabling Act 'enabled' the executive power and effectively eliminated the two chambers as active players in the German representative system – and politics. While their existence was formally protected by the Enabling Act, it will be shown later that, for all intents and purposes, the Act reduced the *Reichstag* to a mere stage for Hitler's rhetorical performances (see Chapter 7).

Hitler never trusted jurists and despised the law. Nevertheless, he made sure that his dictatorship had the appearance of legality. The Enabling Act – which has been labelled the constitution of the dictatorship – was extended twice, in 1937 and 1941. The extension was an empty formal act because the ban on all other parties assured its safe passage through the *Reichstag*. In 1942, the *Reichstag* passed a law giving Hitler the power of life and death over every citizen, effectively extending the provisions of the Enabling Act

---

[46] Officially, '*Gesetz zur Behebung der Not von Volk und Reich*'. See Evans, R. (2003), *The Coming of the Third Reich* (New York: Penguin Press); Kershaw, I. (2015), *To Hell and Back. Europe 1914 – 1949* (New York: Penguin), 142 ff and 283 ff.

[47] Enabling Act of 23 March 1933, Article 2.

[48] *Ibid*, Article 3.

for the duration of the war. But why did he bother having the Enabling Act extended three times? He had established a ruthless, murderous, totalitarian dictatorship; who was he trying to impress with this quasi-constitutional manoeuvre? What purpose could the Enabling Act serve after the *Reichsrat*, representing the states, had been abolished – notwithstanding that Article 2 of the Enabling Act protected the existence of this institution, and that the Law for the Reconstruction of the *Reich* (1934) had done away with federalism, transferring and centralizing the powers of the states in the hands of the *Reich* and leaving the *Reichsrat* impotent?

The constitutional projects of authoritarian regimes discussed here, albeit briefly, avail themselves very selectively of the conventional rhetoric and instruments of political authoritarianism. They are not very explicit about purposes and audiences. In Chapter 8, I will offer some ideas on how to deal with them more systematically.

2. CONSTITUTIONAL WORLD-MAKING

Constitutions are more than texts or projects. Some are weak; some make things happen. Their performative power is not self-executing, though. It crystallizes in the way they claim, through interpretation and application, to represent reality and contribute constructively – and not unrelated to artistic activity – to 'world-making'.[49] They notably transform a population into a 'people' as *pouvoir constituent* and agent and object of self-government. They turn a piece of land into a 'territory'; declare territory and government a 'state'; and alter a plurality of social groups and classes, organizations and individuals into a 'nation' (or another unified construct, such as a state or union).[50] They convert things we say into opinions and what we own into property. Even constitutional definitions become dogmatic or commanding.

Constitutional world-making operates with a vocabulary and abides by the rules of a grammar that cannot be unlocked and understood through reading alone: texts must rather be unpacked and interpreted. Thus, constitutions become more or less impressive *commanding* texts. The charters of autocracies, whatever their worth, are no different.

From a distance, constitutions can be recognized as performing their world-making with authority – a quality and relationship that will be explained in Chapter 3. 'Higher law' accentuates the elevated status of constitutional norms. 'Fundamental' or 'basic law' refers to the *authoritative* distribution of

---

[49] Goodman, N. (1978), *Ways of Worldmaking* (Cambridge, MA: Hackett).

[50] Constitutions lend a political-legal form to modern types of the 'society of individuals' – Elias, N. (2010), *The Society of Individuals* (Dublin: UCD Press).

rights and freedoms, distinction of social values and allocation of powers to agents and agencies of a state, union or supranational government. Beyond the juridical terminology, constitutions can be read as scripts for the resolution of basic social conflicts or instruction manuals for the operation of government.

Apart from world-making with authority, the appeal of constitutions is predicated on their versatility and their peculiar combination of magic and deceit.[51] Their versatility is brought to bear in diverse modes of application. They became a signum of modernity, regardless of fundamental laws that preceded the constitutional 'threshold era' from the end of the eighteenth century to the first decades of the nineteenth century. The Virginia Bill of Rights and the US-American Declaration of Independence started the ball rolling in 1776. The French Rights Declaration followed in 1789. Then came Haiti's Constitutions of 1801 and 1805, commencing a century of experiments – notably in Europe[52] and Latin America[53] – constituting absolutist and constitutional monarchies, presidential and parliamentary democracies, empires and republics, military regimes and despotism, centralized nation-states and federal unions, and more.

According to a conventional reading, constitutions 'lay down' the principles, institutional arrangements and procedures of authoritative decision-making with which societies seek to manage the problems of self-government and social integration. Due its transformative force, the constitutional project is therefore of interest for authoritarian regimes; even more so as these regimes – as will be shown later – cope with the contradictory nature of modern sociality and integration by shifting it towards homogenous communities of tribes, religions and cultures, and by excluding strangers and other groups they consider to be deviant or to undermine the universalization they seek to promote through the constitution.

Like any other government, autocracies have to deal with *authority* that generates and legitimizes binding decisions, as well as *integration* – that is, finding a way to bring about social cohesion.[54] For these purposes, constitu-

---

[51] For a more detailed discussion, see Frankenberg (n 3), Ch 1.

[52] See Frankenberg (n 3), 156 ff.

[53] From 1810 until 2015, 195 constitutions were counted among 18 Latin American countries; Negretto, G. and Couso, J. (2018), 'Constitution-Building Processes in Latin America', Discussion Paper 3 (Stockholm: International IDEA); Gargarella, R. (2013), *Latin American Constitutionalism 1810–2010. The Engine Room of the Constitution* (Oxford: Oxford University Press).

[54] Frankenberg, G. (2003), *Autorität und Integration* (Frankfurt am Main: Suhrkamp). See, for instance, Constitution of Malaysia, Number 160B: 'Where this Constitution has been translated into the national language, the Yang di-Pertuan Agong may prescribe such national language text to be authoritative, and thereafter if there is any conflict or discrepancy between such national language text and the English language text of this Constitution, the national language text shall prevail over the English language text.'

tions also come in handy for authoritarian regimes. Because of their status as supreme or higher law, situated at the top of the legal hierarchy, they claim higher authority[55] for the institutions of autocracies and protect them from easy revision. To this effect, Article V of the US Constitution originally protected slave-owners and traders from any law that would attempt to curtail the importation of slaves. By the same token, the dual role of the king of Morocco as monarch and spiritual ruler is constitutionally sacrosanct.[56]

After the threshold era, the constitution flourished and proliferated as the globally accepted model for societies to distinguish their political order as monarchic, republican or democratic, liberal or social, based on the rule of law or on the recognition of human rights. Based on their constitutions, states sought access to regional or international organizations, such as the Council of Europe, the Organization of African Unity and the United Nations. It is plausible to assume that autocrats exploit the authority of constitutions for their political world-making, however abhorrent it may be. It will be shown that authoritarian constitutionalism very selectively draws on the arsenal of liberal and democratic constitutionalism, privileging the archetype of the political manifesto, focusing on values and fabricating an imaginary community.

3. BETWEEN MAGIC AND DECEIT

For more than 200 years, constitutional projects have oscillated between the attribution of special powers – which I call 'magical powers' or simply 'magic' – and the fabrication of false facts, such as the inaccurate representation of power.[57] For just as long, regimes of all kinds – especially authoritarian governments – have taken advantage of constitutional enchantment and pretence. The magic that should be inherent in constitutions reveals itself in different forms and abstraction. On the one hand, as mentioned above, it transforms individuals into bearers of rights and, by contract or law, populations of a territory into members of imagined communities ('people'). On the other hand, rule is magically turned into a text. The nation is an imaginary community that one believes to be both sovereign and inherently limited. According to

---

[55] Kelsen, H. (1945), *General Theory of Law and the State* (Cambridge: Harvard University Press).

[56] 'The King, Commander of the Faithful [Amir Al Mouminine], sees to the respect for Islam. He is the Guarantor of the free exercise of beliefs [cultes]. He presides over the Superior Council of the Ulema [Conseil superieur des Oulema], charged with the study of questions that He submits to it' (Article 47 of the 2011 Constitution of the Kingdom of Morocco).

[57] For a more elaborate discussion of magic and deceit, see Frankenberg (n 3), especially Ch 1.

Benedict Anderson, it is imaginary because the members of even the smallest nation usually neither know nor meet nor even hear from most of the other members; though in the imaginations of all, the notion of their connectedness exists and is kept alive. Communities differ not in their authenticity or falsity, but in the style and modality in which they are presented.[58]

The style of that imagination was and is characterized by the constitutional vocabulary: declarations of rights, proclamations of independence or complete constitutions. By sleight of hand, these texts – their rhetoric, supported by rituals and procedures – convert personal rule into the modern, abstract idea of governing (see Figure 1.1): the 'government of laws and not of men'.[59] The magic makes power disappear, depersonalizes rule and transforms the personal duty of loyalty of the ruled to the ruler into abstract legal obedience based on external behaviour: the constitution as another Wizard of Oz.

It was mentioned previously that constitutional speech acts – such as enshrining rights catalogues or values, declaring the people sovereign or turning to history – are performative acts. They communicate ideas (popular sovereignty or democratic dictatorship, equal freedom or liberation from slavery); they open up new horizons (constitutional monarchy or democratic dictatorship). They also initiate events, such as referenda, elections or states of emergency. It is therefore not inappropriate to say that the people do not declare or constitute *themselves*, but are rather constituted by the constitution, empirically by the constitutional elites, at the moment of the declaration.[60]

Constitutional magic works depending on how norms, ideology, myths and the symbolic dimension in general are brought into play. Subsequently, it seems, bills of rights, judicial decisions, doctrines, conventions, even unwritten constitutions, formulas such as 'king/queen-in-Parliament' and concepts such as constitutional state or constitutional democracy participate in the aura of the magical in different ways (for example, see Figure 1.2).

This aura, of course, is ultimately a deception or illusion. Common examples include the mantra of US constitutionalism that the Constitution is colour-blind; or the counter-mantra of the Haitian Constitution (1805); or the Syrian despot's attempt to conjure a constitutional moment during his merciless war against his own people. With borrowings from their holy scriptures,

---

[58] Anderson, B. (1983), *Imagined Communities. Reflections on the Origin and Spread of Nationalism* (London: Verso).

[59] Constitution of Massachusetts, Part I, Article XXX. See Franz Neumann (1980), *Die Herrschaft des Gesetzes*, (Frankfurt am Main: Suhrkamp).

[60] See Derrida, J. (2002), 'Declarations of Independence', in: *id*, *Negotiations: Interventions and Interviews, 1971–2001* (Stanford: Stanford University Press), 46 ff.; and de Ville, J. (2008), 'Sovereignty without Sovereignty: Derrida's Declarations of Independence', in: 19 *Law and Critique*, 87 ff.

Source: Bibliothèque Nationale de France, Paris. https://gallica.bnf.fr/ark:/12148/btv1b6954300h.r=le%20roi%20et%20la%20charte?rk=42918;4/ (last accessed 7 March 2019). I thank Daniel Schulz for directing my attention to this print. See Schulz, D. (2018), '*Verfassungsbilder: Text und Körper in der Ikonographie des demokratischen Verfassungsstaates*', in: 46 *Leviathan*, 71 ff.

Figure 1.1 Transforming rule into text – Le Roi et la Charte

the Soviet cadres enthroned and legitimized themselves owing to their superior knowledge as executors of historical laws of socio-economic progression and political development – as per socialist legality. The wealthy elites of the founding states of the United States elegantly but quite authoritatively translated their particular economic interests and demands towards the absent people, by proxy, into the rhetoric of universal guarantees.

There are other, less well-known references to the belief in the constitutional spell and the deception hidden under the (semantic) surface or in the background. Even under Japanese occupation, the 1943 Constitution of the Philippines called on the support of divine providence and – perhaps invigorated thereby – proclaimed its independence. In a moment of exuberance, a Chinese observer of the Japan-Russian War ultimately attributed the victory of the imperial military regime of Japan to its constitution. The power of

Note: © Janina Focke, photographer, reproduced with kind permission.
Source: Novastan.org, www.novastan.org/de/kirgistan/kirgistan-amtseinfuhrung-von-sooronbaj-dscheenbekow/ (last accessed 14 December 2019).

Figure 1.2 A magic moment – soldiers of Kyrgyzstan bring the constitution to the inauguration ceremony, 24 November 2017

a constitution, according to one historian, 'equals the power of one million soldiers'.[61] Magic.

These examples indicate that the study of constitutions – of *all* constitutions – should equip itself with realism and combine it with a critical approach. For what appears to be linguistic magic could soon be lost in the thicket of ideology, myth, strategy or empty talk. When dealing with the charters of autocracies, realism and sobriety are particularly in demand; but they are also more easily invoked than practised. Like all constitutions, the authoritarian ones are overloaded with narratives and ideology. They tell founding myths, which one might not readily believe; refer back to experiences that reflect only a segment of history; contain political visions and fears; offer an interpretative grid for the interpretation of reality recorded with interest; and ultimately establish a framework of legality of uncertain strength and substance.

[61] Wu, J. (2005), *Studien zur Rechtsphilosophie* (Beijing: Qinghua University Press).

Neither an exact description of the world we live in nor a diagram of the actual functioning of political institutions can be expected from constitutions. In this respect, the term 'operating manual of the state' has not only a polemical but also an ironic meaning. Above all, the centres of power are not accurately localized in any constitution; and notably liberal constitutions remain silent about the power of private property. Constitutions should therefore be read not as blueprints, but preferably as narratives or, contingent on their fuzziness, *aspirational* texts that point to the future and indicate what societies or their elites have in mind – for example, Cuba's determination 'never to return to capitalism'; Rwanda's commitment to 'prevent and punish the crime of genocide'; Pakistan's 'unrelenting struggle against oppression and tyranny'; or Belarus's defence of its 'independence and territorial integrity'.

At the same time, constitutional documents may provide clues as to how societies and their elites or leaders want to manage the government's business – or try to hide their interests, intentions and stratagems. Examples include the following

> [N]ever again be struck by the horrors of war through the actions of the government …[62]

> In the coming years, the fundamental task of the nation is to concentrate its forces on socialist modernization. Under the leadership of the Chinese Communist Party and the guidance of Marxism-Leninism and Mao Zedong's thinking, the Chinese people of all nationalities are following the socialist path …[63]

While authoritarian regimes can be expected to assume and not discuss the (constitutional) legitimacy of their power, they generously invoke some kind of community to provide individuals and groups with the phantasm of a cohesive collective. There are different options to proceed down this path of magical transformation: a 'more perfect union'[64] and 'nation'[65] appear to have been evoked as standard communities.[66] While authoritarian regimes adopt the common rhetoric ('people', 'nation', 'republic', 'union'), on closer scrutiny their constitutions shift the emphasis from the (ritually affirmed) rights of the individual to the privileged interests of the community. The Chinese Constitution conjures up the 'Chinese people of all nationalities'. Hungary's Basic Law celebrates the 'intellectual and spiritual unity' of the nationalities that 'live with us', thus revealing the beginnings of a strategy of repelling

62 1947 Constitution of Japan.
63 1982 Constitution of the People's Republic of China, Preamble.
64 1787 Federal Constitution of the United States.
65 For example, 1789 French Constitution and 1853 Argentine Constitution.
66 Echoed by the 'ever closer union of the peoples of Europe' (EU Treaty 1992).

refugees and migrants. Indonesia's Constitution affirms 'faith in the One and Only God, just and civilized humanity, Indonesia's unity and democratic life'. The Iranian Constitution (1979/1989) sites the God-fearing people in the cross-border, religiously founded *Ummah* – the community of all Muslims. North Korea transforms the 'People's Republic' into the 'socialist fatherland'. So far, so innocent or symbolic.

The next step, however, treats the demands of the community with partiality. Subtly and deceitfully, the Chinese Constitution distinguishes 'sacred public property' from citizens' 'lawful property' (Article 13), and combines every citizen's enjoyment of rights with obligatory legal-constitutional duties (Article 33). Iran's Constitution denies individuals and groups 'the right to infringe in the slightest way upon the political, cultural, economic, and military independence or the territorial integrity of Iran under the pretext of exercising freedom' (Article 9). The North Korean Constitution fosters 'a world outlook centered on people' (Article 3) and a 'people-centered (social) system under which the working people are the masters of everything and everything in society serves them' (Article 8). In consequence 'the rights and duties of citizens are based on the collectivist principle: "One for all and all for one"' (Article 63). More cautiously, the Hungarian Constitution proclaims in its Preamble: 'We hold that individual freedom can only be complete in cooperation with others.'

How can one take constitutions seriously without being tricked by the motives and strategies of autocrats that inform them? How can attempts to harness the magic of constitutions be distinguished from outright deceit? It seems evident that a mere examination of constitutional texts is not sufficient; this must be complemented by a contextual analysis. Nonetheless, one begins with the text itself. Whether written in good faith or in bad faith, the constitutions of authoritarian regimes are related to their context and examined, as far as possible, at the levels of regime and rhetoric. Taking these texts seriously requires, first, a conceptual clarification of authority and authoritarianism. In order to avoid dismissing the constitutions of authoritarian regimes merely as deviations from the constitutional ideal of liberalism, attention then turns to authoritarian elements of liberal constitutional theory and practice.

4. BASIC CONSTITUTIONAL PATTERNS

The diversity of constitutions can be captured in four archetypes that allow for numerous hybrids: constitution as manifesto, contract, statute (higher law) and programme or plan. Needless to say, these archetypes or dominant patterns characterize only the basic structure of constitutions. They have a different use value in authoritarian settings.

The *contractual* archetype functions as a real pact of allegiance among sovereign princes (eg, the 1871 Constitution of the German Empire), a treaty of the union of sovereign states forming a federation (eg, the original 1787 US Constitution without the Bill of Rights; the Federation of Malaysia), a supranational confederation (eg, the Commonwealth) or a similar interconnection of states (the European Union). The constitutional contract structures the *pouvoir constituant* as an internal relationship between discrete contractual parties, which are usually signatories ('We the Undersigned') representing the members of the union, federation or confederation. As regards their content, constitutional contracts focus on organizing institutions and allocating powers. If demarcating territory and borders is problematic, these become constitutional issues – in particular, in partitioned and internally fragmented countries.[67]

When constitutions result from revolutionary struggles, political liberation movements or other social processes, they often do so in the style and wording of a *political manifesto.* Manifestos come across as ceremonial, apodictic, unilateral declarations that contain generally accepted messages about historical experience, political vision and the actors' intentions. The form suggests evidence, the content truth – such as the classic introduction to Virginia Bill of Rights in its first article:

> That all men are by nature equally free and independent, and have certain inherent rights, of which, when they enter into a state of society, they cannot, by any compact, deprive or divest their posterity; namely, the enjoyment of life and liberty, with the means of acquiring and possessing property, and pursuing and obtaining happiness and safety.

It is typical of manifestos that (in most cases, self-declared) representatives *declare* and *proclaim* (rather than explain) in the name of a collective – preferably the nation; some invoke the world – what historical truth, theoretical insight[68] or simple necessity commands. This means that manifestos are moulded by their authoritarian style:

> We, therefore, the *Representatives* of the United States of America, in General Congress, Assembled, appealing to the Supreme Judge of the world for the rectitude

[67] For further details, see Frankenberg (n 3), 223 ff.

[68] 'Under the leadership of the Communist Party of China and the guidance of Marxism-Leninism, Mao Zedong Thought, Deng Xiaoping Theory and the important Theory of "Three Represents", the Chinese people of all nationalities will continue to adhere to the people's democratic dictatorship, follow the socialist road...' – 1982 Constitution of the People's Republic of China, Preamble. North Korea trusts the 'genial' theoretician Kim Il-sung (1972/2016 Constitution).

> of our intentions, do, *in the Name, and by Authority of the good People of these Colonies*, solemnly publish and *declare* ... [69]
>
> I will cease to exist before I yield to a connection on such terms as the British Parliament propose; and in this, I think *I speak the sentiments of America.*[70]

Compared to other constitutional charters, the manifesto remains rudimentary; addresses common goals and values, consented rights and principles; but abstains from making concrete statements or laying down rules concerning the organization of government. In contrast to negotiated contracts of more or less equal partners, the unilateral, top-down speech acts, references to necessity and history as well as value paternalism are likely to appeal to constitutional elites of authoritarian systems:

> We are proud that our king Saint Stephen built the Hungarian State on solid ground and made our country a part of Christian Europe one thousand years ago...
>
> We honour the achievements of our historical constitution and we honor the Holy Crown, which embodies the constitutional continuity of Hungary's statehood and the unity of the nation.[71]

In the neighbourhood of the political manifesto resides the constitution as a *plan* or *programme* of socio-economic development. Real existing socialism developed this archetype to perfection as a kind of five-year plan. Under the guidance of historical and dialectical materialism, the socialist cadres translate the laws of scientific socialism and the necessities of a planned economy into constitutional documents with a limited lifespan.[72] Their accessory connection with ideological parameters and the (officially determined) stages of socio-economic and political development submit programme/plan constitutions to frequent revisions, which document, for example, the transition from 'dictatorship of the proletariat' to 'people's democracy', then 'socialist democracy' and finally 'communist democracy'.

The *coded constitution* or constitution as a statute of higher law represents the most complete or comprehensive pattern, as will be discussed below. It has proliferated worldwide and may be considered superior to the other

---

[69] *A Declaration by the Representatives of the United States of America*, 4 July 1776, National Archives of the United States, www.archives.gov/founding-docs/ (last accessed 12 December 2019).

[70] Thomas Jefferson [1775], quote from Hazelton, J. (1970), *The Declaration of Independence. Its History* (New York: Da Capo Press), 19 – emphasis added.

[71] 2011/2016 Hungarian Constitution, Preamble.

[72] See Frankenberg (n 3), 46 ff; and Newton, S. (2017), *The Constitutional Systems of the Independent Central Asian States: A Contextual Analysis* (London: Hart Publishing).

archetypes, as it can incorporate contractual, manifesto and programmatic elements within its design.[73] Though the coded constitution, with its four modules (see below), is an instrument of liberal constitutionalism, it has been widely adopted by authoritarian regimes. Nevertheless, this adoption must be analysed very carefully to make allowance for the logic of the diverse models and practices of constitutionalism.

5. READING AUTHORITARIAN CONSTITUTIONS

Constitutions, including those of autocracies, tend to follow a similar structural design, unless they are single-purpose declarations or resolutions. In general, they are deemed (fairly) complete if they are drafted to contain the basic principles and rules for the solution of the essential problems of life in society or in a supranational environment. However, even if the structure and the outward appearance – the textual surface, so to say – are alike, it does not make for an interesting argument to maintain that authoritarian constitutions are not like liberal charters because they do not mean what they say. The standard proof is always freedom of speech. While this may be true, and in many cases it is, a more interesting approach could be to consider *what else* they could mean. To introduce this avenue of investigation, I will examine the basic structure first, in order to discover the spaces and gaps where authoritarianism could creep in. Later, having distinguished the constitution's special features, I hope it will be easier to explain the basic elements – such as rights, values/duties, organization of government and meta-rules that refer to its amendment, review and validity – and how they are modified in authoritarian constitutions.

Most constitutions follow a basic design that is composed of four elements. First, catalogues of *rights*, supported by rule of law principles and procedures, relate to questions of justice. Globally, one registers a variety of answers. Authoritarian regimes may not appreciate rights and procedures because they are intended to limit government. Therefore, it is instructive to look for clauses that confine their scope or that neutralize their normative use value. Constitutions are not always as frank about this as was the 1918 Constitution of the Federated Socialist Republic of Russia: 'Being guided by the interests of the working class as a whole, the Russian Socialist Federated Soviet Republic

73 Preambles tend to follow the style not only of manifestos, but also of constitutional norms that have the character of confessions, such as the Preamble and Article D of the Hungarian Constitution. Programmes that must be implemented by the legislature come in the guise of constitutional mandates or goals, such as the protection of the environment or affirmative action policies.

deprives all individuals and groups of rights which could be utilized by them to the detriment of the socialist revolution.'[74]

In a rather long-winded manner, the Thai Constitution goes about limiting rights and freedoms:

> Any right or liberty stipulated by the Constitution to be as provided by law, or to be in accordance with the rules and procedures prescribed by law, can be exercised by a person or community, despite the absence of such law, in accordance with the intent of the Constitution.[75]

More often, rights are adapted to autocratic purposes by doctrinal schemes, 'concretized' by laws or merely set aside in state practice.

The second element addresses problems of how to promote the common weal. The most popular constitutional mechanisms to achieve this goal are *values* and corresponding *duties.* At times, these are turned into constitutional mandates that address the law-makers or the executive, to protect the natural environment or certain vulnerable social groups. Autocracies are likely to dwell on this module because, by definition, values and duties must be enforced from above. Hence, they come with a hard-coded, authoritarian tendency. Values can do almost everything because they are highly indeterminate and lend themselves to a variety of implementation purposes. Besides, values and duties make crucial contributions to the transformative agendas that governments may pursue. Furthermore, they can be defined to ensure loyalty or mobilize for a collective project (eg, socialism, nationalism), or to further a collective identity or illusory community.[76] Unsurprisingly, authoritarian constitutions have a penchant for values and duties, such as 'national solidarity' (Turkey), 'strength, fidelity and hope' (Hungary), 'equality according to the Sharia' (Saudi Arabia), 'freedom, justice, fraternity and concord'[77] (Tanzania), and 'the well-being and prosperity of Russia'. Romania declares 'loyalty to the country… a sacred duty'.

The third, and often the predominant,[78] element comprises provisions covering the 'constitution of politics' – that is, the organization of government, the party system, elections and so on. This element is likely to be of special interest to autocracies, as long as it meets their increased demand for order. Generally,

---

[74] 1918 Constitution of the Federated Socialist Republic of Russia, Article 2, Number 23.

[75] 2017 Constitution of the Kingdom of Thailand, Section 25.

[76] These aspects of authoritarianism will be discussed later (see Chapter 7).

[77] The word 'concord' suggests that it may be difficult to successfully integrate the 125 ethnic groups and 120 languages spoken.

[78] Notably of the US Constitution of 1787, to which the Bill of Rights was added three years later.

the 'organization of politics' reflects historical experience, political wisdom and statecraft. It converts political visions and anxieties, strategies and plans into the construction of institutions, the allocation of competences, mechanisms of control and procedures for the appointment of decision-makers. The constitutional organization of autocracies is inclined to depend on the basic structure (eg, personal regime, military junta, one-party system) and also the need to camouflage authoritarianism in the context of a democratic environment – for example, as an electoral democracy or a competitive authoritarian system.

The fourth element concerns questions of constitutional validity and addresses the amendment, interpretation, review and protection of constitutions. These seem to be rather technical matters, but they are more than that: as meta-rules, they determine the self-reflexivity and modernity of constitutions. They make sure that constitutions generate their legitimacy on their own terms by marking the people as sovereign and tying any modification or revision to a decision of the sovereign, its representatives or institutions established by the sovereign (constitutional courts). In all probability, authoritarian governments can be expected to change those terms and tap transcendental sources of legitimacy, such as tradition or religion. Thus, Hungary invoked 'our king Saint Stephen [who] built the Hungarian State on solid ground and made our country a part of Christian Europe one thousand years ago'.[79] Turkey cited 'Atatürk, the immortal leader and the unrivalled hero, and his reforms and principles as crown witness of constitutionalism'.[80] Syria's draft Constitution of 2017 refers to 'the responsibility before the past, present and future generations'.

Constitutional patterns and construction elements should not be overrated in terms of what they achieve in the context of a democratic or authoritarian regime. They might clarify the view of the *possible* strategies, intentions and expectations of constitutional elites – no more and no less. It does not make sense to read constitutions of autocracies as charters of rights, however. On the whole, they are likely to be authority 'sensitive' – that is, preoccupied with the establishment of order and the allocation of powers, and interested in guaranteeing rights that would interfere with government. It is instructive to enquire into their mechanisms which defuse the normative force of rights and overwhelm them with common values and duties that privilege the demands of the collective (people) or government.[81] It is also illuminating to explore how political authoritarianism uses constitutions to celebrate and

---

[79] 2011 Hungarian Constitution.

[80] 1982/2017 Turkish Constitution.

[81] For example, the 1992/2013 Vietnam Constitution: 'Human rights and citizens' rights shall only be restricted in imperative circumstances for the reasons of national defence, national security, social order and security, social morality, and the health of

legitimize authority: no presidential inauguration does not at least pretend to follow the constitutional script! Figure 1.2 shows how President Jeenbekov of Kyrgyzstan is 'offered', as it were, the Constitution. And as will be shown later, Hugo Chávez's team in Venezuela went out of its way to comply with the constitutional swearing-in of the new president – in his absence.

the community' (Article 14); 'Citizens' rights are inseparable from citizens' duties' (Article 15); 'The citizen must show loyalty to his Fatherland' (Article 44).

2. Authority/power

The authoritarian character is able to see the world only in the modes of emergency and state of exception. This perspective empowers him to all the measures that lead him step by step out of the framework of humanism and the Enlightenment. There is a revolt not against, but in the name of authority.[1]

1. AUTHORITY AND POWER

Authority and power are related to each other. However, the exact nature of this relationship is controversial. How can these concepts be understood?[2] What is the basis of their relationship? While the sciences (in particular, of politics and law) can be of some help in considering these questions, they are ultimately of limited utility. The sciences do not serve their readership with unambiguous terms or solidly proven insights. As regards power, we learn, among other things, that it is basically a matter of appearance; that it reveals itself in the ability to impose one's own will on others; that it consists of the management of disappointments, the correct handling of 'barons'[3] or the ability to create or destroy something – for example, an order, a constitutional court or a set of institutions.[4] According to Hannah Arendt, power 'springs from the human ability not only to act or do something, but to unite with *others* and to act in accordance with them' by communicating.[5] Max Weber defined the essence of

---

1 Weiß, V. (2017), *Die autoritäre Revolte. Die Neue Rechte und der Untergang des Abendlandes* (Stuttgart: Klett-Cotta), 265 – a very informative study concerning the authoritarian-nationalist networks in Germany.

2 Allen, A. (2016), 'Power', in: *Stanford Encyclopedia of Philosophy*, with a discussion of the main concepts of power.

3 Finer, S.E. (1997), *The History of Government*, vols 1–3 (Oxford: Oxford University Press) suggests that the power of the king depends on the disposition of his barons to implement royal decisions. They must be convinced to follow the king with enthusiasm (the best result), to accept his orders (the second best result, and according to Max Weber sufficient) or at least not to resist them.

4 See Foucault, M. (1977), *Discipline and Punish: The Birth of the Prison* (New York: Vintage); see also Rudolph, E. (2017), *Wege der Macht* (Weilerswist, Velbrück). *McCullough v Maryland*, 17 US 316 (1819) refers to the destructive power of taxation.

5 See Habermas, J. (1994), 'Hannah Arendt's Communication Concept of Power', in: Hinchman, L.P. and Hinchman, S.K. (eds), *Hannah Arendt. Critical Essays* (New

power as the 'probability that one actor within a social relationship will be in a position to carry out his own will despite resistance'.[6] By contrast, sociologist Niklas Luhmann suggested that power derives from neither acting in concert nor imposing one's will: he laconically states that power rather belongs to those who can wait.

Many theoretical paths lead to power. And power follows a variety of paths.[7] Depending on the theoretical perspective, power is a phenomenon of will, language or violence. Whether power is deliberate, communicative or tangible, it is always dependent on authority to determine its practice. More precisely, power takes its bearings from the authority attributed to the ruler; the authoritative way in which it is exercised; the authority of the purpose it serves; and the reactions of those who enter into and sustain a relationship with it – whether obedience, allegiance, acquiescence, consent or endorsement. If one concentrates only on this last aspect, like the philosopher Stein Ringen, then authority depends on the willingness of others to listen, to be persuaded and ultimately to grant it to the party seeking to exercise it:

> No governor has any other authority than that which others see in him. He has the authority he is able to extract from those he wants to lead and which they are willing to award him. Authority enables governors to get others to do for them, but at the same time the governor is at the mercy of those same others for the authority he needs in order to lead. Authority, then, although appearing to belong to the governor, is really a gift from those he wants to exercise authority over. The ultimate power of others is their ability to deny the governor the authority he needs to be able to affect them.[8]

From these conditions to effectively exercise power, it may be concluded that power consists in the ability to produce a normative order[9] in which binding decisions are made. In addition to a general instruction, the binding character of an order and of norms also presupposes that they can be justified to avoid violence and weapons being ennobled as 'arguments'. Thus, state practice and techniques of governing regularly derive their entitlement to exercise power

---

York: SUNY Press); Paretti, G. (2017), 'Arendt on Power and Violence', in: Baehr, P. and Walsh, P. (eds), *The Anthem Companion to Hannah Arendt* (New York: Anthem Press), Ch. 8.

6 Weber, M. (1978), *Economy and Society* (Berkeley: University of California Press), Chapters 1 and 9.

7 Rudolph (n 4).

8 Ringen, S. (2011), 'It's about Authority, Stupid! Having Power is Not Enough to Get Things Done', in: 133 *WZB-Mitteilungen*, 7ff; and id (2008), 'Moving Houses', in: *The Times Literary Supplement*, 4 April, 10 f.

9 Or to change or destroy it. Regarding the normative order of power: Raz, J. (2009), *The Authority of Law* (Oxford: Clarendon Press), 124 ff.

from legitimate – that is, somehow convincingly justified or reasoned – authority,[10] based on the ruler's inauguration and the acquiescence of the ruled.

1.1 Basic Patterns of Authority

Hence, authority establishes a dual relationship between those in power and those who are subject to its exercise. Karl Marx held that a person is 'only king because other people behave towards him as subjects. Conversely, they believe that they are subjects because he is king'.[11] This relationship works if authority is either believed or, in violent or threatening contexts, feared. It is not authority that determines the relationship; rather, the relationship ultimately determines what is considered as authority.

In political and constitutional contexts, authority assumes the basic forms of father, master/lord, leader and judge. These basic constellations of authority are complemented by numerous hybrid combinations that do not fully correspond to any one of them. This also applies to the temporal modalities that Alexandre Kojève linked to these basic forms: father/past, master/present, leader/future and judge/eternity. In authoritarian regimes, leadership regularly pushes itself to the foreground, at times through its references to the future. Bernhard von Bülow, then foreign minister of the German Empire, revealed Prussia-Germany's imperialist foreign policy designs in a *Reichstag* debate on 6 December 1897 when he stated: 'We wish to throw no one into the shade, but we also want our own place in the sun.'[12] In 1933 Adolf Hitler declared in his first radio address: 'Now, German People, give us the time of four years, and then try and judge us.'[13] One might argue that the promise of 'blooming landscapes in East Germany'[14] made in 1990 by former Chancellor Helmut Kohl (against his better judgement, carried away by the historical moment or just carelessly – who knows?) was more original than what von Bülow and

---

[10] From the vast library of authority, see only Marcuse, H. (2007), *A Study on Authority* (London: Verso); Arendt, H. (1954), *Between Past and Future* (New York: Viking) ('What is Authority?'); Kojève, A. (2014), *The Notion of Authority. A Brief Presentation* (London: Verso) (commenting on post-revolutionary Russia); Raz, J. (2009), *Between Authority and Interpretation. On the Theory of Law and Practical Reason* (Oxford: Oxford University Press).

[11] Marx, K. and Engels, F. (1983), '*Das Kapital*' in: *Marx-Engels-Werke* vol 23 (Berlin: Dietz-Verlag), 72 (fn).

[12] Penzler, J. (1907), *Fürst Bülows Reden nebst urkundlichen Beiträgen zu seiner Politik* vol I (Berlin: G. Reimer), 6–8.

[13] See Kellerhof (2017), '*Gebt mir vier Jahre Zeit*, in: *Die Welt*, 30 January.

[14] This promise was arguably intended to brighten up and legitimize the act of an authoritarian-administrative unification. See Wiegrefe, K. (2018), '*Kohls Lüge von den blühenden Landschaften*', in: *Spiegel,* 26 May.

Hitler had to say. To change country and context: by comparison, slogans such as Donald Trump's 'Make America great again'[15] have eroded this reference to the future through overexposure and vulgarized use.

All of this must be taken into account when considering political authoritarianism. Accordingly, in the exercise of political power, *personal* authority – mediated by performance, knowledge, experience, age or similar qualities – generally takes a back seat to *functional* authority, based on professionalism and expertise; and above all to the *positional* authority associated with a rank, position or office. However, this hierarchy is by no means fixed; in autocracies, it may be disrupted or even reversed – especially by charismatic leaders (which is not to say that democratic heads of state do not also tap this source).

Thus, authority relations generally have a reciprocal but asymmetric structure. They are epitomized by the relationship between lordship (master) and bondage (slave).[16] Contingent on the theoretical conception, this relationship is conceptualized as 'affirmed dependence' (Max Horkheimer *et al*), a 'relationship of dependence' (Karl Marx), the 'affirmation of the bearer of authority' (Herbert Marcuse) or the dualism of 'authority without responsibility' and 'responsibility without authority' (Robert Brandom). These variations of the master-slave myth invariably presuppose a certain degree of freedom to bind one's own will by subjection that ties both the slave (subject) to the will of the master (bearer of authority) and the master to the relationship of domination.

On the level of political systems, authority relations affect the practice of governing and ideology – the presumed or law-supported will to make decisions. Authority can be linked to a person (ruler), office, role or institution. On the part of the ruler, it implies a duty to lead and protect, whether by legal commitment or self-obligation. On the part of the subjects, the leader's duty is accompanied and complemented by a corresponding duty of loyalty and obedience. Constitutions may intervene in this complex relationship of authority. Such intervention, however, presupposes a mutual *will to the constitution* and its *recognition* as 'commanding text' that legitimately calls for observance, if not allegiance. Only then can the constitution muster normative power and serve as a relay between leaders and subjects.

---

15 'Let's make America great again!' was also Ronald Reagan's election campaign slogan and also featured in the speeches of other presidents, such as Bill Clinton. See Jouet, M. (2017), 'Trump Did Not Invent "Make America Great Again"', in: *Mother Jones*, January/February 2017.

16 Hegel, G.W.F. (2019), *Phenomenology of the Spirit* [1807] (Cambridge: Cambridge University Press), B.IV.A.

1.2 Recognition and Protection

Across regimes and in diverse cultural contexts, voluntary or forced recognition of political authority expects in return the promise of security. Based on the father/leader's authority, it functions as a draft for the future. Borrowed from the historical legacy of Thomas Hobbes (and others), public security thus occupies the centre of constitutional rhetoric with regard to both state technology and its political legitimation:[17] 'The office of the sovereign, be it a monarch or an assembly, consists in the end for which he was trusted with the sovereign power, namely, the procuration of *the safety of the people…*'[18]

This can be verified both in regimes that label themselves as 'democratic' and in those that either openly call themselves 'illiberal' or could otherwise essentially be described as 'autocratic'.[19]

Security may be promised through a state programme that is variously oriented towards defending territorial borders against external enemies; ensuring peaceful coexistence and social peace within the state (including through the elimination of armed insurgents); or protecting against natural disasters or other chaotic natural events. Security may also be sought through establishing collective alliances or assigning the security function to the military, intelligence services, (border) police, politicians or other authorities. One may therefore conclude that the promise of public safety – whether honest or deceptive – always includes the citizens' obedience as a *quid pro quo*. In the cosmos of liberal constitutionalism, this promise is intended to compensate for the loss of freedom generally associated with it. Not always as clearly as Hobbes would suggest, protection (as per the concept of theoretical realism) is the 'gift' in return for obedience. In the usual and erroneous way, the complex problem of freedom, social cohesion and mutual commitment to common norms is often reduced to the dichotomy of freedom and security.[20]

---

[17] Hobbes, T. (1958), *Leviathan, Parts I and II* [1651] (New York: Bobbs-Merrill), 262; and Skinner, Q. (2008) *Hobbes and Republican Liberty* (Cambridge: Cambridge University Press); Foucault, M. (1991), 'Governmentality', in: Burchell, G. *et al* (eds), *Studies in Governmentality* (Hemel Hampstead: Harvester Wheatsheaf), 87 ff; Bröckling, U. *et al* (2011), *Governmentality – Current Issues and Future Challenges* (New York/London: Routledge); Frankenberg, G. (2014), *Political Technology and the Erosion of the Rule of Law – Normalizing the State of Exception* (Cheltenham: Edward Elgar Publishing).

[18] Hobbes (n 17), 262.

[19] See Alviar Garcia, H. and Frankenberg, G., 'Authoritarian Structures and Trends in Consolidated Democracies', in: Uitz, R. (ed), *Routledge Handbook on Illiberalism* (New York and Oxford: Routledge) (forthcoming in 2020).

[20] For more detail, see Frankenberg (n 17), Ch. 1.

2. AUTHORITARIANISM

Everyday language and scientific discourse do not always distinguish between 'authoritative' and 'authoritarian' in a uniform or sufficiently clear way. 'Authoritarian' can easily be assigned under 'authoritarianism', which thus functions as a kind of umbrella or collective singular covering forms of state, governing practices, rhetoric and ideology. Under this umbrella may be found dictatorial, autocratic, radically nationalist, despotic, illiberal and kleptocratic regimes; and other institutional arrangements, sets of state measures and constitutional cultures that conform to this label. In the following discussion, I use the terms 'authoritarian', 'autocratic', 'despotic', 'dictatorial' and 'tyrannical' synonymously in order to identify those persons or agencies – leaders, cadres, cliques or regimes – to which authority is ascribed through the respective relations of power, and on which constitutions and laws confer powers of command and intervention *vis-à-vis* those who are dependent on instructions and bound to obedience and loyalty. On the other hand, it may be argued that this classification allows the conceptual power of the factual to triumph. That may very well be; but in view of the inconsistent use of 'authoritarian' in everyday language and scientific studies, there is little prospect of defining the variants of authoritarianism in advance. For example, dividing them strictly into autocracies, military regimes, single-party systems, semi-democratic regimes and so on does not have much purchase. And a definition, it seems, would only disguise what must be understood through the study of historical and social contexts and political constellations of authoritarianism.

2.1 Educational Style: Patterns of Attitude

The *Duden Dictionary* defines 'authoritarianism' rather poorly and misleadingly as 'an authoritarian form of government that is not based on a certain ideology' and a 'style of education'. The definition in the *Cambridge Dictionary* is not much of an improvement: 'the belief that people must obey completely and not be allowed freedom to act as they wish.'[21] Dictionaries of psychology tend to emphasize 'a generalized attitude or a system of opinions, attitudes and values',[22] which is followed by a reference (obvious from a scientific perspective) to the 'attitudinal syndrome of anti-Semitism, ethnocentrism, fascism and political conservatism determined by Adorno et al. through

---

21 *Cambridge Dictionary* (2020), https://dictionary.cambridge.org/dictionary/english/authoritarianism/ (last accessed 20 March 2020).

22 Wirtz, A. (ed) (2017), *Dorsch Lexikon der Psychologie*, 18th ed, (Göttingen: Verlag Hogrefe).

interviews and projective procedures and defined with the F/Fascism scale'.[23] This approach focuses on research on the 'authoritarian personality', which was ground-breaking at the time but has long been considered methodologically controversial. Some authors suggest that the 'authoritarian character' may be obsolete,[24] and question whether the (hierarchical and exploitative) parent-child relationship bleeds into political ideology, thus gaining a profile both in private relationships and in public-political discourse. Other authors have developed their own scale (notably Altemeyer), which has not resolved the controversies.[25] To this day, numerous surveys and research projects have investigated authoritarian attitudes among the population, such as the recent authoritarian thought patterns emerging among the young.[26]

The growing presence of authoritarianism in governments and consolidated regimes, as well as in social movements, organizations and populations, raises the question of how to explain the significant increase in anti-democratic and racist attitudes, and in chauvinistic, misogynistic, homophobic and xenophobic rhetoric. Why today are 'strangers' more vehemently rejected, while the approval rate of democracy simultaneously plummets? Recent analyses of authoritarian attitudes and their causes[27] relate them to capitalist incursions on – or 'takings' of – the social, the ambivalence of an 'unlocked' modernity and the decline of the middle classes, which have caused a marked loss of certainty and control and sparked an (undirected) desire to search for new assurances. The result seems to be a willingness to follow authoritarian movements and regimes that come with an anti-elitist and xenophobic agenda, and that position themselves aggressively against the (possibly ambivalent) offerings of liberal democracy.[28]

---

[23] Adorno, T.W. et al (1950), *The Authoritarian Personality* (New York: Harper & Brothers); Adorno (1995), *Studien zum autoritären Charakter* (Frankfurt am Main: Suhrkamp). For a critique of the original research design, see Altemeyer, R. (1981), *Right-Wing Authoritarianism* (Winnipeg: University of Manitoba Press); id. (1988), Enemies of Freedom. *Understanding Right-Wing Authoritarianism* (San Francisco: Jossey-Bass).

[24] Decker, O. et al. (2012), '*Das Veralten des autoritären Charakters*', in: Friedrich-Ebert-Stiftung (ed), *Die Mitte in der Krise. Rechtsextreme Einstellungen in Deutschland 2010* (Berlin: zu Klampen), 29 ff.

[25] This is not the place to resolve them; and nor do I feel competent to tackle that task.

[26] See Brähler, E. and Decker, O. (2018), *Flucht ins Autoritäre: Rechtsextreme Dynamiken in der Mitte der Gesellschaft* (Giessen: Psychosozial-Verlag).

[27] Heitmeyer, W. (2018), *Autoritäre Versuchungen* (Berlin: Suhrkamp) with further references.

[28] Heitmeyer (n 27), 86 f; Dörre, K. (2012), '*Landnahme und die Grenzen kapitalistischer Dynamik. Eine Ideenskizze*', in: *Initial – Berliner Debatte,* 24 July, www.linksnet.de/artikel/27742 (last accessed: 26 June 2019).

The analysis of authoritarian constitutionalism inevitably relegates action orientations and patterns of attitude of individuals or groups to a back seat. Instead, what might be called systemic dispositions are considered when discussing authoritarian techniques of governing, the ownership concept of power, participation as complicity and the cult of immediacy – all of which open out into delusions of community. A spotlight is shone on the power-holders and their constitutional strategies and tactics. This leaves unanswered the question of why the power-givers suffer to languish in the shadows cast by repressive, patronizing institutions in the pre-political space, which fails to nurture resilient democrats.

2.2 Authoritarian Forms of Governance

In political science and its neighbouring sciences, authoritarianism is predominantly discussed as an anti-democratic alternative, whose current variants (under the *topos* of 'new authoritarianism') do not necessarily rely on the widely used primitive-repressive style of government, but rather prove to be thoroughly adaptable and functionally flexible forms of governance.[29] Therefore, democratically disguised types of political authoritarianism are particularly difficult to grasp. On the surface, they maintain their constitutional appearance and, so far as unavoidable, expose themselves to the risk of elections in systems ranging from electoral democracy to competitive authoritarianism. Their democratic indifference prevents them from trying out other possible forms of rule (eg, elitism, entrepreneurship) that could hide behind the mask of democracy. And they do not address the illiberality of the liberal order or the devastation wrought under the banner of freedom (eg, climate change, poverty, irresponsibility of economic power).

Political science analyses of authoritarianism either concentrate (as comparative regime theory) on *forms* of state or government and their classification, distinguishing between democracy and authoritarianism (and sometimes also totalitarianism);[30] or (for those guided by a *normative* compass) examine selected institutions that are predominantly taken from the liberal-democratic paradigm – especially elections and political competition, separation of powers, and the judicial review of governmental and administrative measures.

---

[29] Bank, A. (2009), '*Die Renaissance des Autoritarismus*', 10 ff; Köllner, P. (2008), '*Autoritäre Regime – Ein Überblick über die jüngere Literatur*', in: 2 *Zeitschrift für Vergleichende Politikwissenschaft*, 351 ff, 357.

[30] Influential: Linz, J.J. (2000), *Totalitarian and Authoritarian Regimes* (Boulder: Lynne Rienner); also Brooker, P. (2000), *Non-democratic Regimes: Theory, Government, and Politics* (New York: St Martin's Press) with further references.

Almost inevitably, approaches to authoritarianism that focus on how institutions are constructed and government is run, and on the normative underpinnings, operate with a Western bias. Autocratic regimes are not critically examined as phenomena in their own right, but are rather viewed through the perspective of political liberalism as deficient, deviant or illiberal democracies. Exemplary statements include: 'autocratic government is *not* bound by any legal provisions that limit the use of state power'; 'authoritarian state power is *not* legally accountable'; and 'in autocratic regimes, proper succession to office is *not* guaranteed by legal means'.[31]

While these statements can certainly be empirically validated, problems arise when it comes to the method of strategic comparison. Such comparisons of political-legal systems are inevitably informed by the familiar (liberal) model, from which they derive their (normative) criteria. The comparatist both begins and ends the analysis from the established (Western-liberal) perspective within which he or she is contextualized; a perspective which is impervious to the influence of new information and insights from outside its own knowledge base.[32] I endeavour to avoid the hegemonic nature of such comparisons by not establishing a doctrine of forms of democratic or non-democratic rule. Instead, I focus on state practice and governing techniques, as well as on institutional structures and symbolic representations, with the aim of foregrounding the features of political authoritarianism and authoritarian constitutionalism: an informal, opportunistic style of governing; power as private property; participation as complicity; and the cult of immediacy.[33]

2.3 Authoritarian Practices of Power and Political Technology

Authoritarianism of state practice – whether in old or new garb – and authoritarian rhetoric as its linguistic expression, often clothed in constitutional apparel, point to the exercise of power. Without pre-empting the discussion

---

[31] For example, Perlmutter, A. (1981), *Modern Authoritarianism: A Comparative Institutional Analysis* (New Haven: Yale University Press), 1981, 1; Bredies, '*Verfassungen ohne Konstitutionalismus: quasikonstitutionelle Institutionalisierung des Autoritarismus in Osteuropa*', in: 8 *Totalitarismus und Demokratie*, 133 ff, 139. Further references follow in Chapter 3.

[32] From a very different perspective and for a quite different purpose: Haraway, D. (1988), 'Situated Knowledges: The Science Question in Feminism and the Privilege of Partial Perspective', in: 14 *Feminist Studies*, 575 ff. For a more detailed discussion of strategic comparison see Frankenberg, G. (1985), 'Critical Comparisons. Re-Thinking Comparative Law', in: 26 *Harvard International Law Journal*, 411 ff.

[33] See Chapters 4 to 7. See also the related characterizations by Geddes, B. (1999), 'What Do We Know About Democratization After Twenty Years', in: 2 *Annual Review of Political Science*, 115 ff.

of the essential characteristics of authoritarianism, it may be said that power is exercised in the style and towards the ends of authoritarianism where public debate on the common affairs of society is either stifled altogether or strictly regulated by the powers that be; and, more importantly, where it is a criminal offence or politically dangerous to question the legitimacy of rule – that is, to pose the democratic question.[34]

While authority produces relations that rest – in a well-functioning democracy at least – on the voice and agency of the people, who recognize leaders for their prestige, legal legitimacy, charisma or competence, authoritarian alliances are more likely grounded on acclamation and, once the performance is over, leave the people with a sense of loss and powerlessness. Without a doubt, a multitude of models of state practice and styles of political rhetoric come under the umbrella of authoritarianism. They demand that one provide for a critical analytics that can accommodate the many shades of autocracy. Hence, one cannot comfortably rely on dichotomizing definitions or the (instructive, but controversial) classifications offered by comparative political science and commit oneself in advance to a certain typology, such as autocracy versus dictatorship or fascism versus right-wing populism.

Nevertheless, the following variants of authoritarianism (which arise rather frequently) may be contrasted at least analytically, even if they evolve into hybrids in the 'real life' context of power: *personalistic* authoritarianism (leader principle or leadership cadre, sultanate); *one-party* rule; *clan* rule (oligarchy, sheikdom, warlordship); *military* junta; *theocracy*; and autocratic *corporatism*. Admittedly, these models offer at best initial access and a first take; they do not constitute a viable basis on which to give these diverse regimes a more precise, empirically informed profile. A different methodological path is therefore chosen here: I treat 'authoritarian', 'autocratic', 'dictatorial' and so on as synonyms, unless a more precise characterization is called for by certain contexts and constellations. For that (limited) purpose, signs, criteria and transitions are discussed first; followed by an attempt to demarcate totalitarianism from authoritarianism and a (hopefully less futile) endeavour to profile populism. The main part of this book is then devoted to a more thorough discussion of four crucial constructive elements of authoritarianism.

2.4 Signs, Criteria and Transitions

As a rule, commanders in chief, leadership cadres or parties do not brandish the self-description 'authoritarian' in front of them like a monstrance – with the

---

[34] See Rödel, U., Frankenberg, G. and Dubiel, H. (1989), *Die demokratische Frage* (Frankfurt am Main: Suhrkamp).

exception of the demonstrative illiberal show-off, in the mould of Hungary's Viktor Orbán, Poland's Jarosław Kaczyński or the Philippines' Rodrigo Duterte, who has proudly compared himself to Hitler. At first glance, even constitutions do not yield enough reliable information (if any) about the imperative or democratic quality of state practice – especially since regimes that in essence are authoritarian are regularly labelled 'democratically elected' or 'republican'; adorn themselves with catalogues of fundamental rights (keeping duties in the background); and, as far as possible, clothe their practice in non-autocratic garb. However, transitions to autocracy are most clearly found in governmental practice; although they can also be observed in rhetoric such as programmatic statements, official announcements or public justifications, and also – albeit somewhat hidden – in constitutions.

In particular, indications of authoritarianism include the following: access to political decision-making centres is sealed off and the public space is strictly sequestered; oppositional behaviour is routinely checked; and publicly expressed doubts about the political status and legitimacy of those in power and their claim to obedience are penalized. For authoritarianism, as mentioned above, cannot allow the democratic question[35] – the permanent and systematic challenging of legitimacy. With bans on the expression of opinion and assembly, and the execution of criminal offences such as incitement to riot, breach of the peace and high treason, the switch is thrown, as it were, from agency and voice of the citizenry to acclamation and even passivity; from public discourse to forced (tacit) consent.[36] A strong indicator of authoritarianism is whether citizens are degraded to subjects[37] who are bound to renounce the right to determine for themselves what justice and a good life mean to them, and are ordered to desert the public sphere, disappear through internal emigration or even exit the state altogether. In the following chapters, I aim to show that authoritarian state practice and rhetoric are designed to set the agenda and, if need be, delimit the communicative world of those subjects who are manipulated or forced to accept domination while sharing, as accomplices, an imaginary community with their leaders.

---

35 See Rödel *et al* (n 34) – inspired by Lefort, C. (1994), *L'invention démocratique: Les limites de la domination totalitaire* (Paris: Fayard).

36 Anyone who operates with the concept of populism would be well advised to pay attention to this aspect (more on this later).

37 Identifiable, for example, by exit bans and the denial of the right to return, illustrated by the plight of the Palestinian refugees. See, B. (1987), *The Birth of the Palestinian Refugee Problem* (Cambridge: Cambridge University Press).

2.5 Authoritarian Legitimacy

In relation to political regimes, the authoritative/authoritarian distinction also presupposes that rule can be characterized as legitimate – or not. Following Max Weber, tradition, charisma, and rational legality come into question as ideal-typical candidates of legitimate authority. They are based respectively on an everyday belief in the venerable nature of everlasting traditions; on an extraordinary devotion to the holiness, heroic power or exemplary nature of individuals and the commands they issue; or on a sober belief in the legality of established (normative) orders and the right of those appointed by them to exercise dominion.[38] In contrast, philosophical discourses that follow Thomas Hobbes largely base the legitimacy of ruling normatively on consensus and contract; public reason and debate; democracy and people's sovereignty; trust and real discourse; and deliberation.[39] Where they raise questions of legitimacy, theories of the state and constitutional doctrines consistently derive the answers from the sovereignty and constitutionality of government and its composition through democratic elections (if their correct implementation can be assumed).[40]

By stark contrast, political legitimacy in the practice and propaganda of authoritarian regimes, parties and movements is oriented towards the problems of ambivalent, insecure modernity, and the promise of overcoming them. What is decisive for legitimacy is not, in the main, their conformity with the constitution or their general acceptance in a normatively ambitious sense; but rather the plausibility of interpretative offers that aim to exorcise uncertainty among their followers through conspiracy theories or through the mobilizing power of strategic concepts that appeal to simple minds and are intended to compensate for the loss of control – such as 'America first', 'Austria first', 'Foreigners out' or 'We're taking back our country'.[41] Finally, opening the valves to hate speech may also have a legitimizing effect, allowing accumulated anxieties and inse-

---

[38] Weber, M., *Economy and Society*, III, § 2 and § 10.

[39] Peter, F. (2017), 'Political Legitimacy', in: *Stanford Encyclopedia of Philosophy*, https://plato.stanford.edu/entries/legitimacy (last accessed 25 December 2019); Anscombe, G.E.M. (1981), 'On the Source of Authority of the State', in: *Ethics, Religion, and Politics* (Collected Philosophical Papers: Vol. 3) (Oxford: Blackwell), 130 ff; Estlund, D. (2008), *Democratic Authority* (Princeton: Princeton University Press); Habermas, J. (1996), *Between Facts and Norms* (Cambridge: MIT Press); Pitkin, H. (1965), 'Obligation and Consent I', in: 59 *American Political Science Review*, 991ff.

[40] Kelsen, H. (2005), *General Theory of Law and State* (Piscataway Township: Transaction Publishers).

[41] For examples, see Heitmeyer (n 27), 265 f; Frei, N. et al. (2019), *Zur rechten Zeit. Wider die Rückkehr des Nationalismus* (Berlin: Ullstein), 161 ff.

Source: © Max Frankenberg 2020.

Figure 2.1 *Leviathan's bitter irony and tragedy*

curities to be unloaded onto out-groups. US President Donald Trump not only presents a smokescreen of nationalism, tribalism, xenophobia, anti-elitism and an advice-resistant economic 'drive' (see Figure 2.1), but also demonstrates to traditional political representation and the established political class that the party is over, and that authoritarian governing supported by social media is in.

3. TOTALITARIAN POWER SCHEMES

Despite the obvious problems of definition and the endless scientific controversy, a clear distinction may be drawn between authoritarian and totalitarian systems. Totalitarianism is usually introduced as a distinctive form of ramped-up authoritarianism. Its power emerges from standard autocracies through discrete structural elements, and is characterized by the intensity of repressive techniques of governing and a hermetic ideology.[42] In relation to

42 See Marcuse, H. (1968), 'The Struggle Against Liberalism in the Totalitarian View of the State', in: *id*, *Negations: Essays in Critical Theory* (Boston: Beacon Press), 3 ff; Kellner, D. (ed), *Technology, War and Fascism: Collected Papers of Herbert Marcuse* (Vol 1) (London and New York: Routledge); and Linz (n 30). Critical: Poulantzas, N. (1972), *Pouvoir politique et classes sociales,* vol. II, Paris: Maspero, 118 ff.

Italian fascism, but above all to National Socialism and Stalinism,[43] Hannah Arendt identified certain structural components that define a system of total rule – a system of world interpretation (ideology) with a claim to absoluteness, organized as a mass movement for the purpose of exercising terror:

> The essence of totalitarian rule, then, is not that it curtails or eliminates certain freedoms, nor that it eradicates the love of freedom from human hearts; but only that it locks people as they are into the iron band of terror with such force that the space of action, and this alone is the reality of freedom, disappears.[44]

In totalitarian systems, therefore, terror not only constricts systemic criticism, intimidates and eliminates oppositional thought and bans organizations; but also rises to become the most important instrument of power, the instrument of conformity. Regimes reveal their totalitarian tendencies through ubiquitous terror and violent social control, and bring to bear the submission of people in all areas of life according to a hermetic world view.[45] This does not rule out the possibility that totalitarian regimes may display specific features – for instance, of a nationalism that mobilizes the population and could therefore be (misleadingly) portrayed as 'populist'.[46] Ultimately, however, totalitarianism reveals its ugly face through ethnic and political purges, deportations and mass murder in the name of promoting social hygiene, establishing (racial) purity and eradicating social ambivalence.

In contrast, Claude Lefort and Marcel Gauchet argued that totalitarian regimes are not only identified by the hermetic ideology they propagate and their practice of total terror in executing a 'secularized religion'.[47] In fact,

---

[43] From a socialist perspective, Karl Kautsky formulated an incisive critique of Soviet-style communism: 'Fascism is nothing but the counterpart of Bolshevism, Mussolini only Lenin's monkey'; id (1930), *Der Bolschewismus in der Sackgasse* (Berlin: Dietz), 102.

[44] Arendt, H. (1951), *The Origins of Totalitarianism* (New York: Schocken); Neumann, F. (2009), *Behemoth. The Structure and Practice of National Socialism 1933–1944* (Chicago: Ivan R. Dee, Inc.).

[45] Different regimes that executed an ideology through terror are analysed by, for example, Jäckel, E. (1999), *Hitlers Herrschaft. Vollzug einer Weltanschauung*, 4th ed (Stuttgart: DVA); Figes, O. (2007), *The Whisperers. Private Life in Stalin's Russia* (New York: Metropolitan Books); Kiernan, B. (2002) *The Pol Pot Regime. Race, Power and Genocide in Cambodia under the Khmer Rouge, 1975–79*, 2nd ed (New Haven: Yale University Press). See also Nisbet, R. (1953), 'Ideology and Terror: A Novel Form of Government', in: 15 *The Review of Politics*, 303 ff.

[46] Germani, G. (1978), *Authoritarianism, Fascism, and National Populism* (New Jersey: New Brunswick), 95 f.; Diehl, P. and Cavazza, S. (2012), 'Editorial: Populism and Fascism', in: 9 *Totalitarismus und Demokratie*, 207 ff.

[47] Aron, R. (1985), 'L'avenier des religions séculières', in: *Commentaire*, Nr 28–29, 369 ff.

these regimes must be understood above all as agents and institutions of an 'anonymous intentionality' aimed at realizing a society that is at one with and transparent to itself, in which all clashes of interests and divergences as to what constitutes a good life have been completely stamped out.[48] The phantasm of this society stifles the never-ending questioning of the legitimacy of rule and power in a democracy, supplanting it with the incessant and vicious stigmatization and elimination of its (presumed) enemies – thus giving the democratic question a Schmittian response.[49] The 1918 Constitution of Russia – a likely frontrunner in enemy naming – reflects the sombre scenario of a world full of foes: 'propertied classes', 'the exploiters', 'parasitic strata of society', 'landowners', 'the bourgeoisie' and more. By the same token, this spectre dictates that subjects be submitted to the imperatives of necessity and the 'laws' of history, which are prompted by the dominant ideology. This is why totalitarian regimes are inclined to invade society with restrictive and even racist laws, such as prohibitions on residence, occupation or marriage.[50] Accordingly, albeit in a more cryptic wording, the constitutions of such regimes require citizens, for instance, to 'observe the socialist standards of life'.[51]

Totalitarian regimes are invariably organized pursuant to the principle of leadership and/or a one-party system. Both morph the phantasm into a doctrine, which is put in the service of a comprehensive scheme of governing: 'Everything in the state, nothing outside the state, nothing against the state.'[52]

---

48 See Lefort, C. (1986), *The Political Forms of Modern Society: Bureaucracy, Democracy and Totalitarianism*, (Cambridge: MIT Press); Gauchet, M. (2010), *L'avènement de la démocratie*, vol iii: *À l'épreuve des totalitarismes, 1914–1974* (Paris: Gallimard); Rödel *et al* (n 34), Chapter IV.

49 Almost modest (which it was not), Stalin's Constitution (1936): 'Persons committing offenses against public, socialist property are enemies of the people' (Article 131). For an analysis of authoritarianism and its 'enemies', see Altemeyer, R. (1988), *Enemies of Freedom: Understanding Right-Wing Authoritarianism* (San Francisco: Jossey-Bass).

50 For example, the Nazi Act for the Protection of German Blood and Honour, 15 September 1935, RGBl I S 1146; the Prohibition of Mixed Marriages Act (55/1949) and the Natives Laws Amendment Act (54/1952) of the Apartheid regime in South Africa.

51 Article 82 of the Constitution of the Democratic People's Republic of Korea. More low-key, the 1992/2013 Basic Law of Saudi Arabia lays down in Article 34: 'Defending the Islamic faith, the society and the homeland shall be the duty of each and every citizen.' Likewise, the 2017 Constitution of Thailand obliges citizens in a general way 'not to participate in or support all forms of dishonest act and wrongful conduct' (Section 50, Number 10).

52 Mussolini, B. (1925), 'Per la medaglia dei benemeriti del comune di Milano', in: Opera Omnia, vol 21, 425. See Gentile, E. (2005), *The Origins of Italian Fascism 1918–1925* (New York: Enigma Books).

Finally, the phantasm produces the idea of an incorporated society whose gory aesthetic is expressed in the 'endless drama of the healthy social body' that 'defends itself against parasites in its search for purity'.[53] The imagination of a society that is literally at peace with itself because it is cleansed and has done away with all conflicts of interest and 'people of foreign origin' is drastically expressed in official announcements of fascist regimes. Robert Paxton therefore defines fascism as an 'obsessive preoccupation with the decline, humiliation or victimhood of a community', which is revealed in compensatory 'cults of unity, strength and purity'.[54]

In contrast, autocracies of the 'regular' kind that do not – or not completely – subscribe to totalitarian hermeticism and repression must at least accommodate electoral politics and deal with a real existing society (in some way or other), rather than a fantasy. They need to address conflicts of interest and recognize (to a certain extent) pluralism and opposition, rather than assuming homogeneity – if only for the purpose of identifying the opposition and neutralizing 'dangerous elements'. It is therefore necessary to turn to the authoritarian way of claiming and enforcing power below the level of the totalitarian. Typically, autocratic rhetoric echoes a crucial aspect of totalitarian ideology by privileging the presumed interests of the community, and above all its security. 'The welfare of the people takes precedence over the selfishness of the individual!' 'Public good goes before self-interest!'[55] 'You are nothing, your nation is everything!'[56] 'One for all, all for one!'[57]

Where omnipresent coercion, brute force and inequality must be 'argued away', the community – the 'political-ideological unity of the whole people' (in the North Korean Constitution) – is invariably invoked as the bearer of the general interest or common good. Rather concisely, and almost discreetly,

---

[53] Lefort (n 35). For a not altogether different interpretation, see Stanley, J. (2018), *How Fascism Works. The Politics of Us and Them* (New York: Random House).

[54] See Paxton, R. (2005), *The Anatomy of Fascism* (New York: Vintage).

[55] Anti-capitalist, anti-Semitic nationalist slogans that were adopted (not only) by Hitler's party, the NASDAP – see *Das 25-Punkte-Programm der Nationalsozialistischen Deutschen Arbeiterpartei,* 24 February 1920, www.documentarchiv.de/wr/1920/nsdap-programm.html (last accessed 28 December 2019). For a defence of self-interest, see Maitland, I. (2002), 'The Human Face of Self-Interest', in: 38 *Journal of Business Ethics*, 3ff.

[56] Nazi propaganda meant to justify the 'Euthanasia Programme' – that is, the systematic murder of people with disabilities (in 1939) – Aly, G. et al. (1994), *Cleansing the Fatherland: Nazi Medicine and Racial Hygiene* (Baltimore: Johns Hopkins University Press).

[57] The Constitution of the Democratic People's Republic of Korea (Article 63) adopted the slogan of Alexandre Dumas' 'Three Musketeers' (1844) ('*Unus pro omnibus, omnes pro uno*'). See also the Swiss Confederation.

the 1924 Constitution of the Union of Soviet Socialist Republics propagated a 'family concept', even though only federalism and the vertical separation of powers had to be justified: 'Finally, the Soviet Union, which according to its class nature is internationally building up Soviet power, is pushing the toiling masses of the Soviet republics on the path of unification into a socialist family.' Likewise, the North Korean Constitution praises Kim Il-sung, the founder of North Korea, for having 'transformed the whole society into one big family, united with one heart and soul' (Preamble). The Constitution of the Islamic Republic of Iran, understandably, relies on a religious community (*ummah*):

> From the point of view of Islam, the state does not emerge from class thinking or the hegemony of individuals or groups, but it is the implementation of the political ideal of *a people who are equally oriented in religion and way of thinking*, who organize themselves in order to pave the way to their ultimate goal – the way to God – in the process of spiritual and ideological development.[58]

4. HOBBES' QUESTION

Both totalitarian and authoritarian regimes (and also, *mutatis mutandis*, democratic ones) are confronted with the question of how the passions and interests of individuals, the excessive energies and initiatives of civil society, can be permanently tamed and brought under control. This question is generally informed by sociological theorems on the irrationality of collective actors and their threatening actions, or by sociological analyses of the clash of interests (see Chapter 6, Section 2). Thomas Hobbes pursued this emphatically in his contractual state theory and political philosophy.[59] His position should not be too hastily dismissed as reactionary. First, he recognized conflict and developed a theory – in particular, in the Elements of Law. Second, compared to later contributions to the discourse on the irrationality of collective protest, Hobbes' treatment of the topic is almost enlightened. His questioning of how the collective energies of the people, once unleashed, can be disciplined – how the genie can be bottled again – is not necessarily autocratic.

During and after the French Revolution, the intellectual spokespersons of the Restoration and Counter-Revolution lashed out against the uprisings. Depending on the historical-political context, they held ready the answers to Hobbes' question that they deemed appropriate. Traumatized by the terror of the Jacobins, the Catholic Counter-Revolutionaries of the nineteenth century

---

58 Preamble, Constitution of the Islamic Republic of Iran 1979 – emphasis added.

59 Hobbes, T. (1958), *Leviathan* (Indianapolis: Bobbs-Merril), Chapter XIV; *id* (2008), *The Elements of Law, Natural and Politic* [1650] (Oxford: Oxford World's Classics), Chapters 15, 17 and 19.

embellished their images of revolting citizens with religious metaphors and apocalyptic visions. For Joseph de Maistre, a Catholic enemy of the revolution of the first hour, the French Revolution was 'something devilish that distinguishes it from everything that has been and will ever be experienced'.[60] Donoso Cortés likewise sketched out the conditions that he feared would ensue once the legitimacy bases and structures of order had been destroyed by revolutionaries, and predicted where help would come from: 'Mankind is a ship thrown aimlessly into the sea, loaded with a rebellious, vulgar, forcibly recruited crew that roars and dances until the wrath of God pushes the rebellious rabble into the sea so that silence may reign again.'[61]

Today, the diagnoses of these enemies of the revolution – who were not necessarily thinking of an ecclesiastical order – find approval, if at all, on the fringes of political geography, towards the extreme right. While current criticisms of democracy and protests draw on other sources – mostly nationalism – it is true that the idea of the angry, mindless mob has withstood the test of time. Latter-day Horsemen of the Apocalypse usually lack the religious overtones and are less graphic than Donoso Cortés, de Maistre or Burke.[62] Their tone is congenial, though they claim to be appalled and enraged by the irrationality of a society that abolishes itself and surrenders to Islam,[63] irresponsible elites,[64] the European Union or whatever. Where de Maistre and Cortés ultimately heroically invoke the power of religion and the 'dictatorship of the dagger' against the revolting rabble, today's self-appointed speakers for an enraged citizenry often demand, in the spirit of a nationalist petty bourgeoisie,[65] that immigration be stopped (or even reversed) immediately; that Muslim females

---

60 De Maistre, J. (1797), *Considérations sur la France* [1796] (London: Bâle), 1797, 76. See Schmitt, C. (2005), *Political Theology. Four Chapters on the Concept of Sovereignty* [1922] (Chicago: University of Chicago Press), Chapter 4 ('The State Philosophy of the Counterrevolution'); Burke, E. (1955), *Reflections on the Revolution in France* (Indianapolis/New York: Bobbs-Merrill).

61 Cortés, J. D. (1854), *Obras* I (Madrid: Tejado), 192.

62 More moderate in his rhetoric, but adamant as regards the evils of the revolution – and also not averse to religion as a force of order, Burke (n 60), especially 189 f and 198 f.

63 Sarrazin, T. (2010), *Deutschland schafft sich ab* (New York: Random House).

64 I will return to the theme of participation and collective action in Chapter 6.

65 See also Hall, S. (1979), 'The Great Moving Right Show', in: *Marxism Today*, 14 ff; Eribon, D. (2009), *Retour à Reims* (Paris: Fayard).

be prevented from wearing headscarves; that fertility be encouraged;[66] and that Western culture be saved.[67]

According to Joseph de Maistre's counter-draft to the social contract, 'Democracy… has a shining moment, but… one must pay dearly for it'.[68] He thus opened a discourse that has accompanied democracy since the dawn of modernity. This discourse is led by those who see in the enterprise of (self-) government 'the ruin of every legitimate order' and for whom democracy always remains a 'synonym of abomination', because political power 'should legitimately belong to those persons' who are called to leadership by birth or status, merit or ability.[69] Not all of the authors quoted above participate in the eulogy of the authoritarian. Quite a few of today's Horsemen devote themselves to denigrating one or another minority, to which they attribute responsibility for impending doom. This gives them increased media presence and high print runs for their books. The more moderate proponents tend to regard democracy as a state event and therefore demand a state-sponsored attitude, not without lamenting a lack of authoritarianism.

5. SPECTRUM OF AUTHORITARIANISM

Autocratic programmes and propaganda, movements, regimes and leaders have been on the rise for years, both nationally and globally.[70] They erode the standing of democratic governance and exploit its problems.[71] Depending on

---

66 The lonesome alerter, Thilo Sarrazin, remains in the apocalyptic waters of his literary success and these days – less religiously, but in the defensive spirit of the counter-revolutionaries – calls for a reversal of the trend to prevent 'conquest by fertility' as a result of Muslim immigration and the 'hostile takeover'. His Islamophobic biologism echoes the discourses on vitalism and social discipline under National Socialism and neo-National Socialism. See 'Germany is Becoming Islamophobic', in: *Spiegel International*, 31 August.

67 For references see Al-Azm, S.J. (2004), 'Islam, Terrorism and the West Today', in: 44 *Die Welt des Islams*, 114 ff.

68 De Maistre, J. (1992), *De la souveraineté du peuple: Un anti-contrat social, Étude sur la souveraineté* [1794], (Paris: Presses Universitaires de France).

69 Rancière, J. (2011), *Der Hass der Demokratie* (Berlin: August Verlag), 2011, 8. This discourse is quite vividly illustrated by Edmund Burke (n 60), who finds fault with a great many aspects – notably the composition of the National Assembly and the dominance of lawyers in the representation of the *Tiers État* (p 194 f.).

70 See the references in the Introduction and in Chapter 1.

71 A global, empirically informed panorama is offered by: Diamond, L. *et al* (eds) (2016), *Authoritarianism Goes Global: The Challenge to Democracy* (Baltimore: Johns Hopkins University Press); Thompson, M.R. (2004), 'Pacific Asia After "Asian Values": Authoritarianism, Democracy, and "Good Governance"', in: 25 *Third World Quarterly*, 1079 ff; King, S. J. (2009), *The New Authoritarianism in the Middle East*

their definition and agenda, they are accompanied by different practices and rhetoric,[72] symbolic representations[73] and conceptual disguises[74] that cover a broad spectrum of regimes: bureaucratic and competitive authoritarianism;[75] oriental despotism;[76] personalist or developmental dictatorship; autocracy; elitism; one-party rule; military juntas; right-wing communitarianism; right-wing or left-wing populism;[77] Bonapartism;[78] police states; arbitrary rule; technocracies; economic authoritarianism; authoritarian national radicalism;[79] 'dual states';[80] neopatrimonialism; and kleptocracy.[81] Other manifestations of political authoritarianism are often favoured by presidential systems.[82]

---

and North Africa, (Bloomington: Indiana University Press); Borejsza, J.W. *et al* (eds) (2006), *Totalitarian and Authoritarian Regimes in Europe* (Oxford/New York: Berghahn Books); O'Donnell, G.A. (2007), 'The Perpetual Crisis of Democracy', in: 18 *Journal of Democracy*, 5 ff; and Geddes (n 33).

72 See Kennedy, D. (2019), 'Authoritarian Constitutionalism in Liberal Democracy', in: Alviar and Frankenberg (eds), *Authoritarian Constitutionalism – Comparison and Critique* (Cheltenham: Edward Elgar Publishing).

73 Regarding the iconography of Hugo Chavez' authoritarian regime: González-Jácome, J., 'Authoritarianism and the narrative power of constitutionalism in Venezuela', in: Alvia and Frankenberg (eds) (n 72).

74 A rich survey is provided by Linz (n 30); Bogaards, M. and Elischer, S. (2016), 'Competitive Authoritarianism in Africa Revisited', in: 10 *Zeitschrift für Vergleichende Politikwissenschaft*, 5 ff; Levitsky, S. and Way, L.A. (2010), *Competitive Authoritarianism. Hybrid Regimes After the Cold War* (Cambridge: Cambridge University Press).

75 *Impressive*: Levitsky and Way (n 75).

76 See the thoughtful study by Sultany, N. (2017), *Law and Revolution: Legitimacy and Constitutionalism After the Arab Spring* (Oxford: Oxford University Press).

77 See the discussion and references below.

78 Instructive and insightful the historical reconstruction and critique of Bonapartism by Mérieau, E. (2019), 'French Authoritarian Constitutionalism and its Legacy', in: Alviar and Frankenberg (eds) (n 72),185 ff.

79 Heitmeyer (n 27), 231 ff.

80 Fraenkel, E. (2010), *The Dual State: A Contribution to the Theory of Dictatorship* (Clark: The Law Book Exchange, Ltd).

81 See Scott Newton's in-depth analysis of kleptocratic regimes in Central Asia: (2017), *Constitutional Systems of the Independent Central Asian States: A Contextual Analysis* (Oxford: Hart), and 'Plus ça change… the riddle of all Central Asian constitutions', in: Alviar and Frankenberg (eds) (n 72), 209 ff.

82 Linz, J.J. (1994), *The Failure of Presidential Democracy* (Baltimore: The Johns Hopkins University Press); Görgens, M. (2017), *Die Präsidentialismus-Falle* (Saarbrücken: AV Akademikerverlag). See also the exemplary study concerning affinity presidentialism and authoritarianism in Mexico by Alterio, A.M. and Niembro Ortega, R. (2018), 'Constitutional Culture and Democracy in Mexico – A Critical View of the 100-Year-Old Mexican Constitution', in: Graber, M. *et al* (eds), *Constitutional Democracies in Crisis?* (Oxford: Oxford University Press), 139 ff; Gargarella, R.

The picture becomes even more confusing where these variants evolve into hybrids. For example, Italy was governed (if one can call it that) by a combination of a peculiar kind of populism (*Cinque Stelle*) and authoritarian-xenophobic nationalism (*Lega*) – linked by anti-elitism, economic insecurity and a strong anti-EU sentiment – in a coalition that collapsed after a year.[83] In Austria, posh 'salon populism', represented by the glib federal chancellor and his conservative party, joined forces with the stale, xenophobic-authoritarian 'Alpine nationalism' of the *Freiheitliche Partei* (FPO), until a scandal[84] in 2019 brought down the FPO leader and the honeymoon ended after two years. These coalitions illustrate how authoritarianism – like a chameleon – changes its colour and appearance from one context to another. It flexibly adapts the rules of its grammar to escape critical scrutiny that might otherwise reveal how much today's authoritarian regimes appropriate elements of modernity, such as rational bureaucracy and centralized government; and how intensively they participate in – indeed, depend on – the liberal world order, financial flows, investment plans and value chains, while simultaneously pretending to fight them. Geographically, these models range from Azerbaijan to Poland; from Egypt to Swaziland; from North Korea to Singapore. They include Erdoğan's supposedly 'competitive authoritarianism' and Vladimir Putin's mix of autocracy and 'vertical', 'managed democracy'.[85] Some movements start out on the democratic side, but then lose themselves in nationalist Caesarism (Juán Peron, Hugo Chávez); others, such as repressive kleptocracies, demonstrate only greed rather than confused idealism from the very beginning.

In short, from the perspective of conceptual history,[86] authoritarianism inscribes itself in the book of modernity as a collective singular that encompasses a plurality of heterogeneous phenomena. Just a few years after the

---

(2013), *Latin American Constitutionalism 1810–2010. The Engine Room of the Constitution* (Oxford: Oxford University Press), 157 ff.

[83] See the election results of September 2019: https://europarl.europa.eu/election-results-2019/de/nationale-ergebnisse/italien/2019-2024 (last accessed 29 December 2019). Also, for the history and programme of *Cinque Stelle*: Tronconi, F. (ed) (2016), *Beppe Grillo's Five Star Movement. Organisation, Communication and Ideology* (London: Routledge).

[84] Obermayer, B. and Obermayer, F. (2019), *Die Ibiza-Affäre. Innenansichten eines Skandals* (Cologne: Kiepenheuer & Witsch).

[85] Esen, B. and Gumuscu, S. (2016), 'Rising Competitive Authoritarianism in Turkey', in: *Third World Quarterly*, 1581 ff; Petrov, N. and McFaul, M. (2018), 'The Essence of Putin's Managed Democracy', https://carnegieendowment.org/2005/10/18/essence-of-putin-s-managed-democracy-event-819 (last accessed 26 December 2019).

[86] Koselleck, R. (2006), *Begriffsgeschichten: Studien zur Semantik und Pragmatik der politischen und sozialen Sprache* (Berlin: Suhrkamp); and Müller, J.-W. (2014), 'On Conceptual History', in: McMahon, D.M. and Moyn, S. (eds), *Rethinking Modern European Intellectual History* (Oxford: Oxford University Press), 74 ff.

beginning of the 'long 19th century',[87] political-revolutionary authoritarianism, in the form of *Terreur*, followed by Napoleon's military dictatorship; and Bonapartism[88] a few decades later overshadowed the glory of democratic revolutions. Throughout the nineteenth century and thereafter, it was followed by the colonial and imperialist regimes – often passed over in 'Western' academic discourse – which from then on accompanied modernity as nightmares in theory and above all in practice.[89] In the following, we will try to identify the different models of authoritarianism. Numerous examples will be discussed – although not comprehensively analysed – and further studies of them are encouraged.

6. AUTHORITARIANISM AS PATHOLOGY

In clinical terms, authoritarianism can also be diagnosed as a pathology[90] – a pathological manifestation of self-government. Thus, authoritarianism provides patterns of government that can be deduced from the joint occurrence of various virulent symptoms, such as manipulated elections with highly implausible results;[91] governing by decree, following the model of the

---

[87] Hobsbawn, E. (1962), *The Age of Revolution, 1789-1848* (London: Weidenfeld & Nicolson); Burke, E. III (2004), 'Modernity's Histories: Rethinking the Long Nineteenth Century, 1750–1950', https://escholarship.org/uc/item/2k62f464#page-1 (last accessed 29 December 2019).

[88] Marx, K. (1937), *The Eighteenth Brumaire of Louis Bonaparte* [1851/1852] (Moscow: Progress Publishers). See Mérieau (n 78).

[89] For an overview: Gilmartin, M. (2009), 'Colonialism/imperialism', in: Gallaher, C. *et al* (eds), *Key Concepts in Political Geography* (London: Sage), 115 ff; Osterhammel, J. (2005), *Colonialism: A Theoretical Overview*, 2nd ed (Princeton: Markus Wiener Publishers); Knight, F.W. (2000), 'The Haitian Revolution', in: 105 *American Historical Review*, 103 ff. Davis, M. (2000), *Late Victorian Holocausts* (London: Verso); Marsh, K. (2013), *Narratives of the French Empire: Fiction, Nostalgia, and Imperial Rivalries, 1784 to the Present*, (Lanham: Lexington Books); Anghie, T. (2005), *Imperialism, Sovereignty and the Making of International Law* (Cambridge: Cambridge University Press).

[90] For a critical analysis of the patterns of authoritarianism: Adorno, T.W. (1970), '*Die Freudsche Theorie und die Struktur der Faschistischen Propaganda*', in: 24 *Psyche*, 486 ff; see also Brown, W. *et al* (2018), *Authoritarianism. Three Inquiries in Critical Theory* (Chicago: University of Chicago Press); Gordon, P.E. (2016), 'The Authoritarian Personality Revisited: Reading Adorno in the Age of Trump', in: *boundary*, 15 June.

[91] Results are implausible to begin with if only candidates of one party are standing for election; if candidates are only allowed to stand for election with the approval of the government (Rwanda 2017); or if opposition candidates are arrested, excluded or intimidated. The results are also implausible if they suggest a manipulated count. At a rare moment of a constitutionally fixed plausibility flaw, the preamble of the *Constitution of*

Weimar emergency decrees pursuant to Article 48, paragraph 2 of the Weimar Constitution, 1919;[92] imprisonment without trial; little or no protection for minorities; little or no tolerance of oppositional opinions and programmes. Other symptoms include gender inequality, which betrays an intimate relationship between authoritarianism and patriarchy;[93] manipulation of the rules of political responsibility and accountability; extension of the terms of office;[94] recourse to a quasi-dynastic principle in regulating succession; and rigid administration and constriction of the public sphere. Furthermore, authoritarian regimes reduce the density and efficiency of judicial review of state measures, and often replace them with appeals to the population to support political decisions and projects. They habitually declare a state of exception and impose emergency measures, frequently designed to manage economic crises. Last not least, authoritarianism tends to enforce a political criminal law that punishes dissent as high treason[95] and deviations from state religion as blasphemy or defamation.[96] Almost without exception, xenophobia and homophobia, anti-Semitism and misogyny, and more recently Islamophobia are venomous ingredients of authoritarian politics. Thus, the demonization of others – out-groups, strangers, minorities – functions as a toxic agent of negative integration.

Were one to conduct a pathological inquest, the variants of authoritarianism would be characterized by clusters of disease patterns or syndromes, each of

---

the Islamic Republic of Iran (1979) mentions the approval it received by referendum: 98.2 per cent!

[92] *Rule by decree* will be discussed in Chapter 4, Section 4.

[93] Brandt, M. J. and Henry, P. J. (2012), 'Gender Inequality and Gender Differences in Authoritarianism', in: 38 *Personality and Social Psychology Bulletin*, 1301 ff.

[94] I return to this aspect of authoritarian practice later (Chapter 5). A recent, and certainly not the last case was Xi Jinping, who had his term limit lifted in March 2018 with the blessing of the (docile) National People's Congress of China. This permitted him to preserve the trinity of his functions as chairman of the Communist Party, head of the Military Commission and president.

[95] For high or war treason, the German *Wehrmacht* courts imposed about 25 000 death sentences from 1933–45 and executed about 18 000–22 000 of them. See Messerschmidt, M. (2005), *Die Wehrmachtjustiz 1933–1945* (Paderborn/Munich/Vienna/Zurich: Schöningh); Jahn, M. (2004), *Das Strafrecht des Staatsnotstandes* (Frankfurt am Main: V. Klostermann).

[96] While in more secularized societies initiatives prevail that try to get rid of blasphemy laws, theocracies and other countries with a state religion affirm them – see Temperman, J. and Koltay, A. (2017), *Blasphemy and Freedom of Expression: Comparative, Theoretical and Historical Reflections after the Charlie Hebdo Massacre*, (Cambridge: Cambridge University Press). In Pakistan, one of the frontrunners, blasphemy carries the death penalty – see Talbot, I. (1998), *Pakistan, a Modern History* (New York: St. Martin's Press), 282.

which combines in different ways three particularly striking symptoms: first, a deep mistrust of dissent and opposition; second, an equally deep aversion to political risks inherent in genuine (democratic) competition; and third, a dogmatism that does not tolerate ambiguity and rejects any kind of co-determination powers as well as mutual obligations. Regardless of how they are combined, these basic symptoms form and inform the clinical diagnosis of political authority infected by authoritarianism. However, one must take into account that in each national context, an autocrat is further shaped by the given political constellation and culture, social forces and economic imperatives. A threatening authority presented itself in a fascist leader cult in Germany and Italy. The corporative *Estado Novo* of Portugal received support from the Catholic Church in an unholy alliance with the secret service and the military.[97] South Africa's apartheid regime relied on a legal framework blended with a racist agenda that guided brutal state practice and extinguished dissent.[98] Likewise, the institution of slavery and white supremacy in the southern states of the United States owed its long life to prejudice, economic interests and the Jim Crow Laws.[99] Militarism infected dictatorial juntas in Greece, Argentina, Chile, North Korea, Myanmar and numerous other countries around the world. The charismatic Gamal Abdel Nasser – head of a one-party system he founded and a military clique he commanded – assumed power in Egypt in 1952, crushed the opposition (the Muslim Brotherhood) and set up an authoritarian regime. In 1958 he declared a state of emergency and then pursued his politics and ideology, based on a mix of nationalism, pan-Arabism and anti-colonialism, with remarkable popular support after nationalizing the Suez Canal and implementing land reforms.[100] Once her charisma had faded away and her nationalism had lost much of its attraction, Indira Gandhi tried to wield power based on repression and a state of exception; today's president of India, Narendra Modi, combines dogmatic Hindu nationalism with emergency powers drawn from a normalized,[101] yet undeclared state of exception which

---

[97] Costa Pinto, A. (1996), *Salazar's Dictatorship and European Fascism: Problems of Interpretation* (New York: Columbia University Press).

[98] Davis, D. (2019), 'Authoritarian Constitutionalism: The South African Experience', in: Alviar and Frankenberg (n 72), 57 ff.

[99] Frederickson, G.M. (1981), *White Supremacy: A Comparative Study in American and South African History* (Oxford: Oxford University Press).

[100] Vatikiotis, P.J. (1991), *The Modern History of Egypt. From Muhammad Ali to Mubarak*, 4th ed (Baltimore/London: The Johns Hopkins University Press); Edel. M. and Josua, M. (2018), 'How Authoritarian Rulers Seek to Legitimize Repression: Framing Mass Killings in Egypt and Uzbekistan', in: 25 *Democratization*, 882 ff.

[101] The concept of normalization of the state of exception is discussed at great length in Frankenberg, G. (2014), *Political Technology and the Erosion of the Rule of Law. Normalizing the State of Exception* (Cheltenham: Edward Elgar Publishing), Chapter 1.

he brings to bear by proxy against the opposition, critical media and, above all, the Muslim population.[102]

7. FAREWELL TO 'POPULISM'?

Today, 'populism' pervades the media, the public and science, relatively unchecked; and occupies a broad conceptual field with blurred borders. In this field, empty phrases and buzzwords frustrate attempts to arrive at an appropriately precise, empirically informed understanding of this complex phenomenon. It might be helpful to clarify the discourse, abandon the concept of populism and look for other terms. However, it seems unlikely that 'populism' could be replaced in the academic discourse, media commentaries or political pamphlets.[103] Nonetheless, there is a lot to be said for attempting to distinguish between the various iterations of 'populism'. The term calls for historical memory and regional differentiation; for attention to its programmatic diversity, cultural specifics and political economy. Its indeterminacy resists definition and analytical clarity, very much like the proverb has it: jelly

[102] Bhowmick, N. (2020), 'Why this Indian State is Witnessing the Country's Most Violent Anti Citizenship-Law Protests', in: Time, 1 January; Filkins, D. (2019), 'Blood and Soil in Narendra Modi's India', in: *The New Yorker*, 2 December.

[103] Concerning both the ambiguity and attractiveness of populism and its strained relationship to democracy and constitutionalism, see, from the hardly manageable bulk of literature: a helpful, clear and insightful introduction: Mudde, C. and Roviro Kaltwasser, C. (2017), *Populism: A Very Short Introduction* (Oxford: Oxford University Press). The contributions of Canovan, Laclau and Germani qualify as more elaborate, classic texts: Canovan, M. (1981), *Populism* (New York: Harcourt Brace Jovanovich); *id* (1999), 'Trust the People! Populism and the Two Faces of Democracy', in: 47 *Political Studies*, 2 ff; Germani, G. (1978), *Authoritarianism, Fascism, and National Populism* (Piscataway Township: Transaction Publishers); Laclau, E. (1977), *Politics and Ideology in Marxist Theory: Capitalism, Fascism, Populism* (London: NLB/Atlantic Highlands Humanities Press); *id* (2005), *On Populist Reason* (London: Verso). B. Moffitt contends that populism is a political style and pays attention to the populist use of social media: Moffitt, B. (2016), *The Global Rise of Populism: Performance, Political Style, and Representation* (Stanford: Stanford University Press), 2016. J.–W. Müller focuses on the moral claim of many populist movements and governments that they represent the authentic people and describes how, once in power, they turn authoritarian: Müller, J. –W. (2016), *What is Populism?* (Philadelphia: University of Pennsylvania Press). Philipp Manow analyses the North-South split of populism and relates it to its political economy: (2018) *Die Politische Ökonomie des Populismus* (Berlin: Suhrkamp). A concise set of criteria is developed by Vorländer, H. (2011), 'The Good, the Bad and the Ugly', in: 8 *Totalitarianism and Democracy. An International Journal for the Study of Dictatorship and Liberty*, 187 ff.

cannot be nailed to the wall.[104] At best, the main modalities of its use or lines of discourse can be profiled here,[105] albeit briefly.

7.1 Populism as a Style of Political Mobilization

To begin with, populism designates a style that movements or parties use to mobilize potential followers (eg, the population at large; the underclass; farmers) and to put issues on the political agenda that are widely negated. Generally, it is designed to encourage apathetic or excluded social groups or classes to take their interests in their own hands and participate in politics. This style of mobilization features direct addresses to the people and relies on rhetoric or (promised) incentives that have popular appeal – notably welfare programmes, social benefits or tax cuts. In Argentina in the late 1940s and early 1950s, Peronism succeeded in mobilizing not only the unions, but also, in particular, the *Descamisados*[106] (the Shirtless), turning this term of derision into one of pride and honour. Peronism has been described as a blend of labourism, nationalism and corporatism, combined with a socially progressive agenda.[107] Apologists of Peronism also characterize the agenda as populist, insofar as it mobilized the masses (workers), and especially the most vulnerable social groups. While observers and academic analyses have mixed opinions on Chavismo policies, in particular his brand of socialism, they would recognize that Hugo Chávez initially attempted to mobilize Venezuela's poverty-stricken population in the early years of his political career.[108]

A current example of this mobilization strategy is the *Podemos* ('We can') party in Spain. It began as a protest movement to transform indignation into political change (*Mover ficha: convertir la indignación en cambio politico*), enjoyed success in the elections and became a coalition partner in government.[109]

---

[104] Berlin, I. (1967), 'To Define Populism', in: *The Isaiah Berlin Virtual Library*, 1ff, http://berlin.wolf.ox.ac.uk/lists/bibliography/bib111bLSE.pdf/ (last accessed 26 June 2019).

[105] For new ideas that helped me revise the first version (in *Autoritarismus, Verfassungsrechtliche Perspektiven*), I have to thank Scott Newton.

[106] For example, Evita Peron's Speech to the *Descamisados* on 17 October 1951, www.marxists.org/history/argentina/peron/1951/speech.htm (last accessed 29 December 2019).

[107] James, D. (1988), *Resistance and Integration: Peronism and the Argentine Working Class, 1946–1979* (New York/Cambridge: Cambridge University Press).

[108] Hawkins, K.A. (2016). 'Chavismo, Liberal Democracy, and Radical Democracy', in: 19 *Annual Review of Political Science*, 311 ff.

[109] Mudde, C. (2015), 'The problem with populism', in: *theguardian.com*, 17 February; Cini, M. and Perez-Solorzano Borragan, N. (2016), *European Union Politics*, 5th ed (Oxford: Oxford University Press).

Where there are no 'castaways', no civilian deserters in large numbers, the myth of the 'people' still functions as a mobilization narrative, because it is structurally presented to exclude those who do not belong to the real 'true' people (eg, migrants, refugees, even elites). This style of mobilization and its translation into governmental action are discussed in Chapters 6 and 7. Special attention will be paid to the point at which democracy-enhancing mobilization evolves into democracy-denying demobilization of the people.

7.2 Populism as Strategy

Related to the style of mobilization, populism can also denote a strategy for gaining political power, as in the case of the Populist Party in the United States at the end of the nineteenth century, which was considered a left-wing and agrarian populist movement.[110] The strategic component or modality of populism can be observed in many movements through the world, such as Peronism in Argentina; *Chavismo* in Venezuela; the *Rassemblement National* in France; the Alternative for Germany; and, on the surface, Donald Trump's election campaign.

Populism as strategy follows a *plan* to participate in the political process with the aim of transforming a movement into a party (even if its character as a movement is to be preserved). These movement organizations launch election campaigns in order to obtain a position of power, securing a presence on representative bodies and holding government offices. To this end, one of the central goals of the Populist Party in the United States was to create a coalition between the farmers in the South and West and the urban labourers in the Midwest and Northeast. However, the party did not have the necessary organization or resources to muster support in urban areas. (Arguably, the party would have needed a Bernie Sanders figure to mobilize the urban population.) Its leadership divided, its agenda and strategy unclear, the Populist Party disbanded in 1908.

7.3 Populism as Ideology

Populism is often said to have no ideology, or only a 'thin' ideology.[111] Obviously, the 'thickness' or 'thinness' depends on the definition of ideolo-

---

[110] Lawrence, G. (1978), *The Populist Moment: A Short History of the Agrarian Revolt in America* (Oxford: Oxford University Press).

[111] Stanley, B. (2008), 'The Thin Ideology of Populism', in: 13 *Journal of Political Ideologies*, 95 ff; Mudde, C. (2004), 'The Populist Zeitgeist', in: 39 *Government and Opposition*, 542 ff; Laclau, *On Populist Reason*, 117 f.

gy.[112] 'Thick' would probably require a comprehensive worldview and a fairly systematic, if not hermetic theory (eg, historical materialism, socialism or neoliberalism). Rather than demanding an all-inclusive theory or programme, I suggest – following Eagleton – that a set of ideas qualifies as an ideology if it has 'enough cognitive content to help organize the practical lives of human beings'[113] and 'works' as an interpretive framework. Accordingly, there is not a comprehensive world vision to be found in the programmatic texts and pamphlets of Trump's election campaign or governing agenda; however, he invites his followers to embrace the ideology of white supremacy and American hegemony. Similarly, the *Sverigedemokraterna* (Swedish Democrats), the *Dansk Folkeparti* (Danish People's Party), *Lega* and *Cinque Stelle* (in Italy), *Fidesz* and *Jobbik* (in Hungary), and *Prawo i Sprawiedliwość* in Poland offer a rudimentary anti-elitist, xenophobic, nationalist interpretive framework. The *Partido Socialista Unido* in Venezuela – at least before its fragmentation – and especially Perón's *Justicialista* have more to offer in terms of programmatic ideas and ideology. Nevertheless, most of today's aggressive nationalist authoritarianisms come with weird, fragmentary and dangerous programmes that qualify as ideology: a set of ideas through which social actors make sense of the world, define their enemies and embrace a (mostly right-wing) political agenda.

If such conceptual modesty (or naivety?) can be accepted for the time being, it is easy to see that most populist movements and parties – without presenting a precise explanation of why things are the way they are – propose how 'we the people' should see and understand the world, albeit in a selective, sketchy way.[114] Many populists want to engage their audience in a Manichean – that is, ideological – discourse of politics as the inevitable struggle between the (good) 'mythical' people 'down here' and the (evil) elites, bureaucrats (eg, in Brussels or Washington), rulers (in Paris or Berlin) or technocrats (in the World Trade Organization, the International Monetary Fund or the World Bank) 'up there'.[115] This discourse is currently fuelled in particular by radically nationalist movements, parties and regimes in Hungary, Poland and several EU member states; as well as by *Podemos* (Spain), some of the *gilets jaunes* in France, Geert Wilders' *Volkspartij voor Vrijheid en Democratie* in the Netherlands and more. In other parts of the world, the nationalist Manichean

---

[112] I side in the following, though neither very closely nor religiously, with Eagleton, T. (2007), *Ideology. An Introduction* (London: Verso).

[113] Eagleton (n 112), 27.

[114] Albertazzi, D. and McDonnell, D. (2008), 'The Sceptre and the Spectre', in: *id* (eds), *Twenty-First Century Populism. The Spectre of Western European Democracy* (London: Palgrave MacMillan), 1 ff.

[115] Mudde (n 111); Vorländer (n 103).

tableau draws on religion and ethnicity. In India, the Modi regime not only propagates Hindu nationalism, but also combines it with Hindu supremacy, to the disadvantage of the Muslim population.[116] In ideological contrast, Turkish President Erdoğan is bent on the re-Islamization of Turkey, without a clearly supremacist agenda.

Another crucial element of populist (nationalist) ideology is the invocation of a deeply divided society. Thus, Donald Trump has always tried to persuade his followers that the United States is divided two camps: the good people in his heartlands and the corrupt elites and intellectuals in New York, Hollywood and Washington, who will not acknowledge that the country is being menaced by illegal Mexican immigrants and Muslims. Likewise, the Brexit protagonists in Britain and President Erdoğan in Turkey (especially after the 2016 coup) conjured up the image of a deeply divided society.

Populists – or as I prefer, authoritarian nationalists – almost invariably blend this Manichean worldview with apocalyptic visions of the homeland being overrun and occupied by 'others'. India's Prime Minister Modi wants India to demonstrate strength and power over its rivals and enemies – particularly (Muslim) Pakistan, after a decades-long territorial dispute and recurrent flashes into violence, and the Muslim community in the country. Trump decries illegal Mexican migrant workers coming from the south and Muslim refugees threatening the United States from outside. Orbán fantasized about a 'Soros Plan' to flood Europe, and in particular Hungary, with 2 million Muslim refugees. Erdoğan has turned the Turkish army against the Kurds, even though they were previously allies in bringing down ISIS.

Thus, populists structure the world and produce a corresponding mindset by incessantly telling those who will listen how to make sense of politics, the opposition, capitalism, immigration, Islam and so on. The political success of Trump, Erdoğan, Orbán, Chávez, Maduro and Modi demonstrates how these basic ideological modules (one is tempted to invoke Marx's concept of false consciousness) can be produced and reproduced, and their content disseminated. Sometimes local specifics are added to the Manichean world, such as the narrative of a heroic past – think of the Hungarian nation in the time of St Stephen or the conservative Bolivar lending his image of *libertador* to socialist Chávez[117] – or the promise of a golden future.

---

[116] Subramanian, S. (2020), 'How Hindu supremacists are tearing India apart' in: *The Guardian*, 20 February.

[117] See González-Jácome (n 73).

7.4 Populism as Discontent

Populism – or at least some of its strands – can also be more precisely read as the expression of a diffuse unease or discontent that is triggered especially by a feeling that things (work, status, life) are out of control. Even if not clearly articulated, this discontent can be understood as a critique of the globalizing and totalizing dynamic of neo-liberalism. More specifically, it is directed against the incursions of authoritarian capitalism into non-capitalist terrains, as social relations, education and health systems are increasingly economized and cannibalized.[118] Such incursions also extend to politics, as reflected in the adaptation of political decisions and rhetoric to economic imperatives.[119]

Populist discontent often results from the feelings of insecurity and loss of control caused by these incursions. It is usually experienced at the margins of society by those who perceive themselves (for good reason) as the 'losers of modernity'. In many countries, it has also permeated the middle classes, who are or feel threatened by an 'accelerated capitalism' that invalidates their qualifications, undermines their social status and has sent them drifting downstream.[120] This is why they object to cosmopolitanism, universalism and other liberal stances, and reject with anger and fear the ambivalence of modernization, dreading the onslaught of capitalism. In consequence, the media and academia tend to name its bearers, such as Trump voters in the US rust belt or protest movements in Germany: angry or enraged citizens who have been neglected or left behind and who, as marginalized groups, must cope with precarious living conditions (real or imagined) or with the repercussions of infrastructure projects.

This brand of populism is primarily directed against what are seen as the political and legal failures of irresponsible economic and political elites and incompetent members of the political class. *ANO 2011*, the 'Movement of Dissatisfied Citizens', organized protests in the Czech Republic against 'the corruption of the system' and 'Brussels bureaucracy'. It still identifies as

---

[118] Harvey, D. (2006), *The Limits to Capital* (London: Verso); Heitmeyer (n 27), 118 ff.

[119] Angela Merkel's idea that democratic decision-making must be 'in conformity with the market' indicates how far the economization and 'taking' of the political has progressed. Less obvious, but far-reaching is TINA ('there is no alternative') – originally claimed by Margaret Thatcher but also practised elsewhere – a maxim that indicates a triumph of economic imperatives over the political.

[120] Movarelli, M. (2019), 'The success of populism, and why it's all about the middle class' in: *euroactiv.com*, www.euractiv.com/section/economy-jobs/opinion/the-success-of-populism-and-why-its-all-about-the-middle-class/ (last accessed 5 January 2020); Rothstein, B. and Steinmo, S. (2018), '"Us Too!" – The Rise of Middle-Class Populism in Sweden and Beyond', in: 19 *Social Europe*, 595 ff.

a political movement rather than a political party, even though it is currently a coalition partner in government and its founder and leader, multi-millionaire Andrej Babiš, is the prime minister.[121] Populism as discontent is also illustrated by *Lega* in Italy and by Bolsonaro's Alliance for Brazil, which decries same-sex marriage and homosexuality, abortion, affirmative action and drug liberalization. In the absence of a viable, attractive social democracy that might channel this discontent, demagogues such as Trump, Orbán, Salvini, Maduro, Duterte and Bolsonaro can play the crowds to their advantage. And in the next election or referendum, they convert this anger into votes or support for their politics.

7.5 Populism as a Rhetoric of Resentment and Identity

If used in relational terms, populism characterizes a rhetoric of resentment that invokes 'the people', who rally behind the flag of national patriotism or illiberalism against 'others' whom populists wish to exclude from the community. References to the 'authentic people' should not be overrated, however. Instead, leaders of 'populist' movements and parties, who are out to foment resentment, adopt 'the people' as a pretext for talk of nationalist identity and a cover narrative for inciting anger.

While discontent operates in a vertical direction against those in power, resentment focuses first horizontally on potential social allies (eg, the middle class; the 'losers'; the xenophobes), then downward on those who do not belong 'here' because they come from elsewhere (strangers; foreigners; migrants; refugees; clans) or who live 'here' as minorities but, from a majoritarian view, should not. The latter do not belong because they are different or look different; or because they deviate from accepted norms of sexual, political or other behaviour, or from the accepted faith. The targets of resentment are always minorities. Consequently, populist resentment is charged with possessive pronouns and tends to appropriate nation, society or people: 'We are the people – and who are you?'[122] 'We want our country back'; 'Bring back our country'.[123] However, these grand identities – nation, people, society, religious community and so on – are proxies for what resentment actually reclaims: safety, control, cultural hegemony and a (more) homogenous society.

---

[121] Heinrich Boell Foundation ed. (2013), 'Political earthquake in the Czech Republic: Rejection of established parties', 28 October.

[122] Turkey's President Erdoğan, cited by Djavadi, A. (2016), '"Who Are You?" How Erdoğan Has Lowered the Tone of Turkish Politics', in: *Turkey Notebook*, August 2016. See Holtmann, E. et al. (2006), *Die Droge Populismus. Zur Kritik des politischen Vorurteils* (Wiesbaden: VS Verlag).

[123] Slogans of the *Alternative für Deutschland*.

Resentment cannot be fed by prejudice alone, but must be continually recharged by anti-minority events (e.g. diatribes on social media against homosexuals or Jews), taboo breaking through abusive language (eg, Holocaust denial), protests (eg, anti-Semitic rallies; national consultation in Hungary against George Soros' plan to relocate millions of refugees in Europe)[124] and even violence (eg, arson attacks on the homes of refugees in Germany and pogroms against Muslims in India).[125]

For the critics of populism, resentment is expressed in generalizing, moralizing labels, such as 'racist', 'fascist' and 'neo-Nazi'. These may well be empirically correct, but they contribute little to understanding the deeper problems of those who feel marginalized. Labelling will not help to overcome resentment, let alone heal the ruptures.[126]

7.6 Populism as a Style of Governing

Populism is not only a phenomenon of protest, a psychological disposition (discontent or resentment) and a strategic attitude in politics, but also a style of governing that reveals itself in state practice.[127] Two aspects are striking here, which will be discussed more thoroughly in later chapters. On the one hand, plebiscites are privileged over electoral politics, or elections are manipulated and thus turned into *de facto* plebiscites – a style that can be traced back to Bonapartism. While Marx understood Bonapartism as the bourgeoisie's toleration of an authoritarian regime that favoured bourgeois class interests and supported its 'social domination', today's Bonapartist plebiscites in autocracies[128] echo the crisis of representative democracy and the welfare state (and social democracy) – and lend themselves to nationalist politics. (For more details on this, see Chapter 6.)

---

124 'National consultation on "Soros plan" extended', in: *Budapest Business Journal*, 27 November 2017, https://bbj.hu/news/national-consultation-on-soros-plan-extended_142127/ (last accessed 30 December 2019).

125 Shah, F. (2020), '"The Government Has Done This": Inside India's Muslim Pogrom', in: *The Nation*, 5 March, www.thenation.com/article/world/india-delhi-violence (last accessed 9 March 2020).

126 Heitmeyer (n 27), 14 ff; Manow (n 103), 26 ff.

127 Canovan, M. (2002), 'Taking Politics to the People: Populism as the Ideology of Democracy', in: Mény, Y. and Surel, Y. (eds), *Democracies and the Populist Challenge* (New York: Palgrave), 25 ff; Jun, H. (2004), '*Populismus als Regierungsstil in westeuropäischen Parteiendemokratien*', in: Decker, F. (ed), *Populismus – Gefahr für die Demokratie oder nützliches Korrektiv?* (Wiesbaden: Springer), 233 ff.

128 A motley group including, among others, Hungary (Orbán) and Venezuela (Chávez).

On the other hand, populist governance features a peculiar method of communication. Leaders have a preference for bypassing the institutionalized channels of addressing the people. On the side of the state, they ignore or circumvent parliaments and party committees; on the side of society, they avoid the media (unless under governmental control). Instead, they communicate through top-down monologues – at rallies, on television, in social media – directed at their followers or society at large. The cult of immediacy that they establish and exploit will be reviewed in Chapter 7.

7.7 Populism as a Category of Political Geography

Populism also functions as an indicator that positions a movement, party or regime within the coordinates of traditional political geography. Whereas it seems fairly evident that politically, the terms 'left' and 'right' no longer mean what they did at the time of the French Revolution,[129] the media and participants in the academic discourse on populism freely refer to 'right-wing populism' and 'left-wing populism'. Thus, right-wing extremists such as *Vlaams Belang* (Belgium), the *Rassemblement National* (France), *ANO 2011* (Czech Republic) and the *Alternative für Deutschland* may be distinguished from left-wing movements such as early Peronism (Argentina), *Chavismo* (Venezuela) and *Podemos* (Spain).[130]

Often, this kind of labelling appears to be a (vain) attempt to exorcise radical nationalism and ban 'right-wing populism' from the liberal camp, despite the fact that there is a significant intersection between authoritarian capitalism and 'right-wing populism'.[131] As shorthand, these labels may be unavoidable at times and useful in quickly charting movements and agendas. However, one might still argue for a more precise identification: for example, 'nationalist', 'xenophobic', 'misogynist', 'homophobic', 'anti-Semitic' or 'Islamophobic' instead of merely 'right-wing'; and 'nationalist', '(eco-)socialist', 'social democratic'/'liberal', 'unionist' or 'authoritarian' instead of merely 'left-wing'. I would further argue that it is utterly inappropriate to trivialize organizations and leaders that practise or condone hate speech and pave the ground for hate crimes as 'populist'.

---

[129] Gauchet, M. (1996), 'Right and Left', in: Nora, P. (ed), *Realms of Memory I: Conflicts and Divisions* (New York: Columbia University Press), 248 ff; Bobbio, N. and Cameron, A. (1997), *Left and Right: The Significance of a Political Distinction* (Chicago: University of Chicago Press).

[130] Priester, K. (2012), *Rechter und linker Populismus: Annäherung an ein Chamäleon* (Frankfurt am Main: Campus Verlag).

[131] Wilkinson, M. (2019), 'Authoritarian Liberalism as Authoritarian Constitutionalism', in: Alviar and Frankenberg (n 72), 317 ff.; and Heitmeyer (n 27).

7.8 Making Sense of Populism

If one does not want to drop the term 'populism' altogether, it may be illuminating to bear in mind the aforementioned ways in which the concept is used and, in particular, to distinguish a democracy-enhancing, populist drive to mobilize marginalized, disenfranchised groups of society from strictly authoritarian, xenophobic, corporatist, anti-institutionalist, socialist, conservative or other agendas. In this regard, it is crucial to identify the point at which and the reasons why mobilization is discontinued and replaced by repressive governing techniques; and when and how popularity and unity with the people turn into sheer demagogy and camouflage.

Those who find populism analytically useful are further invited to distinguish between populist movements, parties, governments and consolidated regimes. It is likely to make a difference whether populist ideas and strategies are articulated by protest movements or are being pursued by the state as government policy; whether they have already consolidated themselves as a regime or must be accommodated as partners in a coalition government; whether changes in rhetoric and compromises as regards strategy and agenda may be required; and whether there is a general willingness to be moderate. Instructive cases in point would include the ideological development of *Podemos*[132] in Spain, *ANO 2011* in the Czech Republic, *Cinque Stelle* and *Lega* in Italy, *Chavismo* in Venezuela and Peronism in Argentina.

Moreover, populism's ubiquity and indeterminacy demand that attention be paid – aside from their radically nationalist leanings – to specific programmatic components. Examples include Trump's racist supremacism and tribalism (the importance of being white);[133] Orbán's more than latent anti-Semitism (revealed in election campaigns and national consultations);[134] Maduro's siege mentality and discrediting of 'enemies' in Venezuela;[135]

---

[132] Sola, J. and Rendueles, C. (2018), 'Podemos, the upheaval of the Spanish politics and the challenge of populism', in: 26 *Journal of Contemporary European Studies*, 99 ff ; Rodríguez Teruel, J. (*et al*) (2016) 'Fast and Furious: Podemos' quest for power in multi-level Spain', in: 21 *South European Politics and Society*, 561 ff.

[133] Serwer, A. (2019), 'The President's Pursuit of White Power', in: *The Atlantic*, January; Coates, T. (2017), 'The First White President', 7 September.

[134] Echikson, W. (2019), 'Viktor Orbán's anti-Semitic problem', in: *Politico*, 13 May.

[135] Kurmanaev, A. and Herrera, I. (2019), 'Venezuela's Maduro Cracks Down on His Own Military in Bid to Retain Power', in: *The New York Times*, 13 August; 'Mastermind or scapegoat? Besieged South American leaders blame Venezuela's Maduro for historical wave of unrest', in: *The Washington Post*, 31 October 2019.

Erdoğan's ethno-nationalist persecution of Kurds in Turkey;[136] and Modi's Hindu-nationalist and anti-Muslim bigotry in India.[137] There are many further examples that go beyond the scope of 'populism' and will be discussed later under the auspices of authoritarianism and its variants.

Finally, comparable to the argument above regarding authority, the *relationship* constituted by so-called 'populism' and its dynamics must be taken into account. It seems plausible to ask whether the populism of a political chief, clique, regime or party exhausts itself in unilateral measures and rhetoric that impress a docile audience; or whether it enters into a dialogue with the people and relies on their willingness to listen and be persuaded. In short, the question here is whether 'populism' is about authoritarian power or authoritative power.

8. REINTRODUCING AUTHORITARIANISM

In light of the authoritarian xenophobic nationalism known as 'right-wing populism' which is currently rampant in Europe, and also the wide spectrum of heterogeneous authoritarianisms, I need to reduce the complexity somewhat. In the following chapters, I avoid, as far as possible, the unqualified use of 'populism'. Instead, I will reintroduce 'authoritarianism' and 'authoritarian constitutionalism'. Generally speaking, 'political authoritarianism' is identified here as a configuration of strategy, ideology,[138] propaganda and practical performance – a complex ensemble shaped by the respective socio-economic environment, cultural dispositions and political constellations. Special attention is paid to the latter, because of their proximity to the constitution. These constellations give rise to diverse techniques of governing, styles of representation and normative or other justifications of domination, each of which – in its own way – is constituted by a mix of several basic elements. After examining liberal constitutionalism and its 'authoritarian moments' (Chapter 3),

---

[136] Burc, R. (2019), 'The Long Kurdish Struggle', in: *The New York Times*, 22 October; Ashdown, N. (2019), 'Erdogan Wants to Redraw the Middle East's Ethnic Map', in: *Foreign Policy*, 8 November.

[137] Filkins, D. (2019), 'Blood and Soil in Narendra Modi's India', in: *The New Yorker*, 13 December; Chaudhary, A. and Marlow, I. (2019), 'Why India's Modi Has His Country's Muslims Worried', in: *The Washington Post,* 13 December.

[138] I do not share the view that authoritarianism replaces ideology with mentality. See Linz, J.J., (1975), 'Totalitarian and Authoritarian Regimes', in: Greenstein, F.I. and Polsby, N. (eds), *Macropolitical Theory: Handbook of Political Science* III (Reading: Addison-Wesley), 175 ff. At any rate, authoritarianisms do not renounce ideology, if one understands the latter (as I have argued above) as a pattern of interpretation, each of which is connected with certain value systems, thus forming a frame of reference for making sense of the world.

I shall examine the four most striking elements[139] – presented here as a critical analytics – that contribute to the strength and, arguably, the fascination of authoritarian regimes.

First (and almost trivially), authoritarianism is marked by an executive style of governance (Chapter 4). However, it not only operates in the modality of repression, but by the same token, is also productive: 'it traverses and produces things',[140] such as knowledge and even pleasure (for followers at least). This style is shaped by constitutional opportunism, prefers informalism and routinely comes with a security agenda.

Second, many authoritarian regimes and leaders can be recognized by their concept of political power as private property (Chapter 5). The spirit and practice of private ownership, rather than trust or a public law entitlement, come to the fore in the management of power (notably term limits), decisions on succession and the appropriation of public goods and moneys (kleptocracy).

Third, the chapter on participation as complicity (Chapter 6) discusses how authoritarianism exploits the crisis of representative democracy and transforms political action (eg, demonstrations, elections) into support for the regime.

Fourth, this peculiar type of participation is complemented by a communicative style that disposes of intermediary institutions and media, then creates a cult of immediacy (Chapter 7) aimed at spawning fantasies of an illusory communality between leaders and followers.

---

[139] This is not to deny that authoritarianism, especially authoritarian constitutionalism, can also be described and classified differently. See, for example, Brooker, P. (2009), *Non-Democratic Regimes*, 2 Aufl (New York: Palgrave), 9, 1 ff and 16 ff, who distinguishes monarchy, one-person rule, military government and one-party systems; also O'Donnell, G. (1979), *Modernization and Bureaucratic Authoritarianism: Studies in South American Politics* (Berkeley: University of California Press), and Linz (n 138).

[140] Foucault, M. (1980), 'Truth and Power', in: *Power/Knowledge. Selected Interviews and other Writings 1972 – 1977*, Gordon, C. (ed) (New York: Pantheon Books), 109 ff/119.

3. Authoritarian moments of liberal constitutionalism

Iliacos intra muros peccatur et extra.[1]

The orthodoxy of both political liberalism and liberal constitutionalism treats their authoritarian sibling – or neighbour? – as neither an 'essentially controversial concept'[2] nor a phenomenon of its own right that is to be taken seriously. It is usually dismissed as a travesty or as a deceptive ensemble of norms, principles and practices that mimics a 'Western' vocabulary, but lacks the proper spirit that supports the framework of legality. This orthodoxy – the mainstream in constitutional theory and comparative law – cultivates a naïve notion of Western law and Western constitutionalism without being aware of the attendant ethnocentric connotations. Inevitably, this means that all – at first sight – 'non-Western' constitutions are not perceived as unfamiliar or alien charters, accompanied by equally exotic theories and therefore examined with particular intensity; but are rather discredited as liberalism's evil or cagey 'other'. Authoritarian constitutionalism is thus viewed solely in the light of an (idealizing) liberal-democratic projection. This chapter aims to counteract such 'Westernization' and normalization: first, with a brief critique of the Anglo-European colonization of the constitutional world, followed by a review of authoritarian moments in the liberal-democratic world of constitu-

[1] 'Within and without the walls of Ilium (Troy) there is sin.' Quintus Flaccus Horaz, *Episteln*, quoted after *Brockhaus' Kleines Konversations-Lexikon* (2011), 5th ed, vol 2 (Leipzig: F.A. Brockhaus), 368.

[2] According to Gallie, W.B. (1956), 'Essentially Contested Concepts', in: 56 *Proceedings of the Aristotelian Society*, 167 ff, the disputed term must designate or acknowledge a certain phenomenon ('appraisiveness'); it must be complex in itself – that is, have several definitional components ('internal complexity'); it must be describable in different ways, whereby the different accentuations give rise to different meanings ('diverse describability'); it must be open – that is, subject to modification, for example, in response to changing historical circumstances ('openness'); and it must be recognized as disputed by those involved in the discourse ('reciprocal recognition'). These criteria are easily met by both constitutionalism and authoritarianism, as will be shown in the following chapters.

tional theory and practice, which demonstrates that both inside and outside the walls of liberalism, there is sin.

1. LIBERAL COLONIZATION OF THE CONSTITUTIONAL WORLD

It is no coincidence that ethnocentrism is sprawling on the Western divan – that is, strikingly evident in European countries and the United States. Why should law and constitution be exempt from this approach? One of the 'masters of comparative law', René David, set the marker for 'Western law' that constitutional comparatists, relying on a fuzzy and incoherent epistemology and methodology, adopted without hesitation. In his essay on the 'Concept of Western Law', René David – to this day an influential figure in the French interpretative community – defends with remarkable self-confidence and lack of critical reflection the hegemonic view of things and the authoritarian attitude it supports. He considers an essential attribute of 'Western' civilization to be the role that law is supposed to play in societies:

> As Westerners, we have an ideal: a society that is dominated as much as possible by law... This ideal is undoubtedly imperfectly realized to varying degrees in our present societies, but we strive for its progressive realization, and for societies that reject the idea of law, we can only imagine that anarchy, arbitrariness and chaos reign there.[3]

The problem with such ideological statements is that they combine naivety with a unitarizing approach. As a result of this combination, constitutional theory and constitutional comparison derive their information and evaluations mainly from the experience and ideas of half a dozen reasonably politically stable, economically prosperous liberal democracies. Non-European and non-American texts and traditions are denied the 'same discursive dignity'. Certainly, the cradle of modern constitutionalism has long been sited in Virginia, Philadelphia and Paris. But colonialism has continued by other means: the Central European-American privileging of the interpretive pattern of freedom and limited and lawful government has left other variants, such as egalitarian or transformative constitutionalism, in the shadows.

After the constitutional experiments of the nineteenth century,[4] it is hardly plausible to assume that authoritarian constitutions have nothing to contribute

---

[3] David, R. (1983), 'On the Concept of "Western" Law', in: 52 *Cincinnati Law Review,* 126 ff

[4] More on this later. See Frankenberg, G. (2018), *Comparative Constitutional Studies – Between Magic and Deceit* (Cheltenham: Edward Elgar Publishing), 156 ff.

to the understanding of constitutionalism as a combination of constitutional theory, practice and culture. However, this is precisely what standard textbooks and monographs can be charged with: they remain firmly within the narrow confines of the liberal paradigm and seek to bring the world of the constitutional under cognitive control, primarily from the perspective of the jurisprudence of the US Supreme Court.[5] This is supplemented by the jurisprudence of some other – 'Western' – constitutional courts, such as Germany's Federal Constitutional Court, the *Court constitutionelle* in France, and sometimes the constitutional courts of Italy and South Africa, and – more recently –the *Corte Suprema Justicia* of Colombia.[6] The focus is always directed to the practice and problems of judicial review. Methodologically, this type of comparison not only concentrates on the centre (the West), its institutions and its view of the problem, at the expense of the periphery (the rest), but also operates on the assumption that the areas of agreement and convergence have significantly more weight than important forms of contextual, structural or functional diversity.[7] By concentrating comparisons on the established liberal operation, authoritarian ways of dealing with constitution are automatically left outside the spectrum of attention.

Ethnocentrism[8] manifests itself not only in the privileging of one's own ethnicity (nation, people, social group) and a hostile attitude towards phenom-

---

5 The title of David Fontana's otherwise very informative and thorough analysis, 'The Rise and Fall of Comparative Constitutional Law in the Postwar Era', in: 36 *Yale International Law Journal* (2011), 1 ff, suggests that he investigates the rise and fall of the whole discipline. However, the author deals almost exclusively with the era of the Warren court and the pre- and post-Warren period in the United States.

6 For example, Finer, S.E. et al. (2006), *Comparing Constitutions* (Oxford: Clarendon); Murphy, W. and Tanenhaus, J. (1977), *Comparative Constitutional Law: Cases and Commentaries* (London: Palgrave Macmillan); Jackson, D.W. and Neal Tate (eds) (1992), *Comparative Judicial Review and Public Policy* (Santa Barbara: Greenwood Press); Dorsen, N. et al. (2016), *Comparative Constitutionalism,* 3rd ed (Eagan: West Publishing Co). A wider spectrum and more differentiated methodological considerations are offered by Jackson, V.C. and Tushnet, M. (2014), *Comparative Constitutional Law*, 3rd ed (New York: Foundation Press).

7 For further unitary approaches, see David (n 3); Mauro Cappelletti, M. (ed) (1978), *New Perspectives for a Common Law of Europe* (Leyden: Sijthoff); critical Teitel, R. (2004), 'Comparative Constitutional Law in a Global Age', in: 117 *Harvard Law Review,* 2570 ff; Frankenberg (n 4), 74–84; Frankenberg (1985), 'Critical Comparisons – Rethinking Comparative Law', in: 26 *Harvard International Law Journal*, 411 ff and (2016), *Comparative Law as Critique* (Cheltenham: Edward Elgar Publishing); Legrand, P. (2001), 'The Return of the Repressed. Moving Comparative Legal Studies Beyond Pleasure', in: 75 *Tulane Law Review*, 1033 ff and (2016), 'Negative Comparative Law', in: 10 *Journal of Comparative Law*, 405 ff.

8 The concept was made popular by Sumner, W.G. (1906), *Folkways* (New York: Ginn & Co). For the more recent debates, see Reynolds, V. *et al* (1987), *The*

ena of foreign law, but also in the fact that unfamiliar behaviour or aspects of foreign cultures are interpreted through the lens of one's own culture, tradition or common sense, thus self-referentially exporting familiar values and ideas. The foreign 'other' is seen as a deviation from the known that deserves less attention than the own because it is inferior, less developed, derivative and marginally significant. Ethnocentrism is the result one can expect when comparative analyses of cultural artefacts, such as constitutions or laws, go on a 'strategic trip': the strategy being that researchers of the foreign mentally and cognitively 'never leave the train' and operate only on the basis of their settled (and unshakable) knowledge.[9] As examples, 'civilization' in the nineteenth and twentieth centuries was defined by the schools of comparative law as essentially white, male and Christian; and the predominant view of constitutionalism tended – and still tends, despite the growing number of dissidents – to consider the world from a liberal position[10] or to operate from the totalizing position of a Western-style constitution. René David was convinced that:

> the idea of the rule of law is a concept shared by Western nations. This is the idea that the countries of Africa and Asia support when, in order to assert their desire to 'westernize', they take inspiration from models provided by the nations of Western Europe or the nations of common law. [11]

From this, one can easily conclude that the representation of the constitutionally different, unfamiliar or foreign was – and still is – normative from the beginning. No matter how interesting, exotic or enigmatic a foreign constitu-

---

Sociobiology of Ethnocentrism (Athens: University of Georgia Press). 'Ethnocentrism' in: *Dictionary of Race, Ethnicity and Culture* (London: Sage Publications Ltd, 2003); Kinder, D.R. and Kam, C.D. (2009), *Us Against Them: Ethnocentric Foundations of American Opinion* (Chicago: University of Chicago Press).

9 'Settled knowledge does not *grow*' – Popper, K. (1994), *The Myth of the Framework: In Defence of Science and Rationality* (London/New York: Routledge), 156.

10 Notably dominated by the concept of globalized US-American constitutionalism: Ackerman, B. (1997), 'The Rise of World Constitutionalism', in: 83 *Virginia Law Review*, 771 ff. It is the point of reference for Kim Lane Scheppele's rich and in-depth analysis of 'Autocratic Legalism' (2018), in: 85 *The University of Chicago Law Review*, 545 ff. See also Pech, L. and Scheppele, K.L. (2017), 'Illiberalism Within: Rule of Law Backsliding in the EU', in: 19 *Cambridge Yearbook of European Legal Studies*, 3 ff; see the introduction and narrative of decay by Ginsburg, T., Huq, A.H. and Versteeg, M. (2018), 'The Coming Demise of Liberal Constitutionalism?', in: 85 *The University of Chicago Law Review*, 239 ff; and the counter-narrative presented by Epstein, R. (2018), 'The Wrong Rights, or: The Inescapable Weakness of Modern Liberal Constitutionalism', in: 85 *The University of Chicago Law Review*, 403 ff.

11 David, 'The Concept of 'Western' Law', 131. Dorsen et al. invoke 'the universal ideal of constitutionalism' in the teacher's manual for the textbook *Comparative Constitutionalism*.

tion may be, the own and the familiar are inevitably evaluated more positively. The constitutions of authoritarian regimes thus have a hard time finding a place in a world dominated by the liberal paradigm, let alone achieving the equal discursive dignity necessary for critical analysis. In order to grant them this status, especially in the open space of critique, and at the same time to undermine the notion that they are 'other', we will now consider the arguments through which authoritarian constitutionalism is expelled from the accepted space of investigation.

The need to find a position from which authoritarian constitutionalism is not examined and criticized merely as a derivative phenomenon is supported by its diversity and global spread.[12] There is a presumption that the discursive hegemony of liberalism could obscure what is hidden both in the autocratic heart of darkness and behind the liberal glamour: in each case, an ambivalence or paradox that could be a key to better understanding both authoritarian and liberal constitutionalism.

2. A CRITIQUE OF LIBERALISM'S DEFENSIVE RHETORIC

2.1 Constitutionalism 'in the Proper Sense'

Boldly Anglo-Eurocentric, liberal orthodoxy operates with the concept of constitutionalism 'in the proper sense'.[13] This brand of authentic constitutional theory and practice comprises the complex of liberal ideas, ideals and ideologies and the combination of practices and patterns of government that reside behind the stockade of legality, and occupy an area where the authority of any government ideally derives from, and finds its limits in, basic laws and fundamental rights and the rules of a system of competences. This orthodoxy is based on the polished Anglo-Eurocentric constitutional history. It almost obsessively[14] privileges a constitutionalism of rights.[15] Rights are understood

---

[12] Similarly: Niembro Ortega, R. (2016), 'Conceptualizing authoritarian constitutionalism', in: 49 *Verfassung und Recht in Übersee*, 339 ff.

[13] From the hardly manageable literature on the marking of 'authentic constitutionalism': Dicey, A.V. (1914), *Introduction to the Study of the Law of the Constitution*, 8th ed (London: Macmillan); McIlwain, C.H. (1947), *Constitutionalism: Ancient and Modern* (Ithaca: Cornell University Press; Duverger, M. (1944), *Les constitutions de la France* (Paris: Presses Universitaires de France); Grimm, D. (2016), *Constitutionalism – Past, Present and Future* (Oxford: Oxford University Press).

[14] Gargarella, R. (2013), *Latin American Constitutionalism 1810–2010. The Engine Room of the Constitution,* (Oxford: Oxford University Press), vii, notes an 'obsessive attention to issues of rights'.

[15] In their empirical study, David Law and Mila Versteeg measure 'constitutional compliance' consequently with reference to the 'rights performance' of states: Law,

as negative competences of the state and as positive competences that enable the civil and political use of freedom. In contrast, social entitlements and basic rights, as well as redistributive policies of the welfare state, recede into the background.

Democratic constitutionalism as an ideal type differs from this model by a different focus and accentuation: it is less concerned with the rights of the possessive or non-possessive but vulnerable individual, and therefore aims not to prevent intervention – that is, the defence against unlawful state encroachments – but rather to enable and safeguard civic action and political active status through the guarantee of freedoms and the institutionalization of procedures that are intended to guarantee the 'state-generating legal status'[16] and active civic competence.

Viewed from the high ground behind the stockade, the constitutions of authoritarian regimes are argued down to the level of deviant or deficient forms of liberal and/or democratic constitutionalism in democratically not fully developed or failed states.[17] At worst, they are seen against the background of totalitarian regimes.[18] At best, they appear in this perspective as transitional phenomena that have yet to develop towards fundamental rights, the separation of powers and free elections.

The thesis of an 'authentic'[19] or 'proper' constitutionalism (which inevitably implies that there are also 'inauthentic' or 'improper' ones) is based on the condensed conception of an institutional and legal arrangement that forges a liberal political order based on a framework of legality – constitutional democracy – formerly known as a free republic. From this perspective, constitutionalism is thus coextensive with the canonical elements of liberalism: enforceable (basic) rights, free and fair elections, separation of powers, judicial review of governmental and administrative measures, and so on. In short: rule

---

D.S. and Versteeg, M. (2013), 'Sham Constitutions', in: 101 *California Law Review*, 863 ff.

[16] See Denninger, E. (1990), *Der gebändigte Leviathan* (Baden-Baden: Nomos), 1990, 9 ff; and Preuß, U.K. (1974), *Legalität und Pluralismus* (Frankfurt am Main: Suhrkamp).

[17] To the concept: Chomsky, N. (2006), *Failed States: The Abuse of Power and the Assault of Democracy* (New York: Henry Holt & Co); Breede, H.C. (2017), *The Idea of Failed States* (New York: Routledge) .

[18] See Somek, A. (2003), 'Authoritarian Constitutionalism: Austrian Constitutional Doctrine 1933 to 1938 and Its Legacy', in: Joerges, C. and Singh Ghaleigh, N. (eds), *Darker Legacies of Law in Europe: The Shadow of National Socialism and Fascism over Europe and its Legal Traditions* (Oxford: Hart Publishing), 361 ff; see also Niembro Ortega (n 12).

[19] Instructive, if read as a critique of ideology: Adorno, T.W. (1973), *The Jargon of Authenticity* (Evanston: Northwestern University Press).

of law and democracy. The actual constitutionalism functions as an elaborate update of the conceptual amalgamation of John Locke's 'limited and lawful government', Thomas Paine's 'power with... right', Immanuel Kant's 'constitutional state'[20] and James Madison's moderate suspicion[21] which is targeted against majorities – all of this translated into the constitutional law of our time and adapted to the respective national context. In his *Second Treatise*, John Locke sketched out what James Harrington had previously propagated as the 'empire of laws'[22] and later, with more ideological momentum, circulated worldwide as the 'government of laws and not of men' (Article 30 of the 1780 Constitution of Massachusetts). This ensemble of philosophical and juridical ideas comes with an impressive pedigree and brings forth the liberal paradigm of constitutionalism[23] – and also bears the defensive semantics that banish improper constitutionalism from the world of study as a phenomenon of no interest.

2.2 Constitutions without Constitutional Culture

From the liberal perspective, the 'inauthentic' or 'improper' constitutions of authoritarian regimes qualify at best as 'constitutions without constitutionalism', because they lack the setting of a constitutional culture and the spirit and ideas that could guide 'genuine' constitutional usances.[24] This is another way

---

[20] Locke, J. (1960), *Two Treatises of Government* [1689] (New York: The New American Library); Paine, T. (2012), *Rights of Man. Being an Answer to Mr. Burke's Attack on the French Revolution* [1792] (Cambridge: Cambridge University Press); Kant, I. (1976), '*Metaphysische Anfangsgründe der Rechtslehre*' [1797] in: id, *Studienausgabe*, vol IV, Weischedel, W. (ed) (Frankfurt am Main: Suhrkamp); Ripstein, A. (2009), *Force and Freedom: Kant's Legal and Political Philosophy* (Cambridge: Harvard University Press).

[21] Hamilton, A., Madison, J. and Jay, J. (1961), *The Federalist Papers* [1787/1788] (New York: The New American Liberary).

[22] Harrington, J. (1992), *The Commonwealth of Oceana and A System of Politics* [1656], Pocock, J.G.A. (ed), (Cambridge: Cambridge University Press).

[23] Holmes, S. (2012), 'Constitutions and Constitutionalism', in: Rosenfeld, M. and Sajó, A. (eds.), *The Oxford Handbook of Comparative Constitutional Law* (Oxford: Oxford University Press), 198 ff.

[24] For example, Brown, N.J. (2002), *Constitutions in a Nonconstitutional World* (Albany: State University of New York Press); Okoth-Ogendo, H. (1993), 'Constitutions Without Constitutionalism: An African Political Paradox', in: Douglas Greenberg *et al* (eds), *Constitutionalism and Democracy: Transitions in the Contemporary World* (New York: Oxford University Press), Chapter 4; Chen, A.H.Y. (2014), 'The Achievement of Constitutionalism in Asia – Moving Beyond "Constitutions Without Constitutionalism"', in: *id* (ed), *Constitutionalism in Asia in the Early Twenty-First Century* (Cambridge: Cambridge University Press), 4 ff; Bredies, I. (2011), 'Verfassungsen ohne Konstitutionalismus: quasikonstitutionelle Institutionalisierung

in which authoritarian charters are denied any constitutional qualification and accordingly are variously dismissed as 'paper constitutions', 'mere parchment limitations of power', 'Potemkin villages', 'dishonest promises' or 'façades'. With mild disdain, some authors suggest that these constitutions are '*de jure*, but not *de facto*' – 'aspirational texts' that ultimately go nowhere from a normative viewpoint.[25] It is sometimes acknowledged that, while the constitutional conformity of governmental actions can be guaranteed, legal authority and the application of constitutional provisions by no means correlate with the principle of constitutionalism, correctly understood as limited and lawful government: 'Constitutions without constitutionalism do not curb authoritarian rule, but make it possible in the first place.'[26]

These semantics regularly take account of non-Western systems only – above all, the constitutions of socialist regimes[27] (albeit now somewhat out of vogue); next, of the constitutions of the Arab and African world;[28] and then – to a lesser extent at present – the constitutions of Latin American states. The idea of 'constitutions without a constitutional culture' was originally based primarily on the non-enforceability of rights and deficits in the separation of powers in centralist or one-party states, or on the disintegration of democracy and liberalism: '[T]he two strands of liberal democracy, interwoven in the

---

des Autoritarismus in Osteuropa', in: 8 *Totalitarismus und Demokratie*, 133 ff. Critical: Prembeh, H.K. (2007), 'Africa's "Constitutionalism Revival": False Start or New Dawn?', in: 5 *International Journal of Constitutional Law*, 469 ff; and the thoughtful and incisive critical study by Sultany, N. (2017), *Law and Revolution: Legitimacy and Constitutionalism After the Arab Spring* (Oxford: Oxford University Press); and *id* (2019), 'Arab constitutionalism and the formalism of authoritarian constitutionalism', in: Alviar and Frankenberg, *Authoritarian Constitutionalism – Comparison and Critique* (Cheltenham: Edward Elgar Publishing), 292 ff.

25 See Murphy, W.F. (2007), *Constitutional Democracy: Creating and Maintaining a Just Political Order,* (Baltimore: Johns Hopkins University Press), 14; Sajó, A. (1999), *Limiting Government: An Introduction to Constitutionalism* (Budapest: Central European University Press); Sartori, G. (1962), 'Constitutionalism: A Preliminary Discussion', in: 56 *American Political Science Review*, 853 ff; Greenberg, D. *et al* (eds) (1993), *Constitutionalism and Democracy, Transitions in the Contemporary World* (New York: Oxford University Press). For more interesting perspectives and interpretations, see Ginsburg, T. and Simpser, A. (eds) (2014), *Constitutions in Authoritarian Regimes* (Cambridge: Cambridge University Press); and notably Sultany, *Law and Revolution: Legitimacy and Constitutionalism After the Arab Spring* (n 24).

26 Bredies (n 24) 134.

27 For an implicit critique of this literature, see Scott Newton's diagnosis of Soviet constitutionalism: Newton, S. (2017), *The Constitutional Systems of the Independent Central Asian States. A Contextual Analysis* (Oxford: Hart); Frankenberg (n 4), 46 ff (analysis of socialist programme constitutions).

28 Brown (n 24), xiv and 9–10.

Western political fabric, are coming apart in the rest of the world. Democracy is flourishing; constitutional liberalism is not.'[29]

The façade theorem and related labels are based on two highly problematic conclusions. First, they reduce constitutionalism *per se* – that is, any constitutional theory and practice – to the liberal paradigm, and here in particular to compliance with rights, their enforceability, judicial control and effective power-limiting functions. Thus, other grammars of the constitutional are ignored, which are more egalitarian (Haiti 1805, South Africa 1996, Bolivia 2009) or which are not concerned with staving off interventions (of the state), but rather aimed at stabilizing or improving social conditions by promoting emancipation through state intervention.[30] The following passage in a decision of the Supreme Court of Kenya, which can also be found analogously in the rulings of the South African Constitutional Court, is quite instructive:

> Kenya's Constitution of 2010 is a transformative charter. Unlike the conventional 'liberal' Constitutions of the earlier decades which essentially sought the control and legitimization of public power, the avowed goal of today's Constitution is to institute *social change* and *reform,* through values such as *social justice, equality, devolution, human rights, rule of law, freedom and democracy*...[31]

The problem of the liberal paradigm and its mechanisms of denial is obvious: they paralyze the constitutional imagination and do not allow other ideas of constitutional theory, practice and culture to be recognized as 'constitutional'. Obviously, liberal orthodoxy can do little with dramatically divergent views on the meaning and purpose of constitutions, such as the following:

> Lenin and the Bolshevik Party believed that the constitution is not only a legal act but also a major political document. The Party regarded the constitution as a ratification of the gains of the revolution and also as a proclamation of the fundamental aims and objectives of building socialism.[32]

---

[29] Zakaria, F. (1997), 'The Rise of Illiberal Democracy', in: 76 *Foreign Affairs*, 22 ff, 23.

[30] Regarding the transformative constitutionalism: Klare, K. (1998), 'Legal Culture and Transformative Constitutionalism', in: 14 *South African Journal on Human Rights*, 146; Klug, H. (2000), *Constituting Democracy: Law, Globalism and South Africa's Political Reconstruction* (Cambridge: Cambridge University Press); Davis, D. (2019), 'Authoritarian Constitutionalism – the South African Experience', in: Alviar and Frankenberg (n 24), 57 ff

[31] Supreme Court of Kenya, *Speaker of the Senate & Another v Attorney-General & Another & 3 Others,* paragraph 51 – quoted by Kibet, E. and Fombad, C. (2017), 'Transformative Constitutionalism and the Adjudication of Constitutional Rights in Africa', in: 17 *African Human Rights Journal*, 340 ff.

[32] Brezhnev, L. (1977), *On the Draft Constitution of the Union of Soviet Republics* (Moscow: Foreign Languages Publishing House), 10.

To resurrect Leonid Brezhnev as a flawless constitutionalist would be quite absurd. Nevertheless, it is important to open our eyes to socialist programme charters and their specific functions.[33] That these – because they do not correspond to the liberal paradigm – have a purely symbolic meaning as façades from the outside, and an instrumental meaning as tools of social control from the inside, says little about them and is actually a fairly trivial observation. And one wonders why communist one-party systems which, through the police, military and secret services, have far more powerful and far-reaching instruments through which to control behaviour and ensure loyalty would fall back on the modest services that constitutions can offer. Moreover, it is not obvious whom such constitutional manoeuvres would (or could) deceive; this is the final point (Chapter 8) I will address, in an attempt to pin down the purposes of constitutions and their audiences. Until then, the reference to the task of ratifying social developments should therefore be taken quite seriously, because it in no way diminishes a critical approach. In addition, one might ask whether a constitution could not contribute something to mobilizing the population towards a given (positive) ideology.[34]

Second, reducing non-liberal constitutions to mere façades or deceptions in turn suggests that liberal-democratic constitutions are genuine/authentic/proper law (and not mythical founding narrative, rhetoric or ideology), and keep their promises with neither distortion nor deficit. A thorough search for the sites of power in liberal constitutions would suggest otherwise. Only naïve positivism, however, could tempt one to read liberal constitutions as political maps with a reasonably tight grip on reality. Few would disagree, I hope, with the view that liberal constitutionalism turns a clouded eye to political power[35] and a blind eye to private power – its formation, exercise and distribution; and is anything but 'colour blind'[36] with regard to race and skin colour, as myth would have it in the United States since the much-criticized decision of *Plessy v Ferguson* (1896)[37] – a landmark ruling that distorted the meaning of

---

33 Frankenberg (n 4), 46 ff; Newton (n 27), 86 ff

34 See Bui, T.H. (2013), 'Liberal Constitutionalism and the Socialist State in an Era of Globalisation: An Inquiry into Vietnam's Constitutional Discourse and Power Structures', in: 5 *Global Studies Journal*, 43 ff.

35 Reading, for instance, the US Constitution is not very illuminating about the powers of the president.

36 Sealing, K.E. (1998), 'The Myth of a Color-Blind Constitution', in: 54 *Washington University Journal of Urban and Contemporary Law*, 157 ff; and Gotanda, N. (1991), 'A Critique of "Our Constitution is Color-Blind"', in: 44 *Stanford Law Review*, 1 ff.

37 *Plessy v Ferguson* 163 US 537 (1896). The case originated in 1892, when a citizens' committee brought Louisiana's Separate Car Act (1890) to court. The law required that all railroads in the state provide 'equal but separate accommodations' for

the 'equal protection' clause of the Fourteenth Amendment to accommodate racial segregation.[38] In *Plessy*, the US Supreme Court had to rule on the constitutionality of segregation. The majority of the judges affirmed this with the following argument:

> A statute which implies merely a legal distinction between the white and colored races -- a distinction which is founded in the color of the two races, and which must always exist so long as white men are distinguished from the other race by color -- has no tendency to destroy the legal equality of the two races... The object of the [Fourteenth A]mendment was undoubtedly to enforce the absolute equality of the two races before the law, but in the nature of things it could not have been intended to abolish distinctions based upon color, or to enforce social, as distinguished from political equality, or a commingling of the two races upon terms unsatisfactory to either.

Judge Harlan was the sole dissenter, who upheld the liberal credo (bravely in the context of *Plessy*) against the majority of judges:

> Our Constitution is color-blind, and neither knows nor tolerates classes among citizens. In respect of civil rights, all citizens are equal before the law. The humblest is the peer of the most powerful. The law regards man as man, and takes no account of his surroundings or of his color when his civil rights as guaranteed by the supreme law of the land are involved.[39]

This ruling was passed more than a century ago and was subsequently revised step by step,[40] but it is still of pressing relevance.[41] Racism is entrenched in the most diverse constitutional states, including the United States.[42] In addition to

---

white citizens and non-whites ('coloreds'). Passengers were not allowed to enter compartments other than those allocated to them on the basis of race.

38 'All persons born or naturalized in the United States, and subject to the jurisdiction thereof, are citizens of the United States and of the State wherein they reside. No State shall make or enforce any law which shall abridge the privileges or immunities of citizens of the United States; nor shall any State deprive any person of life, liberty, or property, without due process of law; nor deny to any person within its jurisdiction the equal protection of the laws.' (Section 1 of the 14th Amendment).

39 *Plessy v Ferguson*, 537, 559 (1896).

40 In the 1950s, *Plessy* was repealed by decisions that declared racial segregation unconstitutional: *Brown v Board of Education of Topeka*, 347 US 483 (1954). See Balkin, J.M. (2002), *What Brown v. Board of Education Should Have Said* (New York: New York University Press).

41 Alexander, M. (2012), *The New Jim Crow* (New York: The New Press).

42 Allen, T. (1994/1997), *The Invention of the White Race*, 2 vols (London: Verso); Bonilla-Silva, E. (2018), *Racism without Racists: Color-Blind Racism and the Persistence of Racial Inequality in the United States,* (Lanham: Rowman & Littlefield Publishers, Inc).

race, property/class, ethnicity, religion, political conviction and gender – constitutional axes of inequality – remain relevant as constitutional issues.[43] There is therefore no reason to understand the liberal paradigm as a complete and realized programme, much less to immunize it against criticism. For a robust analysis of authoritarian (as well as liberal and democratic) constitutions, it is therefore advisable not to assume the purity and innocence of liberal constitutionalism – for example, the absence of strategic motives and political agendas. For this reason, I remain aloof from the Manichean image of good versus evil constitutions and pose, in relation to *all* constitutions, the following questions.

First, do they refer to a concrete (and not just idealized) state practice?[44] Second, what types of state practices and state techniques elude the respective constitutional matrix?[45] Third, what kinds of state practices require a constitutional theory that lies beyond the liberal paradigm and is more precisely tailored to its basic features?

These questions will guide the following considerations. They assume that constitutionalism can refer to diverse theories and practices: constitutionalism (1) oriented towards limiting government, as well as (2) promoting the transformation of society and increasing political authority;[46] (3) instrumental for the pursuit of certain goals (order, discipline), as well as (4) symbolic, geared towards mobilizing people and propagating a collective idenwtity; (5) cynical-bad faith (constitutions as deceit, ideology), as well as (6) normative good faith (constitutions as freedom-enhancing, democracy-supporting). These central questions seem significant because it is interesting to consider what authoritarian rulers might expect from a constitution.

---

43 Daniels, J. (1997), *White Lies: Race, Class, Gender and Sexuality in White Supremacist Discourse* (New York: Routledge); Irving, H. (2008), *Gender and the Constitution. Equity and Agency in Comparative Constitutional Design* (Cambridge: Cambridge University Press); Röhner, C. (2019), *Ungleichheit und Verfassung - Vorschlag für eine relationale Rechtsanalyse* (Frankfurt am Main: Velbrück).

44 State practice is used as a synonym for (hierarchical but also non-hierarchical) 'governance': Mayntz, R. (2009), *Über Governance* (Frankfurt am Main: Campus).

45 Concerning state techniques or political technology see Frankenberg, G. (2014), *Political Technology and the Erosion of the Rule of Law. Normalizing the State of Exception* (Cheltenham: Edward Elgar Publishing).

46 Similar: Brown (n 24), xiii and 3 ff.

3. AUTHORITARIAN FOUNDING MOMENTS OF LIBERAL CONSTITUTIONALISM

'Gallery of shame'[47] or business as usual of liberal constitutionalism? Probably neither, if one traces authoritarian moments of liberalism. And yet both premises are in evidence when one considers the ambivalence of the liberal paradigm and seeks out the skeletons that are hidden in its closet. Gallery of shame, because authoritarianism is regularly denied from the inner perspective; and business as usual, insofar as the ambivalences of liberalism are put into theory by constitutions. Denial, however, is given a high priority in particular by protagonists of liberal constitutionalism: denial as silence or clothed in the semantics of defence that argue away authoritarian structures (and sins) or justify then as inevitable, necessary or at least practical.

Denial begins at the first constitutional moment: the 'hour zero' of a founding event that concludes a constitutional debate with a commanding gesture. The *pouvoir constituant*, usurped by self-proclaimed elites or occupied by appointed or elected representatives of the democratic sovereign, submits the draft of the basic agreement to the electorate or its deputies in Parliament, who then vote on it. Once adopted, the constitution enters into force. In this mutual promise, if the image of a social contract is fitting, everyone is included. Even minorities that lost the vote and future generations (for obvious reasons) must surrender, at least for the time being. They owe, like all others, a modicum of constitutional obedience.

Constituting is a performative act: it creates a community by ennobling the population that inhabit a certain area as 'people' and persons, groups in power as 'government'. It transforms the country – that is, a territory with people who are governed into a 'state'. By the same token, these definitions and transformations are acts of structural force: 'The violent structure of the founding act holds a silence.' The 'settlement' by constitutional law, 'the origin of authority is in itself a groundless violence'.[48] Eritrea – not a role model of liberalism – is one of the very few countries to acknowledge this character of constitutions: '[T]he constitution we adopt will be an agreement between us and the government, which we will shape according to our free will, to serve as a means of governing this and future generations…'[49]

---

[47] 'Gallery of shame' is how Duncan Kennedy ironically describes my study of liberalism's authoritarian moments (or rather, the result); *id* (2019), 'Authoritarian Constitutionalism in Liberal Democracy', in: Alviar and Frankenberg (n 24), 173 and 175.

[48] Derrida, J. (1990), 'Force of Law: 'Mystical' Foundation of Justice', in: 11 *Cardozo Law Review*, 921 ff.

[49] Preamble, 1997 Constitution of Eritrea.

Those who do not wish to follow Jacques Derrida and Walter Benjamin into the haze of the mythical[50] and instead prefer to stay on an empirical path will find that the construction and adoption of constitutions are consistently in the hands of elites. At the Constitutional Convention of 1787 – as previously during the deliberations of the Declaration of Independence in Philadelphia in 1776 – it was not 'the good people' of the New England states who assembled there, but always white, wealthy men: landowners, merchants and financiers (see Figure 3.1).[51] That some of these framers were also slaveholders is not a trivial aspect of the founding.[52] Other moments of constitution-making were more or less conspiratorial. The participants met then, as now, but not always in public.

Source: Ullmann Medien, Klass. Neu-Engl-A-So04-D.

Figure 3.1 *White, wealthy men constituting the people*

[50] Benjamin, W. (2003), 'Critique of Violence', in: *id, Reflections, Essays, Aphorisms and Autobiographical Writings*, Demetz, P. (ed) (New York, Schocken Books), 277 ff.

[51] For references, see Beard, C.A. (2017), *An Economic Interpretation of the Constitution of the United States* [1913] (New York: Routledge); and Levy, L.W. (ed) (1969), *Essays on the Making of the Constitution* (Oxford: Oxford University Press).

[52] Klarman, M.J. (2016), *The Framers' Coup: The Making of the United States Constitution* (Oxford: Oxford University Press), especially 257 ff; Zinn, H. (2015), *A People's History of the United States* (New York: Harper); and, of course, the controversial but inspiring study by Beard (n 51).

The extremely successful Philadelphia Style found many imitators. In the course of constitutional history, however, the constitutional elites underwent a change of form. The representatives of the aristocracy, clergy and the (big) bourgeoisie were replaced by political elites as early as the 'threshold period' of constitutionalism – for example, in the United States and France.[53] In the course of the nineteenth century, the national political class dominated the experiments of new or re-constitutionalization. In the twentieth century, elitism took on a colour increasingly dyed by political parties. Party delegates began to consult experts, such as the 'committees of experts' that prepared the Weimar Constitution in 1918 and the 'committees of experts' that shaped the German Basic Law in 1948.[54] After the collapse of Stalinist state socialism, legal consultants were engaged on constitutional and legal projects in the countries of Central and Eastern Europe.

Elites always bring to bear their own interests, views, experiences, agendas, expertise and sometimes their reputation as opponents of a replaced regime in the proceedings of the conventions they dominate. Empirically, the act of constituting was and is predominantly not a self-binding act of the democratic sovereign 'people' in the singular or the plural, but rather an external binding through proxies who speak and decide for the people. Therefore, constitution-making implies the exclusion of those who ultimately neither implicitly nor actually agree with the event and its outcome.

One may consider this operation pertinent or even unavoidable in terms of the division of labour. One can also acquire a democratic taste for it as a reasonable division of labour, because the non-participating people must first be 'constituted' by, and in the act of constituting, the constitution. Once constituted, the people can subsequently correct the exclusion and catch up on the founding by claiming their citizens' rights through protest and other forms of activism.[55]

However, all this can be left aside here. What is at stake is merely the identification (not the condemnation) of an authoritarian moment in liberal constitutionalism, an ambivalence in the founding act. It is revealing that the authoritarian valence is hardly mentioned in historical accounts and is rarely mentioned in the liberal theories of the founding act.

---

[53] With further references and detailed information: Fitzsimmons, M.P. (1994), *The Remaking of France: The National Assembly and the Constitution of 1791* (Cambridge: Cambridge University Press).

[54] Kurtenacker, S. (2017), *Der Einfluss politischer Erfahrungen auf den Verfassungskonvent von Herrenchiemsee* (Munich: H. Utz Verlag).

[55] See Rödel *et al* (1989), *Die demokratische Frage* (Frankfurt am Main: Suhrkamp), 71 ff.

Germans experienced a special variant of covenant authoritarianism, as it were *ex negativo*: in 1990 they were refused what the Basic Law promised. They had just fulfilled their original obligation and unified: 'The entire German people remain called upon to complete the unity and freedom of Germany in free self-determination.'[56] Instead of happily proceeding along the path laid out by Article 146 of the Basic Law in its original version of 1949 and 'freely deciding' to adopt a new, all-German constitution, the unification was administratively accomplished[57] by the accession of the five 'new *Länder*' – a process that a teacher of constitutional law cynically described as a 'failed secession'.[58] One might more aptly say that Germans were deprived of a constitutional debate – in vain lamented by quite a few, barely noticed by most and welcomed by even fewer.[59] The protagonists of the administrative solution immediately opened the arsenal of justification: among other things, they argued that there had been insufficient time to conduct a constitutional debate and a referendum; that the Basic Law was, after all, a solid, widely accepted constitution (which nobody denied); and that a re-founding of the Federal Republic of Germany would have implied a renegotiation of the treaties with the European Union. There may indeed have been good reasons for the 'simple', administrative implementation of the unification; however, they were never explained or discussed publicly in the spirit of a constitutional debate. Even today, the two Germanys sometimes seem to be looking for the missing link that a new constitution could have provided. If the small and internally torn Albania, after the end of a brutal dictatorship and under more difficult political and social circumstances, allowed such a debate,[60] why not the hyper-stable Federal Republic of Germany? So the fact remains that the

---

56 Preamble of the German Basic Law (1949).

57 Pursuant to Article 23 of the Basic Law in its original version: 'For the time being, this Basic Law shall apply in the territory of the Länder of Baden, Bavaria, Bremen, Greater Berlin, Hamburg, Hesse, Lower Saxony, North Rhine-Westphalia, Rhineland-Palatinate, Schleswig-Holstein, Württemberg-Baden, and Württemberg-Hohenzollern. In other parts of Germany it shall be put into force on their accession.'

58 Isensee, J. (1990), '*Abstimmen, ohne zu entscheiden?*', in: *Die Zeit*, 9 June, www.zeit.de/1990/24/abstimmen-ohne-zu-entscheiden (last accessed 1 January 2019); *id* (1990), '*Ist das Volk untergegangen?*', in: *Der Spiegel*, 21 September; see also Frowein, J.A. *et al* (1990), *Deutschlands aktuelle Verfassungslage* (Berlin/New York: W. de Gruyter).

59 See also Deutscher Bundestag (ed) (1996), *Materialien zur Verfassungsdiskussion und zur Grundgesetzänderung in der Folge der deutschen Einigung: Anhörungen und Berichterstattergespräche* (Berlin: Deutscher Bundestag).

60 Frankenberg, G. (1997), 'Stranger than Paradise. Identity & Politics in Comparative Law', in: *New Approaches to International and Comparative Law*, No 2 *Utah Law Review* 1997, 1 ff.

draft constitution prepared at the 'round table' was documented, but not really discussed in public.[61]

This means that decisions to found a polity or even an election may very well be experienced by the losers as a violent exclusion. They have no choice but to wait on the sidelines for the chance to establish a different authority, more conducive to their interests and plans, when power relations change (which they can bring about under favourable conditions). Thomas Jefferson may have had this in mind (or was it the guilty conscience of a member of the victorious US constitutional elite?) when he declared: 'The tree of freedom must be refreshed from time to time with the blood of patriots and tyrants.'[62]

4. THE PREROGATIVE AND LEGISLATIVE TECHNIQUES OF GOVERNING

While the authoritarianism of the founding moment is guarded like a secret in the citadel of liberalism, the discourse on the prerogative takes place quite openly in the light of the interested (professional) public – not, however, under the rubric of authoritarianism. This tradition of frankness was established by one of the most influential founders and theorists of liberalism, John Locke. In the second of his *Two Treatises of Government*, he guides his readers through the authorities that he (not too differently from Hegel) considers to be important – monarch, father,[63] judge and legislator[64] – first in the semi-natural state and then in the semi-social state. 'Semi' because women, mothers, slaves do not have full status in this patriarchal-possessive predator-prey system. Locke's attention is concentrated on the legislative technique of governing,[65] with a different vocabulary framed by the concept of the rule of law. The constitutional design of the institutions (separation of powers) and competences (especially of the legislature), and in particular the supremacy of the legislature

---

[61] The draft discussed at the 'Round Table' is documented with an introduction by Ulrich K. Preuß in: (1990), *Kritische Justiz*, 222 ff; see also Preuß, U.K. (1990), *Revolution, Fortschritt und Verfassung* (Berlin: Wagenbach).

[62] Thomas Jefferson: 'The tree of liberty must be refreshed from time to time with the blood of patriots and tyrants.' (Letter to William Stephens Smith, 13 November 1787).

[63] He recognized that it should be about parents, but he seems to overlook this and the other side of the social theory narrative: subjugation. See the classic critique by Pateman, C. (1988), *The Sexual Contract* (Stanford: Stanford University Press), especially 3 and 19 ff

[64] Locke, J. (1967), *Two Treatises on Government* [1689], Laslett, P. (ed) (Cambridge: Cambridge University Press), Chapter XIV.

[65] Frankenberg (n 45), Chapter I.

(Sections 149–57), seems to be tailored to the secular interests of the developing (possessive) bourgeois society:[66]

> I take political power to be a right to make laws—with the death penalty and consequently all lesser penalties—for regulating and preserving property, and to employ the force of the community in enforcing such laws and defending the commonwealth from external attack; all this being only for the public good.[67]

Locke imposes strict limits on the legislative power:

> The legislative power of every commonwealth, in every form of government, is subject to the following limits to the trust that is put in them by the society and by the law of God and the law of nature. First, they are to govern by published established laws, not to be varied in particular cases, but to have one rule for rich and poor, for the favorite at court and the peasant at his plough. Secondly, these laws ought to be designed for no other ultimate purpose than the good of the people. Thirdly, they must not raise taxes on people's property without their consent, whether given directly or through deputies. This is relevant only for governments where the legislature is always in existence, or at least where the people haven't made any provision for some part of the legislature to be chosen, from time to time, by themselves. Fourthly, the legislature must not transfer the power of making laws to anyone else, or place it anywhere but where the people have placed it.[68]

This sounds promising. After Locke places the general law in the position of the central, formerly monarchical and absolute authority, and with it the core of 'lawful government', there follows a surprising (at least retrospectively) return to tradition and *Realpolitik*, through which he changes the architecture of the constitution. On the threshold of modernity, he in turn introduces the prerogative familiar from monarchical times:[69]

> When the legislative and executive powers are in distinct hands (as they are in all moderated monarchies and well-formed governments), the good of the society requires that various things should be left to the discretion of the executive. The legislators can't foresee and make legal provision for everything that may in future be useful to the community, so the executor of the laws—having the power in his hands—has by the common law of nature a right to make use of it for the good of

---

66 Concerning the controversy about Locke's 'possessive individualism', see: MacPherson, C.B. (2011), *The Political Theory of Possessive Individualism – Hobbes to Locke* (Oxford: Oxford University Press); and for a different perspective, see Tully, J. (1980), *A Discourse on Property, Locke and his Adversaries* (Cambridge: Cambridge University Press).

67 Locke, J. (n 64) *Second Treatise*, Chapters 1, 3.

68 Locke, J. (n 64) *Second Treatise*, Chapters 11, Section 142.

69 Brooks, C.W. (2008), *Law, Politics and Society in Early Modern England* (Cambridge UK: Cambridge University Press).

> the society in many cases of difficulty where the existing law doesn't deal with the difficulty—until the legislature can conveniently be assembled to make laws that do. There are many things that the law can't possibly provide for, and those must be left to the discretion of him who has the executive power in his hands. Indeed, it is appropriate that the laws themselves should in some cases give way to the executive power, or rather to the fundamental law of nature and government that: All the members of the society are to be preserved as much as may be...[70]
>
> The word 'prerogative' is the name for this power to act according to discretion, for the public good, without the support of the law and sometimes even against it.[71]
>
> This power, while employed for the benefit of the community and in accordance with the trust and purposes of the government, is an undoubted prerogative that the executive has, and it is never called into question.[72]

Locke's introduction of the prerogative deserves to be quoted at some length, because it breaks through the legislative technique of the state and makes the autocratic valence of liberal constitutionalism in the modern narrative quite obvious and in need of justification. Locke relieves himself of this burden in a normative way by referring to the natural law of self-preservation, and in a pragmatic-empirical way by pointing out problems that are unforeseeable for the legislature.

From that point onwards, both *topoi* accompany like a shadow the further development and metamorphoses of the regulatory model of liberalism as it is embedded in the regimes of law-rule, such as rule of law, the *État de droit, estado de derecho, Rechtsstaat* and its relatives.[73] It is particularly evident in times of crisis. We will see that the protagonists of these models, in all their variations, rationalize the executive branch's exceptional powers time and again by bringing into play the unpredictability of social emergencies and unforeseeable crises and, correspondingly, the fragmentary nature of a legal system; or else by trivializing them as ordinary contributions to public security.[74] The coronavirus pandemic is the latest, albeit most dramatic crisis of the

---

70 Locke, J. (n 64), *Second Treatise*, No 159.

71 Locke, J. (n 64), *Second Treatise*, No 160.

72 Locke, J. (n 64), *Second Treatise*, No 161. See the in-depth analysis of the prerogative in Loughlin, M. (2010), *Foundations of Public Law* (Oxford: Oxford University Press), 377 ff with further references.

73 As had been pointed out already by Herbert Marcuse (1979), '*Der Kampf gegen den Liberalismus in der totalitären Staatsauffassung*' [1934], in: *id*, *Schriften*, vol 3 (Frankfurt am Main: Suhrkamp), 21.

74 This usually happens when the state of exception is extended: see, for example, Jacquin, J.-B. (2017), 'L'intégralité du projet de loi du gouvernement pour banaliser les mesures de l'état d'urgence', in: *Le Monde,* 8 June, www.lemonde.fr/libertes-surveillees/article/2017/06/08/l-integralite-du-projet-de-loi-du-gouvernement-pour

regulatory model that Locke tried to bring home to his contemporaries. We will return to this crisis later when discussing the state of exception.

The arguments of both unpredictability and self-preservation undermine the liberal-legal model's claim to regulate *all* essential conflicts and problems of life in society, while at the same time compromising its formal-rational authority. Martin Loughlin precisely elaborates the tension between norm and exception (not only in Locke's work). However, he tries to offset the authoritarian aspect of this political-legal dynamic by introducing the 'extraordinary sovereign' as a 'matter of sociological necessity'.[75]

Whatever one wants to call it – ambivalence, the combination of two antithetical narratives or constructive contradiction – from the very beginning, the liberal citadel has a deep crack in its masonry, creating inroads for a personal, arbitrary, executive style of governing that eludes the constraints of the model. To use another metaphor: the prerogative becomes a Trojan horse that sneaks diverse authoritarian moments into the inner sanctum of liberality. In the following, three forms of authoritarian statehood will be briefly introduced: the dual state, the deep state and the state of exception. Subsequently, modified variants of the prerogative, more limited in range, will be discussed.

5. THE PREROGATIVE IN THE DUAL STATE AND DEEP STATE

Ernst Fraenkel introduced the concept of the dual state in 1940/1941 as a matrix for the analysis of the Nazi regime,[76] which Franz Neumann described as a structurally amorphous behemoth.[77] The 'dual state' refers to the coexistence of the executive prerogative state that rejects all formal rationality and the normative state, designed to regulate and bind state activity through norms, but where 'there is always a reservation (lurking): the consideration of political expediency'.[78] Thus, the dual state appears to be a schizophrenic version of liberal democracy that resides well outside the liberal paradigm, combining

-banaliser-les-mesures-de-l-etat-d-urgence_5140602_5109455.html (last accessed 1 January 2019).

[75] Loughlin (n 72), 383–87. The ambivalence of this construction of the prerogative is brought to the fore by Mansfield, H.C. (1993), *Taming the Prince: The Ambivalence of Modern Executive Power* (Baltimore: Johns Hopkins University Press), 181 f.

[76] Fraenkel, E. (1969), *The Dual State* (New York: Octagon Books).

[77] In contrast, Neumann, F. (2009), *Behemoth - The Structure and Practice of National Socialism 1933–1944* [1944] (Chicago: Ivan R. Dee, Inc), accentuated the lack of structure of the Nazi regimes, the manipulation of the masses through terror in legal form and above all the totalitarian monopoly economy ('command economy').

[78] Fraenkel (n 76).

legality and expediency. On closer scrutiny, it is not all that alien to a liberal order.

Depending on the situation in a dual state, expediency transcends the legal boundaries of areas of competence and standardized procedures, and undermines judicial controls. And apart from the legal matters of the capitalist economic order, the normative state, according to Fraenkel, never operates on safe ground, but is always threatened by the dynamics of the action state (of measures). Within the sphere of power of the Nazi regime, the prerogatives of the leader and the party worked towards the 'complete elimination of the inviolability of law' and any predictability of state action. The *Reichstag* Fire Decree of 28 February 1933[79] and the Enabling Act that followed in March 1933 testify to the dynamic of the executive state. They morphed into the *de facto* constitutional charter of the Third Reich on the ruins of the suspended and demolished Weimar Constitution, and on the basis of the prerogatives of terror.

If one removes the dual state from its original, fascist context and looks for transgressions of the boundaries of what Fraenkel called the 'normative state' – that is, rule of law – as well as the triumph of expediency over legality, this concept loses the features of the extraordinary, or even the totalitarian. Its structures and dynamics can be discerned, if only in rudimentary shape or in differing forms, in inherently consolidated liberal democracies which are led by their governments into 'wars on terror', 'wars on organized crime' and so on.[80] The dual state reappears as a security state, choking what were once consolidated law-ruled democracies, such as Australia, Belgium, France, Germany, Britain, Israel and the United States.[81]

---

[79] Decree of the *Reichspräsident* for the Protection of People and State, 28 February 1933, which was followed by the Law to Remedy the Distress of People and Reich, an amendment passed on 23 March 1933 that suspended crucial parts of the Weimar Constitution and is regarded as the constitution of the Nazi regime (Enabling Act). For background information, see Evans, R.J. (2003), *The Coming of the Third Reich* (New York City: Penguin Press); Kershaw, I. (2016), *To Hell and Back. Europe 1914–1949* (London: Penguin Books), 208 ff.

[80] For a more detailed discussion, see Frankenberg (n 45), Chapters V and VI with further references. Concerning abuses in counter-terrorism, see Human Rights First (2004), *Getting to Ground Truth: Investigating U.S. Abuses in the 'War on Terror'* (New York: Human Rights First); Savage, C. (2009), 'Obama's War on Terror May Resemble Bush's in Some Areas' in: *The New York Times*, New York, 17 February; Norton-Taylor, R. (2008), 'Response to 9/11 was "huge overreaction"', in: *The Guardian*, London, 18 October.

[81] Wolfendale, J. (2007), 'Terrorism, Security and the Threat of Counterterrorism', in: 30 *Studies in Conflict & Terrorism*, 75 ff.

Recent forms of the 'deep state'[82] relate to both the dual state and the behemoth. While the dual state houses a prerogative state (of measures) and a normative state (of norms and regulations) under one roof, patterns of the deep state come under the guise of republican rhetoric or in the context of monarchies. They are often structured as networks that operate quite prerogatively in the arcanum of constitutional-liberal statehood. If one steers clear of conspiracy theories,[83] deep states or 'double governments' are disconnected – one might say lobotomized – from official institutions and decision-making procedures. They are conceptually suited to capture extra-legal and non-public governmental action that typically takes place in backrooms and eschews parliamentary control or judicial review.

The term 'deep state' is believed to have its origins in a secret society founded by Mustafa Kemal Atatürk in 1923. It seems to be alive and well in Turkey, albeit under a different guise:

> The deep state is Turkish shorthand for a faceless clique inside the Turkish state that has, some claim, held the reins of real power throughout the republic's 84-year history. There are some who see it on a continuum with the shady networks that 'took care of business' (including, some believe, the Armenian business) in the last years of the Ottoman Empire. The deep state is held to be based in the army, but closely linked with the National Intelligence Service (MIT), the judiciary, and (since the 1960s) the mafia.[84]

Likewise, the military-industrial complex in the United States developed and relied on deep state networks in the 1950s and 1960s to channel military and weapons industry interests and demands to Congress and presidential administrations.[85] Today's deep states have proliferated globally, and range from the Thai deep state[86] to the 'vertical democracy' that Vladimir Putin established in Russia alongside the official institutions of government, but beyond public scrutiny – the composite appears to function more like an

---

[82] Defined by Lofgren, M. (2013), *The Deep State: The Fall of the Constitution and the Rise of a Shadow Government* (London: Penguin). See also, from an anarchist perspective, Lindsay, J.R. (2013), *The Concealment of the State* (London: Bloomsbury).

[83] And by the same token, if one steers clear of Trump's diaphanous polemics against an 'entrenched bureaucracy' or critical media. See Kolb, M. (2018), '*Die gefährliche Theorie von Amerikas , "deep state"* ', in: *Süddeutsche Zeitung,* 10 March.

[84] Freely, M. (2007), ', in: 36 *Index on Censorship*, 15 ff.

[85] Mills, C.W. (1959), *The Power Elite* (New York/Oxford: Oxford University Press); Hennes, M. (2003), 'Der neue Militärisch-Industrielle Komplex in den USA', in: Bd 46 *Aus Politik und Zeitgeschichte.*

[86] Mérieau, E. (2016), 'Thailand's Deep State, Royal Power, and the Constitutional Court (1997–2015)', in: 46 *Journal of Contemporary Asia*, 445 ff.

imitated democracy.[87] The term is also applied to the hypertrophic, networked security apparatuses of numerous countries. As a rule, the institutions and groups of a government associated with the deep state act in conjunction with top functionaries from high finance and business (eg, the weapons industry) beyond formal democratic procedures and institutions. They function as contemporary, pluralistically composed prerogative bodies in the shadow of the constitutional state because the interests they represent shy away from the light of the public.

6. PREROGATIVE AS STATE OF EXCEPTION

In a state of exception,[88] violence and mystery unite. This is where the prerogative finds its feet. In a totalizing way, the exceptional or emergency situation withdraws from the rule of law and from Fraenkel's normative state, and opens up an almost unlimited domain for the prerogative. The law abdicates, while the prerogative comes into play. This moment, which is also one of raw masculinity, irresistibly attracts certain types of intellectuals. One of them dissolves the ambivalence of the extraordinary at the expense of law. Another plays off law against politics and the judgment against the decision.[89] Yet another privileges 'beautiful literature' over constitutional law. Aesthetes 'feel attracted to the orgiastic cult of the exception'.[90] Bohemians like to play with fire. The intellectual as Catholic praises the exceptional affair over the boring quotidian of marriage. So, the exception has the charm of borderline experience. It offers what the brittle normal case (marriage, law) lacks: a gloomy scenario that can be splayed out into apocalyptic visions. The exception radiates a romantic irony for the paradoxical and a perfection of power that no one must answer

87 One hesitates to apply the term 'democracy' to Russia's 'Putinstate', though. Mommsen, M. and Nußberger, A. (2007), *Das System Putin: Gelenkte Demokratie und politische Justiz in Russland*, München: Beck; Neumann, I.B. (2004), 'Deep Structure, Free-Floating Signifier, or Something in between? Europe's Alterity in Russia', in: Goff, P.M. *et al* (eds), *Identity and Global Politics* (New York: Palgrave Macmillan), 9 ff.

88 The following considerations continue my discussion of the normalization of the state of exception: Frankenberg (n 45), Chapters I and IV; and (n 4), Chapter 8. See also Greene, A. (2018), *Permanent States of Emergency and the Rule of Law* (Oxford: Hart Publishing) with many references.

89 Schmitt, C. (2006), *Political Theology. Four Chapters of the Concept of Sovereignty* (Chicago: University of Chicago).

90 Isensee, J. (2002), 'Normalfall oder Grenzfall als Ausgangspunkt rechtsphilosophischer Konstruktion?', in: Brugger, W. and Haverkate, G. (eds), *Grenzen als Thema der Rechts- und Sozialphilosophie* (Stuttgart: Franz Steiner Verlag), 51 ff/67. Critical: Bredekamp, H. (2008), *Der Künstler als Verbrecher* (Munich: Carl-Friedrich-von-Siemens-Stiftung).

for. However, these male fantasies miss some of the crucial features of a state of exception.

First, a 'state of emergency' cannot be defined without a loss of determinacy. The loss is signalled by metaphors that immediately come to the fore: 'hour of the executive', 'necessity knows no law' or – more technically – 'legal civil war'. Apart from law/constitution, a series of unpredictable normative points of reference come into play to qualify exceptional situations: self-preservation, *force majeure*, (bio-)politics, ('war on') terror and more.[91] In consequence, the discourse of exception covers a variety of fields of application: the state of exception can, first of all, aim to address an actual emergency caused by the onset of *force majeure* – hurricane, tsunami, earthquake, pandemic – or by industrial catastrophes induced by human unreason, which as a memento bear the name of the site of the disaster, such as Chernobyl, Seveso, Fukushima, Bhopal and many more.

Second, the state of emergency serves as a surrogate for the normal legal regime (or law of normalcy). It is declared or decreed when the circumstances are presented in such a way, or present themselves in such a way, that it seems practically impossible to control them by recourse to the elements of normal law (eg, rights, constitution, jurisdiction, legislation). Whoever declares a state of emergency promises to do what is not or may not be covered by 'regular' legal powers in order to control the unleashed forces. As a rule, this applies to political crises and extraordinary threats that measure up to *force majeure* because they factually or allegedly overstep the standard legal framework and security practices. In state practice, terrorist attacks and political unrest in particular, where they imply a catastrophic disruption of public order, routinely trigger the suspension of fundamental rights, which is complemented by the grant of special powers to the security forces, such as curfews, night-time arrests, detention of suspects without trial, demarcation of security zones, bans on assemblies, intensified interception and surveillance measures, lockdowns, and government by decrees. Such exceptional measures are easily adopted when anticipated in the constitution or in law. In liberal settings, they must be justified and limited in duration.

Third, exceptionalist rhetoric can seek to 'talk up' an emergency situation in order to bring special powers into play in the context of a liberal regime, if necessary while maintaining constitutional forms and procedures – albeit reduced to their outward appearance. The 'pretext of emergency law'[92] is

---

[91] See Mbembe, A. (2003), 'Necropolitics', in: 15 *Public Culture*, 11 ff.

[92] Such pretext, according to Kant, would not even entertain an extra-legal justification. See Maus, I. (1992), *Zur Aufklärung der Demokratietheorie* (Frankfurt am Main: Suhrkamp), 107 ff – *'Notrecht' und Gewalt.*

invoked by those who seek to implement extra-legal measures – for instance, to crack down on political opposition, apply cruel and inhuman punishments or avail of other techniques of raw power as law.[93] This pretext has a long and gory pedigree; its protagonists – its executioners, rather – and their origins are evenly distributed across all continents. The assumption of an exceptional situation and the ensuing practice of emergency law are evidenced in detention centres, colonies, prisons, show trials and purges of the civil service; and (less palpably violently) in censorship and intimidation.

Fourth, US President Trump recently added a new example to the long history of imaginary states of exception. *Uno actu*, he declared a state of emergency on the southern border of the United States while also publicly admitting that there was no such thing.[94] Wielding his extensive emergency powers[95] – upheld by the National Emergencies Act of 1976 – he tried unsuccessfully to undermine the budgetary authority of Congress to obtain budget funds for the construction of a border wall. The Democratic Party congresspersons and legal experts considered this action unconstitutional,[96] with good reason – which did not help much.

6.1 Constitutionalizing the Exception?

In an emergency, the irregular side of power emerges.[97] Where it goes beyond technical disaster control, it wages an ostensibly secret war against society that is nonetheless in full view. In a democracy, this open secret – that its stability in exceptional circumstances depends on a radically anti-democratic practice – must be covered up at all costs. Political irregularity – whether a state of exception, deep state or prerogative – must never be allowed to reveal itself as such. John Locke therefore carried the monarchical prerogative inconspicuously in the shadow of the liberal paradigm and left the door open for politics to decide at its discretion – even arbitrarily – whenever the law should fail.[98] Regimes

---

93 Philippe Sands' analysis of US-governmental practices in Guantanamo is impressive and depressing: Sands, P. (2008), *Torture Team, Deception, Cruelty and the Compromise of Law* (London: Penguin Books).

94 Baker, P. (2019), 'Trump Declares a National Emergency and Provokes a Constitutional Clash', in: *The New York Times*, 15 February.

95 Goitein, E. (2019), 'The Alarming Scope of the President's Emergency Powers', in: *The Atlantic,* February 2019, www.theatlantic.com/magazine/archive/2019/01/presidential-emergency-powers/576418/ (last accessed 24 February 2019).

96 Savage, C. (2019), 'Presidents Have Declared Dozens of Emergencies, but None Like Trump's' in: *The New York Times*, 15 February.

97 Horn, E. (2013), *The Secret War: Treason, Espionage and Modern Fiction* (Evanston: Northwestern University Press).

98 Locke, J. (n 64), Chapter XIV, § 160.

that take no prisoners, isolate their victims, torture and murder them in secret prisons and try to erase all traces of their existence – such regimes do not lean on Locke, of course, but invoke the necessity of self-preservation. This should be recalled when the concept of (undisguised) authoritarianism is examined.

The fact that lawlessness, at the price of loss of a regime's reputation and legitimacy, must be hidden could be taken to weigh in favour of going one step further than Locke and legalizing the prerogative to constitutionally contain the state of emergency.[99] The first question is how – or rather where – the state of emergency can be situated in relation to the legal order: inside or outside? Different approaches and arguments have been proposed to 'constitutionalize' the state of exception. They can be reduced to three major options: general clause, model structure or typification.

A *general clause* has a very broad scope of application. It establishes a state of exception whenever a certain condition occurs, such as a grave danger or catastrophe. The general clause is quite indeterminate and therefore eludes judicial control. For example, Article 15 of the European Convention on Human Rights (ECHR) allows the high contracting parties to take 'measures which deviate from the obligations provided for in this Convention, but only to the extent strictly required by the situation'[100] (what else?) and respecting other obligations under international law. According to the ECHR, the triggering condition would be a threat to the life of the nation from war or other public emergency. In a similar way, the Turkish Constitution lists 'war, mobilization, martial law or a state of emergency'. Apart from its lack of certainty, Article 154 of the 2014 Egyptian Constitution – typical in this respect – reflects another weakness of many general clauses: they are short and leave it to the ordinary legislature to get caught in the traps of exception/rule or 'tragic choices'.[101] Article 77 of the Italian Constitution offers a rather vague and inconclusive general clause:

> When the Government, in case of necessity and urgency, adopts under its own responsibility a temporary measure, it shall introduce such measure to Parliament for transposition into law. During dissolution, Parliament shall be convened within five days of such introduction.

---

99 See the classical study by Rossiter, C. (1948), *Constitutional Dictatorship: Crisis Government in Modern Democracies* (Princeton: Princeton University Press). Instructive, arguing in the shadow of 9/11: Gross, O. (2003), 'Chaos and Rules: Should Responses to Violent Crises Always be Constitutional?', in: 112 *Yale Law Journal*, 1014 ff; see also Loughlin (n 72), 396 ff.

100 Adopted almost *verbatim* by a string of national constitutions – for example, Article 15 of the Turkish Constitution (1982).

101 For example, Article 67 of the Constitution of Cuba (1976/2002).

In contrast, some authors prefer and constitutions contain a more elaborate *model structure* for the management of exceptional situations.[102] The 1949 Indian Constitution, for instance, provides such a structure, which is defined by fairly detailed procedural provisions and allocations of power for all cases of 'grave emergency' (Articles 352 ff). Whereas this approach does not succumb to a Schmittian 'epiphany of sovereignty', it still registers the state of emergency in the statist tradition and explains the need for a model regulation as an attempt to stop any gap in the constitutional order. However, it is fairly obvious that this strategy is likely to backfire. Sooner or later, the unpredictability of a (further) exceptional situation will catch up with the model structure and reveal new gaps therein (Chernobyl and Fukushima are instructive cases). Since normal situations and states of emergency each have their time,[103] as discussed above, the assumption of an incomplete legal order may result in an 'infinite recourse to ever more meta-emergency rights of the state'.[104]

The German Federal Republic's emergency laws of 1968 illustrate a third approach to make exceptional situations constitutionally manageable and controllable, through *typification*. Cases of defence (Articles 115a ff), tension (Article 80a), natural disasters and accidents (Article 35 II-III), armed insurrection (Article 87a IV) and internal emergency (Article 91) are obviously based on (partly faded) historical models. In addition, there is the almost forgotten legislative state of emergency (Article 81): the parliamentary democratic alternative to Article 48 of the Weimar Constitution, which declares the federal government and the *Bundesrat* as substitute legislatures in case of dysfunction of the *Bundestag* – not really a state of emergency after all. The German Basic Law lacks a clause that allows for the declaration of a state of exception other than in specifically enumerated cases; unlike, for instance, the Colombian Constitution, which extends the use of 'emergency powers' beyond war and riots ('state of disturbance') to other unnamed events ('events different from those provided in Articles 212 and 213').

Typifying exceptional situations can bring up (usually painful) collective historical experiences.[105] Needless to say, the utility of approaches that tie

---

[102] For references, see Frankenberg (n 45), 189 ff.

[103] Forsthoff, E. (1963), '*Der introvertierte Rechtsstaat und seine Verortung*', in: 2 *Der Staat*, 385 ff/397.

[104] See Augsberg, S. (2009), '"Denken vom Ausnahmezustand her". Über die Unzulässigkeit der anormalen Konstruktion und Destruktion des Normativen' in: Arndt, F. *et al* (eds), *Freiheit – Sicherheit – Öffentlichkeit,* (Baden-Baden: Nomos), 17 ff/26.

[105] Against the backdrop of the Pinochet dictatorship, the Constitution of Chile (2012) tries to rather precisely list (in Articles 32 ff) extraordinary situations: external/internal war, internal commotion, emergency, public calamity, state of siege, state of catastrophe, state of exception.

emergencies to an enumerative list is limited: natural disasters generally appear to strike society in a uniform manner, but their infinite, destructive consequences are unpredictable. Man-made nuclear and industrial disasters – and even more so politico-military disasters – differ considerably according to what triggers them, and the extent and nature of the devastation they cause. The 2020 coronavirus pandemic[106] raged from country to country without following the pattern of earlier epidemics and, by contrast, forced scientists and politicians to learn as events unfolded and develop strategies of coping: which measures to take, how best to contain the pandemic, how to trace infection chains and so on. Thus, historical situations are increasingly becoming markings without value; however, they still open the door to authoritarianism, as we shall see.

Worldwide, most constitutions provide for emergency regulations.[107] Most of them opt for one of the three models – general clause, model structure or typification[108] – or hybrids thereof. All of them differ from the 'dual state', in that a state of emergency is formally declared and is usually limited in duration – a formalism that is intended to ensure the primacy of the normal constitution or pacify the population. In practice, however, states of exception can be extended almost indefinitely. The prime example perhaps is Egypt, which from 1958 until 2012 was governed essentially on the basis of emergency laws; the short-lived lifting of those laws was followed by the imposition of new or identical emergency measures in 2012 and 2013.

6.2 Normalizing the State of Exception

To be within the range of a constitution, the declaration of a state of exception must be temporary and transitional, and must limit the extraordinary powers. Often, however, these extraordinary 'states' are extended. It is crucial to analyse how such extensions affect constitutions and how these selective breakdowns of democratic regimes are camouflaged. It has been argued that temporary suspensions and extensions such as the *état d'urgence* in France,

---

[106] World Health Organization (2020), 'Rolling update on corona virus disease (COVID-19)', 20 March – www.who.int/emergencies/diseases/novel-coronavirus-2019/events-as-they-happen (last accessed: 23 March 2020).

[107] Negretto, G.L. and Rivera, J.A. (2000), 'Liberalism and Emergency Powers in Latin America: Reflections on Carl Schmitt and the Theory of Constitutional Dictatorship', in: 21 *Cardozo Law Review*, 1797 ff.

[108] Frankenberg (n 4), Chapter 8 with further references; and Ramraj, V.V. (ed) (2008), *Emergencies and the Limits of Legality* (Cambridge: Cambridge University Press); Pasquino, P. (2004), 'The Law of the Exception: A Typology of Emergency Powers', in: 2 *International Journal of Constitutional Law*, 210 ff.

which was extended six times from November 2015 until 2017, and the state of emergency in Turkey, which ended in 2018 after seven extensions, damage the constitutional order and cultures. For who would trust a constitution that seems to be valid only 'until suspended', as happened in Turkey or Egypt? Obviously, the declaration of a state of exception or emergency cannot be simply undone with another declaration. It has been argued that the declaration of a state of exception leaves behind a 'zombie' constitution[109] after it is lifted; and one might add, the longer, the 'zombier'. Constitutional cultures are likely to erode when states of exception are repeatedly extended. In order to come to terms with the trauma of the exception, a constitutional 'cooling period' is needed, during which confidence can be rebuilt in the reliability of the new constitution and the functioning of its institutions and norms.

To avoid trauma and the need to resort conspicuously to extraordinary powers, thus upsetting or calling into question the legitimacy of the normative order, liberal-democratic and authoritarian regimes alike try to bypass a formal declaration by incorporating authorization for 'necessary measures' into the legal corpus. In particular, anti-terror surveillance measures and other restrictions of freedoms are transferred to the regular security and police laws, and are thus 'normalized'. At times, normalization leaves its traces in the semantics of security laws – see the discussion of 'combat' regulations and programmes below. In general, however, lawmakers can rely on the force of normalization and the habituation effect it yields. The German minister of health may have overstretched this force recently: to combat the coronavirus pandemic more efficiently, he introduced radical revisions to the Law for the Protection against Infections.[110] The new Section 5(2), which empowers the minister to rule by decree, has all the ingredients of a normalized state of exception: in 'epidemic situations of national dimension', those decrees may diverge from and functionally replace other public health laws. The minister can operate beyond parliamentary control and beyond the borders of the Basic Law; and the revision comes with neither transparent criteria nor determinate purposes. Will the Federal Diet acquiesce to this self-disempowerment?

6.3 Layered Emergencies

The United States offers yet another emergency regime: a layered concept of emergency regulations. The Constitution names a few of the classic situations that qualify for the declaration of a state of exception, and allocates

---

[109] I borrow this term from Augsberg, S. (n 105), 17 ff.

[110] *Infektionsschutzgesetz*. See Gärditz, K.F. and Meinel, F. (2020), 'Unbegrenzte Ermächtigung?', in: *Frankfurter Allgemeine Zeitung*, 26 March, 6.

to Congress the power to 'declare war', 'suppress insurrections and repel invasions' (Article II, Section 8, numbers 11 and 15). Yet the president (and Congress) have the power to declare a national emergency. While not uncontested, this is generally grounded on the notion of 'executive power' and/or the role of head of government and chief commander as an *implied* decisional authority.[111] For quite some time, US presidents have no longer had to rely on implied powers, because plenty of Congress statutes authorize or can be read as authorizing presidential emergency action. Here is a quote from the quite shocking Senate Report:

> Since March 9, 1933, the United States has been in a state of declared national emergency. In fact, there are now in effect four presidentially proclaimed states of national emergency: In addition to the national emergency declared by President Roosevelt in 1933, there are also the national emergency proclaimed by President Truman on December 16, 1950, during the Korean conflict, and the states of national emergencies declared by President Nixon on March 23, 1970, and August 15, 1971.
>
> These proclamations give force to 470 provisions of Federal law. These hundreds of statutes delegate to the President extraordinary powers, ordinarily exercised by the Congress, which affect the lives of American citizens in a host of all-encompassing manners. This vast range of powers, taken together, confer enough authority to rule the country without reference to normal constitutional processes.
>
> Under the powers delegated by these statutes, the President may: seize property; organize and control the means of production; seize commodities; assign military forces abroad; institute martial law; seize and control all transportation and communication; regulate the operation of private enterprise; restrict travel; and, in a plethora of particular ways, control the lives of all American citizens.[112]

There are many more statutes that a US president can feel empowered by without (always) having to worry about 'being stabbed in the back by the judiciary'.[113]

---

[111] Edelson, C. (2013), *Emergency Presidential Power: From the Drafting of the Constitution to the War on Terror* (Madison: University of Wisconsin).

[112] Senate Report 93-549 (1973), *Emergency Powers Statutes. Provisions of Federal Law Now in Effect* – https://archive.org/stream/senate-report-93-549/senate-report-93-549_djvu.txt (last accessed: 11 January 2020).

[113] For the range of judicial reactions to presidential emergency decrees: *Youngstown Sheet & Tube Co. v Sawyer*, 343 US 579 (1952) (Truman lost because the court limited the power of the president to seize private property); and *Korematsu v United States*, 323 US 214 (1944) (Franklin D Roosevelt won because the court upheld the exclusion and detention of Japanese Americans from the West Coast Military Area during the Second World War).

7. 'MILITANT DEMOCRACY' AND EXECUTIVE PRIVILEGES

7.1 Militant Democracy

Below the threshold of the state of exception, the prerogative is traded in smaller coins. The measures and institutions are mainly pooled there for the benefit of the executive branch. 'Executive privilege', 'executive authority' or – more technically – the 'competence to determine guidelines of policy' come under different names, but cannot deny their affinity to the prerogative (and some even the unruly side of the dual state).

The concept of 'militant democracy' has a better ring. It was originally engineered in the laboratory of political science and sociology to denote a democratic regime that could (or should be able to) defend itself against tyrannies such as Hitler's fascism: '[D]emocracies that have gone fascist have gravely sinned by their leniency.'[114] Since then, it has been detached from this context and adopted by a number of countries of liberal-democratic extraction as an authoritarian instrument to combat 'anti-democratic' political movements – that is, political extremism.[115] Article 16 of the French Constitution includes a general clause:[116]

> Where the institutions of the Republic, the independence of the Nation, the integrity of its territory or the fulfillment of its international commitments are under serious and immediate threat, and where the proper functioning of the constitutional public authorities is interrupted, the President of the Republic shall take measures required by these circumstances...

---

[114] The classical readings are Loewenstein, K. (1937), 'Militant Democracy and Fundamental Rights', in: 31 *American Political Science Review*, 417 ff and 638 ff, at 638 f; and Mannheim, K. (1943), *Diagnosis of Our Time. Wartime Essays of a Sociologist* (London: Paul, Trench, Trubner & Co).

[115] References in Sajó, A. (ed) (2004), *Militant Democracy* (Utrecht: Eleven International Publishing). See Venice Commission (1999), Guidelines on Prohibition and Dissolution of Political Parties and Analogous Measures, adopted by the Venice Commission at its 41st plenary session (CDL-INF (2000)1). See Appendix I, Prohibition of Political Parties and Analogous Measures, for an overview of restrictions concerning political party activities in national law, based on a survey of 40 countries, www.venice.coe.int/docs/2000/CDL-INF(2000)001-e.asp (last accessed 8 July 2020). See also Müller, J-W. (2014), 'The EU as a Militant Democracy, or: Are There Limits to Constitutional Mutations within EU Member States?', in: 165 *Revista de Estudios Políticos (nueva época),* 141 ff; Wagrandl, U. (2018), 'Transnational militant democracy', in: 7 *Global Constitutionalism*, 143 ff.

[116] 'Political parties and groups shall... respect the principles of national sovereignty and democracy.' (Article 4 of the Constitution of 1958).

The Italian Constitution contains a specific norm to prohibit a resurgence of fascism: 'It shall be forbidden to reorganize, under any form whatsoever, the dissolved Fascist party.'[117]

The arsenal of 'militant democracy' contains a wide range of powers of surveillance and repression, including the possibility of banning parties and associations that are radically critical of the political system (which are regularly labelled 'enemies of the constitution' or 'extremists'). In consequence, political competition is curbed once these 'elements' are excluded from elections or denied public appearances. In addition to the possibility of banning associations and declaring parties unconstitutional, the German Basic Law provides for the forfeiture of fundamental rights of political communication, including the right of asylum – which has not gained any practical or instrumental importance since 1949, but which is sometimes mobilized in the political rhetoric of the parties.[118]

Justifications of the restriction of fundamental rights and of party bans consistently refer to the immanent limits of political freedom ('no freedom for the enemies of freedom') and the protection of democracy. That one may not be allowed to demand, in the name of democracy, to destroy it or hand it over to its destroyers is reminiscent of John Locke's natural law right to self-preservation. The autocratic, internal tendencies of democracies[119] to restrict political pluralism, of ruling majorities to get rid of political minorities and of governments to extend their powers in the name of security are vividly described by Stephen Holmes in his review of militant democracy:

> Roughly speaking, the concept of "militant democracy" refers to the capacity of modern constitutional democracies to defend themselves against domestic political challenges to their continued existence as democracies. Must a democratic system stand idly by and watch antidemocratic forces gather strength? Must liberal constitutions, because they support tolerance and openness, function as suicide pacts, preventing effective self-defense? Joseph Goebbels believed that the answer was "yes" to both questions: "It will always be one of the best jokes of democracy that it gives its deadly enemies the means to destroy it."
>
> The correct answer is "no." Constitutional democracies can and do act preemptively; for instance, by banning extremist parties while they are still relatively weak. Endangered democracies can curtail freedom of speech, freedom of association, and associated political rights to vote and compete for office and still remain recogniz-

[117] Compare XII. Transitional and Final Provisions of the Italian Constitution, 1947; Article 16 of the Constitution of the French Republic, 1958.

[118] Read Articles 9 II, 21 II and 18 of the Basic Law of the Federal Republic of Germany.

[119] Pildes, R.H. (2003), 'The Inherent Authoritarianism in Democratic Regimes', in: Sajó, A. (ed), *Out of and Into Authoritarian Law* (New York: Kluwer Law International), 125

> ably liberal and democratic. To be sure, honest debate remains possible about the most effective and least restrictive ways of defending democracy against its most virulent enemies.[120]

Holmes overlooked, however, the dynamic of militant democracy that begins with a defence against extremism, continues as a 'war on terror' or a 'war on organized crime' and ultimately evolves into the security state[121] and 'combat law'.[122]

7.2 Militant Executive

Not unlike events of militant democracy, the routines of liberal law-rule are disrupted (or at least interrupted) by moments when the executive branch claims privileges – not rights or legal powers – to reject the legitimate demands of parliament, the judiciary, the media or the public. In most cases, heads of government or government agencies defend their information and files like private property, which they guard against any access by holding up 'shields', claiming 'executive privileges' or invoking 'executive authority'.[123] The (ultimately unsuccessful) refusal of the Nixon government to hand over to the courts presidential tapes on the Watergate scandal[124] and the landmark controversy concerning the Pentagon Papers are notorious examples of this.[125] The US Supreme Court affirmed the existence of a 'qualified privilege' regarding the Watergate tapes, but did not rule out inspection, provided that it could be proven that the disputed material was of 'substantial importance' for legal proceedings. In its *Pentagon Papers* decision, the US Supreme Court upheld the right of the *New York Times* and the *Washington Post* to publish classified material on the war in Vietnam. 'Executive authority' succumbed to the First Amendment freedom of speech (and the press).

---

120 Holmes, S. (2006), 'Review', in: 4 *International Journal of Constitutional Law*, 586 ff.

121 Foucault, M. (2008), *Security, Territory, Population: Lectures at the Collège de France, 1977–1978* (New York: St. Martin's Press); Michaels, W. (2005), *No Greater Threat: America since September 11 and the Rise of the National Security State* (New York: Algora Publishing). For a historical perspective on the rise of the security state, see Kazin, M. (2017), *War Against War: The American Fight for Peace, 1914–1918* (New York: Simon & Schuster).

122 Frankenberg (n 45), Chapters V and VI.

123 Cox, A. (1974), 'Executive Privilege', in: 122 *University of Pennsylvania Law Review*, 1384 ff; Savage, C. (2017), 'Explaining Executive Privilege and Sessions's Refusal to Answer Questions", in: *New York Times*, 15 June. See also *Chavez v Public Estates Authority*, GR No 133250, 9 July 2002 (Philippines).

124 *United States v Nixon,* 418 US at 713–14 and on Watergate: Cox (n 123), 1406 f.

125 *New York Times, Co. v United States*, 43 US 713 (1971).

Similar privileges to shield executive decision-making processes and secrecy of documents are claimed to prevent the judicial review of human rights violations and criminal actions committed by the military,[126] or to cover up the activities of the secret services. In court proceedings against the extreme right-wing National Socialist Underground (NSU), which was charged with nine murders, the German secret services refused to disclose information and their involvement. They invoked the confidentiality of their sources, which they had to protect, and of course the public weal – respectively, the integrity of the state.[127] After the murder of a politician, the same authorities initially decided that the NSU files should remain under lock and key for 120 years. Only after massive protests was the duration of the classification limited to 40 years. Following the logic of security and secrecy, the authorities wrote another chapter on the topicality of the prerogative for a regime of liberal-democratic constitutionalism.

8. SILENCE AND DISCRETION

Derrida's statement that 'The violent structure of the founding act holds a silence' and his reference to 'The silence that is walled up in the violent structure of the founding act'[128] can be applied *mutatis mutandis* to the jurisdiction of high courts and constitutional courts. In all law-rule regimes, courts are required and expected to argue, perform reasoned elaboration and give reasons for their decisions. Therefore, a court's simple ruling that 'the case is not accepted' or 'the case is submitted for appeal' qualifies as a privilege – the privilege of not having to give reasons. It is clearly an authoritarian moment in the citadel of liberal law, because courts exercise the prerogative to remain silent and hence cannot be held accountable for a decision – or even for the logic of a ruling.[129]

Supreme or constitutional courts that specialize in constitutional law must cope with high expectations: they are expected to answer nothing less than the

---

[126] Pereira, A.W. (2005), *Political (In)Justice: Authoritarianism and the Rule of Law in Brazil, Chile and Argentina* (Pittsburg: University of Pittsburg Press).

[127] Von der Behrens, A. (2018), 'Das Netzwerk des NSU, staatliches Mitverschulden und verhinderte Aufklärung. Plädoyer vom 29. November und 5. Dezember 2017', in: *id* (ed), *Kein Schlusswort. Nazi-Terror. Sicherheitsbehörden. Unterstützernetzwerk. Plädoyers im NSU-Prozess* (Hamburg: VSA Verlag), 197 ff; Pichl, M. (2018), 'Von Aufklärung keine Spur: 20 Jahre NSU-Komplex', in: 8 *Blätter für deutsche und internationale Politik*, 111 ff.

[128] Derrida (n 48).

[129] Wilkinson, J.H. (1989), 'The Role of Reasons in the Rule of Law', in: 56 *University of Chicago Law Review*, 779 ff; Levin, J.K. (1962): 'Certiorari' in: *American Jurisprudence*, 2nd ed, vol 14 (Eagan: West Publishers).

'ultimate questions'. Their reputation, authority and power hinge upon their rulings.[130] As tribunals of the highest instance and last resort, they are not only overburdened with hopes, but also flooded with cases; fundamental rights lawsuits are particularly attractive and common. For example, constitutional complaints before the German Federal Constitutional Court account for about 96 per cent of all its cases. Of 228 501 complaints filed since 1951, however, just 2.3 per cent have succeeded.[131] In itself, this does not validate the charge of authoritarianism. Filter systems of admissibility are elementary components of the law; and it is also obvious that vexatious or unfounded motions fail or are settled during the proceedings. What is striking, however, is the decision as to which appeals (and cases) are admitted at all, are granted certiorari[132] or are rejected without any argument. If only about 70 to 90 of 5000 to 6000 constitutional complaints are accepted by a high court and the overwhelming majority are rejected without a single word beyond 'not accepted', this can hardly be justified as the result of routine admissibility checks or of the politics to relieve the court of some of its burden, since every motion must be examined and is evaluated (by law clerks) anyway.[133] Not dignifying a serious complaint with even a brief statement characterizes the violent structure of high court decision-making. Like any other autocrat, the court conceals its reasons, albeit with statutory blessing.

8.1 Discretion and Margins of Appreciation

Less spectacularly, but quite efficiently, a prerogative 'writ small' runs through governmental, administrative and judicial decision-making: discretion. This resembles the prerogative's little brother, guarded by law and doctrine, normalized and firmly integrated into all standard systems of liberal-democratic constitutionalism. It may be small, but it comes in large quantities. Broken down and distributed among myriads of rules – a doughnut's hole, as Dworkin

---

[130] See the seminal analysis by Hirschl, R. (2007), *Towards Juristocracy. The Origins and the Consequences of the New Constitutionalism* (Cambridge: Harvard University Press).

[131] *Bundesverfassungsgericht, Jahresstatistiken 2017*, www.bundesverfassungsgericht.de/DE/Verfahren/Jahresstatistiken/2017/gb2017/A-I-1.pdf?__blob=publicationFile&v=2/ (last accessed 11 March 2019).

[132] Kennedy, T. (1993), 'First Steps Towards a European Certiorari?', in: *European Law Review* 18 (1993), 121 ff.

[133] Lorenz, P. and Sehl, M. (2018), 'Weg von der Praxis des leeren Blatts?', in: *Legal Tribune Online* 16 November, www.lto.de/recht/justiz/j/bundesverfassungsgericht-verfassungsbeschwerde-nichtannahme-ohne-begruendung-pflicht/ (last accessed 11 March 2019).

argued,[134] where judicial review is reduced or ends – it presents itself as 'discretion', 'margin of appreciation', 'prerogative of assessment', 'administrative choice' or 'judicial consideration' – residual arbitrariness ennobled by doctrine.

While the legislature's prerogative of assessment moves legislative decisions (laws) to a certain extent away from the constitutional court's review, by the same token it favours democracy. In the Council of Europe, the 'margin of appreciation' doctrine[135] grants the ECHR states much broader freedom of assessment and decision in the application of the ECHR, especially regarding moral and ethical questions, such as whether to allow a crucifix in the classroom or to fire a headscarf-wearing teacher. Interestingly enough, on questions of national security or the application of basic criminal procedural rights, the margin is comparatively narrow. Strictly speaking, it is a space to be filled by interpretation, which is primarily effected through the method of balancing. A judicial margin of appreciation is therefore a rather distant relative of the prerogative and more a method than a norm conferring powers.

Discretion as the (almost) ultimate freedom to make decisions is primarily a domain of the administration in a variety of legal systems.[136] Discretion, one might argue, pluralizes the venues of decision-making and thus enhances democracy. Administrative discretion is not free, as it was called in the early days of the rule of law, but is rather bound by law, and must be exercised accordingly. Decision-makers must also justify their choice of a measure taken pursuant to the purpose of the law that grants discretion and always observe the principle of proportionality. Discretion empowers in two respects: an agency is entitled (1) to act or not act at all, and (2) to choose between different types of conduct – that is, to choose how to act (eg, measures, decisions). Discretionary powers are considered necessary throughout – for example, to enable police forces, in accordance with a general clause, to react flexibly to a dangerous situation ('...can take the necessary measures to avert a danger...'), or to decide on individual cases.

---

[134] Dworkin, R. (1978) *Taking Rights Seriously* (Cambridge: Harvard University Press).

[135] See Brems, E. (1996), 'The Margin of Appreciation Doctrine in the Case-Law of the European Court of Human Rights', in: 56 *Zeitschrift für Auslandisches Öffentliches Recht und Völkerrecht*, 248 ff; and Council of Europe, 'The Margin of Appreciation', www.coe.int/t/dghl/cooperation/lisbonnetwork/themis/ECHR/Paper2_en.asp/ (last accessed 5 January 2020).

[136] Rabin, J. (2003), 'Administrative Discretion' in: *Encyclopedia of Public Administration and Public Policy* (New York: Dekker), 35 ff; Figuereido, M. (2018), 'Administrative Discretion: A Comparative Analysis', https://blog-iacl-aidc.org/blog/2018/5/17/administrative-discretion-a-comparative-analysis (last accessed 5 January 2020).

Regardless of all practical considerations – and even if discretionary limits and obligations are carefully maintained (above all by the law in question and constitutional principles) and, in addition, no discretionary errors are committed – discretion remains a candidate for the 'gallery of shame' in liberal democratic constitutionalism, because it provides authoritarian moments, albeit in single cases. Discretion withdraws the bureaucratic-administrative rule of expertise and routine – always selectively and only to a certain extent – from the scrutinizing gaze of third parties; the density of judicial control[137] is significantly reduced and the separation of powers is partially suspended. What remains in a discretionary situation is a remnant of the 'ultimate responsibility' for which no one is responsible, insofar as legal norms grant agencies a certain leeway that comes with the power to choose and decide. Thus, in a new guise, distributed among countless norms, legally restrained, in individual cases the prerogative of power survives.

In short, the classic powers of the liberal paradigm and even the constitutional courts have their own areas of retreat, where they evade and avoid the controlling access of law-rule. This may very well be explained as being more or less justifiable or necessary, expedient or unavoidable.[138] Nevertheless, discretion and the more conspicuous specimens of the prerogative are small or large escapes into the shadowy empire of the authoritarian.

---

[137] Treves, G.E. (2011), 'Administrative Discretion and Judicial Control', in: 10 *The Modern Law Review*, 1486 ff. Concerning judicial discretion, see Vaishnav, S. and Marwaha, K. (2015), 'Judiciary: A Ladder between Inevitable Administrative Discretion and Good Governance', in: 2 *International Journal of Multidisciplinary Approach & Studies*, 63 ff.

[138] Shane, P.M. (2013), 'The Rule of Law and the Inevitability of Discretion', in: 36 *Harvard Journal of Law & Public Policy*, 21 ff.

4. Political technology of authoritarianism

Whatever it takes.[1]

It would be nice to think that America is protected from the worst excesses of Trump's impulses by its democratic laws and institutions.[2]

To contain the coronavirus pandemic in India, the Modi regime recommended traditional homeopathic remedies and Ayurveda until the middle of March 2020. Less than two weeks later, it locked down the country and ordered the police to beat up anyone who was seen in the streets.[3] Autocrat Alexander Lukashenko suggested that people should work in the countryside, drive tractors and remain positive to stabilize their immune systems and keep the pandemic out of Belarus.[4] Likewise, US President Trump first promised that the 'foreign virus' would disappear 'miraculously' when the temperature outside increased, then declared a state of exception and, while also issuing decrees, suggested that people drink bleach to protect against the virus. Aside from denial and idiocy, these examples show that authoritarianism – even in times of danger – cannot be identified by repressive techniques of governing alone, but has also stored flexible instruments in its armory.

---

1 From a speech of former president of the European Central Bank Mario Draghi (2012), aimed at calming the financial world following the crisis of the banking system.

2 Gotein, E. (2019), 'The Alarming Scope of the President's Emergency Powers', in: *The Atlantic*, January/February.

3 Chandna, H. (2020), 'Modi govt again advises homoeopathy for COVID-19, suggests sipping water boiled with tulsi', in: *The Print*, 18 March; https://theprint.in/health/modi-govt-again-advises-homoeopathy-for-COVID-19-suggests-sipping-water-boiled-with-tulsi/383363/ (last accessed 27 March 2020).

4 'Belarusian leader proposes "tractor" therapy for virus', in: *Euractiv*, 16 March 2020; www.euractiv.com/section/coronavirus/news/belarusian-leader-proposes-tractor-therapy-for-virus (last accessed 28 March 2020).

1. NARRATIVES AND EXPERIMENTS

Modernity proposes a blend of narratives. These contain condensed insights gained primarily from experiences and experiments that gave rise to disappointment or hope, fear or confidence. Constitutionalism is one of these narratives. Its stories tell of such experiences – some bitter, some promising, all valuable – of successful and failed attempts to establish authority and restrain power. The library of constitutionalism – shorthand for the theory and practice embedded in a constitutional culture – contains many reports on its shelves, from tragedy to farce. This variety documents historical defeats and victories, deceptions and enlightenments; and again and again confirms the widespread belief in the magic of constitutions.[5] No wonder that the collective singular of constitutionalism covers a wide spectrum of diverse regimes and their equally diverse techniques of governing.

The early constitutions of the late eighteenth and early nineteenth centuries reflect the struggles against feudal and colonial rulers, absolutist monarchy and other *ancien régimes*. They reflect the attempts to abolish or at least limit the privileges of rulers and old elites, to establish new elites and, more generally, to grant the (tax-paying, male) members of the bourgeoisie equal rights and authorize them as political sovereign and *pouvoir constituant*. At the same time, however, they set new axes of inequality along the borders of property and social class, national belonging and foreignness.[6]

To give a brief overview: the French Constitutions of 1791 and 1814 established constitutional monarchies. The Constitution of Year I (1793) contained far-reaching provisions for democratization and the distribution of wealth. But just two years later, before it could have a lasting effect, it was supplanted by a new constitution, which established the Board of Directors. There followed the Constitution of 1799, which legitimized Napoleon's *coup d'état* and sanctioned his military dictatorship. After a series of further constitutional reforms, the Bonapartist Constitution of the Second Republic (1848) again provided some revolutionary impetus. Eventually, the Constitution of the Fifth Republic

---

[5] See Chapter 1, Section 3; and the more detailed discussion in Frankenberg, G. (2018), *Comparative Constitutional Studies – Between Magic and Deceit* (Cheltenham: Edward Elgar Publishing), Chapter 1.

[6] Marx, K. (1975), 'On the Jewish Question', in: Marx, K. and Engels, F., *Collected Works*, Vol 3 (London: Lawrence & Wishart), 146 ff. See also Röhner, C. (2019), *Ungleichheit und Verfassung – Vorschlag für eine relationale Rechtsanalyse* (Weilerswist: Velbrück Verlag).

followed in 1958. Its presidential system bears the signature of Charles de Gaulle, former general and then president.[7]

Constitutional developments in other countries, with the exception of the United States, were also quite rocky. In the laboratory of constitutionalism, during the 'long' nineteenth century, there was a great restlessness and willingness to experiment – especially, though not exclusively, in Europe and Latin America.[8] This continued into the twentieth century, after two world wars and in an age of decolonization and post-socialist reconstruction.[9] Liberal and illiberal, monarchist and non-monarchist frameworks were set up around the world to abet political authority, to cloak it in the mantle of legitimacy and to rein in self-rule, driven by popular sovereignty and democracy, through the flexible instruments of constitutionalism. This pliability allowed for ideological legends to accommodate almost every kind of authority and construction of legality, and diverse techniques of governing. However, for all this diversity, legal authority – the alloy of authority and law – consistently emerges as a defining characteristic of constitutionalism, especially where charisma and violence alone are insufficient.[10]

The *dispositif*[11] of authoritarian constitutionalism, regardless of its variations, encompasses an ensemble of discourses, forms of knowledge and institutions, regulatory decisions, political strategies and normative positions. This *dispositif* informs a technique of governing ('*Staatstechnik*' or 'political technology') that combines constitutional opportunism with a specific security agenda and imperative, and often informal actions that consistently privilege the executive. For the purposes of this study, I define techniques of governing (or 'political technology')[12] as encompassing the totality of practices, norms

---

7 See Mérieau, E. (2019), 'French Authoritarian Constitutionalism and its Legacy', in: Alviar, H. and Frankenberg, G. (eds), *Authoritarian Constitutionalism – Comparative Analysis and Critique* (Cheltenham: Edward Elgar Publishing), 185 ff.

8 For a more elaborate discussion, see Frankenberg (n 5), Chapter 5, with further references; and Gargarella, R. (2013), *Latin American Constitutionalism, 1810–1910: Social Rights and the 'Engine Room' of the Constitution* (Oxford: Oxford University Press).

9 Bos, E. (2004), *Verfassungsgebung und Systemwechsel: Die Institutionalisierung von Demokratie im postsozialistischen Europa* (Wiesbaden: Springer VS).

10 'Charisma' is defined as belief in extraordinary power and leadership; see Weber, M. (1978), *Economy and Society* (Berkeley: University of California Press).

11 I borrow the concept from: Foucault, M. (2004), 'Security, Territory, Population', in: *id*, *Ethics: Subjectivity and Truth* (New York: The New Press), 73; *id* (2008), *Dispositive der Macht: Über Sexualität, Wissen und Wahrheit,* (Berlin: Merve); and Vismann, C. (2011), *Medien der Rechtsprechung*, Kemmerer, A. and Krajewski, M. (eds) (Frankfurt am Main: S. Fischer), 17 ff.

12 For want of a more precise term, I use 'technique(s) of governing' and 'political technology' as synonyms for the German '*Staatstechnik*'.

and principles, forms of knowledge and skills, calculations, strategies and tactics that state (or international) actors and institutions bring to bear in their operations of social control, threat aversion, risk management and so on.[13]

Authoritarian power – whether instituted, acquired or usurped – invariably executes the rules of this political technology provided by the *dispositif.* Its grammar links Machiavellian and Hobbesian elements and agendas. Under current conditions, and depending on the context and political constellation, these connections generate a mix and remix of autocracy and democracy; of oppression and tolerance; of law-rule and arbitrariness.

1.1 Justifying Behaviour Control

The security apparatus of authoritarian regimes, adapted to today's requirements, covers a wide range of different forms of preventive and repressive control of social behaviour. The available measures bring disciplinary power and bio-power to bear, as well as techniques of control in welfare settings.[14] Hence, contemporary versions of authoritarian constitutionalism work with justifications that regularly claim to promote the security and welfare of the community. These objectives are defined top-down, often clothed in vague notions of secondary virtues, such as order and loyalty. Progress,[15] welfare, peace and public security are helpful as *passe-partouts* to fill constitutional value spots. The security agenda of authoritarian regimes and the justification of repressive measures have a momentum that transcends tangible reality – for example, when tradition or necessity is brought into play. Here are some samples from the arsenal of autocratic justifications: Franco's followers believed his dictatorial regime justified because it 'installed the just order of things' and did what was necessary for the 'good of Spain', out of 'patriotic duty'.[16] Venezuela's President Maduro legitimized his emergency decrees on the grounds of 'defend[ing] the peace and security of the people'. Hungarian

---

13 Frankenberg, G. (2014), *Political Economy and the Erosion of the Rule of Law. Normalizing the State of Exception* (Cheltenham: Edward Elgar Publishing), Chapter I.

14 Foucault, M. (1977), *Discipline and Punish. The Birth of the Prison* (New York: Pantheon Books); *id, The Birth of Bio-Politics: Lectures at the Collège de France 1978-1979* (London: Palgrave Macmillan); see the illuminating analysis by Lemke, T. (2019), *Critique of Political Reason. Foucault's Analysis of Modern Governmentality* (London: Verso).

15 Brazil's national motto, *Ordem e Progresso* ('order and progress'), nicely captures the ambivalence of both maxims of Auguste Comte's political positivism, when industrialization and technical progress are combined with a strong executive power, including the support of the military. An ideological aid for the Bolsonaro regime.

16 Ell, E. (2019), '40 Jahre nach dem Ende der Franco-Diktatur: "Der Tote packt den Lebenden"', in: *RT Deutsch*, 14 January, https://deutsch.rt.com/europa/82353-40

Prime Minister Viktor Orbán invoked the defence of 'European Christian values'[17] to justify in his repressive decrees the inhumane treatment of refugees. In March 2020 he sought to ramp up his autocracy to a dictatorial level through a kind of 'Enabling Act' that would allow him to govern by decree without parliamentary control until the 'end of the emergency caused by the Corona-pandemic'.[18] Turkish President Erdoğan announced, when declaring a state of emergency, that it would be imposed as a temporary measure to achieve 'welfare and peace'. The list is endless. And the justifications always follow the logic of 'needs must when devils drive' or 'necessity knows no law'.[19]

Authoritarian leaders, cliques and parties have an inherent emergency mind set. To help avert extraordinary dangers, constitutions are expected to provide special powers for crisis management alongside regular powers for the management of normal situations. To this end, the charters of autocracies offer techniques of governing drawn from a rich pool of emergency-related instruments, as will be shown later.

2. CONSTITUTIONAL OPPORTUNISM

After a mental update to take into account the differences between Machiavelli and (present-day) Machiavellianism,[20] *The Prince*[21] can function as a manual that guides today's autocrats on how states can be ruled top-down, and on the different instruments and tools that can be used to acquire and secure power.

2.1 Once Again: Whatever it Takes

The 'golden rule' of Machiavellian opportunism[22] is extremely topical: always do what circumstances demand for the acquisition, preservation and protection

---

-jahre-nach-franco-diktatur-der-tote-packt-den-lebenden-i/ (last accessed 13 January 2019).

17 See Pichl, M. (2019), 'The Constitution of False Prophecies: The Illiberal Transformation of Hungary', in: Alviar and Frankenberg (n 7), 240 ff.

18 Walker, S. (2020), 'Hungary to consider bill that would allow Orbán to rule by decree', in: *The Guardian*, 23 March.

19 With many references: Frankenberg (n 13), Chapters 4 and 5.

20 Bock, G., Skinner, Q. and Viroli, M. (eds) (1999), Machiavelli and Republicanism (Cambridge: Cambridge University Press); Frankenberg (n 13), Chapter I.

21 Machiavelli, N. (2019), *Der Fürst* [1532], E. Rudolph (ed) (Hamburg: F. Meiner;) (2005), *The Prince with Related Documents*, Connell, W.J. (trans and ed) (Boston: Bedford/St. Martin's Press).

22 Without engaging in the controversy as to whether *The Prince* should be read as a political satire, a manual of carefully crafted advice to arm the people against

of your assets, using all strategic options and tactical tricks that you deem opportune. This logic was adopted by the president of the European Central Bank (ECB), Mario Draghi, when he set out to address the euro financial crisis in 2012, vowing that he would do 'whatever it takes' to protect the single currency.[23] His successor, Christine Lagarde, intervened in the coronavirus crisis with less rhetorical aplomb when launching the ECB's Pandemic Emergency Purchase Programme, declaring that 'Extraordinary situations call for extraordinary measures' and adding: 'We are determined, within the limit of our mandate, to use the full potential of our possibilities.'[24] Other governments echoed Lagarde's rhetoric when implementing their own measures to mitigate the fallout from the coronavirus crisis.

In a constitutional environment – and except in a crisis situation such as the coronavirus pandemic – Machiavellian opportunism (both Draghi's formula and Lagarde's version) must generally be toned down, adapted and modified according to normative and situational requirements – even by political actors who generally do not care much about constitutional restraints. On the whole, the compliance of autocrats depends on the theory and practice of constitutionalism that they consider expedient to safeguard their status and interests – in Machiavellian terms, the stability of order, their position of power and sometimes peace.[25] If the forcible elimination of rival elites is forbidden by circumstances and the co-option of oppositional movements does not work, respect for the constitution – or at least an appreciation of its manipulative potential – can gain in importance.

Many autocrats, almost like *The Prince*, find constitutions useful as a guide – a kind of *vade-mecum* that provides valuable services for the efficient exercise of power. In keeping with Machiavellian strategy, constitutions can paint a casually unprincipled style of ruling in a thin coat of legality, applying a subtle veneer of respectability and legitimacy. This explains why authoritarian heads of government willingly follow the traditions ritually practised in liberal-constitutional states and take the oath to the constitution at their inauguration, adorn their office walls with it and brandish it as a badge of their

---

government or a shockingly immoral text to instruct the prince (Lorenzo di Medici), I use it to illustrate political and constitutional opportunism. See Rudolph, E. (2019), '*Einleitung*', in: Machiavelli (n 21) *Der Fürst*, VII ff; and Connell, W.J. (2013), 'Dating The Prince: Beginnings and Endings', in: 75 *Review of Politics*, 497 ff.

[23] 'Within our mandate, the European Central Bank is ready to do whatever it takes to preserve the euro. And believe me, it will be enough.' ECB President Mario Draghi (2012), speech at the Global Investment Conference, London, 26 July,

[24] *Spiegel online*, 13 March 2020, www.spiegel.de/wirtschaft/unternehmen/corona-krise-die-ezb-geht-all-in-a-49f2fc85-eb3f-488f-bdc1-85b968157bc0/ (last accessed 24 March 2020).

[25] Machiavelli (n 21), *Der Fürst*, Chapter IX ff.

Source: 37902672 picture alliance / dpa / EFE / Harold Escalona. With friendly permission.

Figure 4.1 *President Hugo Chávez upholding 'his' constitution*

propriety (see Figure 4.1), only to ignore or disrespect it at the next possible occasion.[26] Thus, constitutional opportunism allows once crowned, and today mostly uncrowned, heads of state to document their title of power and conceal their autocratic state practice.

Hugo Chávez, for example, positioned himself within the legal framework of demonstrative, formal-constitutional opportunism at his solemn inauguration as president of Venezuela. He initially was ready to take the oath to the constitution; however, in an original adaptation of Napoleon's self-coronation, he set an autocratic counterpoint by authorizing himself to alter the oath and announce his constitutional agenda:

> I swear before God, I swear before the Fatherland, I swear before my People that, on the basis of this doomed constitution, I will push ahead with the necessary democratic transformations so that the Republic will have a Magna Carta that is in keeping with the new era.

In line with Machiavellian constitutional opportunism, autocrats who need to keep up appearances must (at least rhetorically) pledge their commitment to legality. That is why heads of state tend to emphasize the constitutionality of their decrees, insisting that they are availing of constitutional instruments, procedures and forms of action or explicitly and legally granted special powers – even when they manifestly are not. They often justify state action on the

---

26 I owe the reference to the constitution as a 'handrest' during inaugurations – for example, of Charles de Gaulle – to Schulz, D. (2018), 'Verfassungsbilder: Text und Körper in der Ikonographie des Verfassungsstaates', in: 46 *Leviathan*, 71 ff.

imperative to ensure public security or stabilize the economy. As previously mentioned, Hitler extended the Enabling Act three times. Likewise, after the attempted coup in 2016, Erdoğan extended the state of exception seven times. Putin claimed that his tandemocracy, transferring presidential power in name only to Medvedev, was constitutional. Venezuelan leaders argued that the transfer of power from Chávez to Maduro, and, by implication, their tactic of denying Chávez's availability to serve in 2013 so as to preclude the president of the National Assembly from becoming interim president, was constitutional.[27] Xi Jinping had his term limit lifted by formally changing the Chinese Constitution.

Despite his 'authoritarian instincts' and actions, US President Trump has adopted a different style. Although in the first year of his presidency, Trump declared each of his decrees to be constitutional, he subsequently seemed to march to a different drum. He called the emolument clauses 'phony' (they essentially prohibit the president from profiting from office via foreign or domestic governments), then ironically used the formula 'I Hereby Order' and declared a non-state of exception to get the construction of the wall at the Mexican border 'done faster, that's all'.[28] It seems that Trump has sold his mockery of legality to his constituency quite effectively: thus far, his followers have accepted his opportunism as necessary to deal with and, if circumstances require, circumvent the Washington elite.

Viktor Orbán recently demonstrated his Machiavellian style once again by using the coronavirus pandemic as a pretext to step up his autocracy and dismantle the representative system. As per the Machiavellian maxim, 'Never waste the opportunity of a good crisis',[29] he sent a draft bill to Parliament that would considerably augment his powers in a state of emergency: if approved, the government will in future be able to extend emergency measures indefinitely without having to worry about interventions by the deputies, and people will be held criminally liable for spreading 'fake' or 'dangerous' news.[30] Considering that Orbán's *Fidesz* party commands a comfortable two-thirds majority in the Hungarian Parliament and is unlikely to restrain its leader, these unlimited extra powers for emergency situations seem to be more symbolic than instrumental. They symbolize that Orbán is empowered to run the country in good times and in bad from his home office.

---

[27] Articles 231 and 233, Section 2 of the Constitution of Venezuela.

[28] National Emergency Concerning the Southern Border of the United States (Proclamation 9844), in: *The Guardian*, 23 August 2019.

[29] 'Orbán Using Coronavirus Crisis to Cement Power, Critics Say', in: *Balkaninsight*, 25 March 2020, https://balkaninsight.com/2020/03/25/orban-using-coronavirus-crisis-to-cement-power-critics-say (last accessed 28 March 2020).

[30] Donald Trump would be well advised to avoid travelling to Hungary.

2.2 Interest of the Ruler 'in Himself'

In Russia, as in other authoritarian regimes, updated Machiavellian techniques of governing come coated in the thin veneer of constitutionalism. They convert the ruler's interest 'in himself' into *raison d'état.* This pays off in robust political-economic benefits for leaders, elites and other hegemonic utility maximizers. Insofar as transitions occur – from revolutionary socialism to dictatorial rule (Ortega in Nicaragua); from mobilizing the poor and 'shirtless' to autocratically de-mobilizing them (Chávez in Venezuela, Perón in Argentina); from parliamentary democracy to presidential autocracy (Erdoğan); from a precarious constitutional state to a 'vertically directed democracy' (Putin) – they must be justified so as to pass the test of public scrutiny. (Parliamentary democratic systems also have their Machiavellian moments: opportunism notably lends itself to justify anti-terror or other anti-crisis measures. More recently, this has manifested itself in attempts to shut down public debate before it even begins by invoking the 'TINA' rule: 'there is no alternative' to the policy decision being implemented).[31]

2.3 Of Enemies

Enemies always appear to provide helpful assistance when it comes to justification. Where natural disasters or other exceptional situations are not at hand, constitutional opportunism resorts to naming and blaming internal or external enemies, perceived or imagined. Dignified by Carl Schmitt's *Concept of the Political*,[32] the defamation and 'othering' of enemies has become a standard tool of autocratic governance. The enemy is used to create a national self-image that relies on distinguishing 'who is in' from 'who is out'. The enemy is also held responsible for disaster. Islam is commonly invoked as an enemy in Europe, triggering apocalyptic visions and boosting the profiles of conservative nationalists and right-wing extremists.[33] In its fight against Muslims, the

---

[31] 'TINA' is credited to British premier Margaret Thatcher. See Séville, A. (2017), There is no alternative. *Politik zwischen Demokratie und Sachzwang* (Frankfurt/New York: Campus Verlag).

[32] Schmitt, C. (1996), *The Concept of the Political* (Chicago: University of Chicago Press); see Altemeyer, B. (1988), *Enemies of Freedom: Understanding Right-Wing Authoritarianism* (San Francisco: Jossey-Bass). Critical: Frankenberg (n 13), Chapter 4.

[33] *Apocalypse Now!* seems to be the favourite topic of German writers against the Islamic 'colonization' of their lifeworld – for example, Thilo Sarrazin sees a 'hostile take-over' of countries such as Germany: Sarrazin, T. (2018), *Feindliche Übernahme* (*How Islam Impedes Progress and Threatens Society*) (Munich: FinanzBuch Verlag). Likewise, Ulfkotte, U. (2015), *Mekka Deutschland. Die stille Islamisierung*

Austrian Freedom Party invoked the 'Battle of Vienna' of 1683, which finally ended the Ottoman siege at the gates of the city. Likewise, Hungarian Prime Minister Viktor Orbán proclaims that Muslim refugees cannot be integrated and are a security risk because they bring terrorism into the country.[34] In a national consultation, he charged Jewish entrepreneur George Soros with planning to resettle 2 million (Muslim) refugees throughout Europe, including in Hungary.

In Western European states, 'Islam' or 'Muslims'[35] currently shape perceptions of reality much as did 'the Russians' in the West and 'the imperialist Americans' in the East during the Cold War.[36] The voices of Stop Islamisation of Europe, the American Freedom Defense Initiative and other organizations with anti-Islam(ist), radically nationalist agendas[37] are echoed by anti-Westernism – notably anti-Americanism – in the East and Middle East.[38] Anti-immigrant fervour and Islamophobia have increased in Britain, emboldened by Boris Johnson's endorsement; and in other European countries in response to the so-called 'refugee crisis'.[39] In India, Prime Minister Modi's regime is ravaging the foundations of secularism and openly inciting violent Islamophobia.[40]

More recently, the coronavirus crisis appears to have diverted the rhetoric of autocrats from Islam towards a new enemy. Donald Trump repeatedly referred to the pandemic as the 'Chinese virus' or 'foreign virus', and charged China

---

(Rottenburg: Kopp Verlag); and Schwarzer, A. (2010), *Die große Verschleierung – Für Integration, gegen Islamismus* (Cologne: Kiepenheuer & Witsch).

34 See Pichl, M. (2019), 'The constitution of false prophecies: the illiberal transformation of Hungary', in: Alviar and Frankenberg (n 7), 240 ff.

35 Sokolowsky, K. (2009), *Feindbild Muslim* (Berlin: Rotbuch Verlag); for a more apologetic reading, see Lewis, B.W. (1993), *Islam and the West* (Oxford: Oxford University Press). Lewis also criticizes Said, E.W. (2003), *Orientalism* (London: Penguin Books), as 'anti-Western'.

36 White, R.K. (1991), 'Enemy Images in the United Nations-Iraq and East-West Conflicts', in: Rieber R.W. (ed), The Psychology of War and Peace (New York: Plenum Press); and Frei, D. (1985), *Feindbilder und Abrüstung. Die gegenseitige Einschätzung der UdSSR und der USA* (Munich: UNIDIR).

37 Ernst, Carl W. (2013), 'Introduction: The Problem of Islamophobia', in: Ernst. C. (ed), *Islamophobia in America: The Anatomy of Intolerance* (London: Palgrave Macmillan).

38 O'Connor, B. (2007), *Anti-Americanism: In the 21st Century* (Westport: Greenwood Publishing Group); Ansary, T. (2009), *Destiny Disrupted: A History of the World Through Islamic Eyes* (New York: Public Affairs).

39 'What Do Europeans Think About Muslim Immigration?' in: Chatham House, 7 February 2017 www.chathamhouse.org/expert/comment/what-do-europeans-think-about-muslim-immigration/ (last accessed 28 September 2018).

40 Waikar, P. (2018), 'Reading Islamophobia in Hindutva: An Analysis of Narendra Modi's Political Discourse', in: 4 *Islamophobia Studies Journal*, 161 ff.

with covering up the outbreak.[41] The Chinese government responded in kind and blamed the United States for its careless handling of the coronavirus. For its part, the Iranian government laid the blame for the virus squarely at the doors of Israel and the United States.[42] This pattern of blaming a foreign country as the origin of a deadly disease or epidemic has played out over centuries. The 'Spanish flu' – an influenza with an unusually high mortality rate – did not originate in Spain.[43] Syphilis was called the 'French disease' – arguably because the first well-recorded European outbreak occurred in 1495 among French troops besieging Naples, Italy, where it may have been transmitted to the French via Spanish mercenaries. A recent study absolves the 'New World of being the birthplace of syphilis'.[44] Like coronavirus, syphilis has also been labelled the 'English disease', the 'Persian fire' and more, depending on prejudice and politics.

Defaming critics and opposition movements as enemies helps to mobilize supporters and signals to the opposition that proposals of compromise are not on offer. Hysteria about an external threat is often used to deflect from and justify secrecy and suspicion, open discrimination and covert action; to mobilize for national unity and policies that suppress dissent; and very often to distract attention from domestic problems. Though usually motivated by (unitary) nationalist[45] sentiment, declarations of hostility destroy the texture of a democratic culture of debate. This is why democratic constitutionalism focuses on equality of social and political relations, even in controversies, and avoids the concept of the enemy. 'Enemy' talk and fantasies indicate that societies, political classes or leaders are transitioning towards radical political factionalism and the asymmetric treatment of followers and critics, whereby constitutional rules are only occasionally observed, according to the maxim of opportunism.

---

[41] Collins, S. (2020), 'Trump says China "should have told us" about coronavirus', in: vox.com, 23 March.

[42] Aarabi, K. (2020), 'Iran Knows Who to Blame for Virus: America and Israel', in: *Foreign Policy*, 19 March.

[43] Various studies locate the origin in the armies of the First World War, the United Kingdom, the United States or China. We will probably never know.

[44] Regarding the fascinating and never-ending debate on the origin of syphilis: Diamond, J. (1997), *Guns, Germs and Steel* (New York: W.W. Norton); and Tampa, M. et al (2014), 'Brief history of syphilis', in: 7 *Journal of Medicine and Life*, 4 ff.

[45] For a very informative overview and further references, see Smith, A.D. (2017), *Nationalism: Theory, Ideology, History* (2nd ed) (Cambridge: Polity Press).

3. INFORMALISM

The ritual of constitutional forms and procedures conceals the fact that authoritarian regimes generally operate in the shadow of norms and constitutions,[46] and prefer the informal exercise of power. Anti-formalism loosens the ties to the legality that autocrats are only too happy to use as a cover in everyday life to silence doubts about their legitimacy. In striking contrast to the formalized assumption of power through inauguration, the informal exercise of power takes place quietly in the darkness of authoritarian constitutionalism. Of course, a folksy costume is occasionally adopted, in the spirit of opportunism.

3.1 In the Shadow of Legality

A costume that barely hides vice or constitutional violations is a flimsy masquerade: the population applauds the abuse of power by their leaders and relishes their disregard for legality as an entertaining spectacle. Italian Prime Minister Silvio Berlusconi served as a depressing example of popular constitutional opportunism of this kind during his terms of office. In default of a majority to call him to account for his politics, time and again he introduced laws that granted him amnesty or, after his most recent electoral win, immunity from criminal prosecution. His preference for informality was expressed in his marked disdain for legality and the courts, as well as his televised political peepshows, with the Italian people as complicit onlookers. Informality and opportunism met with broad approval from one part of the electorate, which interpreted Berlusconi's casualness and illegal actions as signs of brio; and with resignation from the other part, which had long given up expecting anything serious from his government. Many Italians savoured the entertainment; many more were inured to it; and only a critical fringe took offence to the dismantling of the Italian Constitution and its political and legal institutions. Berlusconi's success and self-assessment did not suffer when critical observers charged him with transforming Italy's fragile parliamentary democracy into a sultanate.[47] Since the social sciences and the courts had not yet been subsumed into his entertainment complex, their reports and critiques were of no concern to Berlusconi.

Insofar as a Machiavellian style reaches constitutional limits, the scripts of fun and games *à la* Berlusconi, or dictates of raw power and expediency as seen elsewhere – even if occasionally varnished with Machiavellian virtues – must be adapted to each context and generally masked in pseudo-constitutional

[46] On the normative side of Fraenkel's dual state, so to say.

[47] Sartori, G. (2009), *Il Sultanato* (Rome: Laterza).

terms and forms. For this masquerade to work, regimes tend to invoke necessity or claim the prevalence of a given security agenda. Once authoritarian power is safely consolidated, more pragmatic explanations will suffice. The latter was the case when Chinese head of state Xi Jinping recently lifted the constitutional two-term limit on the presidency.[48] In a show of concord, the almost 3000 members of the National People's Congress agreed to allow him be president for life. The official, quite pragmatic reasoning was that the office of president should be aligned with Xi Jinping's two other permanent leading positions as secretary general of the Communist Party and chairman of the Central Military Commission. Since 'real' political power comes from those other two roles, one might dismiss this as symbolic[49] and seek comfort in the concept of the 'King's Two Bodies':[50] while no one can predict when his natural body will end, the lifespan of Xi's symbolic (political) body may be shorter, as it is tied to his standing as party chief.

Vladimir Putin has perfected the combination of constitutional opportunism with a penchant for the informal to create what may be called an imitated democracy. The former high-ranking intelligence officer is particularly well practised in nonchalant informality and demonstrated this at the expense of the already fragile reputation of the 1993 Constitution – and democracy – of the Russian Federation.[51] At the end of his second presidential term in 2008, he sent straw man and confidant Dmitry Medvedev into the race for office and had himself appointed as a 'godfather' prime minister, who pulled all the strings behind the scenes. Given that in Russian elections, promising opponents are eliminated through fabricated criminal charges, staged criminal proceedings, arrests and even murder, Putin was subsequently able to be 're-elected' to the presidency without any problems. This all happened in accordance with the constitution, which has been reduced to a paper tiger, largely stripped of its

---

[48] Article 79 of the Constitution of the People's Republic of China.

[49] Observers disagree: Li, E.X. (2018), 'Why Xi's lifting of term limits is a good thing', in: *The Washington Post*, 2 April; Buckley, A. and Wu, A. (2018), 'Ending Term Limits for China's Xi is a Big Deal. Here's Why', in: *The New York Times*, 10 March.

[50] The body natural and the body politic – see Kantorowicz, E. (2016), *The King's Two Bodies – A Study in Medieval Political Theology* (Princeton: Princeton University Press).

[51] Dawisha, K. (2014), *Putin's Kleptocracy: Who Owns Russia?* (New York: Simon & Schuster); Politkovskaya, A. (2007), *Putin's Russia* (New York: Holt & Co).

normative core to allow for Putin's informal power management. With utter conviction, the 'guardian of the constitution'[52] commented innocently:

> The Constitution clearly states: two terms in a row. I am now elected for the second time. As you know, I have been President twice before, but had to interrupt because the Constitution does not allow a third consecutive term. That's all.[53]

Putin – the master of de-formalization – claimed that he had always respected the constitution and would always abide by it. The mastermind of an extra-constitutional 'vertical of power' and chain of command[54] that encompass all state organs further announced that he would give up his presidency in 2024. This is another autocratic gesture: declaring that *he* would decide when to step down. He changed his mind, though, and followed Xi Jinping's example, as will be shown later.

Informal political technology is most apparent in the style of governing. As a follow-up to the discussion on authority/authoritarianism in the previous chapter, aspects of political performance are now presented that further illustrate the widely practised informality of authoritarian political technology and share an *internal* authoritarian tendency: the normalization and perpetuation of a state of emergency 'on the quiet',[55] networks operating in secret and without rules (the deep state) and the introduction of 'combat laws'.

3.2 Informality and the State of Exception

Informality – the twin of opportunism – is characterized by the fact that the techniques of autocratic governing and autocratic constitutions undermine the fundamental distinction between norm and exception by authorizing a wide range of extraordinary powers and measures, and by eroding a 'culture of (constitutional) formalism'[56] that could help to mediate between commitment

---

[52] Article 80, paragraph 2 of the 1993 Constitution of the Russian Federation.

[53] Bartlett, W. (2012), 'The Constitutionality of Vladimir Putin's Third Term', in: Brookings, 9 March, www.brookings.edu/opinions/the-constitutionality-of-vladimir-putins-third-term (last accessed 8 January 2020). See also Articles 1 and 81, Section 3 of the Constitution of the Russian Federation.

[54] In her book *Putin's Russia*, the journalist Anna Politkovskaya – murdered in 2006 (on Putin's birthday) – characterized the Russian democracy as a conglomerate of Mafia entrepreneurs, agencies of the administration of justice and the state power.

[55] See Chapter 3, Section 3.

[56] Alluding to Koskenniemi, M. (2009), *The Gentle Civilizer of Nations. The Rise and Fall of International Law 1870–1960* (Cambridge: Cambridge University Press), 2009, 500; and *id* (1999), 'Between Commitment and Cynicism: Outline for a Theory of International Law as Practice', in: *Collection of Essays by Legal Advisers of*

and cynicism or promote a spirit of resistance in civil society and a responsible style of government; and might prevent the self-fulfilling prophesy that 'emergency powers would tend to kindle emergencies'[57] – that is, once these powers are allocated, they will be used.

The informal side of emergency laws and their execution is particularly evident in the ritual extension and arbitrary explanation of states of exception. Whatever the rationale, the extension turns the original imposition, limitation and justification of the state of exception – which was intended to restrain those in power – into a pattern without value. The following examples illustrate the diversity of deformalized extraordinary state practices.

3.2.1 Example 1: de-formalizing by normalizing

To begin with, allow me to refer to a simple case. A state of emergency was announced in France in 2015 and then extended six times until it was finally replaced by a revised anti-terror law, which incorporated some of the provisions of the previous *état d'urgence*. Once again, the 'war on terror' served as an engine of *normalization*. In France, this dynamic is enhanced by an authoritarian presidential system that allows the president to dissolve Parliament and empowers him to issue legislative decrees.[58] Although the French network of security regulations allows the president to do 'whatever it takes', Emmanuel Macron – perhaps to compensate for never having done national service or to increase his chances of re-election – has repeatedly declared a state of war ('*Nous sommes en guerre*')[59] against an 'invisible enemy'. In a manner that combined silliness and hazard, he positioned himself as the commander-in-chief in a battle against the coronavirus and called for the general mobilization of a society that was beginning to fall apart at the seams.

After the failed *coup d'état* of 2016, a state of emergency was declared in Turkey and then extended seven times, moving the regime towards a caliphate. No sooner had the Turkish Constitution been suspended than Erdoğan introduced drastic constitutional changes, imposing a semi-dictatorial presidential system that departed from the authoritarian Kemalist project of modernizing

International Organizations and Practitioners in the Field of International Law (New York: United Nations), 495 ff.

57 US Supreme Court J. Jackson, in the *Youngstown* decision, quoted by Gotein, E. (2019), 'The Alarming Scope of Presidential Emergency Powers', in: *The Atlantic*, January/February.

58 Articles 12 and 38 of the 1958 Constitution of France.

59 Pietralunga, C. and Lemarié, A. (2020), '*"Nous sommes en guerre": face au coronavirus, Emmanuel Macron sonne la "mobilisation générale"*', in: *Le Monde*, 17 March, www.lemonde.fr/politique/article/2020/03/17/nous-sommes-en-guerre-face-au-coronavirus-emmanuel-macron-sonne-la-mobilisation-generale_6033338_823448.html (last accessed 26 March 2020).

Turkey towards anti-secularism.[60] Previously, hundreds of journalists had been arrested and massive purges had been carried out, affecting the judiciary, public services, the police and the military, and neutralizing alleged opposition members, civil servants, judges and lawyers. Based on reliable reports, at least 130 000 people lost their jobs. The latest wave of dismissals, which affected almost 20 000 state employees, was executed two weeks before emergency measures were discontinued.

Under cover of the state of exception, Erdoğan staged a counter-coup that was much more successful than the original 'coup'. After winning the national elections, he lifted the state of emergency, in compliance with the formal requirements; but most of its provisions had already been transferred into the corpus of ordinary law. The extraordinary powers morphed into the law of the status quo – to all intents and purposes, they were *normalized* by a constitutional coup. Today's anti-terrorist laws contain provisions that might very well be more restrictive than the extraordinary measures taken during the state of exception.

3.2.2 Example 2: routinizing the exception

In Egypt's recent history, emergency laws have become more engrained than perhaps in almost any other country.[61] Originally enacted by President Gamal Abdel Nasser in 1958 to neutralize the old power elites, Emergency Law 162 remained in force until 1964, when it was suspended; it was reintroduced in 1967 as a result of the Six-Day War. The Emergency Law extended police powers, suspended constitutional rights, legalized censorship and abolished the principle of *habeas corpus*. It limited non-governmental political activity, curbed the freedoms of political communication (speech, assembly, association), and prohibited unregistered financial donations. It permitted indefinite detention without trial and hearings of civilians by military courts. Over time, the Emergency Law was stripped of its formal properties. Even when Nasser's successor, Anwar as-Sadat, was in power, it remained – externally – an important instrument for securing his authority. When in May 1980 the Emergency Law was temporarily suspended, it had already been transformed into a mere

---

[60] 'The Republic of Turkey is a democratic, secular and social state governed by the rule of law; bearing in mind the concepts of public peace, national solidarity and justice; respecting human rights; loyal to the nationalism of Atatürk, and based on the fundamental tenets set forth in the Preamble.' Article 1, Section 1 of the 1982 Constitution. See Clayer, N. *et al* (eds) (2018), *Kemalism: Transnational Politics in the Post Ottoman World*, (London: I.B. Tauris).

[61] Kassem, M. (1999), *In the Guise of Democracy: Governance in Contemporary Egypt* (Reading: Garnet & Ithaca Press); Kirkpatrick, D.D. (2012), 'Egypt Reimposes Martial Law, Ahead of Closely Watched Ruling' in: *The New York Times*, 14 June.

ritual. After the assassination of President Anwar as-Sadat on 6 October 1981 by fundamentalist members of the Egyptian armed forces, the Emergency Law was reintroduced in a new guise and with extended powers by as-Sadat's successor, Husni Mubarak, to resolve the explosive domestic political situation (Law 560/1981).

The Emergency Law has been extended several times since then. During his campaign for re-election as president (2005), Mubarak maintained that he would replace it with a new anti-terror law. Instead, in May 2006, May 2008 and most recently May 2010, he had the Emergency Law extended, each time for another two years.[62] After the fall of Mubarak, state practice changed only slightly: the ruling military council took the attacks on the Israeli embassy on 9 September 2011 as an opportunity to extend the Emergency Law further, contrary to earlier promises. The official justification followed the usual pattern: in the face of terror, the threat to national security and public order demanded that all articles of the Emergency Law be applied in full. On 4 June 2012, after its temporary repeal, a further turnaround occurred. Minister of Justice Adel Abdel Hamid issued Decree 4991, which again enacted the very measures and sanctions that were previously thought to have had been abandoned. Surprisingly, the decree was based on Law 25 on Military Justice of 1966. The pattern was repeated in March 2020, when the Cabinet of Prime Minister Mustafa Madbouli approved the extension of the state of exception, randomly and conveniently combining terror and the coronavirus crisis:

> All of you are aware of the magnitude of the threats and turmoil that still afflict the Arab region, the Middle East, and the entire world. Amid these [circumstances], we are faced by those who plan to destabilize the state. But, we do not fear any threat or maliciousness to our homeland.[63]

These examples demonstrate the empty formalism of declarations and justifications. They were and still are thoroughly devoid of normative elements: without binding procedures and controllable arguments, they illustrate a basically informal state practice in Egypt.

3.2.3 Example 3: the undeclared state of exception

In India – generally known as the world's largest democracy – the regime of Narendra Modi provides another example of the informality of authoritarian

---

62 Rutherford, B.K., (2013), *Egypt after Mubarak: Liberalism, Islam, and Democracy in the Arab World* (Princeton: Princeton University Press).

63 *Egypt today*, 3 May 2020, www.egypttoday.com/Article/1/85383/Egypt%E2%80%99s-PM-State-of-Emergency-declared-to-face-COVID-19 (last accessed 16 July 2020).

regimes by operating on the basis of an undeclared state of exception.[64] Learning from the disastrous experience of Indira Gandhi in 1975, Modi refrained from suspending the Constitution *in toto.* While Indira Gandhi had formally declared a national state of emergency and ultimately lost power, Modi and his henchmen ordered extraordinary measures – such as arrests without a court order and press censorship – against critics of the regime and oppositional groups, on the basis of security regulations and criminal law. Modi's government revoked the autonomous status of Jammu and Kashmir,[65] and antagonized the predominantly Muslim population living there, on the strength of his more than two-thirds majority in India's National Parliament.[66] By the same token, he introduced amendments to the Citizenship Act[67] that laid out a path to Indian citizenship for illegal migrants of the Hindu, Sikh, Buddhist, Jain, Parsi and Christian faiths, but excluded Muslims.

Originally, the Modi regime propagated the narrative that a line had to be drawn between the 'true Indians' and their 'enemies' – public intellectuals, Muslims, Dalits, Communists and other dissidents. Modi singled out these enemy groups to legitimize his politics, but was careful not to affect his party base on the one hand and to ensure sectoral support in the regions of India on the other. In 2019, Modi launched a more deliberately Hindu-nationalist[68] agenda and openly moved against the Muslim community. As the Indian government most likely expected, the Citizenship (Amendment) Act sparked

---

[64] See Nielsen, A.G. (2018), 'An Authoritarian India Is Beginning to Emerge', in: *The Wire,* 31 August; and 'Modi has drawn many lessons from Indira Gandhi's Emergency – save one', in: *Scroll.in,* 8 April 2019, https://scroll.in/article/892576/modi-has-successfully-drawn-several-lessons-from-indira-gandhis-emergency-save-one/ (last accessed 14 January 2019).

[65] Article 370 of the Constitution of India.

[66] See the in-depth, yet concise analysis by Kaushik, A. (2029), 'Constitutional Exceptionalism in Kashmir', in: *Verfassungsblog*, 25 October, https://verfassungsblog.de/constitutional-exceptionalism-in-kashmir/ (last accessed 26 March 2020).

[67] The bill amends the Citizenship Act of 1955 to give eligibility for Indian citizenship to illegal migrants who are Hindus, Sikhs, Buddhists, Jains, Parsis or Christians from Afghanistan, Bangladesh or Pakistan, and who entered India on or before 31 December 2014 – but not to Muslims. The bill makes no mention of other persecuted groups and in particular Muslims, however. The Office of the United Nations High Commissioner for Human Rights criticized the act and called it 'fundamentally discriminatory in nature'. The High Commissioner added: 'Although India's broader naturalization laws remain in place, these amendments will have a discriminatory effect on people's access to nationality.' See 'The Citizenship (Amendment) Act, 2019', in: *The Gazette of India*, 12 December 2019.

[68] Gettleman, J. *et al* (2019), 'Under Modi, a Hindu Nationalist Surge Has Further Divided India', in: *The New York Times*, 11 April; Mehta, P.B. (2020), 'Hope, Fear, Anger: Will this be the decade we finally come to terms with our reality?', in: *Indian Express*, 1 January.

vehement protests nationwide, which cut across religious, ethnic and class boundaries. In turn, the protests served as a pretext for massive police (over) reaction, with many casualties and more than 1000 arrests. Moreover, extremist Hindu-nationalist groups – acting like paramilitary Nazi storm troopers – felt called upon to defend, by proxy, the Hindu-nationalist project, invading university campuses and attacking demonstrating students and bystanders.[69] Without declaring a state of exception, simply by laying the foundations for violence, the Modi regime pursued its Hindu-nationalist agenda.

The Indian government likewise did not declare a state of exception, but deployed extraordinary measures in response to the coronavirus crisis. Initially, the government played down the pandemic and officially advised that the virus be treated with homeopathy and Ayurvedic, plant-based remedies.[70] The government left it up to individual states to deal with the situation themselves, and Kerala duly declared a state of exception. As the number of coronavirus cases increased dramatically, the national government resorted to recommending social distancing, staying at home and the usual arsenal of extraordinary public health measures, such as lockdown.

3.2.4 Example 4: faking the exception

One might think that the US Constitution is not a suitable example of either informal or executive-authoritarian technology, since the power of the executive seems to be adequately contained. Congress has the authority to make provisions for the establishment, organization and arming of militias; to suppress insurrections; to declare wars and repel invasions; and to address militant protests.[71] The fact that the president is commander-in-chief of the armed forces and the national militia ensures the conscientious enforcement of the law. Given that he or she has the power to 'fill all civil servant posts that become vacant during the Senate vacations by means of the official mandate that expires at the end of the next session', one might readily concede to him or her without necessarily thinking this in any way authoritarian (as long as he or she does not adopt the Trumpian style). Pursuant to a formalist reading of the Constitution, this system of legitimate organized violence and emergency measures in times of crisis is basically in the hands of Congress: Congress can suspend the 'writ of *habeas corpus*' and the right of a detainee to immediate judicial review if public security so requires in case of rebellion or invasion.

---

[69] 'India: largest protests in decades signal Modi may have gone too far', in: *The Guardian*, 20 December 2019; Human Rights Watch, 'India: Deadly Force Used Against Protesters', 23 December 2019.

[70] Wallen, J. (2020), 'Indian state declares emergency after third confirmed coronavirus case', in: *The Telegraph*, 3 February.

[71] Article I, Section 8 and Article II of the US Constitution.

Hence, arguably Congress – not the president – should call up the 'Militia of the Several States' to enforce the law, suppress riots, repel invasions and handle other extraordinary situations. Still, the president has the power to declare a state of national emergency.

However, when it comes to how powers are allocated in exceptional situations, the written US Constitution provides only a fragmentary script. This is why, time and again, presidents have claimed 'inherent powers to act beyond ordinary legal limits in an exigency'. Such implied emergency powers were invoked to intern members of the enemy forces in Japan, regardless of their citizenship;[72] to carry out wiretapping without court order; and to use torture during the Iraq war and after 9/11.[73]

While those claims have tended to fare poorly, at least when challenged in court,[74] presidents find themselves on firmer legal ground when they rely on statutes through which Congress has authorized the executive branch to act in emergencies. And there are quite a few of these. The Brennan Institute reported that in the 200 years since the Insurrection Act of 1807, presidents have issued some 123 emergency laws to combat insurrection and other political crises,[75] including the Communications Act of 1934/1942 to control communications; the International Emergency Economic Powers Act of 1977, which authorizes the president to block transactions, freeze accounts and confiscate property in emergency situations; and the PATRIOT Act of 2001, which confers broad powers to combat terrorism.

Through the National Emergencies Act of 1976, Congress made (what soon turned out to be) a vain attempt to formally end the emergencies declared in previous decades and to limit future ones. However, the informality of the extraordinary ultimately proved stronger. At the last count, a remarkable 30 'states of emergency' were still in force in the United States.[76] Instead of

---

[72] *Korematsu v United States*, 323 US 214 (1944). See also *Trump v Hawaii*, No 17-965, 585 US ___ (2018), concerning Presidential Proclamation 9645 of 24 July 2017 ('Protecting the Nation from Foreign Terrorist Entry into the United States').

[73] Sands, P. (2008), *Torture Team: Uncovering War Crimes in the Land of the Free* (London: Penguin).

[74] Savage, C. (2019), 'National Emergency Powers and Trump's Border Wall', in: *The New York Times*, 7 January.

[75] See Goitein, E. (2019), 'In Case of Emergency', in: *The Atlantic*, 1.

[76] Goitein (n 2). See 'Special Committee on the Termination of the National Emergency' of the 93rd Congress (1973 to 1975). For a more optimistic account with little empirical backing, see Ackerman, B.A. (2007), *Before the Next Attack: Preserving Civil Liberties in an Age of Terrorism* (New Haven: Yale University Press), 124: 'The National Emergencies Act of 1976 terminated all existing emergencies…' Rather problematic are the plans and measures concerning Continuity of Operations, a governmental initiative pursuant to US Presidential Policy Directive 40, which aims to ascertain

documenting the viability of the 'emergency constitution', euphemistically argued for by liberal constitutional lawyers,[77] they provide insight into the dark world of informal authoritarianism, far removed from the spotlights of liberal constitutionalism. To these one must add the peculiar state of exception on the southern border of the United States, which President Trump both declared and simultaneously denied. He could learn from other regimes that playing with the state of exception is one aspect of how fascism operates.

3.3 Networks in the Deep State

Within the framework of authoritarian constitutional opportunism, informality has both a procedural and an institutional dimension. In both dimensions, all forms of public control are played off against the informal networks and channels of patriarchal masculinity.[78] Paradoxically, the epitome of such 'unbound', non-institutionalized networks – the opposite of 'delegative democracy'[79] – are military juntas and their secret brotherhoods, otherwise obsessively trained to obey and intent on preserving the external form. Such regimes have included the Greek colonels (1967–74); the Argentine military dictatorship (1976–83); the military junta in Myanmar; and military regimes in Africa and Latin America. They placed little emphasis on international recognition and publicity, let alone democracy. Instead, they established informal networks, enhanced cooperation with other secret services and colluded with consultants and expert bodies – such as the Chicago Boys, willing helpers of Chile's General Pinochet and other Latin American dictators[80] – in the back

---

that governmental agencies can exercise their essential functions 'under a broad range of circumstances'.

[77] It is hardly convincing when Bruce Ackerman argues for an 'emergency constitution' and its mid-range advantages: 'So the emergency constitution offers a trade-off of sorts—a reduction of due process in the short run, followed by its enhancement over the middle run' (Ackerman, *Before the Next Attack*, 114).

[78] The connection between management, organization and masculinity is analysed and submitted to critique by Collinson, D. and Hearns, J. (1996), *Men as Managers, Managers as Men. Critical Perspectives on Men, Masculinities and Managements* (London: Sage). See Valdés, J.G. (1995), *Pinochet's Economists. The Chicago School in Chile* (Cambridge: Cambridge University Press).

[79] O'Donnell, G. (1994), 'Delegative Democracy', in: 5 *Journal of Democracy*, 55 ff.

[80] These willing helpers turned Chile's dictatorship and other autocracies into laboratories of neoliberal political experiments. However, Nobel Prize winner Gary Becker argued that in retrospect, 'the willingness of the Chicago Boys to work for a cruel dictator and develop a different economic approach' was 'one of the best things that could happen to Chile'. He held that 'Chile went from being a pariah state controlled by a dictator to an economic role model for all developing countries', and that 'its achievements

rooms of their already shady regimes, beyond parliamentary, judicial, media or other control. Likewise, McKinsey celebrates its cooperation with China, unfazed by reports of the detention of Uyghurs in 're-education' camps;[81] and pursues consultancy projects with other autocracies, such as Russia, Malaysia and Saudi Arabia, undaunted by reports of corruption and cruelty.[82]

Informality functions as a medium that connects the different elements of the network structure of the deep state, like synapses.[83] It allows for the flexible fine-tuning of the logic and arguments of secret services, other agencies and consultants that operate *in arcanum*, in a largely unregulated space. Thus, it is virtually impossible to hold the actors of the deep state accountable for any actions or decisions. In consequence, they can let themselves be guided primarily by expediency rather than legality.

It is less well known that the agents of the deep state cooperate across borders and in a 'de-constitutionalized' realm with other (foreign) data services through intelligence networks, such as Five Eyes[84] or PRISM; exchange data; develop and deploy joint surveillance systems; and attack infrastructure.[85]

---

became even more impressive when the government was transformed into a democracy'. Quoted by Montecinos, V. and Markoff, J. (2009), *Economists in the Americas* (Cheltenham: Edward Elgar Publishing); Valdés, J.G. (1995), *Pinochet's Economics. The Chicago School in Chile* (Cambridge: Cambridge University Press).

[81] Officially called 'vocational education and training centres' by the Chinese government. See Zenz, A. (2019), 'Brainwashing, Police Guards and Coercive Internment: Evidence from Chinese Government Documents about the Nature and Extent of Xinjiang's "Vocational Training Internment Camps"', in: 7 *Journal of Political Risk*, 1 July.

[82] Bogdanovich, W. and Forsythe, M. (2018), 'How McKinsey Has Helped Raise the Stature of Authoritarian Governments', in: *The New York Times*, 15 December; Jones, C.W. (2019), 'What Happens When Consultants Work for Authoritarian Regimes', in: *Harvard Business Review*, 8 April; Dunn, C.W. (2019), 'How the Private Sector Supports Authoritarian Regimes in the Arab World', Arab Center Washington DC, 30 January.

[83] See Chapter 3, Section 3. O'Connor, K. *et al* (2019), 'Open Government in Authoritarian Regimes', in: 1 *International Review of Public Policy*, 65 ff.

[84] Cox, J. (2012), *Canada and the Five Eyes Intelligence Community* (Toronto: Canadian International Council).

[85] For obvious reasons, not secret service cooperation, but attempts at their control are published: Born, H. *et al* (2015), *Making International Intelligence Cooperation Accountable* (Oslo: Printing Office of the Parliament); Belgian Standing Intelligence Agencies Review Committee *et al* (2018), 'Strengthening oversight of international data exchange between intelligence and security services', May 2019.

4. RULE BY DECREE

Governing by decree is common and well-practised worldwide. A decree is underpinned by law that binds a governmental agency to the regular normative order, and thus rule by decree falls under the delegated powers of the executive. Technically, the decree is a fairly common form of governmental or administrative action. It is used as a flexible and accelerated tool in – or arising from – the legislative technique of governing. Rule by decree has an invaluable advantage: normally, it is removed from parliamentary debate and control (although not from judicial scrutiny), and thus flirts with authoritarianism.

In the first half of the twentieth century, the notorious Article 48, Section 2 of the Weimar Constitution gave decrees a bad name as emergency instruments and highlighted the risks of their application. First, Article 48, Section 2 – or rather, its frequent use – handed over the parliamentary governments of the first German republic to the already well-endowed executive power. Ultimately, this type of rule by emergency decree surrendered the eviscerated Republic to an authoritarian clique of nationalists, and *de facto* destroyed Constitution and enabled the Nazi regime.

The fate of the Weimar Constitution illustrates what I have previously called an internal authoritarian tendency within the decree. Article 48 tied any recourse to the instrument of emergency decrees to the existence of a 'serious disturbance or threat to public safety and order'. Rather than invoking a state of siege or exception, the article worked with a wording that dates back to the General Prussian Land Law of 1794 and the general clause of the Prussian police law.[86] Thus, Article 48, Section 2 oscillated between emergency law and ordinary law. However, it lacked a semantic structure and determinacy that could have limited its application to genuinely exceptional situations. In consequence, the power of the *Reichs-präsident* to issue '*Notverordnungen*' could be mobilized at will in all kinds of situations, ranging from a temporary failure to act on the part of the legislature to national security threats and often to economic crises – for example, to secure the gold reserve of private banks. Ultimately, the ominous article morphed into an all-purpose weapon of autocratic statehood. In 1931 alone, 34 laws were passed by the *Reichstag*, contrasted with 44 emergency decrees of the executive.

---

[86] In the Austrian December Constitution of 1867, Section 14 was considered an 'emergency provision'. It was invoked several times when the Parliament of the Habsburg Monarchy was suspended (*Stillstellung*). Karl Kraus called this provision the 'constitutional hernia bandage laid out for the state'. Kraus, K. (1988) 'Das provisorische Österreich', in: *Die Fackel* Number 6, 13.

This is where the relationship between *rule by decree* and the type of authorization (enabling) law that was common long before the Weimar era becomes apparent. The latter breaks and sets aside the constitution. The collision with the constitution is considered acceptable only because the legislature is involved and the law is intended to be temporary. However, this form of special delegated power indicates the breakthrough of a new constitutional political principle of extraordinary importance that is particularly popular in times of war and crisis: necessity.

The tragedy of the Weimar Republic, and in particular the devastation caused by the decrees of a totalitarian regime, did not affect the fate of this technique of governing. On the contrary, executive agencies around the world have continually glided into the grey zone between the normal and the extraordinary, using decrees in order to accelerate and implement decisions.

Between 1938 and 1942, the Daladier government repeatedly asked the French National Assembly to be granted special powers to intervene in the economic and financial crisis, to 'strengthen its defence force' and to wage war. This decree practice favoured demands for an authoritarian reorganization of the Third Republic. Yet it came to a halt with the Constitution of 1958, after the 'failure' of the Fourth Republic to end the war in 'French Indochina'. With the installation of presidentialism,[87] the French Constitution became semi-authoritarian. During the Algerian crisis, the first prime minister – later President Charles de Gaulle – had special powers granted in 1961 to combat the *Organisation de l'Armée Secrète* for an initial period of six months. These allowed him to govern largely in a domain outside of parliamentary control in the final years of the war – especially since the National Assembly had adjourned and legislative power had been transferred to the executive during this period.[88]

A change of scenery: in 2007, at a solemn ceremony, the Venezuelan National Assembly – that is, the supporters of President Hugo Chávez – granted him special powers for 18 months. The aim was to enable him to implement his 'socialist revolution'. Once the parliamentary deliberations had ended, the deputies gathered in the centrally located Bolivar Square in Carácas to ceremonially grant him – in an act of 'parliamentarism of the street' – the power to govern the 'Bolivarian Republic' by decree.[89] Chávez's version of 'twenty-first century socialism' included, among other things, deciding on

---

87 See Articles 12, 13 and 16 of the French Constitution (1958).

88 Noyer, A. (1966), *La sûreté de l'État (1789–1965)* (Paris: IGDJ).

89 The members of Parliament were exclusively Chávez supporters because of the boycott of the 2005 election by the opposition.

distribution measures, abolishing the independence of the Central Bank and nationalizing the telecommunications and energy industries.

Pursuant to Article 2 of the US Constitution, the president controls the instruments of executive order and proclamation. This possibility to enact measures in place of laws is in itself tailored to the business of government leadership in the narrower sense.[90] If the frequency of its use alone provides valid evidence of a Hobbesian authoritarian style of governing, then F.D. Roosevelt clearly leads the 'Leviathan scale', with 3522 executive orders issued – albeit spread over a little more than three terms of office. He is followed by Woodrow Wilson (1803), Calvin Coolidge (1203) and Theodore Roosevelt (1081).[91] The current president, Donald Trump, celebrates in the media the signature of his numerous executive orders as an authoritarian pose.[92] He seems to be fast catching up with the leaders, far outdoing the rather reserved decree practice of his predecessors (Obama, Bush, Clinton).[93] After initially and for far too long downplaying the coronavirus crisis, Trump finally issued a series of decrees on national defence, the allocation of public health resources and more.[94]

4.1 Combat Laws

Over the decades, in many states, a security policy and security law paradigm that plays into the hands of political authoritarianism has developed the modality and rhetoric of 'combat laws'. These fly under the banner of the 'war on terror' – sometimes in tandem with the 'war on organized crime'.[95] In the wake of assassinations and terrorist attacks, a sober assessment of the threat situation appears to fade into the background. The militant rhetoric reminds societies that they are at war against crime and terrorism. The political class therefore

---

[90] Based on Article 2 (enforcement authority) and the explicit or implicit authority derived from Congress laws (delegated legislation).

[91] See, in general, Mayer, K.R. (2002), *With the Stroke of a Pen: Executive Orders and Presidential Power* (Princeton: Princeton University Press).

[92] On 18 March 2020, President Donald Trump invoked the Defense Production Act, 50 USC §§ 4501, et seq, to confront the spiralling coronavirus crisis. He has been labelled the 'executive order president' by Riesche, S. (2018), 'Der Dekret-Präsident', in: *Frankfurter Allgemeine Zeitung*, 27 January.

[93] Between taking office on 20 January 2017 and December 2019, Trump enacted 137 executive orders.

[94] Butzel Long, 20 March 2020, www.butzel.com/resources-alerts-Defense-Production-Act-The-Manufacturing-Impact.html/ (last accessed 25 March 2020).

[95] See United Nations Security Council Resolution 1368 of 11 September 2001, www.un.org/press/en/2001/SC7143.doc.htm/ (last accessed 16 July 2020). See also Makarenko, T. (2004), 'The Crime-Terror Continuum: Tracing the Interplay between Transnational Organized Crime and Terrorism', in: 6 *Global Crime*, No 1, February, 130 ff.

favours a combat approach to phenomena considered dangerous, rather than their regulation or prohibition,[96] to demonstrate strength and activity.

In the liberal context, combat is reserved, strictly speaking, for warfare and therefore requires special entitlements granted by the law of war.[97] And combat-like police operations, such as shoot to kill (not merely to disable), must be justified as use of force necessary to defend or rescue a person.[98] In contrast, authoritarian regimes come with a 'combative' – that is, an emergency – mind-set, and their police laws are likewise geared towards emergencies of all kinds. Hence, combat becomes a matter of routine. In the name of public security, it is in keeping with the authoritarian *dispositif* to fly the military flag, as it were, and to wage war against (not merely prevent) dangers, threats and risks. Since most autocrats see the world from the perspective of a state of exception, they are 'by nature' attuned to militant interventions in crisis-ridden social processes and spheres. Where a constitution-based security law must conceal or circumstantially explain the transition from regulation and danger prevention to combat and risk prevention, the security laws of authoritarian regimes are in any case geared towards the anticipation of extreme danger. Extensive monitoring and control of potential threats, sweeping interventions, blanket measures and measures triggered by weak suspicions are all integral to autocratic legality.

5. HERMENEUTICS OF SUSPICION

In contrast to tangible, clearly recognizable encroachments on freedom and physical integrity (eg, arrests, searches and seizures), surveillance measures are designed to provide secondary behaviour control through the recording of movements and social contacts – secondary because surveillance operates on the quiet and beyond cognitive awareness. The inner tendency of secret inspections, wiretapping and monitoring is inherently imperious, because these measures of the thought police are to a large extent removed from judicial review, moving them into the vicinity of an Orwellian, totalitarian regime in which all citizens are monitored for loyalty to the system.[99]

---

[96] For a detailed discussion, see Frankenberg (n 13), Chapter VI.

[97] For a critical review: Kennedy, D. (2006), *Of War and Law* (Princeton: Princeton University Press).

[98] The online *Collins Dictionary* (2019) defines 'shoot to kill' as 'shooting by soldiers or police that is intended to kill rather than disable ... when a suicide attack is deemed to be imminent' (London: HarperCollins Publishers).

[99] Orwell, G. (2008), *1984* (London: Penguin Books).

In autocracies, these emanations of the hermeneutics of suspicion[100] have long since become integral to the techniques of governing. In a digitalized world, informational interventions have become more diverse and refined, and even less tangible, through the use of modern technology and social media that enhance their authoritarian character. While the collection of personal data from undercover agents and informants is more reminiscent of Orwell's world, a new age has dawned, in which computer systems, the Internet and social media have outpaced traditional telecommunications and video surveillance of public facilities and spaces. Highly invasive information technology and pervasive social media have comprehensively infiltrated the capillaries of everyday life. A 'government of codes and not of men' has already spread like a network for gathering information about society, its groups and individuals. At the same time, surveillance has been normalized and integrated into the standard systems of police law and official state powers. Personal data is collected and stored everywhere – not always for good reason; exchanged between authorities beyond the horizons of (judicial and other) control; kept on file and retrieved when necessary (or not). The prevention of abstract risks has taken the lead, bowing to the imperatives of hyper-preventive internal security agendas.

The normalization and fine tuning of surveillance and social control are still evolving. Social media and their use by the state open up opportunities that Orwell could never have envisaged. China has propelled the authoritarian hermeneutics of suspicion in a frightening totalitarian direction, through the combination of facial recognition systems with big data analysis technology.[101] The social credit system is an example of China's 'top-level design' approach. It is coordinated by the Central Leading Group for Comprehensively Deepening Reforms. The Chinese government has not only started to monitor minorities (notably, but not exclusively, the Uyghurs) that might prove 'problematic' for the regime[102] and to expose opposition members; it has also combined Big Data with Big Brother in a comprehensive social scoring scheme and social credit system[103] that analyses, evaluates and sanctions citizens' behaviour.

---

[100] Introducing the hermeneutics of suspicion: Ricœur, P. (2008), *Freud and Philosophy. An Essay on Interpretation*, Savage, D. (transl) (New Haven: Yale University Press).

[101] Botsman, R. (2018), 'Big data meets Big Brother as China moves to rate its citizens', Wired, www.wired.co.uk/article/chinese-government-social-credit-score-privacy-invasion/ (last accessed 10 January 2020).

[102] Detaining them in 're-education camps' – Brophy, D. (2005), 'Taranchis, Kashgaris, and the "Uyghur Question" in Soviet Central Asia', in: *7 Inner Asia BRILL*, 16 ff.

[103] Stanley, J. (2015), 'China's Nightmarish Citizen Scores Are a Warning for Americans', in: *American Civil Liberties Union*, 5 October.

The normalization effect of such secondary behavioural control is fully exploited here to promote an all-round controlled, state-supported existence in a 'well-ordered community'.[104] The main objectives of social scoring are 'trustworthiness' and 'sincere conduct' – that is, conformity. These criteria are addressed at individuals, market participants, companies and, ultimately, the administration. Under this project, which has already been implemented in some provinces, data collection will be established for all Chinese citizens, to reflect their reliability and creditworthiness (eg, 'easy lending for the trustworthy'; 'easy debt issuance for the trustworthy'). According to the logic and guidelines of social scoring, behaviours are evaluated either positively or negatively. Breach of trust is strictly sanctioned. Black sheep who deviate from the norm – for example, by excessive computer gaming, disorderly driving or frequent changes of partner – must reckon with point deductions and restrictions to their freedom of movement (including financial movement). For loans, 'social assessment inquiries' are already conducted in one province. As things currently stand, anyone who has opposed a court decision can be excluded from flight bookings. As of June 2019, according to the National Development and Reform Commission of China, 26.82 million air tickets and 5.96 million high-speed rail tickets had been denied to people who were deemed 'untrustworthy' and blacklisted. In April 2019, the People's Bank of China announced that a new version of the personal credit report – described as 'more detailed, more comprehensive and more precise' – would be launched to collect more personal information. The system has also been used to rate individuals on their internet habits (eg, excessive online gaming reduces one's score), personal shopping habits and a variety of other personal habits and wholly innocuous acts without any impact on the wider community.

The designation of the agency that is implementing the social scoring system – the State Council Guiding Opinions concerning Establishing and Perfecting Incentives for Promise-keeping and Joint Punishment Systems for Trust-Breaking, and Accelerating the Construction of Social Sincerity – as well as the logic and structure of the system and the imperative style, is reminiscent of Orwell's 1984 and the 'terror of virtue' of the Cultural Revolution:

> Strengthen social restrictions and punishment for trust-breaking acts. Fully give rein to the role of all kinds of social organizations in guiding social forces to broadly participate in the joint punishment for trust-breaking. Establish and perfect trust-breaking reporting mechanisms, encourage the public to report grave

---

[104] Meissner, M. (2017), 'China's Social Credit System: A big-data enabled approach to market regulation with broad implications for doing business in China', www.merics.org (last accessed 10 January 2020).

> trust-breaking acts by enterprises, and maintain the secrecy of information of the reporting person.[105]

Citizens who do not live up to the standards set by the agencies guiding social forces and score 'low' will experience problems in all aspects of life – not only obtaining bank loans, but also getting a promotion, travelling and even low internet speeds.

6. CO-OPTING AND NEUTRALIZING THE JUDICIARY

> Just cannot believe a judge would put our country in such peril. If something happens blame him and court system. People pouring in. Bad!
>
> When a country is no longer able to say who can, and who cannot come in & out, especially for reasons of safety & security - big trouble!
>
> The opinion of this so-called judge, which essentially takes law-enforcement away from our country, is ridiculous and will be overturned!
>
> What is our country if a judge can stop a Homeland Security travel ban?[106]

These tweets of US President Trump nicely characterize the relationship between genuinely authoritarian leaders and the judiciary. Such leaders do not accept judicial review if it challenges their actions – such as Trump's decrees concerning immigrants from several Islamic countries and deferred action for childhood arrivals. Insofar as courts are institutionally, functionally and politically independent, they have the power to act as a countervailing force, to thwart government policies and curb authoritarian impulses. In a preventive defensive manoeuvre, autocracies pursue a dual strategy of neutralizing judges. (The aspect of 'sanding down' the judiciary as an intermediary set of institutions will be discussed in conjunction with the cult of immediacy in Chapter 7.) In presidential systems, the judiciary is already an endangered

---

[105] From: State Council Guiding Opinions, 23 December 2016, https://chinacopyrightandmedia.wordpress.com/2016/05/30/state-council-guiding-opinions-concerning-establishing-and-perfecting-incentives-for-promise-keeping-and-joint-punishment-systems-for-trust-breaking-and-accelerating-the-construction-of-social-sincer/ (last accessed 17 July 2020).

[106] Some of the many tweets from President Trump in which he has attacked the judiciary, notably the Ninth Circuit, D.J. Trump, @realDonaldTrump, 4 and 5 February 2017. See Brennan Center for Justice (2017), 'In His Own Words', 5 June.

species, because the right to have the final say is based on the power of competing institutions.[107]

The neutralization of the judiciary usually starts with the intimidation of judges or mobilization of public opinion against the courts, which Trump's tweets were intended to achieve. The formal and institutional strategy is usually geared towards dictating or changing the composition of courts by hand-picking judges who are loyal to the system and getting rid of those who are unruly or unreliable. While authoritarian leaders in general focus on the higher courts, especially constitutional or supreme courts, Viktor Orbán's *Fidesz* party also targeted the lower courts.

A more discreet but no less effective approach is to force judges into early retirement. If these measures are not possible or do not work, there is still the possibility of 'court-packing' – that is, adding selected judges to the 'sitting judges', who cannot easily be removed. Court-packing is generally connected to Franklin D. Roosevelt, although his plan to 'pack' the US Supreme Court to save the New Deal fell through during the legislative process.[108] And finally, where judicial conformism cannot be achieved through discipline, circumstances permitting, there is always the possibility to threaten with punishment.[109]

Hungary, Poland, Egypt and Venezuela provide ample illustration of the efforts of governments to haul the courts over the coals of autocracy and thus 'thin out' or offset judicial review. In Hungary, the government disempowered the formerly influential Constitutional Court through a constitutional amendment that thoroughly undermined its authority. This (fourth) amendment of 2013 supplemented the new Basic Law, which had only been in force since early 2012. Among other things, the amendment limited the Constitutional Court's right to review to procedural aspects. The amendment also provided that the president of the National Judicial Office, appointed by Orbán, had the power to assign certain cases to specific courts of her choice. This establishment of 'special courts' was explicitly criticized by the European Commission

---

[107] See Kennedy, D. (2019), 'Authoritarian Constitutionalism in Liberal Democracies', in: Alviar and Frankenberg (n 7), 161 ff.

[108] For a conventional, informative description, see White, E.G. (2000), *The Constitution and the New Deal Court: The Structure of the Constitutional Revolution* (Cambridge: Harvard University Press). Kennedy (n 107) provides a different interpretation and more references.

[109] Poland's ruling PiS seemed to have planned to go down that road: the country risked leaving the European Union because of the ruling nationalists' project that would allow judges to be fired if they questioned the legitimacy of the government's judicial reforms. See 'Poles protest bill aimed at punishing judges', Euractiv, www.euractiv.com/section/justice-home-affairs/news/poles-protest-bill-aimed-at-punishing-judges (last accessed 17 December 2019).

– to no avail. Recently, the Orbán government toyed with and then gave up another idea: the introduction of new (administrative) courts in parallel with the existing courts, thus reducing the latter's mandate and tying the special courts to the Ministry of Justice.[110] It is clear to see that this would have allowed the regime to fill the administrative courts with judges of its own choice. Finally – concerned about or perhaps simply avoiding another confrontation with the European Commission and Parliament – Orbán abandoned this project.

Hungary found a 'legitimate' heir in the European Union, or at least an ally and imitator, in the shape of Poland. For several years, the opposition in Poland and the European Commission have raised concerns about the restructuring of the judiciary by the right-wing conservative government of the Law and Justice Party (PiS) – in particular, the subordination of the Supreme Court to the government and the forced retirement of 24 out of 74 active judges, as well as the introduction of new retirement rules in the ordinary courts.[111] In December 2017, for the first time in EU history, the European Commission initiated 'rule-of-law proceedings' pursuant to Article 7 of the Treaty on European Union against Poland for possible threats to EU fundamental values (Article 2 of the Treaty on European Union) – in this case, the rule of law.[112] While normal infringement proceedings must ultimately be decided by the European Court of Justice, the Article 7 approach sounds more dramatic that it actually is: it could lead to the withdrawal of voting rights in the extreme case. However, the Treaty sets high hurdles: apart from formal and procedural provisions (ie, consultation of Poland; consent of the European Parliament), a four-fifths majority in the European Council (Article 7(1)) or unanimous decision (Article 7(2)) is required. Given the political constellations in the member states and the European Council, such majorities, let alone unanimity, would be nigh on impossible to achieve.

Manipulating and adjusting the screws of the judicial system is a popular instrument of securing power that is used by authoritarian regimes the world over. Thus, the government of Egyptian President Mursi followed the example of Orban's *Fidesz* Party in Hungary and PiS in Poland, and lowered the

---

[110] 'Hungary Creates New Court System, Cementing Leader's Control of Judiciary', in: *The New York Times,* 12 December 2018.

[111] Sledzinska-Simon, A. (2017), 'The Polish Revolution: 2015–2017', in: *ICONnect*, 25 July, http://perma.cc/T2ZC-XVJK/ (last accessed 3 November 2018).

[112] 'On a reasoned proposal by one third of the Member States, by the European Parliament or by the European Commission, the Council, acting by a majority of four fifths of its members after obtaining the consent of the European Parliament, may determine that there is a clear risk of a serious breach by a Member State of the values referred to in Article 2. Before making such a determination, the Council shall hear the Member State in question and may address recommendations to it, acting in accordance with the same procedure.' Article 7, Section 1 of the Treaty on European Union.

retirement age of judges in order to fill the judiciary with its own followers.[113] In Venezuela, Hugo Chávez established a Constitutional Convention of his sympathizers after changing the electoral regulations, which immediately adopted a constitution that suited him. His successor Maduro offset the opposition's election victory in 2015 and bypassed the Parliament by setting up a Constituent Assembly to authenticate his policies.[114] After the election victory of the revolutionary platform that supported him, Rafael Correa – barely inaugurated as president of Ecuador – followed the example of Chávez and convened a constituent assembly to have a constitution tailored to his liking. In Turkey, President Erdoğan had the number of members in the Court of Cassation reduced by law from 516 to 310, and in the Council of State from 176 to 116. The High Council of Judges and Prosecutors, quite firmly in government hands, has since been responsible for the election of these judges. After the attempted coup in 2016, Erdoğan shored up his power position by politically 'cleaning up' the judicial system and rewriting the Turkish Constitution.

These highlights from state and judicial practice do not, of course, mean that political authoritarianism is always out to disempower the judiciary. If one does not allow oneself to be guided too much by the electoral model, and takes into account the fragmentation of the power apparatus and the respective elites, the judiciary can also come into view as a disciplining agency in support of autocrats. History shows that courts are not always and *per se* shelters of (anti-authoritarian) resistance, such as the Ninth Circuit that Trump condemns so vehemently. In the context of a political culture shaped by tradition and obedience, it is rather unlikely that judges will take offence at the executive's pretensions to power. A depressing example of judicial conformism is the jurisdiction in Nazi Germany.[115]

In very different contexts and with different motivations, Thailand's Constitutional Court operates within the deep state to maintain its hegemonic position and accommodate the powers that be.[116] In Turkey, Erdoğan deployed a bundle of autocratic measures against the judiciary – from intimidation via

---

[113] See Risley, D. (2015), 'Former President Morsi's Attacks on the Judiciary, and Judicial Backlash', in: *Egypt Justice,* 10 June, http://perma.cc/75FP-BF3G/ (last accessed 3 November 2018).

[114] Corrales, J. (2015), 'Autocratic Legalism in Venezuela', in: 26 *Journal of Democracy*, 37 ff.

[115] Koch, H.W. (1997), *In the Name of the Volk: Political Justice in Hitler's Germany* (London: I. B. Tauris & Co Ltd).

[116] Mérieau, E. (2016), 'Thailand's Deep State, Royal Power and the Constitutional Court (1997–2015)', in: 46 *Journal of Contemporary Asia*, 445 ff.

changes in the law to outright purges.[117] In Pakistan, the Federal *Sharia* Court and, in individual cases, religious extremists may bring judicial dissenters on course. However, the regime cannot trust blindly that the judiciary will comply. Recently, Pakistan's Supreme Court overturned two blasphemy convictions, abolished the death penalty and contributed significantly to protect (religious) minorities.[118]

In short, depending on the context and political constellations, courts may dare challenge authoritarianism and draw the line. However, they may also very well function as compliant instruments of social control and as extended arms of the regime.[119] In that case, they can help to present the regime's agenda within the framework of the law, eliminate the opposition and cloak it in the mantle of legitimacy conveyed by legality – whether through decisions in the regime's favour, non-decisions or years of protracted proceedings.

---

[117] 'Erdogan's Purges Leave Turkey's Justice System Reeling', in: *The New York Times*, 21 June 2019.

[118] Akins, H. (2019), 'Policy Update: Pakistan's Blasphemy Law', www.uscirf.gov/sites/default/files/2019%20Pakistan%20Blasphemy.pdf/ (last accessed 10 January 2020).

[119] Ginsburg, T. and Moustafa, T. (eds) (2008), *Rule by Law. The Politics of Courts in Authoritarian Regimes* (Cambridge: Cambridge University Press).

5. Authoritarian power as private property

…a freelancer who is now receiving a pension, who had been very successful in his career and had accumulated assets during his lifetime for an orderly retirement.[1]

Autocrats of all persuasions[2] tend to regard office and position as their private property,[3] and to dispose of them in the manner of proprietors. The idea that political power is entrusted for a limited period and must be accounted for as a matter of public law is completely alien to them. In contrast, the resources of the office (whether president, chancellor, prime minister or junta chief) are considered – not only in patrimonial systems – to be assigned to the decisional authority of a leader, group (clique, clan, family) or party. The persons who have complete control over a polity, state or government – whether by election, delegation or usurpation – thus consider themselves entitled to determine what should be done with their manor. In exercising this authority, those persons do not deem themselves to be acting as agents, representatives or officials of the society; but rather to be acting on their own authority. And they are also quite different from the seigneurial monarchs[4] whom Jean Bodin has described.

In discussing these arguments, I will focus Max Weber's description of patrimonialism[5] with regard to the following three aspects. First, I argue that authoritarian constitutionalism is characterized by an *intimate dualism* of

[1] Bank information on Chilean dictator Augusto Pinochet.

[2] Including those who started out as liberal democrats and then wanted more than the usual perks.

[3] Waldron, J. (2004/2020), 'Property and Ownership', in: Zalta, E.N. (ed) *Stanford Encyclopedia of Philosophy – Edition 2020*, https://plato.stanford.edu/cgi-bin/encyclopedia/archinfo.cgi?entry=property (last accessed 17 July 2020).

[4] Jean Bodin described seigneurial monarchies in (1955), *Six Books of the Commonwealth* (Oxford: Basil Blackwell) as ruled by the owners of all the land, and saw the only European examples in Turkey and Muscovy. Since then, political science (and its predecessors) has tended to looked for patrimonialism mainly in Africa and Asia.

[5] Max Weber characterizes 'the genuinely patrimonial office' by its 'political administration [that] is treated as a purely personal affair of the ruler, and political power is considered part of his personal property'. Weber, M. (2019), *Economy and Society* (Cambridge: Harvard University Press), § 10.

power and property. This dualism comes into play in the concept of power as well as the symbolic *dispositive*, which includes the manner in which the 'position of power'[6] is occupied and closed to other contenders. Second, as far as circumstances permit, autocrats derive from this notion of power their right to decide high-handedly on the duration of their term of office and to determine who will be their successor. Hence, succession is a personal matter. Third, not content with the psychological revenue they derive from commanding or oppressing others, or with mere perks, some autocrats seek to appropriate all forms of state capital – all public goods available within their grasp – for their own private benefit. They flagrantly indulge in despotic practices, shamelessly seizing everything of value that state, economy and society have to offer. In short: governing as enrichment.

1. THE SYMBOLIC *DISPOSITIF* OF AUTOCRACY

Autocracy shuns or destroys altogether the imagination of political power as a symbolically empty space that can be periodically occupied and reoccupied. Instead, autocrats – crowned or uncrowned – bask in the pleasantly cool shadows of the throne. Rulers who are secular renegades of the absolutist king parasitically feed on monarchy's symbolic resources. Military dictator and consul for life Napoléon Bonaparte started the ball rolling when, after his 'election' as emperor and anointment, he allowed Pope Pius VII to lift the crown from the altar. But then, in a demonstration of his worldly power, he took the crown himself and proceeded to crown himself and his wife Joséphine. The pope was quite stunned that this crucial part of his job had been taken out of his hands.[7] Napoléon's brazen move was imitated several times in the nineteenth and twentieth centuries;[8] and was echoed once again both when Hugo Chávez boldly rephrased his first oath of office and when, in the absence of the moribund re-elected president, his followers were symbolically sworn in.

Without title, autocrats hijack the heritage of the *ancien régime* and close the centre where political decisions are made. They reserve the ownership of

---

6 Following Claude Lefort's concept of the political. Lefort, C. (1988), *Democracy and Political Theory* (Cambridge: Polity Press). See Flynn, B. (2005), *The Philosophy of Claude Lefort* (Evanston: Northwestern University Press).

7 Pope Pius VII was allowed, however, to anoint the emperor and bless his insignia of power. See Zamoysk, A. (2018), *Napoleon: A Life* (New York: Basic Books).

8 After two denominationally motivated self-coronations of Prussian Kings Friedrich I and Wilhelm I, Reza Pahlavi assumed the crown of the shah of Persia in 1967. Ten years later, then president of the Central African Republic Jean-Bedel Bokassa crowned himself emperor.

power for themselves and occupy the place of power by their own usurped right. Depending on the situation, they subsequently transfer this right of ownership according to hereditary or electoral monarchical practice, thus ensuring the endurance of their political heritage and the continuity of autocracy. They justify the acquisition and exercise of power with fictions of the symbolic unity of leadership and people. The national community and the leader as the embodiment of the spirit of the 'community of racial and political associates'[9] appear as vulgar, sometimes fascist versions of the doctrine of the two (or three) bodies of the 'king'.[10] In addition to the inevitably natural and mortal body of the leader, there is the political body – which has the priceless advantage of being infallible and undying in its public function, because it is purely symbolic. This second body – less mystical in today's autocracies than in medieval kingdoms – is said to embody the people, the community, as *body politic*. The result is a 'mortal God' almost like Thomas Hobbes' *Leviathan*. The symbolic representation of the people will be discussed in detail later in the context of the cult of immediacy (Chapter 7). After the break with representation tailored to republican democracies, the autocrat and centre of the cult returns to the image of the body of the people he represents, like *Leviathan* on the frontispiece of Hobbes' treatise.[11]

Authoritarian regimes seal off the political decision-making centre and place the public sphere under curatorship, just as a proprietor excludes others from possession. Inspired by Claude Lefort's theory of democracy, it could be said that autocrats take possession of positions which authorize them to make binding decisions with one hand, while annexing the symbolically empty 'place of power' with the other. And they do so permanently, and not just temporarily. In consequence, they generally accept neither the uncontrolled

---

[9] Concerning the '*Gemeinschaft der rassisch und politisch Zusammengehörigen*': Konitzer, W. and Palme, D. (eds) (2016), *'Arbeit', 'Volk', 'Gemeinschaft': Ethik und Ethiken im Nationalsozialismus* (Frankfurt am Main: Campus); Schyga, P. (2015), *Über die Volksgemeinschaft der Deutschen. Begriff und historische Wirklichkeit jenseits historiografischer Gegenwartsmoden* (Baden-Baden: Nomos).

[10] See the intriguing study by Kantorowicz, E. (2016), *The King's Two Bodies. A Study in Medieval Political Theology* [1957] (Princeton: Princeton University Press); also Santner, E.L. (2011), *The Royal Remains: The People's Two Bodies and the Endgames of Sovereignty* (Chicago: Chicago University Press). Critical of Kantorowicz: Marek, K. (2009), *Die Körper des Königs. Effigies, Bildpolitik und Heiligkeit* (Paderborn: Fink Verlag).

[11] Regarding the symbolic representation of the ruler: Diehl, P. (2014), '*Die repräsentative Funktion des Körpers in der Demokratie*', in: Brodocz, A. *et al* (eds), *Die Verfassung des Politischen – Festschrift für Hans Vorländer* (Wiesbaden: Springer VS), 113 ff.; Rödel, U. *et al* (1989), *Die demokratische Frage* (Frankfurt am Main: Suhrkamp).

risk of losing power (through elections or open voting) nor the inevitability of conflict, and preclude an analysis that is sensitized to the symbolism of the (repressive) unity of party/leader/state and society and might decipher and delegitimize despotism. As far as possible, criticism is suppressed, penalized and persecuted, in order to give the affirmation of power all necessary space. The autocrat's claimed prerogative to rule alone and to incarnate the symbolic unity of society cannot be denied or undermined by critique of ideology, for example.

Admittedly, a coup that resets the title of governor and the practice of rule, as well as its symbolic representation, to the level of absolutist princes – that is, private owners – can succeed only in a largely secularized environment. Moreover, such leaders, cliques and clans must hide their all too profane monetary interests, and either conceal or justify the property-like power position for which they strive. And one must assume that the constitution will not ultimately frustrate the coup.

Concealment and magic were the modalities of Bashar al-Assad's 2012 'constitutional reform'. Through his hand-picked constitutional committee, he had clauses deleted which provided that his Baath Party would play the central role. In fact, power had been in the hands of both the Assad clan and the Baath Party before – and it remained there notwithstanding the reforms. This gesture of hypocritical humility disguised the fact that the despot had magically[12] gained considerable power. As president of the state, he headed the executive (Article 83) and appointed the prime minister and ministers (Article 97). At the same time, he could access the legislative power and dissolve the Parliament (Article 111). As if that were not enough, he also controlled the judiciary by appointing the members of the Constitutional Court – which, incidentally, had rejected all but three candidates for the upcoming elections.[13] And thanks to his Constitution of Syria, Assad won a third seven-year term in office on 3 June 2014.[14]

---

[12] Carnegie Middle East Center, 'The Syrian Constitution: Assad's Magic Wand', 8 May 2014 – https://carnegie-mec.org/diwan/55541?lang=en/ (last accessed 10 January 2020).

[13] Article 84 of the Syrian Constitution excludes candidates for the presidency who have been convicted of a dishonorable felony, even if they were reinstated. Furthermore, candidates must also have been a resident of Syria for no less than ten years continuously upon being nominated. This disqualifies all former political prisoners and leading member of the opposition who have previously been convicted (on charges of 'weakening national sentiment' and 'spreading false or exaggerated information'), or who had left the country after spending years in jail or been driven into exile during the current conflict.

[14] *Spiegel online*, 24 February 2012 – www.spiegel.de/politik/ausland/syriens-neue-verfassung-assads-reformluege-a-817131.html/ (last accessed 25 December 2018).

Once revolutions have dismantled the absolutist form of government; once liberation has destroyed the neo-absolutism of totalitarian regimes, it is no easy undertaking to transform political power from a title of public law into one of private law held by the 'proprietor'.[15] As two necessary conditions, regimes and rulers must try to neutralize the symbolic *dispositif* of democracy and prevent the explicit self-institution of civil society on the basis of a republican-democratic constitution. Only then can the usurpation of the state as a legal entity and its property-like transfer to a leader, cadre, family, clan or party succeed. And only then can the decisional authority of an autocrat, not legally restricted in his freedom of disposition, be aligned with the privilege and prestige of the lord of the manor or factory owner.

2. AUTHORITARIAN POWER AS A PROPERTY TITLE

Whether the '*Roi Soleil*' Louis XIV knew how to distinguish between himself and the state is debatable. As legend has it, he claimed: 'I am the State.' '*L'État, c'est moi*' would indeed seem a conclusive formula to convey the absolutist centralization of state power at the top and its concentration in a single pair of hands. Through a minor semantic-grammatical intervention, the royal statement becomes '*l'État c'est à moi*' and thus reveals the claim – also attributed to Louis XIV – that the state was his own.[16] Through a (semantic) sleight of hand, the royal power changed from a quasi-public title of monarchic law into a quasi-private legal entitlement. In good time, Louis XIV secured his absolute power by expanding the civil service and the army. For their upkeep and costs, and to finance the opulent expenditure of the court, the king and his advisers thought that a state-controlled, mercantilist economic and trade policy was required.[17] In addition, subduing the oppositional nobility[18] and not convoking the Estates-General helped Louis XIV to realign the borders of his power. Accordingly, he was able to execute his confessional policy[19] and celebrate

---

[15] Waldron (n 3). The shirt-sleeved rentier capitalist and President Trump should know a thing or two about this.

[16] On his deathbed, he is said to have expressed himself in a more differentiated way about absolutism: '*Je m'en vais, mais l'État demeurera toujours.*' To be translated as: 'I go away [or: pass away], but the State remains forever.'

[17] Burke, P. (1992), 'The Fabrication of Louis XIV', in: 42 *History Today*, 24 ff.

[18] Moote, A.L. (1971), *The Revolt of the Judges – The Parlement of Paris and the Fronde 1643–1652* (Princeton: Princeton University Press).

[19] By re-Catholicizing France and revoking the religious and civil rights of Huguenots (1685).

his style of ruling in a manner that corresponded nicely to a landowner's management.[20]

After the long-practised secularization of the foundations of political rule in the wake of revolutionary upheavals, accompanied by philosophical ideas and constitutional ferment and experiments, today's heads of state could hardly afford the latitude enjoyed by Louis XIV (assuming that the tales are true) and openly act as owners of the state under private law – with the probable exception of rulers who have attained the status of sultans or despots of similar hue, whose style of government and concentration of power correspond to the already low expectations of the population. In reasonably consolidated democracies with a fair level of party competition, governors are likely to respect the next round of elections (or conceal corrupt electoral practices) so as to prevent being 'expropriated' by an electoral sovereign that does not agree with the concept of power as property.

In autocratic systems, the idea of an accountable decisional authority delegated *pro tempore* consequently retreats backstage. It is cloaked in Machiavellian concepts, sometimes democratically 'varnished'. To cite an example: Venezuela's President Hugo Chávez pushed through an amendment to the Venezuelan Constitution to lift the limit on his term of office. A president of the Bolivarian republic can now stand for re-election as many times as he likes. The consumptive, already deceptive constitutional precaution against the usurpation of political power has thus come undone in Venezuela.[21] Other examples follow below.

2.1 Dictatorial Centralism

After two – in constitutional terms, astonishingly compliant – changes of power, each at the end of the planned 10-year term of office, in 2018 China opted to return to the model of dictatorial centralism (one is tempted to add, without any need to do so). Following a successful career in the Communist Party, Xi Jinping ascended to the position of 'central leader' in 2016 and – like his North Korean counterpart, Kim Jong-un – soon united in himself the country's most important state offices, becoming general secretary of the Communist Party, president of the state and chairman of the Central Military Commission. In order to transform the concentrated power from a public-law to a quasi-private law title, all that was needed was to remove the limit on

---

[20] After his enthronement in 1661, Louis XIV did not appoint a prime minister, but held the official governmental functions in his own hands.

[21] Article 230 of the Constitution of the Republic of Venezuela (1999/2009) and Article 138 ('A usurped authority is of no effect, and its acts are null and void).

Source: 132536033 picture alliance / AP Photo / Ng Han Guan. With friendly permission.

Figure 5.1 *China's Head of State, Xi Jinping, among his party cadres in the Great Hall of the People, 27 October 2017*

his term of office, which had already been set at 10 years. This was formally done in 2018, in order to fully immunize Xi Jinping against criticism and change (see Figure 5.1). Almost unanimously, the National People's Congress – mainly comprising members of the Communist Party of China and especially its Standing Committee – adopted a corresponding amendment to the Chinese Constitution. The 'collective leadership model', which had previously been based on the fusion of party and state,[22] was thus buried. As long as the Communist Party plays along, the Chinese head of state (and of the party) can now treat his political office like a household owner for life – as long as the party (in practice, the Standing Committee) or rival elites do not 'expropriate' him.

Xi Jinping's strategy has been adopted by many others, including former Haitian dictator François Duvalier (the notorious 'Papa Doc') and Burundi's President Pierre Nkurunziza in Summer 2015, who were both granted a con-

[22] See Article 79 of the revised Chinese Constitution; www.tagesspiegel.de/politik/praesident-auf-lebenszeit-xi-jinping-wird-chinas-neuer-kaiser/21006338.html/ (last accessed 23 November 2018).

stitutional waiver of the limit on their term of office. Nkurunziza decided that the limit of two terms of office did not apply to him and had himself reappointed as head of state through another 'election'; he risked a civil war and ultimately just managed to survive a *coup d'état*.[23] Ugandan President Yoweri Museveni made his time in the resistance against former autocratic President Obote count: he was 're-elected' six times, spending 30 years in office, and is unsurprisingly seeking re-election in 2021. Algeria's President Bouteflika is a special case: after (one is tempted to add: only) four terms in office, he initially moved towards (or was pushed towards by the cadres that support him) a fifth term in Spring 2019 – even though he had not made a public speech since 2012 and it seemed highly uncertain whether he was still in a fit state to hold office. The popular protest movement demonstratively retired him. Since then, other members of his government have come under the scrutiny of a revitalized judiciary.[24]

Alexander Lukashenka – the self-declared 'last dictator of Europe' (if only he knew…) – was able to take up a fifth term as president of Belarus in 2015, unhampered by the Constitution, after elections that were once again highly questionable; and is preparing to run for a sixth term in August 2020. Paul Kagame – who had helped to bring peace to Rwanda after the genocide in 1994 – initially secured overwhelming approval in his election to the presidency (well over 90 per cent); only allowed allies to stand as competing candidates; 'experienced' the murder of opposition politicians and journalists; and in 2015 had the limit on his term of office lifted by a hardly believable majority (98.4 per cent).[25] In Uzbekistan, the winner of the first post-Soviet presidential elections of 1991, Islom Karimov, remained in office until his death in 2016, despite the constitutional limitation of his term to a maximum of 10 years. He repeatedly had his term of office extended by referendum.[26] All of the above leaders and many more – whether constitutionally or by non-constitutional means – subverted the understanding that political power is a position of authority granted in trust for a certain period, which keeps the 'place of power' open. They invariably regarded the office as their own: 'It's private property, stupid!'

If (as is usually the case) the suspension of time limits is accompanied by the bundling of powers – which is euphemistically called 'democratic central-

---

23 In *France24*, 14 May 2015 ('Burundi's Nkurunziza returns after coup attempt').

24 Chikhi, L. and Hamid, A. (2019), 'Beset by protests, Algeria's Bouteflika will not seek new term', in: *Reuters*, 11 March.

25 *The Guardian*, 18 July 2010; www.theguardian.com/theobserver/2010/jul/18/paul-kagame-rwanda-profile/ (last accessed 10 January 2020).

26 Article 90 of the Constitution of Uzbekistan, 1992/2011.

ism'[27] (see below) or is simply accepted as presidentialism[28] – the instruments of the executive, notably emergency laws, take the lead without hindrance, as was seen in the previous chapter. The usual constitutional safeguards against usurpation or hypertrophy of the executive branch will inevitably fail – that is, if they still even exist. Nevertheless, it would be strategically unwise to flaunt absolutist power – let alone claim openly to be the owner of political authority, and not just an official – as this might kindle the aspirations of competing elites and mobilize the opposition to protest. Verbal frankness and *faux pas* are therefore the exception. Mussolini is said to have threatened the Italian Parliament (almost like a homeowner) by boasting that he would turn the building into 'a bivouac for my black shirts [*squadre*]'.[29] Zimbabwe's despot-president Robert Mugabe announced he would never give way to an opposition politician. If not only due to the stubbornness of old age, an authoritarian understanding of ownership of power may also have had its say here.

With the notion of the head of state or government as the owner of political authority – instead of the democratic-sounding servant of the people – popular sovereignty steps aside as the (ideological) matrix for both the staging and the exercise of power. In its stead prevails the logic of private property as the epitome of all decisional powers of the owner – in particular, the right to exclude others from the use or exploitation of property (state, regime, office) or a property right (to make decisions). In the context of an authoritarian regime, power ownership implies the entitlement to create an order according to the tastes of the ruler, shut down competition and eliminate opponents.

Depending on their design and political constellation, constitutions accommodate the understanding of ownership of authoritarian rulers in different ways, as the following examples illustrate – as long as they are not overridden or manipulated beyond recognition. Constitutions may abet the concentration of offices and powers;[30] put up little resistance to the waiver of time limits on political power; make it difficult to hold rulers responsible; or remain silent about abuse. In practice, these strategies are often complemented by disempowering the judiciary.

---

[27] Article 8 of the Constitution of Vietnam, 1992/2013.

[28] Prembeh, H.K. (2008), 'Progress and Retreat in Africa: Presidents Untamed', in: 19 *Journal of Democracy*, 109 ff.

[29] Quoted by Finaldi, G. (2008), *Mussolini and Italian Fascism* (Harlow UK: Routledge, 141).

[30] On the concentration of power in a single pair of hands as a sign of dictatorship, see also the 'state practice' of the (quite paranoid) Albanian dictator, Enver Hoxha, who held the posts of prime minister, foreign minister and defence minister, was also commander-in-chief of the armed forces and secretary general of the Communist Party. The centralization of power schemes in North Korea and China will be discussed later.

The Constitution of the Democratic People's Republic of Korea provides the framework for a 'people's democratic dictatorship' (Article 12), based on the 'political-ideological unity of the people' (Article 10), and takes no precautions against the accumulation of top government offices in a single pair of hands. Quite the opposite: like his ancestors, Kim Jong-un holds a number of posts: first secretary of the Workers' Party, commander-in-chief of the armed forces and – after being elected by the Supreme People's Assembly – first chairman of the National Defence Commission (Article 100) and chairman of the State Affairs Commission. As the 'supreme leader of the Party, the state and the army', he is untroubled by constitutional fetters. At the same time, he has followed the more political than constitutional traces of his grandfather, Kim Il-sung, who was posthumously upgraded to the position of 'eternal president' of the People's Republic. The death of his father made Kim Jong-un a 'great successor and leader of the Party, army and people'. The son and successor of Kim Il-sung was appointed the 'eternal general secretary' and the 'eternal chairman of the National Defence Commission' in April 2012.[31] Kim Il-sung's grandson, Kim Jong-un, is likely looking forward to an eternal title after his death, too.

In the model of dictatorial centralism, the investiture – whether by dynastic succession, election or acclamation – leads to the joined ownership of the supreme authority, whose holder is henceforth distinguished from the circle of constituted powers and acts as the constituent power. In light of the leader's omnipotence (more than supreme), he is not even theoretically accountable to the Supreme People's Assembly of North Korea and limited to a five-year term of office (Article 102). The decisional authority of the 'supreme leader', which is equal in ownership and relieved of concrete responsibility, degrades the 'Supreme People's Assembly' – which is endowed with importance (only) by the text of the Constitution – to an ensemble of supporting actors without state powers.

2.2 Constitutional Coup

After his election as president in 2000, Vladimir Putin faced an extraordinarily fragmented topography of power – a completely destabilized state – and was later targeted by terrorist assaults.[32] Neither, of course, was unfamiliar to him

---

[31] Martin, B.K. (2004), *Under the Loving Care of the Fatherly Leader: North Korea and the Kim Dynasty* (New York: Thomas Dunne Books); Myers, B.R. (2011), *The Cleanest Race: How North Koreans See Themselves and Why It Matters* (Brooklyn/London: Melville House Books).

[32] See Sakwa, R. (ed) (2009), *Power and Policy in Putin's Russia* (New York: Routledge), especially the editor's introduction; a different perspective is presented by Horvath, R. (2013), *Putin's 'Preventive Counter-revolution'* (New York: Routledge).

from his secret intelligence activities and a previous term as prime minister. Political groups, party cadres, regional governors and financial-economic actors competed for influence over the decision-making centre and politics. Separatist efforts fuelled civil wars. Steel barons, oil and gas magnates and bankers with connections to the state apparatus formed a new oligarchy. Under the conditions of limited social pluralism and controlled political competition, it seemed as though Putin was trying to keep all groups at bay with a policy of equidistance. At the same time, he mobilized popular support as an exogenous, but always controlled, power resource. From 2000 to 2018, he completed four terms of office, interrupted by an interim period – again as quasi-presidential prime minister (2008–12) directing his chosen president Dmitry Medvedev, who, as a friend of Putin and chairman of the Gazprom Group's supervisory board, was ideally (un-)qualified for the role. From the outset, Putin pursued a strategy of recentralization and, rather rhetorically, the 'dictatorship of the law'.

After the first – and ultimately failed – attempt during Boris Yeltsin's presidency to unite constitutional law with constitutional reality in post-Soviet Russia, these diverged wildly in the subsequent Putin era. Since then, Putin's Machiavellianism of arcane power (constructed as a 'vertical of power') has been secured by comprehensive controls and domestic intelligence activities, and has infiltrated the structures of a (euphemistically formulated) 'guided democracy'.[33] This regime is characterized by Putin's outsourcing of political decision-making to informal oligarchic circles, and his erosion of both the horizontal and vertical divisions of power in order to prevent other actors from establishing veto positions and/or overseeing the operations of the centre in Moscow. The 'Putinstate' has also relied on the nationalization of the private media and the strict curatorship of the state media and the general public, as well as the elimination, arrest or intimidation of the opposition and the removal of all electoral opportunities for competing candidates.

Comparable to the predisposition for privacy and informal decision-making procedures in financial matters,[34] Putin's imitated or 'guided democracy' –

---

[33] Mohsin Hashim, S. (2005), 'Putin's *Etatization* project and limits to democratic reforms in Russia', in: 38 *Communist and Post-Communist Studies*, 25 ff; see also Mommsen, M. and Nußberger, A. (2007), *Das System Putin. Gelenkte Demokratie und politische Justiz in Rußland* (Munich: C.H. Beck), 32 ff. In 1957 a 'guided democracy' to contain social pluralism had already been proclaimed by President Sukarno in Indonesia.

[34] Regarding informality as a feature of authoritarianism (political – and economic, one might add) see Chapter 4, Section 3. See also Wilkinson, M. (2019), 'Authoritarian liberalism as authoritarian constitutionalism', in: Alviar and Frankenberg (eds), *Authoritarian Constitutionalism – Comparative Analysis and Critique* (Cheltenham: Edward Elgar), 317 ff.

with the axis of the 'vertical of power' running towards him – protects the presidential owner of power from the scrutiny of the public eye, the media and the courts.[35] Among the features of Putin's ruling apparatus – reminiscent of the management of business enterprises – one finds first and foremost the presidential administration, which operates free of laws, and newly created consultative institutions such as the advisory 'State Council' and the 'Chamber of Society'. Authoritarian decision-making structures in companies, and especially in world football association FIFA, are also evoked by the streamlining of the vertical, which has eroded the once strong position of the Council of the Federation and the direct popular election of governors. As a result, Putin has succeeded in transforming the post-Soviet 'dual state' into a dictatorial state shaped by presidential prerogative.

Despite a constitutional design that differs from Chinese or North Korean authoritarianism, and although drafted differently, the concept of ownership of power that underpins the Putinstate is characterized by the fact that the president – although in principle one of the constituent powers – has become *pouvoir constituant* through his state practice based on prerogative (like 'hyper-presidents' elsewhere). Putin decides as sovereign on the interpretation and amendment of the Constitution; the allocation of offices; the dismantling and restructuring of institutions; and the criteria for (and thus the fairness of) elections. It comes as no surprise that Putin orchestrated a major constitutional reform which amounted to nothing less than a constitutional coup: in 2020, the Russian Parliament (*Duma*) agreed to annul his previous terms of office, thus allowing him to run again in 2024 and 2030. Even less surprisingly, the Constitutional Court approved this manoeuvre.

To shift the power/property lens away from global actors: a vertically controlled concentration of power is also in evidence in the government system and practice of Cambodian Prime Minister Hun Sen. Although extremely unpopular with the population – primarily because of his dark past under the Khmer Rouge and his autocratic style of governing – he has been at the helm of the Southeast Asian state for a record-breaking 33 years. Despite a striking lack of charisma, he has always been able to control the opposition, eliminate potential rivals through prosecution or exile, bring the media into line and surround himself with a personal army that almost precludes the possibility of a coup.[36] Moreover, Hun Sen can rely on the support of the economic leaders (*Okhna*) he favours. Like Putin, Hun Sen has also promised on his own initia-

---

35 Taylor, B.D. (2011), *State Building in Putin's Russia. Policing and Coercion after Communism* (Cambridge: Cambridge University Press); Mommsen and Nußberger (n 33).

36 Mehta, H.C. and Mehta, J.B. (1999), *Hun Sen: Strongman of Cambodia* (Singapore: Graham Brash Pte Ltd).

tive to renounce his political property power in 2024; whether, also like Putin, he will renege on this promise remains to be seen.

2.3 Presidential Sultanate

In response to the failed coup attempt of 2016, the state of emergency and the repressive measures of the Erdoğan regime, the Turkish population – albeit by a slim majority – voted for a presidential system. Thus, Recep Tayyip Erdoğan, who had initially been prime minister, became president and proprietor in 2014. Sharing Nicolae Ceauşescu's megalomania and in the spirit of ownership, he had a luxurious palace built for himself at the respectable price of almost half a billion euros – comparable in cost to the luxurious style of Louis XIV and in taste to Ceauşescu's autocratic kitsch. Through this move, Erdoğan proudly stepped out of the shadow of the founder of the Turkish state, Kemal Atatürk. In July 2018, several thousand guests were invited to marvel at his inauguration in the oppressively pretentious palace and took note (as accomplices) of the extension of his term of office,[37] achieved by a change of system. Critics spoke of the enthronement of a sultan-like ruler, who has supreme command over the Turkish army, is the sole head of government and can appoint the majority of constitutional judges, and who commands a solid majority in Parliament based on the alliance between his Justice and Development Party and the ultra-nationalist Nationalist Movement Party. Despite the economic crisis and a foreign debt estimated at $460 billion, Erdoğan was not seriously challenged and was even able to expand his constitutional power base. He replaced the entire board of directors of the Turkish State Fund and appointed himself chairman. By decree, he also authorized himself to appoint the president and vice president of the Central Bank.

In Turkey's hyper-presidential system,[38] the present incumbent need not fear elections. As long as (circumstances permitting) he can imprison opposition members on suspicion and intimidate and censor the press (which he has tried to bring into line through normalized powers of exception), the political risk of electoral defeat and loss of office – that is, the danger of political 'expro-

[37] 'Where the renewal of the elections is decided by the Grand National Assembly of Turkey during the second term of the President of the Republic, he/she may run for the presidency once more' (amended version of Article 116, paragraph 3 of the Constitution of Turkey).

[38] The last revision of the Constitution gave the president considerable powers (Article 104 of the Constitution of Turkey).

priation' – can be minimized; unless the people reimagine the concept of their sovereignty, as was recently the case in the local elections in Istanbul.[39]

3. INGLORIOUS BASTARDS

In the past, power tended to be secured through the privatization of decisional authority and its transfer to private companies[40] – naturally accommodated by an understanding of power as private property. Political decisional authority was shifted to corporations that acted (openly or covertly) as representatives and managers of the state executive. Colonies used to be the preferred parade ground in which to deploy this type of privatized, stately potential – as exemplified by the British East India Company, which made an inglorious name for itself on the Indian subcontinent and in Southeast Asia, especially since the mid-seventeenth century. More latterly, the United Fruit Company sketched out and followed a similar path in the Caribbean. These two companies will be discussed very briefly to illustrate different strategies of privatizing political authority.

3.1 Company State

According to more recent research that examines the company as a political entity, alongside its commercial role for the British Empire, the East India Company proves to be by no means the 'strange absurdity' that Adam Smith once maintained. It was rather quite a modern, government-like institution. Supported by its own financial strength and leverage, administration and army, this company-state exercised sovereign powers quite naturally as property rights. In addition to business, which at times accounted for half of the world's trade, the East India Company annexed important territories, controlled populations, promoted exploitative agriculture, expanded infrastructure, collected taxes and much more.[41] Through corporate sponsorship and the command

---

[39] The Supreme Electoral Council accepted the *extraordinary objection* of Erdoğan's Justice and Development Party (AKP) and ordered a re-run of the elections. In the second round, the AKP lost significantly more votes. See Dündar, C. (2019), '*Die letzten Tage des Sultanats*', in: *Zeit Online*, 26 June, www.zeit.de/2019/27/tuerkei-buergermeisterwahl-istanbul-recep-tayyip-erdogan/ (last accessed 30 June 2019).

[40] Based on new research and with a different emphasis: Stern, P.J. (2011), *The Company-State: Corporate Sovereignty and the Early Modern Foundations of the British Empire in India* (Oxford UK: Oxford University Press); and Chapman, P. (2007), *Bananas: How the United Fruit Company Shaped the World* (Edinburgh: Canongate Books).

[41] Stern (n 40), 24: 'As proprietors, colonial governors and councils were in this sense like manorial lords, who could alienate land, administer justice, exact fines,

transferred to it, or at least exercised in its interests, the company state embodied by the East India Company transformed the idea of political power as private property to *private property as political power*.

3.2 State within a State

The United Fruit Company (since 1985, Chiquita Brands International), a corporation based in the United States, enjoyed a monopoly in the trade of bananas and other tropical fruits in certain regions of the Caribbean and Latin America since the end of the nineteenth century.[42] Throughout the region, it operated as a state-like player because of its significant land ownership, dominant position in the market and control over regional transport networks (rail and shipping). Unlike the East India Company, United Fruit did not act openly in the name of or on behalf of any state. Rather, it always acted in pursuit of its own economic interests – that is, on its own account. In critical situations, it relied on covert or overt support from the US government, its military and/or the Central Intelligence Agency (CIA).[43] On the one hand, the company differed little from a state representation abroad – for example, when negotiating tax privileges or concessions with governments. On the other hand, United Fruit secretly commanded a clandestine service and troops. One example of its concealed operation as a 'state within a state'[44] was the overthrow of the Arbenz government in Guatemala. Authorized by President Truman, the coup was effectively carried out by the CIA and the US army. United Fruit had a significant interest in this coup – in particular, due to the opportunity it afforded to reverse expropriation decisions and industrial safety laws issued by the Arbenz government.[45]

---

and control populations within the bounds of their estates.' See Dirks, N. (2006), *The Scandal of Empire: India and the creation of Imperial Britain* (Cambridge: The Belknap Press of Harvard University Press).

42 Other competitors in the region include Standard Fruit Co (today Dole Fruit Co) and Cuyamel Fruit Co. See Chapman (n 40).

43 There are impressive descriptions in Gabriel García Márquez (1970), *Cien años de soledad* (Buenos Aires: Sudamericana, 1970).

44 Blum, W. (2003), *Killing hope: US Military and CIA Interventions Since World War II* (London: Zed Books), 75.

45 Fraser, A. (2005), 'Architecture of a broken dream: The CIA and Guatemala, 1952–54', in: 20 *Intelligence and National Security*, 486 ff; Schlesinger, S. and Kinzer, S. (1999), *Bitter Fruit: The Story of the American Coup in Guatemala* (Cambridge: Harvard University Press).

As a 'political' company, United Fruit supported autocratic regimes, bribed corrupt governments (hence the term 'banana republics'[46] for countries such as Costa Rica, Honduras, Panama and Guatemala), and had paramilitary units suppress strikes and protests by workers against labour conditions on the plantations. While the secret operations took some time to come to light, United Fruit had already long been criticized for its commercial activities, in which it developed economic enclaves, pursued a strategy of 'shifting plantation agriculture', displaced smaller fruit and banana plantations, and implemented unacceptable wage policies.[47] As a result, Chiquita Brands International has been trying to improve its reputation for years. Overall, United Fruit's practices illustrate how private property assimilates to the authoritarian context and morphs into a state within the state through business influence and with recourse to government assistance.

3.3 McKinsey Governance

Today, private mediation and representation of authoritarian power take place less through borrowed companies, empowered company states and covert representatives than through advisory authorities that are open and transparent only on the surface. McKinsey is one of the global players and leaders in this regard, but by no means the solitary contender in the consulting business.[48] Consultants have no qualms about working for autocrats, as long as the price is right. The clientele of McKinsey, BCG, Bain and others includes the usual suspects, such as China, Saudi Arabia, Russia and Malaysia:

> [A]utocratic leaders from China to Saudi Arabia increasingly rely on experts, especially from top consulting firms, universities, and think tanks in the West. In 2017, the consulting market in the Gulf monarchies topped $2.8 billion, with Saudi Arabia accounting for almost half of that amount.[49]

Consulting firms have no reservations about working for notoriously corrupt or autocratic systems. At a time when democratic values and structures are

---

[46] Coined by Henry, O. (1904), *Cabbages and Kings* (New York: Doubleday, Page & Company).

[47] See Schlesinger and Kinzer (n 47).

[48] Calvert, C.W. (2019), 'All the King's Consultants', in: *Foreign Affairs*, May/June – www.foreignaffairs.com/articles/persian-gulf/2019-04-16/all-kings-consultants (last accessed 13 January 2019); 'How McKinsey Has Helped Raise the Stature of Authoritarian Governments', in: *The New York Times*, 15 December 2018, www.nytimes.com/2018/12/15/world/asia/mckinsey-china-russia.html/ (last accessed 13 January 2019).

[49] Calvert (n 48).

under particularly aggressive attack, they will not hesitate to help authoritarian clients gain prestige and credibility. However, according to their justifications, political agnosticism is their primary virtue: 'Like many large corporations, including our competitors, we try to navigate through a changing geopolitical environment' without supporting or engaging in 'political activities'.[50] Another of their arguments in favour of cooperation with dubious regimes sounds like the 'long march through the institutions' of the 1968 generation or even Willy Brandt's *détente* strategy of 'change through rapprochement': 'Change is best achieved from the inside.'

After all, private government consultancy firms claim to provide the necessary 'expertise' (certainly for no small amount of money). There is no doubt that governments depend on external expertise.[51] Nevertheless, it is problematic when private outsiders covertly become involved in government business: there is an undeniable danger that particular interests will unduly influence the production of state norms and support authoritarian regimes without public control.

4. PASTICHES OF THE DYNASTIC PRINCIPLE

'The King of Cambodia... reigns but does not govern.' He 'shall have no power to appoint his successor'.[52] Thus, the Cambodian Constitution apodictically lays down a basic principle for its elective monarchy. Not a particularly surprising regulation, one might think – at least in a country that once had to cope with the erratic policies of a revered former king (Sihanouk) followed by the murderous Khmer dictatorship of Pol Pot, and that continually lurched between totalitarianism, monarchy and democracy over the last century.[53]

4.1 On Succession and Dynasties

The same provision would be highly unusual, of course, in a constitutional hereditary monarchy, where it is common for one of the variations of the dynastic principle to provide for a property-savvy, political succession (based on the dignity of public law, of course). The following example shows how

[50] Quoted by *The New York Times* (n 48).

[51] Kennedy, D. (2016), *A World of Struggle* (Princeton: Princeton University Press).

[52] Articles 7 and 10 of the Constitution of the Kingdom of Cambodia 1993/2008.

[53] Tully, J. (2005), *A Short History of Cambodia. From Empire to Survival* (London: Allen & Unwin).

this script is defined in the soberly democratic Norway (one mentions it not without irony in the same breath as authoritarian regimes):

> The order of succession is lineal, so that only a child born in lawful wedlock of the Queen or King, or of one who is herself or himself entitled to the succession may succeed, and so that the nearest line shall take precedence over the more remote and the elder in the line over the younger…
>
> The right of succession shall not, however, belong to any person who is not born in the direct line of descent from the last reigning Queen or King or a sister or brother thereof, or is herself or himself a sister or brother thereof.

Only in the case of interrupted succession does the king of Norway has a right of proposal; but even then, as is often the case elsewhere, the final decision lies with the Parliament (*Storting*): 'If there is no Princess or Prince entitled to the succession, the King may propose his successor to the Storting, which has the right to make the choice if the King's proposal is not accepted.'[54]

The constitutions of other monarchies[55] – including parliamentary and absolute monarchies[56] and sultanates[57] – essentially follow this practice of hereditary or elected succession to the throne according to dynastic patterns, with deviations regarding primogeniture, the (matrilineal) right of succession of daughters and women, and the participation of other institutions such as a royal council or parliament. A special case is the Federation of Malaysia, no

---

[54] Articles 6 and 7 of the Constitution of the Kingdom of Norway, 1814. In Thailand, King Rama VI issued a detailed Place Law of Succession BE 2467 (1924), which has guided the practice of succession ever since (Article 20 of the Constitution of the Kingdom of Thailand). See Grossman, N. and Faulder, D. (2011), *King Bhumibol Adulyadej: A Life's Work: Thailand's Monarchy in Perspective* (Singapore/Bangkok): Editions Didier Millet, 325 ff.

[55] For example, succession rules in the Swedish Succession Law of 1810; Section 57 of the Constitution of Spain (1978) and Article 43 Constitution of the Kingdom of Morocco (2011).

[56] Article 5 of the Basic Law of Saudi Arabia (1992): 'The dynasty right shall be confined to the sons of the Founder, King Abdul Aziz bin Abdul Rahman Al Saud (Ibn Saud), and the sons of sons. The most eligible among them shall be invited, through the process of "bai'ah", to rule in accordance with the Book of God and the Prophet's Sunnah… The King names the Crown Prince and may relieve him of his duties by Royal Order.' The Saudi Arabian Constitution is referred to as the 'Basic Law', although in a technical sense it is a constitution, because the *Qur'an* is regarded as the constitution (Article 1).

[57] Articles 5 and 6 of the Constitution of the Sultanate Oman (1996): 'The system of governance is Sultani, hereditary in the male descendants of Sayyid Turki bin Said bin Sultan, provided that whomever is to be chosen from amongst them as successor shall be a Muslim, mature, rational and the legitimate son of Omani Muslim parents. – The Royal Family Council shall, within three days of the throne falling vacant, determine the successor to the throne.'

longer a one-party state, in which the king (*Yang di-Pertuan Agong*) is chosen every five years from among the rulers of the nine sultanates on rotation.[58] One is tempted to identify the sultans as joint owners of the Malaysian kingship. Power, one should add, lies not in their hands, but in the hands of the government.

The Cambodian constitutional norm marks an authoritarian-democratic hybrid regime. It qualifies as a dual state in Fraenkel's sense. Today, the king is spared the marginal role of warming himself on the ashes of a once radiant royal tradition and nostalgically tracing the veneration of his predecessors. In contrast, the decisional authority has been captured – and almost permanently occupied – by an authoritarian head of government, Hun Sen. Despite his *de facto* unchallenged position as power holder, the Constitution denies him the right to transfer his powers a successor selected by him. When the time comes, the longstanding head of government will have to make his proposals to the country's ruling elite.

Where circumstances permit, autocrats adopt the dynastic principle and practice of self-authorization that characterize hereditary monarchies when it comes to the appointment of their successors. In general, the dynastic principle and practice of succession to the throne in non-monarchies bypasses the respective constitution, insofar as rules, procedures and institutions are not provided for. Autocrats therefore base the transfer of power by 'inheritance' – that is, succession to the throne – on a pastiche of the dynastic idea. Without a trace of irony, they imitate the succession to the throne in monarchies and the dynastic principle that legitimizes it. In doing so, they suspend the rotation of the elite, which is possible even in non-monarchies and guarantees periodic change. Party, clan or personal authoritarianism thus opens the door not only to never-ending terms of office, but also to the continuity of authoritarianism, secured by the 'political heirs'[59] of a ruler, whoever they may be: family members, friends or other persons of trust.[60]

The Kim dynasty in North Korea, the Assad clan in Syria and the Saud dynasty in Saudi Arabia – the first in the Stalinist tradition, the other two as oriental counterparts – embody three hard-core versions of dynastic continuity and power descent.[61] They include the targeted murder of potential rivals and critics and, where necessary, the use of extreme brutality to maintain power

---

[58] Article 32, III of the Constitution of the Federation of Malaysia, 1957/2007.

[59] Thus was the name of Ramiz Alia, successor of Albanian dictator Enver Hoxha, when he assumed the leadership of both party and state in 1991.

[60] See the in-depth analysis by Newton, S. (2017), *The Constitutional Systems of the Independent Central Asian States* (Oxford: Bloomsbury), 125 ff.

[61] Martin, B.K. (2004), *Under the Loving Care of the Fatherly Leader. North Korea and the Kim Dynasty* (New York: Thomas Dunne Books), about Kim Il-sung and Kim

and secure property. In comparison, a more moderate pattern is evident in Venezuela, where Hugo Chávez anointed loyal follower Nicolás Maduro as his successor in 2013, and where the latter has since – as is not uncommon in Latin America (see Perón, Kirchner and Ortega) – appointed his wife as a member of the Constituent Assembly for higher offices or even his successor.[62] Likewise, in Nicaragua, the former revolutionary Daniel Ortega – since reborn as despot – has groomed his wife, Rosario Murillo, via the vice-presidency as a potential successor. Both Maduro and Ortega are currently defending their power base against massive anti-dynastic protests. In both countries, it is uncertain whether and for how long the autocratic regime will survive.

4.2 The Bitter Medicine of Power

The usual candidates of trust who are offered 'succession to the throne' in autocracies or who claim to be invested as heads of state surprisingly often include members of the medical profession, if they find themselves close enough to the centre of power (personal physician) or are otherwise well networked within the regime.[63] In Haiti, doctor ('Papa Doc') and former Minister of Health François Duvalier took office as president in 1957, survived a coup, had a number of political opponents assassinated and then won the 1961 election with an official final result of 1.32 million votes – not a single vote against him. He soon went down the road to power as private property and had himself appointed president for life once the Haitian Constitution had been amended in 1964. Through another constitutional amendment, he ensured that his son and playboy ('Baby Doc') – who had shown an impressive lack of interest in pol-

---

Jong-il. Concerning the Assad regime: Yassin-Kassab, R. and Al-Shami, L. (2016), *Burning Country. Syrians in Revolution and War* (London: Pluto Press).

[62] In Nicaragua, Daniel Ortega had the protests bloodily suppressed. More than 300 deaths attest to the regime's shift towards political despotism. See Uprimny, R. (2018), 'Once We Cheered Ortega: Revisiting History in Nicaragua', www.worldcrunch.com/opinion-analysis/we-once-cheered-ortega-revisiting-history-in-nicaragua/ (last accessed 14 January 2020).

[63] It is thus in keeping with tradition that President Trump has just appointed the former White House physician as chief medical adviser and assistant to the president. *Independent* (2019), 'Trump appointed former White House doctor to be chief medical adviser despite ongoing misconduct probe' 3 February, www.independent.co.uk/news/world/americas/us-politics/trump-ronny-jackson-white-house-drunk-doctor-chief-medical-adviser-va-misconduct-drunk-admiral-a8760636.html/ (last accessed 14 January 2020).

itics and the wellbeing of Haiti throughout his life – could assume his father's political heritage in 1971.[64]

Trained as a psychiatrist, Radovan Karadžić was originally a doctor before his meteoric political rise in his home country of Bosnia and Herzegovina after the break-up of Yugoslavia. In 1992, as chairman of the Serbian Democratic Party and one of the spokespersons of the anti-Muslim movement, he was elected president of the Republic of Srpska, which is predominantly inhabited by Bosnian Serbs. No succession, but authoritarianism doubly related to the medical profession: while a fugitive, he worked at a private clinic in Belgrade, specializing in alternative medicine and psychology. Having been caught and transferred to The Hague, on 24 March 2016 he was found guilty by the United Nations War Crimes Tribunal of war crimes during the siege of Sarajevo, crimes against humanity in parts of Bosnia and the genocide in Srebrenica which left 8000 people dead. He was sentenced to a total of 40 years in prison.

In Turkmenistan, the dentist of dictator Saparmurat Nyyazov took the helm when his patient died in 2006: Gurbanguly Berdymukhamedov had already worked his way to the centre of power as minister of health and vice-president. Since taking office, he proved to be a worthy heir: he advanced to fifth place in the list of the world's most evil dictators compiled by US magazine *Foreign Policy 2010*. The World Report 2017 by Human Rights Watch registered Turkmenistan as one of the most repressive and hermetically sealed countries in the world. Reporters Without Borders places the regime at the bottom of a list of 180 countries in terms of press freedom, just ahead of Eritrea and North Korea.[65] Berdymukhamedov's façade of bonhomie hides a regime that meets the basic criteria of a totalitarian police state. He had the constitutional barrier to his re-election lifted after two terms of office (Articles 68 and 70), and thus realized his proprietary title to the presidency in 2016. There is no reason to fear that the constitutional prohibition on the transfer of power will prevent him from one day appointing his successor in office.

4.3 Clans and Democracy

The global history of authoritarianism testifies to a wide range of hybrid versions of 'royal houses'. Not even the United States can be excluded from this; if it were, the family regime of the 45th president would not be out of

---

[64] *The New York Times* called this the most extreme election fraud in the history of Latin America – one might even say worldwide. Regarding the Duvalier family history and the devastating impact, see Abbott, H. (1988), *Haiti: The Duvaliers and Their Legacy* (New York: McGraw-Hill).

[65] Human Rights Watch, *World Report 2017*, www.hrw.org/world-report/2017/country-chapters/turkmenistan/ (last accessed 15 January 2019).

place. Nevertheless, the United States is home to dynastic family clans with a number of post-revolutionary 'ruling houses', such as the Adams, Roosevelts, Kennedys, Bushes and Clintons. Unlike the Tudors or Bourbons, they cannot rely on the intra-family transfer of power because elections punctuate the terms of office. Likewise, India offers the authoritarian democratic dynasty of Nehru-Gandhi.[66] Similarly, the Aquino oligarchy has autocratically dominated Philippine politics and transferred offices intra-clan for some decades.[67] The heads of state of the Central Asian, post-Soviet autocracies have similarly and conspicuously transferred their power to their chosen political heirs (see above), unless death preceded the solemn anointment of the successor.

As once in the Soviet Union, the Communist Party in China (and to a lesser extent in Vietnam) also functions as the original legitimate owner of power, at least by proxy. According to the legal definition of a reversion (*Heimfall*), the party initially acts as the heir of the incumbent whenever the incumbent changes and symbolically occupies the place of power, before transferring it to the new leader. In this way, the party – as elsewhere a clan or family dynasty – guarantees unbroken continuity and prevents a 'terrible interregnum' or power vacuum that might endanger the authoritarian system. To return to the place of power discussed before: where dynasties or quasi-dynasties reign, the place of power[68] is never symbolically empty, either *de facto* or *de jure*. However, the public purse may very well be, as will be shown next.

5. KLEPTOCRACY

Authoritarianism pays off – albeit only for its protagonists; and regularly not by order, but at the expense of society. With its taxes and duties, a society must normally answer for the luxurious lifestyles of leaders and clans, and their excessively costly government. And even after the demise of a regime, the ordinary people must then foot the bill for its 'odious debts'.[69] The practice

---

66 Ali, T. (2005), *The Nehrus and the Gandhis. An Indian Dynasty*, 2nd ed (Clerkenwell/London: Pan Books MacMillan).

67 Hutchcroft, P.D. (1991), 'Review: Oligarchs and Cronies in the Philippine State: The Politics of Patrimonial Plunder', in: 43 *World Politics*, 414 ff.

68 Regarding the *dispositif* of democracy, see Lefort, C. (1986), *Essais sur le politique* (Paris: Seuil); Rödel *et al* (n 11), Chapters III and IV; Diehl, P. (2015), *Der politische Repräsentant und der 'leere Ort der Macht'. Das Symbolische, das Imaginäre und die Demokratie. Eine Theorie politischer Repräsentation* (Baden-Baden: Nomos Verlag).

69 While international law holds governments strictly liable for debts incurred by a predecessor, the doctrine of odious debts (or illegitimate debts) argues – in vain – that they are the private liability of a despotic regime and its partners and accomplices in a technical sense. Therefore, they should not be enforced and 'socialized' like regular

of treating political power as private property is particularly repugnant in the greedy and shameless appropriation of assets and goods that belong to society, not the power holders. This top-down robbery is generally not a grievance that constitutions can correct, let alone prevent. Max Weber describes this in more congenial terms:

> [T]he war hero and his followers... seek prey, the plebiscitary ruler or charismatic party leader material means of their power, the former moreover: substantial glory of his rule to consolidate his prestige as master. What they all scorn – as long as the genuinely charismatic type exists – is: the traditional or rational everyday economy, the achievement of regular 'income through a continuous economic activity geared towards it'.[70]

Weber's characterization reflects his concept of patrimonial government. It does not capture kleptocracy, which post-Weberians often classify under the (rather euphemistic) term of 'patrimonialism' or 'crony capitalism'.[71] Whereas patrimonial leaders – such as the military governors of Indonesia (Sukarno/Suharto) and autocrats Ferdinand Marcos and Rodrigo Duterte in the Philippines – commercialize office and charisma, domination and power,[72] hard-core kleptocrats go one step further and reduce state and society to the prey of the ruler. A distinction between patrimonialism and kleptocracy can be drawn only, if at all, with regard to the extent to which kleptomaniac leaders, clans or cliques feel at liberty to dispose of material means within the sphere of their power, enjoy the material splendour of their rule and consolidate their lordly prestige.

Kleptocracies[73] operate to the detriment of any reasonably reliable constitutional order. They may be compared to operational networks of 'organized

---

debts. See Howse, R. (2007), *The Concept of Odious Debt in Public International Law* (Geneva: UNCTAD); Frankenberg, G. and Knieper, R. (1984), 'Legal Problems of the Overindebtedness of Developing Countries: The Current Relevance of the Doctrine of Odious Debts', in: *International Journal of the Sociology of Law*, 415 ff.

[70] Weber, M. (2019), *Economy and Society* (Cambridge: Harvard University Press), § 10.

[71] Crouch, H. (1979), 'Patrimonialism and Military Rule in Indonesia', in: 31 *World Politics*, 571 ff; and Theobald, who seeks to confine the patrimonial framework to underdeveloped economies – Theobald, R. (1982), 'Patri-monialism', in: 34 *World Politics*, 548 ff; Stiglitz, J. (2002), 'Crony capitalism American style', in: *Project Syndicate*, 11 February.

[72] The personal aspect of power is emphasized by Bakker, J.I. (2006), 'Patrimonialism', in: *The Encyclopedia of Governance* (London: Sage), 668 ff.

[73] 'Kleptocracy', in: *The Oxford English Dictionary,* 1st ed (Oxford: Oxford University Press), 1909; Walker, C. and Aten, M. (2018), 'The Rise of Kleptocracy: A Challenge for Democracy', 29 *Journal of Democracy*, 20 ff; Henry, J.S. (2003), *The*

crime' that specialize in property crimes and official offences, such as theft, robbery, embezzlement, bribery, fraud, money laundering and other forms of corruption.

5.1 A Perverted Hobbesian Right to Everything

With some naivety, one might try to discern some philosophy in the rule of robbers, frauds and bribers. In this regard, one might invoke English philosopher Thomas Hobbes' 'right to everything'.[74] In the state of nature, Hobbes argues, man is driven by desire, fear and reason, and there are no limits to liberty. None of these three elements or drives, he argues, causes man to seek the company of others for anything other than his own advantage. This structure of human appetites in the state of nature inevitably drives them to pursue the 'war of everyone against everyone'. Hobbes concludes with a realistic, 'natural-law' consideration: if one accepts his assumption of psychological egoism, it entails the fundamental right of every person to protect himself against all enemies and to appropriate everything that could serve this protection. In consequence, everyone has a 'right to everything' in order 'to obtain all the means and advantages of war':

> And therefore, as long as this natural right of every man to every thing endureth, there can be no security to any man, how strong or wise soever he be, of living out the time which nature ordinarily alloweth men to live. And consequently it is a precept, or general rule of reason: that every man ought to endeavour peace, as far as he has hope of obtaining it; and when he cannot obtain it, that he may seek and use all helps and advantages of war.[75]

Hobbes continues that this does not exclude peace efforts, but is legitimized 'by the supreme principle of natural law' to defend oneself 'with all available means'. In his *Leviathan*, Hobbes then takes a somewhat surprising, contra-contractual turn, arguing that everyone may renounce this right 'voluntarily, if others [ie, all others] are also willing to renounce [their] right to everything' – 'for the sake of peace and self-preservation'.[76]

Of course, Hobbes' natural right to everything is not at all comparable to the egregious tendency of authoritarian leaders, clans and cadres to enrich themselves in office, or to the privilege that drives them. The structure of

---

Blood Bankers: Tales from the Global Underground Economy (New York and London: Four Walls Eight Windows).

74 Concerning the right to everything: Hobbes, *Leviathan* [1651], Chapter 14 (also for the following quotations).

75 *Ibid.*

76 *Ibid*, p. 100.

the right is quite different: in Hobbes' concept, it operates horizontally and reciprocally; whereas in modern authoritarianism, its application is vertical and imperative. At best, Hobbes' idea of psychological egoism, again reserved for those in power, would fit; or even the metaphor of a kind of asymmetrical state of nature. For it is only a raw state of power that enables kleptocrats to appropriate everything they can get their hands on. Pursuant to kleptocracy's 'natural law', this lordly 'right to everything' requires their subjects not only to accept the robberies and luxuries of such regimes, but also – as we have seen – to pay off their debts in the end.

6. THE CHARM OF AUTOCRATIC BOOKKEEPING

In contrast to Louis XIV, today's autocrats are not overly conspicuous in expropriating from above. While they embezzle, rob, cheat, steal and bribe on the public's dime, they develop different strategies to conceal the sources and sums of illegal income 'in office', in order to maintain a façade of charity and altruism.

Romanian dictator Nicolae Ceauşescu proceeded in a particularly original way: he generously waived his salary and 'dedicated it to the world proletariat'. Yet on his death in 1989, his personal possessions – not counting villas and castles – amounted to more than 9000 items, including furs, paintings and other art. Those assets were valued by the Romanian State Protocol Administration at approximately €1 million; another $400 million was suspected to have been deposited in 'private accounts' abroad.[77]

It is particularly effective to refuse access to information about the income and fortune of leaders – notably to the media, courts, tax authorities and (why not?) the population. Similarly, kleptocrats frequently make great fanfare of modest official salaries, while concealing the (unofficial) income that they actually accrue under the counter, offshore, by proxy or through self-privilege. Under-the-counter income is not easy to detect, but is discussed in Section 6.1. The Panama Papers[78] attest to the popularity of offshore practices. With the right family, clan or accomplice network, wealth acquired illegally or dubiously – by threat, bribery or in some other way – can be concealed simply by transferring it to relatives, friends or intermediaries. Another option is to

---

[77] *Desert News,* 1 January 1990, www.deseret.com/1990/1/1/18839117/wealth-has-lured-many-despots-br-ceausescus-noriega-not-the-only-ones-to-live-extravagantly/; and *Neue Zürcher Zeitung*, 10 December 2006, www.nzz.ch/articleEQFGZ-1.81982/ (both last accessed 13 January 2020).

[78] International Consortium of Investigative Journalists (2016), *The Panama Papers: Exposing the Rogue Offshore Finance Industry*, www.icij.org/investigations/panama-papers/ (last accessed 16 January 2020).

confiscate assets and have 'family' account for them. Both are varieties of the by-proxy method. Similarly, autocrats can use their authority to grant themselves or members of their family, clan or other persons of trust (tax) privileges or, quite openly, special authority to control (or not to control) state finances and to obtain financial immunity.

These strategies are illustrated below through a few examples that typify the greedy, selfish, imaginative and highly profitable exploitation of political power in autocratic systems. These examples reveal quite astonishing elective affinities between regimes that are otherwise at variance. Inevitably, the techniques of concealment and camouflage mean that specific information is often unavailable or unreliable. Since the release of the Panama Papers, it has become widely understood what should be made of the official salary statements and asset lists issued by authoritarian governors: nothing. Consequently, there is a fairly strong case to be made for relying on estimates and minimizing errors by using the most conservative calculations possible. In the following discussion, this is the maxim I have adopted in profiling and comparing some of the world's prototypical authoritarian bookkeepers.

6.1 Secretive Fellows

Information on income and assets, like information on sexual practices, is generally kept out of the public eye or behind closed doors. However, the peculiar strategy of *demonstrative obscuration* peculiar to 'secretive fellows' is not without risk if the addressees – whether the people, supporters, one's own party or the revenue authorities – do not appreciate the ostentatious illegality or condemn the breach of laws and conventions.

One striking example is a refusal to file tax returns or make them accessible to the public during an election campaign. It is quite revealing that, without alienating his fans, Donald Trump steadfastly refused to disclose his taxed income and assets during the last election campaign. Though he promised to do so after the election, he ultimately withdrew this promise with impunity. Oddly enough, however, Trump's 2005 tax return (which was anything but up to date) was leaked to the press in 2017. According to this, Trump had a stated income of $153 million, but offset this against losses of around $100 million.[79] In the end, a tax liability of roughly $36.6 million remained, essentially based

[79] The figures show in general terms that his taxable income (from business, dividends, capital gains, real estate and so on) totalled a little under $50 million, for which he owed $2,450,597; plus $103 million derived from 'other income'. See Stein, J. (2017), 'Read the leaked pages of Trump's 2005 tax returns', in: *vox*, 14 March 2017, www.vox.com/2017/3/14/14930644/msnbc-trump-2005-tax-returns/ (last accessed 20 March 2020).

on the 'alternative minimum tax' (tax rate of 24%). Tellingly, however, this tax was abolished that very same year as part of Trump's tax reforms. Trump's 'definitive net worth' was estimated by *Forbes* in 2019 at roughly $3.7 billion, which corresponded to his personal financial disclosure to the Federal Election Commission in 2016.[80] The *New York Times* reported that part of his wealth (more than $400 million) was transferred from his father's 'good fortune' – presumed to have been the fruits of evasion of gift and inheritance tax.[81] Donald Trump has denied that he or his father ever declared assets at an undervalue to the tax authorities. However, the *New York Times* cited financial documents to refute this claim, including confidential tax returns from Fred Trump and his companies. There is no question that Donald Trump's tax honesty cannot be trusted and that his erratic statements about his assets are worthless.

This lax, selfish handling of publicity and transparency in wealth matters by a holder of power is not without historical precedent. In most other cases, however, income and assets were not demonstratively denied, but simply concealed. It might interest the US president to know that a certain Adolf Hitler, who was registered as a 'writer' with the Munich East Tax Office from 1925–32, was exempted from a tax debt of around 400,000 Reichsmark at his instigation in 1934, soon after he had become *Reichskanzler* (chancellor).[82] Whereas Trump celebrates capitalism and defends his reputation as a successful capitalist,[83] Hitler preferred to flaunt his 'modesty and moral and human character'.[84] In this spirit, he always liked to rhetorically insist that 'the common good goes before self-interest'. Still, he submitted his last tax return

---

[80] See *Investopia*, updated 16 February 2020, www.investopedia.com/updates/donald-trump-net-worth (last accessed 26 March 2020).

[81] Mercado, D. (2019), 'What we might learn from Donald Trump's tax returns if they're released', www.cnbc.com/2019/10/08/what-we-might-learn-from-trumps-tax-returns-if-theyre-released.html/ (last accessed 18 January 2020).

[82] Adjusted for inflation, this would correspond to the purchasing power of approximately €1.6 million today. Evidence: Kellerhoff, S.F. (2016), '*Mein Kampf*'. *Die Karriere eines deutschen Buches* (Stuttgart: Klett-Cotta), also as regards the following; Dominik, N. (2004), '*Wie der Führer seine Steuerschuld los wurde*', in: *Stern*, 17 December, www.stern.de/politik/geschichte/adolf-hitler-wie-der--fuehrer--seine-steuerschuld-los-wurde-3544418.html (last accessed 17 July 2020).

[83] In 2005, Trump sued the author of the book *TrumpNation - The Art of Being Donald*, Timothy O'Brien, and publisher Warner Books for slander, and tried to refute the book's claim that he was not a billionaire. Trump lost in two instances. See Goodman, P.S. (2009), 'Trump Suit Claiming Defamation Is Dismissed', in: *The New York Times*, 15 July.

[84] Stratigakos, D. (2015), 'Hitler at Home', in: https://placesjournal.org/article/hitler-at-home/?cn-reloaded=1/ (last accessed 17 January 2020).

in 1935[85] and then expressly 'agreed' to his tax exemption as *Reich* chancellor and author. The president of the Munich East Tax office who ordered that Hitler's tax debt be waived was paid off: he secretly received 2000 Reichsmark per month tax free in addition to his salary as a civil servant until the end of the war. Hitler's royalties of over 1 million Reichsmark for his bestselling book *Mein Kampf* (*My Struggle*) thus remained secret and never fostered the common good.[86]

Whether North Korean dictator Kim Jong-un receives a salary and how high that might be are unknown, due to a dearth of available information. There are also only estimates of his net worth,[87] which are relatively consistent and amount to the equivalent of $4.2 billion to $5 billion.[88] Of course, Kim Jong-un's lavish lifestyle is hard to conceal and is therefore no secret. It is also very instructive: in one of the world's poorest countries, he owns numerous palaces and villas, private jets, yachts, more than 100 luxury cars and even a ski resort. The bank accounts he maintains all over the world – in Austria, Russia, Liechtenstein, Singapore, Luxembourg and mostly China (no ideological caveats!) – must be added to his 'taxable' income. The sources of his income are international illegal business (eg, smuggling, drugs, counterfeit money) and income from companies he owns. Exiling, imprisoning or executing suspected opponents, while also targeting his country's moneyed elite with asset seizures, may also have advanced his political and financial fortunes.

José Eduardo dos Santos, a former revolutionary hero, ruled Angola for 37 years. According to available information, dos Santos and his power clique robbed the country to the best of his ability during his time in power. He is considered a multi-billionaire; as are his daughter and son. According to research by the *Financial Times*, more than $32 billion disappeared from the state budget between 2007 and 2010. His net worth is estimated in the neigh-

---

85 In the *Hofbräuhaus*, Adolf Hitler had presented the Nazi Party's 25-point programme on 24 February 1920. In this programme, the (equal) rights and duties of citizens were discussed. The slogan 'common good goes before self-interest' can be found in point 24 of the programme. Quoted in www.documentarchiv.de/wr/1920/nsdap-programm.html/ (last accessed: 14 January 2019).

86 According to a documentary on British Channel 5 (*The Hunt for Hitler's Millions*), there is allegedly evidence that Hitler held assets of about 1.1 billion Reichsmarks abroad, which according to today's calculations would be about €4.5 billion.

87 Villasanta, A. (2019), 'Kim Jong Un's Net Worth', in: *International Business Times*, 23 May, www.ibtimes.com/kim-jong-un-net-worth-how-north-koreas-leader-spending-his-billions-2794221 (last accessed 10 January 2020); Frank, R. (2014), *Nordkorea: Innenansichten eines totalen Staates* (Munich: Deutsche Verlagsanstalt).

88 Amounts in foreign currency are converted into euros or US dollars in the following.

bourhood of $20 billion.[89] Due to his close ties to state-owned oil company Sonangol, dos Santos is considered a major beneficiary of oil production in Angola. His eldest daughter Isabel do Santos could easily settle with a net worth of $2.2 billion.

Teodoro Obiang Nquema Mbasogo, who was president of Equatorial Guinea from 1997 until 2017, is not quite in the same league:[90] his wealth is estimated at around €600 million, making him the third richest head of government in Africa. Idriss Deby of Chad, one of the poorest countries of the world, spent 23 years robbing the country of $50 million; while King Mswati III of Swaziland netted $100 million after 28 years in power. In just one year, Kenyan President Uhuru Kenyatta had amassed an astonishing $500 million.[91]

6.2 The 'Brothers Grimm' Method

This combination of a modest official income and a wealth of concealed assets that are hidden from public view is extremely popular. I refer to it as the 'Brothers Grimm' method, alluding to the celebrated authors of fairy-tales.[92] According to this method, Nguyễn Xuân Phúc, prime minister of Vietnam, declares an official salary equivalent to €7735 per year.[93] This is suspiciously modest, albeit about four times the average salary in Vietnam; he can be presumed to have quite successfully disguised his actual income. The same is true of his neighbour and Cinderella counterpart Hun Sen in Cambodia, who likewise earns a modest annual salary of about $27,700. As with other heads of state who follow the fairy-tale method of bookkeeping, the officially stated salary of roughly $20,500 a year that China's Xi Jinping receives makes him

[89] Owusu-Ansah, E. (2014), 'Richest Presidents Africa's Ranked', in: *face2face africa*, https://face2faceafrica.com/article/richest-african-presidents-list/ (last accessed 18 January 2020); magazine *Der Spiegel* reached similar conclusions: '*Afrikas Raubkönige*', in: *Spiegel online,* 22 February 2016, www.spiegel.de/politik/ausland/afrika-die-reichsten-herrscher-des-kontinents-a-1077688.html/ (last accessed 3 January 2020).

[90] *Ortner online*, 25 August 2016, www.ortneronline.at/die-8-reichsten-despoten-afrikas-und-ihr-kontostand/ (last accessed 5 February 2019). See also https://de.wikipedia.org/wiki/Teodoro_Obiang_Nguema_Mbasogo/ (last accessed 17 July 2020).

[91] Owusu-Ansah (n 89).

[92] Zipes, J. (2002), The Brothers Grimm: From Enchanted Forests to the Modern World (2nd ed. Abingdon: Routledge).

[93] *Welt*, 18 August 2017, www.welt.de/finanzen/article167802449/Welche-Regierungschefs-die-hoechsten-Einkommen-haben.html/ (last accessed 15 December 2018).

look like Little Red Riding Hood.[94] His salary is supposed to teach modesty to Chinese officials and citizens: it corresponds to less than three times the average income in Beijing and would hardly suffice to cover his daughter's studies at Harvard University, let alone his family's additional expenses of housing, food and clothing (including indulging his wife's penchant for designer fashion). The presumed other – and real – income of Xi Jinping (and his relatives) has not been fully hidden: in June 2012, Bloomberg learned that this is likely to extend to several hundred million dollars, including properties in Hong Kong worth tens of millions. Current research by investigative journalists has revealed that numerous members of China's political elite operate offshore companies.[95] Recently, Xi Jinping's fortune was estimated at a total of $ 1.51 billion. Officially, however, the man who tops the *Forbes* list of the most world's powerful people ranks considerably lower in financial terms.

In 2015, Kenya's President Uhuru Kenyatta reduced his presidential salary from $14,000 to $11,000 a month, which attracted considerable media attention. However, he has no need to fall back on this 'nest egg': his family holds shares in East Africa's largest dairy company, a hotel chain and a bank. Also included in his fortune is the not inconsiderable inheritance of a property that was illegally appropriated in 1963, estimated at between 1 million and 2 billion square meters (m^2) in size.[96]

According to his own statements in a tax declaration published by Parliament in 2008, Italian Prime Minister Silvio Berlusconi earned more than €23 million that year, ranking him among the European Union's top political earners.[97] His assets – whose (known) sources primarily include media group Mediaset and holding company Fininvest – are estimated at between $7.2 billion and €8.5 billion.[98] The exact origin and extent of Berlusconi's extensive wealth

---

[94] 'No Surprise, Singapore's PM is Still the Highest Salary Among All World Leaders', in: *The Independent*, August, 2019 and *Wageindicator.com.uk* – https://wageindicator.co.uk/pay/vip-celebrity-salary (last accessed 18 January 2020); 'Xi Jinping net worth', in: *Spear's*, 2018, www.spearswms.com/xi-jinping-net-worth/ (last accessed 18 January 2020); the Wage Indicator lists Xi with €17 984: https://wageindicator.de/lohn-gehalt/vip-gehalter/politiker-geh%C3%A4lter per year (last accessed 17 July 2020).

[95] *The Guardian* reported (6 April 2016) that the Panama Papers revealed 'offshore secrets' of China's red nobility.

[96] *Unsere Kirche,* 10 August 2017, https://unserekirche.de/kurznachrichten/reich-und-maechtig-kenias-praesident-kenyatta-vor-zweiter-amtszeit-10-08-2017/ (last accessed 6 July 2019).

[97] Sources: www.stern.de/panorama/steuererklaerung-23-millionen-euro-jahresgehalt-fuer-berlusconi-3571052.html/ and www.finews.ch/themen/high-end/10739-italien-reich/ (last accessed 15 December 2018).

[98] *Forbes*, as of 18 January 2020, www.forbes.com/profile/silvio-berlusconi/#1ab52fee3e8f/ (last accessed 20 January 2020).

– which he acquired to a large extent before taking office as prime minister, but increased considerably during his four terms, and which earned his government the title of 'sultanate' – remain largely unclear today.[99] When analysing this wealth, it should be borne in mind that Berlusconi was convicted of tax evasion and balance-sheet fraud, making him no Snow White – although he has once again adopted the fairy-tale method of the 'Brothers Grimm'.

The wealth of Augusto Pinochet was comparatively modest. Apart from several false foreign passports and other assets, the Chilean dictator had accounts in Switzerland and at the Riggs Bank in Washington, DC. In the United States alone, his liquid assets and those of his family, spread over 128 accounts, amounted to between $50 million and $100 million.[100] However, these often illegal inflows (eg, bribery, money laundering) were difficult to trace, as banks and intermediaries were not only uninterested in revealing them, but also actively involved in covering them up. Notably, the Riggs Bank once issued a statement concerning the owner of one of its accounts (Pinochet) which, in order to protect his anonymity and defend the bank against accusations that it did not investigate suspicions of money laundering, included the following customer profile: '... a freelancer who has since retired, who has had great success in his career and who has accumulated assets during his lifetime for an orderly retirement.'[101]

6.3 The Sprinkler

As is common practice in authoritarian circles, there is no reliable official data on Hun Sen's assets (apart from his fairy tale salary). During his 33 years in office, he has perfected a system of concealing income through asset diversification. The system operates like a sprinkler, one might say. Hun Sen himself, his family and their strawmen – the *Khmer Riche* – have taken almost the entire

---

[99] Benni, S. *et al* (2002), Berlusconis Italien – Italien gegen Berlusconi (Berlin: Verlag Klaus Wagenbach); Ginsborg, P. (2005), *Silvio Berlusconi: Television, Power and Patrimony* (London: Verso Books); Sartori, G. (2009), *Il sultanato* (Rome: Laterza).

[100] See Meinzer, M. (2016), *Steueroase Deutschland: Warum bei uns so viele Reiche keine Steuern zahlen,* 2nd ed (Munich: C.H. Beck).

[101] Quoted by Meinzer (n 100).

economy of Cambodia (one of the poorest countries in Southeast Asia) into self-serving control.[102] As the country's Register of Companies shows:

> at least 27 children, siblings or other close relatives of the head of government control and partially or fully own 114 companies in 17 economic sectors of Cambodia. The registered capital of these companies alone is more than $200 million.[103]

Observers say this is 'just a fraction of the true value of the family's business holdings':[104] an additional $200 million to $4 billion is estimated, but not verified. Considering that Hun Sen was practically broke when he entered politics, he must think that politics pays.

Turkish President Erdoğan is officially listed with an annual salary of just under €108 000.[105] At first glance, this appears to be more realistic (certainly than Xi Jinping's and Hun Sen's annual payroll), while also corresponding to the modest image he seeks to project. However, the Turkish *Official Gazette* also registered the president as having €1.18 million in liquid assets in 2018.[106] In addition, as is widely known, he is the owner of properties worth approximately €850 000, which are not registered in the *Official Gazette*. He also has business holdings and other benefits that amount to €150 million,[107] especially from company shares, management bonuses of nationalized companies, and contributions to his family in the form of shares (son Ahmet), real estate (son Necmettin), the board salaries of the Türgev Foundation (daughter Esra), and salaries as minister (son-in-law Berat Albayrak) or adviser (daughter Sümeyye). Erdoğan has 'sprinkled' his assets in duplicate through intra-family diversification, as well as foreign bank accounts (eg, in Switzerland), offshore trusts (eg, Isle of Man) and business (oil) assets. Erdoğan's net worth is thus

---

102 See Baldwin, C. and Marshall, A., 'Khmer Riche', in: *Reuters*, 16 October 2019.

103 *NZZ*, 11 June 2017, www.nzz.ch/wirtschaft/wirtschaftspolitik/kambodschas-gierige-elite-die-kleptomanen-von-phnom-penh-ld.105044/ (last accessed 14 January 2018).

104 Hunt, L. (2016), 'How Rich Are Cambodia's Hun Sen and His Family?', in: *The Diplomat*, 7 July, https://thediplomat.com/2016/07/how-rich-are-cambodias-hun-sen-and-his-family/ (last accessed 18 January 2020).

105 For details on Erdoğan's salary, see *Vermögen Magazin*, 5 January 2020, www.vermoegenmagazin.de/recep-tayyip-erdogan-vermoegen-und-gehalt/ (last accessed 18 January 2020).

106 Regarding Erdoğan's net worth, see *Celebritynetworth.com*, (2019), www.celebritynetworth.com/richest-politicians/presidents/recep-tayyip-erdogan-net-worth/ (last accessed: 18 January 2020).

107 *Vermögen Magazin*, www.vermoegenmagazin.de/recep-tayyip-erdogan-vermoegen-und-gehalt (last accessed 30 June 2019).

reportedly estimated at around $50 million.[108] Plus in 2018, he appointed himself as head of Turkey's $40 billion sovereign wealth fund.

Very much like Xi Jinping, Hun Sen and Erdoğan, other autocrats take from the country to serve their families – such as the Aquinos in the Philippines, the dos Santos in Angola and Hungarian head of state Viktor Orbán.[109] During his 2009–15 term, Benigno Aquino increased his net worth by a staggering 345.43 per cent[110] to a (comparatively modest) $1.2 million. Since 2010, ten Orbán friends and family have come to control businesses with a net worth of $7.85 billion. Corruption and nepotism are also the handmaidens of the Trump presidency.[111] Donald Trump employs his daughter and son-in-law – allegedly without pay – as top advisers, and his less gifted sons as messengers. Trump's son-in-law received loans for his family's ailing business; and, together with his wife, is not so coincidentally pocketing windfall profits of more than $80 million from around 200 external companies.[112] Their 'honorary' work pays for itself through initiating business deals, purchasing real estate, securing and attracting investments and much more – all on the occasion of their advisory activities on behalf of the government, handsomely remunerated.

Vladimir Putin submits his tax returns each year, which are published on the Kremlin's website.[113] This distinguishes him from Hitler, who had no such website; and Trump, who will not use one. However, the official financial data does not attest to Putin's honesty: officially, his salary increased from about €118 000 in 2015 to €257 300 in 2017, before falling to €119 048 in 2018 (a drop that was not sufficiently explained by the government) and then

---

[108] See www.celebritynetworth.com/dl/putin/ (last accessed 17 July 2020).

[109] According to news reports, Orbán uses public (EU) money to promote projects of his family and friends, www.reuters.com/article/us-hungary-orban-balaton-procurement-exc/exclusive-hungary-premiers-friends-and-family-win-more-and-more-public-business-idUSKCN1GR213/ (last accessed 20 January 2020). The European Anti-fraud Office has recommended that Brussels ask Hungary to repay EU funds totalling more than 4 per cent of the cash Europe gave between 2012 and 2015.

[110] Santos, R. (2016), in: *Rappler.com*, www.rappler.com/newsbreak/in-depth/133069-benigno-aquino-iii-saln-2009-2015-net-worth-growth (last accessed 18 January 2020).

[111] Abrahamson, J. (2018), in: *The Guardian*, 6 March, www.theguardian.com/commentisfree/2018/mar/06/nepotism-corruption-handmaiden-trump-presidency (last accessed 18 January 2020).

[112] *Der Spiegel*, www.spiegel.de/wirtschaft/soziales/donald-trump-und-seine-interessenkonflikte-herrschaft-der-kleptokraten-a-1213319.html/ (last accessed 13 January 2019).

[113] Concerning Putin's and other autocrats' wealth and tax returns: Horcicka, F. (2015), *Das schmutzige Geld der Diktatoren* (Vienna: Knemayr & Scheriau).

rising to $187 000 the following year.[114] The electoral list in Russia further includes under Putin's name an apartment of 77 m^2 and a garage of 18 m^2, which he owns; and a 153.7 m^2 apartment reserved for presidential functions in Moscow. Putin also reported owning three cars and a trailer: two vintage GAZ Volga M21 sedans, a Lada Niva sports utility vehicle and a Skif tent trailer, valued at €800.[115] One might add a modest dacha plot mentioned here and there. It would, of course, be a gross mistake to trust these statements. According to relatively reliable investigations, Putin is also the owner of assets which are hardly commensurate with the salary of his former jobs as secret service officer and politician: a stately row of villas and palaces; four yachts; more than 40 aircraft; several hundred luxury class cars; and shares in several companies, including Gazprom and Surgutneftjets. Due to its complexity and opaqueness, estimates of his wealth vary from €40 billion to €200 billion; €70 billion of personal assets seems to be a realistic estimate. [116] A special investigation triggered by the Panama Papers revealed a $2 billion offshore trail leading to Putin.[117] Even if the most conservative calculation is applied, the question remains as to how these assets were procured and why they have not been declared to the tax authorities (ie, no taxes have ever been paid on them). In his official asset reports, moreover, there is no mention of Putin's long-secret daughter. According to research conducted by news agency Reuters in 2015, her assets – most of which are also attributable to Putin – amount to around $2 billion.

An almost innate understanding of power as property characterizes these crowned heads, who have no need to bend under the yoke of constitutionalism. The 'King of the Poor', Mohammed VI of Morocco (also referred to as the 'Predator King'), is said to have assets of €1.5 billion to €2.5 billion – about 6 per cent of his country's GDP.[118] According to *Forbes*, however, he is far down the list of wealthy royals who have appropriated their country's resources. The top spot is claimed by the king of Thailand, with $30 billion; followed by the

---

[114] Matamoros, C.A. (2019), 'How much does Vladimir Putin earn? Not as much as last year…', www.euronews.com/2019/04/15/putin-s-financial-declaration-reports-a-fairly-unpretentious-salary/ (last accessed 18 January 2020).

[115] *News*, 16 April 2016, www.news.de/promis/855636600/putin-veroeffentlicht-seine-steuererklaerung-so-viel-verdient-der-russische-praesident/1/ (last accessed 18 January 2020).

[116] Dawiska, K. (2015), *Putin's Kleptocracy. Who Owns Russia* (New York: Simon & Schuster); *Forbes Magazine* and *Manager Magazin*, 19 March 2018, www.manager-magazin.de/finanzen/artikel/200-milliarden-dollar-vermoegen-wie-reich-ist-putin-wirklich-a-1018696.html (last accessed 12 December 2018). See www.celebritynetworth.com (n 108).

[117] *The Guardian*, 3 April 2016.

[118] Graciel, C. and Laurent, E. (2012), *Le Roi Prédateur* (Paris: Seuil).

sultan of Brunei, with $20 billion. The queen of England secures a fairly lowly position, with a meagre $450 million.[119]

6.4 Immunization

According to this strategy, offices that might have an interest in investigating or exposing the autocrat's financial assets are filled with confidants, institutionally shielded or corrupted in order to secure financial immunity for him. Hitler bought the silence of the head of the Munich East Tax Office, who wrote off his tax debt, with a monthly pension of 2000 Reichsmark. The original view of this aforementioned tax official, Ludwig Mirre, that Hitler was tax exempt because of his constitutional position also saved the '*Führer*' from having to pay taxes on his property on the Obersalzberg, worth approximately 7.2 million Reichsmark.[120]

Through an artful personnel policy, Turkish President Erdoğan gained control over the country's financial system.[121] He replaced internationally recognized former Minister of Finance Şimşek with his own, barely qualified son-in-law, Berat Albayrak; and, as mentioned, appointed himself as currency guardian. It is unclear to what extent this has accommodated his private financial conduct. Nicolás Maduro took a similar approach and installed his wife's nephew, Carlos Malpica Flores, as treasurer of Venezuela. This was hardly necessary, since the leadership clique around Maduro built up mafia-like structures of 'self-sufficiency' years ago which it has maintained ever since, ensuring its continual enrichment primarily through drug trafficking and black market transactions.[122] According to Transparency International's Corruption Perceptions Index, Venezuela was ranked 160th out of 177 countries evaluated in 2013 and dropped to 168th out of 180 in 2017.

Whether this or a similar strategy is also being pursued by Lee Hsien Loong, the prime minister of the 'dual state' of Singapore, cannot be established beyond doubt. After citizens complained about his high salary, he agreed to a pay cut of more than 30 per cent. He still has a handsome annual income,

---

[119] *Forbes*, 29 April 2011, www.forbes.com/sites/investopedia/2011/04/29/the-worlds-richest-royals/#5b5e3455739f/ (last accessed 20 January 2020).

[120] *Der stern,* 17 December 2004, www.stern.de/politik/geschichte/adolf-hitler-wie-der--fuehrer--seine-steuerschuld-los-wurde-3544418.html/ (last accessed 18 January 2020)

[121] *Wirtschaftswoche,* 10 July 2018, www.wiwo.de/politik/ausland/tuerkei-schwiegersohn-statt-kompetenz/22786100.html/; *Merkur*, www.merkur.de/politik/hitler-seine-riesige-steuerschuld-loswurde-177190.html/ (last accessed 14 January 2019).

[122] *Spiegel online,* 16 May 2018, www.spiegel.de/spiegel/venezuela-der-gangsterstaat-von-nicolas-maduro-a-1207606.html/ (last accessed 15 February 2019).

however – the equivalent of about $1.7 million a year (four times as much as the US president).[123] And before this disclosure is praised as an expression of transparency, it should be highlighted that every inhabitant of Singapore must pay the equivalent of €244 a year towards his salary. It should further be noted that he is also the chair (certainly not unsalaried) of one of the world's largest wealth funds (administering more than €340 billion); and that his wife heads the Temasek sovereign wealth fund, which manages assets of more than €150 billion. Lee Hsien Loong's neighbour – Najib Razak, long-time premier of Malaysia – apparently overdrew his account and the people's goodwill and forgiveness. Surprisingly, he lost the election in 2018 and must now stand trial for stashing away billions of dollars from the 1MDB state fund.[124]

7. THE CONSTITUTION OF AUTHORITARIAN PROPERTY-POWER

Even in autocracies, constitutions sometimes include a number of precautions that, if respected, could not completely frustrate the authoritarian concept of power as property, but at least could limit its scope or make authoritarian asset grabs more difficult. Provisions against the usurpation of power have already been mentioned, but may ultimately be ineffective. More resilient, perhaps, could be term limits, concepts of separated powers or the allocation of powers – in particular, those of the executive. Disregard and amendment of these regulations can hardly be blamed on constitutions – particularly if an autocrat himself is appointed as 'guardian of the constitution' (ie, the proverbial goat is made the gardener).[125] The power-critical function of constitutional jurisdiction works only if it is not overridden by co-opted judges, political manipulation of the agenda of courts or frustration of the right of

[123] *Süddeutsche Zeitung*, 4 January 2012, www.sueddeutsche.de/politik/spitzenverdiener-singapur-kuerzt-die-millionengehaelter-seiner-politiker-1.1250801/ (last accessed 15 December 2018).

[124] For references, see Tew, Y. (2020), *Constitutional Statecraft in Asian Courts* (Oxford/New York: Oxford University Press), Introduction.

[125] For example: the presidents of Uzbekistan (Constitution of 1992/2011, Article 93 No 1), Mali (Constitution of 1992, Article 29 II), Russia (Constitution of 1993/2014, Article 80), Turkey (Constitution of 2017, Article 104), Equatorial Guinea (Constitution of 2012, Article 33) and Zimbabwe (Constitution, Article 90); or the king of Morocco (Constitution of 2011, Article 42).

judicial review,[126] and societies that do not much care one way or the other.[127] Otherwise, constitutions cannot stand a chance against political constellations and social demands, economic imperatives, prevailing indifference and civil desertion; against bribery, nepotism and other forms of corruption. Depending on the circumstances, a constitutional culture may not be able to develop.

Probably no constitution anywhere in the world would sanction a ruler's 'right to everything', thus openly authorizing kleptocracy or providing an amnesty for high-handed raids. Constitutions are powerless against such abuse of the executive or any other state office for personal enrichment. The fact that executive personnel are forbidden to engage in 'commercial', 'lucrative' or otherwise 'profitable' activities in addition to their official duties, or to exercise their power for personal gain;[128] that they are obliged to perform their duties in a virtuous and constitutional manner, and must accept this duty on oath; that they are threatened with criminal prosecution and impeachment if they violate their official duties[129] – all of this may be well and good, but such provisions ultimately ring hollow unless implemented forcefully. Thus far, these clauses in many constitutions have not prevented autocrats from robbing their countries from above. In a kleptocracy, even authoritarian constitutionalism has its limits. In the face of autocrats' greed, authoritarian constitutionalism comes to the end of its strategic logic: greed cannot be constituted.

---

[126] See the critique of the attacks on the constitutional/supreme courts in Hungary, Poland and Venezuela. See Grimm, D. (2016), '*Grenzen der Mehrheitsherrschaft*', in: *FAZ*, 14 January, www.faz.net/aktuell/feuilleton/debatten/dieter-grimm-ueber-das-verfassungsgericht-in-polen-13995517.html/ (last accessed 5 February 2019).

[127] For this reason, caution is called for in attributing the rise of the National Socialist regime offhand to the weakness of the Weimar Constitution.

[128] For example, Constitution of Uzbekistan, Article 91; Constitution of Gambia 2004, Article 68 No 4; Constitution of Gabon 2011, Article 14.

[129] For example, 2015 Constitution of Rwanda, Article 63, No 6 and Article 102, No 6.

6. Participation as complicity

> We must close the borders and then endure the cruel images. We cannot allow ourselves to be blackmailed by the eyes of children.[1]

> Every citizen of the USSR has the right to make proposals to state organs and social organizations for improvement of their activities and to criticize deficiencies in their work.[2]

That authoritarianism comes with a set of autocratic techniques of governing is unsurprising, if one reckons on a certain degree of flexibility ('Whatever it takes!'). Political power as private property can be shown as another plausible feature of many authoritarian regimes. The argument that these regimes rely on popular participation may very well be counterintuitive. It will be discussed in this chapter, which introduces the concept of participation as complicity, geared towards creating a bond of personal loyalty between leaders and followers and serving fantasies of an imaginary national, ethnic, patriotic or religious community.

1. THE AMBIVALENCE OF AUTHORITARIANISM AND PARTICIPATION

1.1 Repression Instead of Participation?

According to popular opinion, autocracies attach little importance to the presence and involvement of citizens in the common affairs of society. Political authoritarianism is thus identified less by mobilizing citizens than by discouraging them from expressing themselves openly; from assembling or founding associations; and from standing in elections with their own candidates. Under this view, authoritarian regimes attempt in every conceivable way to censor

1 '*Wir müssen die Grenzen dicht machen und dann die grausamen Bilder aushalten. Wir können uns nicht von Kinderaugen erpressen lassen*' – vice leader of the right-wing nationalist *Alternative für Deutschland* party and Member of Parliament Alexander Gauland, in a comment on German refugee policy, in: *ZEIT online,* 24 February 2016, www.zeit.de/politik/deutschland/2016-02/alexander-gauland-afd-fluechtlingskrise-fluechtlingspolitik-grenzen/ (last accessed 16 February 2019).

2 1977 Constitution of the Soviet Union, Article 49.

criticism and prevent opposition movements from asserting their ideas of life and of their common business – in short, of the common good – and, according to Kant, from activating the freedom of 'using their own understanding confidently and well in religious matters, without outside guidance'.[3]

In principle, only edifying activity that does not seriously call domination and rule into question is permitted. And in order to ensure such active support – that is, acclamation, applause and ovations – authoritarian regimes carefully orchestrate from above, control, dose and monitor political activity, in order to keep on a course compatible with the interests of the regime; if necessary by coercion and with the help of the security forces. A big hand – yes; a critical word – no.

This assessment of the value and practice of citizens' involvement in politics from the perspective of authoritarian leaders, cadres or parties is backed up by ample evidence worldwide. It is registered and condemned by international organizations, such as the UN Human Rights Commission, Freedom House, Amnesty International, Human Rights Watch and other non-governmental organizations. The media (including Reporters Without Borders) faces the depressing task of opposing the commanders of repression and the persecution of dissidents, press censorship and election rigging, clampdowns, confinements and restraints of freedom as unwanted but tireless witnesses and observers.[4]

Word has long since got around that even elections as a proof of democracy are not very reliable:

> Illiberal democracies may have reasonably free and fair national elections based on broad suffrage, but they do not counteract the tyranny of the majority with effective protections for ethnic and religious minorities or various types of dissenters.[5]
>
> Experts stress that elections alone, without the full democratic range of an independent judiciary, free press and vital political parties, in reality constitute illiberal democracies that still threaten their citizens and neighbors and destabilize their regions.[6]

---

[3] Kant, I. (1999), 'An answer to the question: What is enlightenment?' [1784], in: Gregor, M.J. (ed), *Practical Philosophy. The Cambridge Edition of the Works of Immanuel Kant* (Cambridge: Cambridge University Press), 11 f.

[4] See the annual reports of Amnesty International and Human Rights Watch.

[5] Forsythe, D.P. (2012), *Human Rights in International Relations* (Cambridge: Cambridge University Press), 231; see Alviar, H. and Frankenberg, G., *Routledge Handbook on Illiberalism* (New York and Oxford: Routledge) (forthcoming in 2020).

[6] Henriksen, T.H. (2007), *American Power after the Berlin Wall* (Basingstoke: Palgrave MacMillan).

Here are just a few highlights from widely known authoritarian practice. In late Summer and Autumn 1988, mass executions of political prisoners were carried out daily in Iran's prisons. According to estimates, up to 30 000 people fell victim to this state-organized mass murder. The prison massacre of 1988 is regarded as one of the cruel highlights of the persecution of opponents and dissidents in Iran.[7] Former politicians, journalists and non-violent political opponents have been imprisoned without charge in numerous countries, such as Eritrea.[8] They are held in underground cells or in shipping containers, without sufficient food, clean drinking water or adequate sanitation. Their relatives remain uncertain about their fate. There can be no question of them being legally supported and represented by lawyers. Defenders of human rights and political opposition activists have been persecuted in Cambodia for years. Since the national elections in 2013, the government and the ruling Cambodian People's Party have been exploiting the criminal justice system to intimidate and discriminate against opposition activists and restrict their freedoms.[9] The Cambodian Party for the Rescue of the Nation was founded in 2012 as a democratic opposition party. From the beginning, its activities were suppressed by the Cambodian regime. In September 2017 its chairman, Kem Sokha, was arrested. Two months later, the party was banned.[10]

It is not only in China and Turkey, which are currently enjoying special media attention, that critical journalists live dangerously; and not only in countries of the global South. Of the five countries in which freedom of the press has deteriorated most severely, according to reports from Reporters Without Borders, four are European. This organization sees the combination of politics, business and media as a major problem. The Hungarian government under Viktor Orbán comes under heavy fire for its reprisals against critical media; as do the current governments in Malta, Poland, Slovakia and the Czech Republic.[11] Europe is no sanctuary for the press.

---

7 'Iran: Unrelenting Repression', report by Human Rights Watch, 17 January 2019, www.hrw.org/news/2019/01/17/iran-unrelenting-repression (last accessed 8 July 2019).

8 Amnesty International, *Jahresbericht 2016 Eritrea*, 7 March 2016.

9 Amnesty International, *Report*, 30 May 2017, Index ASA 23/6059/2017/.

10 Amnesty International, *Report 2017/18. Zur weltweiten Lage der Menschenrechte*, 23 May 2018, www.amnesty.de/jahresbericht/2018/kambodscha/ (last accessed 6 July 2019).

11 Reporters Without Borders (2019), *World Press Freedom Index – A Cycle of Fear*, https://rsf.org/en/2019-world-press-freedom-index-cycle-fear (last accessed 22 February 2020).

1.2 Participation Instead of Repression?

That political authoritarianism fears any political participation like the devil fears holy water is denied through quite persuasive arguments. In her influential essay 'What Do We Know About Democratization After Twenty Years?' Barbara Geddes hints at the ambivalent relationship between authoritarianism and participation: 'Authoritarian governments need some support and quite a bit of toleration to stay in power.'[12] Gino Germani – a survivor of aggressive, nationalist populism and fascism in Argentina and Italy – elaborates this ambivalence even more strongly and also emphasizes the usually suppressed valence that favours political participation:

> In its pure form, modern authoritarianism does not reduce individuals to passive subjects; in a sense, it wants them to be citizens. Its goal is not de-politicization (this also happens), but politicization according to a particular ideology. Citizens... must make a choice and acquire a certain conviction, but its content must correspond to the official ideology. There is a choice, but it is openly manipulated. The external controls, repression and terror, are also necessary, but if the totalitarian state is successful, they are mainly applied to a reduced part of the population, mainly the intellectuals.[13]

Norman Spaulding reads Germani's argument that ideological manipulation is the linchpin – at least in totalitarian systems – as confirmation of the privileged position of (liberal) democracy, in which power is derived from a 'truly "free"

---

[12] Geddes, B. (1999), 'What Do We Know About Democratization After Twenty Years?', 2 *Annual Review of Political Science,* 115 ff, 138. This thesis is exemplified by events during the elections in Russia: the presidential election provided the incumbent Vladimir Putin with the desired legitimacy, as expected by the poll results. After the elimination of opposition candidates in the run-up to the election, measures were implemented at several levels to ensure that the election could not change anything in the power structure. At many polling stations, food or underwear could be bought at reduced prices. With music and dance performances in and around the polling stations, a political event turned into a social event. The media close to the government and state media had influenced voters to secure the stability and thus the future of the country by voting for Putin. Election observers were obstructed or threatened. In: *Der Tagesspiegel,* 18 March 2018, www.tagesspiegel.de/politik/praesidentschaftswahl-in-russland-opposition-und-ngos-melden-hunderte-unregelmaessigkeiten/21084470.html/ (last accessed 8 July 2019); and *Bundeszentrale für politische Bildung* (2018), *Präsidentschaftswahlen in Russland 2018. Russland-Analysen* Number 351, 23 March 2018.

[13] Germani, G. (1978), *Authoritarianism, Fascism, and National Populism* (New Brunswick: Transaction Books), 6 ff; also regarding the following arguments. I owe the reference to Gino Germani to Norman Spaulding. Many of the following considerations are inspired by our discussions.

choice'.[14] In this way, Germani preserves the normatively weighty contrast between democracy and authoritarianism, which can also be found in less differentiated theories. In contrast to other authors, Germani in fact assumes that in mass democracies, no sovereign has full control over the population by virtue of the monopoly of 'legitimate violence' (Max Weber) and must therefore grant them – *contre coeur* – voice, choice and agency.

Germani's conception of participation in authoritarianism is based on a strong secularization thesis: after the dissolution of traditional religious, local and status-based restrictions on knowledge, technology and the economy, behaviour in modern societies is regulated primarily within the normative framework of 'elective action' or individual choice; and not, as in pre-modern societies, rather prescriptively by command and prohibition. With the spread of secularization, traditional belief systems have eroded, contributing to the exercise of individual freedom. Thus, the problem of how to integrate a society has intensified, argues Germani. In mass societies characterized by violent repression, it is not possible to maintain social order and build consensus in the long run. Therefore, autocracies also need forms of 'active political participation…, even if these remain to a certain extent merely formal or symbolic'.[15] This argument is confirmed – for a non-secularized regime – by the 2011 Constitution of the Kingdom of Morocco, which postulates in the first sentence:

> With fidelity to its irreversible choice to construct a democratic State of Law, the Kingdom of Morocco resolutely pursues the process of consolidation and of reinforcement of the institutions of a modern State, having as its bases the principles of participation, of pluralism and of good governance.

The counter-position to that of Germani and Spaulding sees the passivity of the population and their retreat from the public sphere or civil desertion[16] as a necessary condition for the stability of authoritarian systems. In particular, totalitarianism needs to generate fear and terror as its elixirs of life, and can therefore rather do without an active citizenry. Depending on the type of regime, manipulated elections may be less important to guarantee stability than terror that ensures acquiescence.

---

[14] Spaulding, N. (2019), 'States of Authoritarianism in Liberal Democratic Regimes', in: Alviar and Frankenberg (eds), *Authoritarian Constitutionalism – Comparative Analysis and Critique* (Cheltenham: Edward Elgar Publishing), 265 ff.

[15] Germani (n 13), 10.

[16] I borrow the concept from Marcel Gauchet's essay: '*Pacification démocratique, desertion civique*', in: *Le débat* 60 (1990), 87 ff.

Germani's analysis better captures the situation in non-totalitarian authoritarianisms, such as Morocco, Erdoğan's Turkey and Orbán's Hungary. But here, too, it would be advisable to 'read' these into the historical and social context and the political configuration in play, in order to understand participatory phenomena. For example, non-participation in elections and the rise of (right-wing) populist parties, as is currently the case in many European countries,[17] could be due to disenchantment with the politics of the elites, a structural crisis of democratic representation or diffuse discontent, rather than a genuine support of authoritarianism. By the same token, those who play their part in national consultations or referendums – as in Hungary or Venezuela – might misunderstand these events as truly democratic proceedings, rather than mere government propaganda. They may overlook both the authoritarian subtext and its implications – that is, the covert call for self-disempowerment.[18]

I will approach the ambivalent relationship between participation and authoritarianism in two steps. First, I assume that the much-discussed crisis of representation – often referred to as the crisis of democracy, 'post-democracy' or 'post-politics'[19] – as well as the failure of the elites can be held partly liable for the upsurge in radically nationalist and xenophobic movements. In a second step, I try to mediate between the controversial positions discussed above by suggesting that in authoritarian constellations, both the elective and non-selective participatory forms are tailored to establish a relationship of complicity between rulers and ruled (Figure 6.1) that creates visions of an imaginary communality. Hence, one may assume that the opportunities for political participation are unequally distributed in all regimes.[20]

---

[17] Hillebrand, E. (ed) (2015), *Rechtspopulismus in Europa. Gefahr für die Demokratie?* (Bonn: Dietz); Wodak, R., Khosravinik, M. and Mral, M. (2013), *Right-Wing Populism in Europe – Politics and Discourse* (London: Bloomsbury).

[18] Regarding national consultations and referenda in Hungary, see Gessler, T. (2017), 'The 2016 Referendum in Hungary', in: 45 *East European Quarterly*, 85 ff.

[19] Crouch, C. (2004), *Post-Democracy* (London: Polity); Farkas, J. and Schou, J. (2019), *Post-Truth, Fake News and Democracy: Mapping the Politics of Falsehood* (Milton Park: Taylor & Francis).

[20] Regarding the unequal distribution of political participation: Dalton, R.J. and Klingemann, H.D. (2019), 'Citizens and Political Behavior', in: *The Oxford Handbook of Political Behavior*, www.oxfordhandbooks.com/view/10.1093/oxfordhb/9780199270125.001.0001/oxfordhb-9780199270125-e-001 (last accessed 22 February 2020); Böhnke, P. (2011), '*Ungleiche Verteilung politischer und zivilgesellschaftlicher Partizipation*', in: 1–2 *APuZ*, 18 ff.

Source: © Photo: Scherl/Süddeutsche Zeitung Photo REF 25812. With friendly permission.

Figure 6.1 *Political participation as complicity? Germans welcome the beginning of the Second World War*

2. NOTES ON THE PSYCHOLOGY OF COLLECTIVE PROTEST

A renaissance of political authoritarianism has been registered worldwide, most notably in Europe.[21] Authoritarian movements and organizations in Austria, Hungary, Poland, Denmark, the Netherlands, the United Kingdom and Italy have not restricted their activities to the streets or parliaments: some have already entered cabinet rooms and government offices. The Alternative for Germany, the Danish People's Party, the National Rally in France, the *Lega* (formerly *Lega Nord*) in Italy, *Vlaams Belang* in Belgium and related parties such as the Swedish Democrats have left the extra-parliamentary arena and moved into parliaments and cabinets.[22] Even there, however, some cultivate

[21] See the references in the Introduction and in Chapter 1.

[22] See the contributions to Hillebrand, E. (ed) (2015), *Rechtspopulismus in Europa. Gefahr für die Demokratie?* (Bonn: Dietz Verlag).

the image and rhetoric of extra-parliamentary protest[23] – at least for the time being. As a rule, these players respond to socially experienced (or imagined) grievances and events with indignation, anger, disappointment, annoyance and insecurity. In terms of emotions and energies, there may be an intersection with left-wing democratic ('populist'?) movements such as the *Descamisados*[24] in Argentina, who were mobilized to protest by the Peronists in the late 1940s, claiming that their shirts were being ripped off; or the *Indignados*[25] in Spain, who were outraged by the austerity policy in 2011–12.

Such emotions are regularly triggered by the (collective) experience of exclusion from political responsibility, or indignation at irresponsible elites and governments that are far removed from the people. More generally, loss of social control and fear of further incursions by capitalism or globalization (see Chapter 2, Section 7) are likely to cause anger, rage or indignation. Such outrage, however, does not mean that engaging in protest is always spontaneous and neither planned nor driven by carefully calculated interests. On the contrary, protest is typically preceded by deliberations and systematic planning that characterize demonstrations as predominantly collective behaviour that is rational, albeit impulsive.

Nevertheless, there is a tendency to reduce rebellious acts against the forces of order to individualism, brand them as irrational and reduce them to the level of disorder (which in turn plays into the hands of authoritarian groups and organizations). Irrationalizing protest or revolts has a long history.[26] One of its fathers was Gustave Le Bon, author of *The Psychology of Peoples*[27] and a prisoner of his views on the February Revolution of 1848 and the Paris Commune of 1871. It is difficult to transfer these biased reflections on the feelings and behaviour of 'the masses' without contextual consideration.[28] Nevertheless, it

---

[23] Stürmer, S. and Simon, B. (2009), 'Pathways to Collective Protest: Calculation, Identification or Emotion? A Critical Analysis of the Role of Anger in Social Movement Participation', in: 65 *Journal of Social Issues*, 681 ff.

[24] The 'shirtless' was the self-designation of Argentine women who were so poor that even their 'last shirt' was taken from them. The first wife of President Juán Perón, Evita Perón, co-opted the term and called herself the 'first shirtless of the country', quoted after 'South America's veto', in: *Der Spiegel*, Number 43, 1947.

[25] Together with *¡Democracia Real Ya!* ('Real Democracy Now!'), they were the 'movement basis' of democratic party *Podemos* ('We can').

[26] The term 'revolt' usually refers to the insurgency of a manageable, because numerically limited, collective – a group of people in a rather local or regional context. In contrast to revolutions, uprisings of slaves, peasants, armies or workers are considered synonymous with revolts, because they lack planning and an elaborated ideological conception.

[27] Le Bon, G. (1898), *The Psychology of Peoples* (New York: Macmillan).

[28] For critical transfers, see Freud, S. (2012), *Group-Psychology and The Analysis of the Ego* (York: Empire Books); Moscovici, S. (1985), *The Age of the Crowd:*

is instructive to note that Le Bon's ideas about common features of collective behaviour seem to be *en vogue* once more: 'impulsiveness', 'irritability', 'exaggeration of feelings' and 'lust for power' are all frequently cited today. Le Bon ascribed to participants in mass actions a considerable reduction in the preconditions of reasoning and assumed that the rational control of behaviour is precluded by 'exuberant emotions', as in 'savages' and 'children'. He argued further that 'absence of judgement' favours collective rebellion: '[T]he less the masses are capable of rational thought, the more they are inclined to action.'[29] This basic assumption of *The Psychology of Peoples* – that irrational emotions drive people to the streets – is not very far from some of the current socio-psychological studies and commentaries that investigate why individuals and movements yield to the authoritarian temptation. Others cite the studies of the Frankfurt Institute for Social Research to explain the appeal of authoritarianism to those who support a strong state and '[despise] democracy and cosmopolitanism, who in a complicated world search for simple answers'.[30] With regard to current problems, still others attribute the flight to 'right-wing populism',[31] xenophobia and nationalism to the unresolved challenges of integrating refugees, the threat of terrorist attacks and the insecurity triggered by global crises. Authoritarian, radical nationalism or right-wing populism is thus seen as a pathological syndrome that above all combines feelings of loss of control with cultural alienation, anti-globalism and anti-elitism, and leads to a growing polarization of society. Ultimately, the two opposing camps have little to say to each other: 'We are the people. And who are you?'[32]

A Historical Treatise on Mass Psychology (Cambridge: Cambridge University Press).

[29] Le Bon (n 27). The racist prejudice is evident.

[30] For example, Werner, H. (2018), '*alles was links ist*', www.harald-werner-online.de/index.php?id=257/ (last accessed 19 August 2018).

[31] The concept of populism was introduced and discussed with many references in Chapter 2, Section 7. For a concise review of current theories of democracy, see Vorländer, H. (2013), '*Krise, Kritik und Szenarien: Zur Lage der Demokratie*', in: 23 *Zeitschrift für Politikwissenschaft*, 267 ff with further references; and *id*, (2010), *Demokratie: Geschichte, Formen, Theorien* (2nd ed) (Munich: C.H. Beck).

[32] President Erdoğan addressing critics during his election campaign in 2014 and invoking a fantasy of genuine representation and purity. See Müller, J.W. (2016), 'Trump, Erdoğan, Farage: The attractions of populism for politicians, and the dangers for democracy', in: *The Guardian*, 2 September, www.theguardian.com/books/2016/sep/02/trump-erdogan-farage-the-attractions-of-populism-for-politicians-the-dangers-for-democracy/ (last accessed 23 February 2020).

3. CRISIS OF REPRESENTATION – RETURN OF AUTHORITARIANISM

3.1 Post-democracy, Post-politics

Pessimistic augurs interpret the protests both on the fringes and in the centre of society as symptoms of decay: against strangers who do not belong 'to the people' or do not belong 'here'; against elites who have no concept of the interests of the population and who lack a sense of responsibility.[33] Traditional parties appear to have lost not only members, but also the power to create a political milieu that could attract and bind a significant part of the population to programmatic ideas and goals. As parties – notably the Social Democratic Party – slid into a crisis, so too did democracy and democratic crisis management, especially in Europe. Hence, the emergence of authoritarianism in many EU member states has not come as a complete surprise.[34] While theories of post-democracy and post-politics cannot be discussed here in detail, some of the results of their analyses can presented in a summary fashion.[35]

First, the crisis that underpins the concept of 'post-democracy' is reflected by changes in political *behaviour*. Declining voter turnouts and loyalty to intermediary organizations (unions, parties), the dwindling membership base of parties and similar are interpreted as indicative of the political mood of a frustrated, disillusioned, politically disenchanted citizenry which has deserted the public arenas to 'bowl alone'.[36] This diagnosis, however, does not sit well with the revival of nationalism and chauvinism, which – not only in numerous European states, but also in the United States – has brought the alleged deserters onto the streets and led to considerable waves of mobilization. Even if one were to see in this a danger to democracy – more precisely, to the established democracy that has fallen into crisis – it would be difficult to

---

[33] Informed by the Trump presidency: Levitsky, S. and Ziblatt, D. (2018), *How Democracies Die* (New York: Broadway Books).

[34] Offe, C. (2016), *Europa in der Falle* (Berlin: Suhrkamp).

[35] See already Rancière, J. (1977), '*Demokratie und Postdemokratie*', in: Badou, A. *et al* (eds), *Politik der Wahrheit* (Vienna: Turia + Kant), 94 ff; Crouch (n 19). Other crisis diagnoses: Wohlin, S. (2017), *Democracy Incorporated: Managed Democracy and the Specter of Inverted Totalitarianism* (Princeton: Princeton University Press); Furedi, F. (2005), *The Politics of Fear* (New York/London: Continuum), criticizing politics and the political class based on an internalized politics of fear.

[36] Putnam, R.D. (2000), *Bowling Alone. The Collapse and Revival of American Community* (New York: Simon & Schuster). Offe, C. (1996), '*Moderne "Barbarei": Der Naturzustand im Kleinformat*', in: Miller, M. and Soeffner H.G. (eds), *Modernität und Barbarei. Soziologische Zeitdiagnose am Ende des 20. Jahrhunderts* (Frankfurt am Main: Campus), 258 ff.

interpret the willingness to confront and revolt against the political class as an authentication of a post-democratic age.

Second, changed *systemic* conditions of politics favour phenomena (at least in theory) of post-democracy. Globalization limits national access to and control of cross-border problems, and increases their complexity. Examples include climate change and environmental pollution; 'organized crime' and terror; migration and production chains; and most recently and dramatically, the coronavirus pandemic. For quite some time, the acceleration and expansion of capitalism has led to spatial and social 'land grabs' and, in response, to feelings of loss of control[37] on the part of citizens. These losses emerge in technical processes, social change and the individual pace of life. On the one hand, these problems pave the way for political decisions to be shifted to supranational or international institutions. On the other hand, they play into the hands of the authority of expertise[38] that removes expert bodies from democratic control. Not only according to the theories of post-democracy, these dismantle democratic standards and empty and devalue representative parliamentary decision-making procedures. Thus, it seems plausible to recognize a crisis of representation that plays into the hands of authoritarian demagogues who claim that they will 'bring the people back in'.

Third, since the collapse of state socialism, ideological conflicts have shifted into the *neoliberal* camp and are discussed from the perspective of 'economizing the political'. This is not unanimously understood to mean that the guiding ideas of neoliberalism are gaining in importance in the political sphere. Above all, neoliberalism tends to push aside the active citizen and enthrone the *homo economicus* – the utility maximizer. Instead of reinvigorating parliamentary co-determination, politicians follow the trend and suggest that it should operate 'in conformity with the market'.[39] The economization of the political undermines an emphatic understanding of democratic self-rule and discourages citizens from engaging in the common affairs of society. Neoliberal topics such as deregulation could be borrowed from the arsenal

---

[37] Heitmeyer, W. (2008), *Autoritäre Versuchungen* (Berlin: Suhrkamp), 119 ff; Harvey, D. (2006), *The Limits to Capital* (London: Verso); Dörre, K. *et al* (2013), *Das Gesellschaftsbild der LohnarbeiterInnen* (Hamburg: VSA Verlag), 29 ff. (concerning capitalist incursions).

[38] See Kennedy, D. (2016), *A World of Struggle – How Power, Law, and Expertise Shape Global Political Economy* (Princeton: Princeton University Press).

[39] Chancellor Merkel – '*Marktkonforme Demokratie? Oder demokratiekonformer Markt?*', in: *FAZnet,* 15 April 2012, www.faz.net/aktuell/politik/harte-bretter/marktkonforme-demokratie-oder-demokratiekonformer-markt-11712359.html/ (last accessed 8 July 2019).

of authoritarian constitutionalism.[40] The same is true for arguments that trade should be liberalized, investments should be protected and fiscal austerity should reign. These further the trend towards the domination of economic elites, governance technicians and experts in the field of democracy, which has favoured a progressive economic 'colonization' of politics,[41] illustrated by the proliferation of economic terminology, the dominance of economic expertise and efficiency calculations as benchmarks for politics.

Finally, the post-democracy thesis can also be validated by the change in techniques of governing, and especially by new surveillance practices and schemes of social scoring such as those discussed above. To the extent that information technology takes the lead, the republican promise of public democratic rule and human rights recedes behind states' and private providers' need to expand their data collections and exchange data. For example, the PRISM surveillance programme is led by the US National Security Agency. According to reports from the *Washington Post* and the *Guardian*, nine of the largest internet corporations – notably Microsoft (with Skype), Google (with YouTube), Facebook, Yahoo, Apple and AOL – are participating in PRISM.[42]

The gloomy and even apocalyptic images of the demise of democracy that theories of post-democracy portray have provoked considerable criticism.[43] They are rejected above all by normative theories of deliberative democracy.[44] This controversy cannot be discussed further here, because it does not relate

---

40 Bruff, I. (2016), 'The Rise of Authoritarian Neoliberalism', 26 *Rethinking Marxism: A Journal of Economics, Culture & Society*, 115 ff; Alviar, H. (2019), 'Neoliberalism as a Form of Authoritarian Constitutionalism', in Alviar and Frankenberg (n 14) 37 ff; and Wilkinson marks this as 'Authoritarian Liberalism as Authoritarian Constitutionalism', in: Alviar and Frankenberg (n 14), 317 ff.

41 Colin Crouch assumes that the state resembles a big corporation that dominates the market (*Post-Democracy*, 109); Claus Offe discusses, with reference to Crouch 'The "post-democratic" superposition of political by economic categories', in: Offe, C. (2008), *Frankfurter Allgemeine Zeitung,* 22 September, 37.

42 Gellman, B. (2013), '*U.S. surveillance architecture includes collection of revealing Internet, phone metadata*', in: *The Washington Post,* 16 June 2013; Hofstetter, Y. (2016), *Das Ende* der *Demokratie* (Munich: *Bertelsmann* Verlag); Rudder, C. (2014), *Dataclysm. Who We Are (When We Think No One is Looking),* (Camarthen: Crown).

43 For critical assessments of post-democracy and for more optimistic appraisals: Cook, J. *et al* (2017), *The State We're In: Reflecting on Democracy's Troubles* (Oxford: Berghahn Books); Ritzi, C. (2014), *Die Postdemokratisierung politischer Öffentlichkeit* (Wiesbaden: Springer VS); Blühdorn, I. (2013), *Simulative Demokratie* (Berlin: Suhrkamp).

44 Goodin, R.E. (2008), *Innovating Democracy. Democratic Theory and Practice after the Deliberative Turn* (Oxford: Oxford University Press); Landemore, H. (2017), 'Deliberative Democracy an Open Not (Just) Representative Democracy', in: 146 *Daedalus*, 51 ff.; Fishkin, J. (2009), *When the People Speak: Deliberative Democracy and Public Consultation* (New York: Oxford University Press).

to authoritarian regimes. Despite conceptual vagueness and shortcomings in empirical justification, however, the 'post-democratic' diagnoses deserve to be taken seriously in view of the rising popularity of authoritarian movements and parties. Whether we are witnessing the historic decline of democracy in general or merely a crisis of established and exercised democratic representation and the system of party competition, the upswing of authoritarianism points to serious phenomena and cannot be dismissed as easily correctable systemic and attitudinal damage, as the following rather tentative and sketchy remarks may indicate. In the following, I assess the diagnoses and consider whether they indicate a crisis of the democratic form of governing or the democratic form of life.[45]

3.2 Crisis of the Democratic Form of Governing

Both at the margins of societies and at their centre, problems of democratic governance play into the hands of right-wing nationalism. The support bases of traditionally strong parties are dwindling and their 'bonding forces' are slackening. Moreover, capitalist incursions into non-economic spheres (education, public health, culture, politics) are increasing. In consequence, social groups feel that they are going to rack and ruin as a result of modernization and globalization, and have been forsaken by the governing elites. They feel – indeed, many are – disenfranchised, and have lost control over their lives. Their social status is threatened. Hence, they succumb to the authoritarian temptation and follow leaders and organizations that promise simple answers, while directing their anger against 'those up there' (eg, in Washington or Brussels) and 'those who do not belong' – immigrants, strangers and all kinds of minorities. Against this backdrop, radically nationalist, authoritarian movements have been able to advance in a number of states, not only infiltrating the margins and strengthening a negligible lunatic fringe, but also exploiting a wider disenchantment with politics and a new demand for an autocratic style of governance. Elites in politics, the media and especially business are believed to operate in an aloof, luxurious parallel sphere; shirk responsibility for wrong decisions ('Dieselgate', the banking crisis, climate change, poverty); and do little to correct the shortcomings of the democratic system. On the contrary, such behaviour generates dichotomous images of society, or at least makes people receptive to Manichean views. From India to Sweden, from the United States to Hungary, this organized resentment has reshaped cabinets and governments.

[45] Regarding the following Vorländer, (n 31), in: 23 *Zeitschrift für Politikwissenschaft*, 267 ff; *id*, *Demokratie: Geschichte, Formen, Theorien.*

The phenomena of crisis must be analysed in each and every context. The divergence between the democratic idea and the democratic form of government has promoted a wide spectrum of political and constitutional authoritarianisms, however. With all due differentiation, some aspects that point to the crisis of democratic governing crop up time and again: futile climate conferences; detached G8/10/20 meetings; interventions of central banks, the International Monetary Fund and the World Bank; austerity policies; irresponsible elites and so on. For quite some time, they have made an astonished audience aware of how – and to what extent – the balance has shifted from popular democratic discussion and parliamentary debate and decision-making to leadership and consultation by experts and committees that are neither sufficiently legitimized nor adequately controlled.[46]

3.3 Crisis of the Democratic Form of Life

Could this crisis affect democracy as a way of life? As we have seen, democracy is not limited to a set of institutionalized procedures for the selection of government personnel (party competition, elections), and for generating and producing generally binding decisions; but also comprises a set of attitudes, performances and ways to solve conflicts and assert interests and lifestyles. The double meaning of politically practised democracy and democracy that is alive in the everyday reflects what Abraham Lincoln may have had in mind in his Gettysburg Address in 1863, when he spoke of the 'government of the people, by the people, and for the people'.[47]

Constitutions have difficulty with everyday practice. Usually, they concentrate on how state power is exercised – by whom, in what form and through which institutions – and how power is allocated and separated. Generally, the people are invoked as the sovereign who generates power as *pouvoir constituant* and then transfers it to the *pouvoirs constitués*. Thereafter, within the state in its legal form, it seems to disappear. Most constitutions can be read as organizational charters. Few approach the idea that democracy could also have meaning as a way of life. John Dewey combined the classic organizational charter *par excellence*, the US Federal Constitution, with the idea of a way of life – albeit from the perspective of pedagogy and ethics: 'The clear conscious-

---

[46] Although representative parliamentary democracy excludes neither *leadership* nor *consultation*, democratic constitutionalism promises discursive mediation, parliamentary feedback and legal control – somewhat magically – in order to prevent authoritarianism from spreading. See, for instance, the regulations of the legislative procedure in most liberal constitutions.

[47] Boritt, G. (2008), *The Gettysburg Gospel: The Lincoln Speech That Nobody Knows* (New York: Simon & Schuster), Appendix B, 290.

ness of a community life, with all that it entails, constitutes the idea of democracy.'[48] If at all, the democratic way of life is expressed more in the abstract spirit or may be inferred from value clusters of a constitution.[49] Unusual, then, is the highly counterfactual commitment of the Egyptian Constitution of 2014: 'We believe in democracy as a path, a future and a way of life.'

A democratic way of living (in society) breaks, or at least strains, the paradigm of liberal constitutionalism by emphasizing the active civic component beyond the confines of official politics: the commitment of individuals or groups both to a society's common affairs, as Marx called it, and also to their own 'private' affairs. Thus, democracy comes to the fore as a form of political coexistence, of shared beliefs and common experiences[50] – not just in the public arenas, but in the contacts and conflicts of the everyday. These contacts and experiences include the way in which social capital is generated by adequately handling conflicts and enduring opposition and diversity – that is, abstaining from all-or-nothing claims and practising what might be called 'relaxed tolerance of difference': other religious habits, contrary political views, other ways of dress (eg, headscarves of teachers), unusual but innocuous social behaviour and so on.[51]

Unless one does not reduce the idea of a democratic way of life to a merely educational project, its political dimensions show both in participation and dispute (agonal dimension) and in the aesthetic-expressive sense of democracy as a 'theatre of passions'.

The critical state of these aspects of the democratic form of life – the agonal and the theatrical[52] – is illustrated by the 'experiences of difference' of those who are alienated from their representatives and the 'system', and at the same time attracted by the rhetoric of authoritarian groups and leaders, because they lack the practice and knowledge of agonal and theatrical democracy.

---

48 Dewey, J. (1927), *The Public and Its Problems* (New York: Holt Publishers).

49 See the Constitution of Bolivia (2009): 'The State adopts and promotes the following as ethical, moral principles of the plural society: *ama qhilla, ama llulla, ama suwa* (do not be lazy, do not be a liar or a thief), *suma qamaña* (live well), *ñandereko* (live harmoniously), *teko kavi* (good life), *ivi maraei* (land without evil) and *qhapaj ñan* (noble path or life).'

50 Dewey, J. (2018), *Democracy and Education* (Gorham: Myers Education Press).

51 Bourdieu, P. (1986), 'The Forms of Capital', in: Richardson, G. (ed), *Handbook of Theory and Research for the Sociology and Education* (New York: Greenwood Press), 241 ff; Frankenberg, G. (2002), 'Tocqueville's Question: The Role of a Constitution in the Process of Integration', in: 13 *Ratio Juris*, 1 ff.

52 These terms are borrowed from Hannah Arendt's political philosophy (see Seyla Benhabib (1993), 'Feminist Theory and Hannah Arendt's Concept of the Public Space', in: 6 *History of the Human Sciences*, 97 ff) and Cornelia Vismann's study: (2011), *Medien der Rechtsprechung* (Frankfurt am Main: Fischer).

The *agonal* aspect refers to the democratic promise to settle disputes publicly, in competition and according to the same rules for all. In order to prevent social conflicts from 'running wild', agonal democracy should provide public arenas and forums, but also institutions and procedures, through which the controversies of those affected can be resolved directly as political issues or mediated by elected representatives. Parliamentary systems use representation to 'shift' conflicts and controversies: to postpone them, to relocate them, to hand them over to competent bodies and thus discipline them, but also to normalize and alienate them.[53] Collective conflicts are shifted from the street, the workplace, the family or the school to the representative bodies, where they are discussed and binding decisions are finally made accordingly. (Individual cases that are not easily negotiable are processed by the judicial system.)

This strategy – democracy as remote control – has its price, which is paid out when those who should be represented in the debates of the representative bodies (eg, parliaments, senates, local councils) feel that their concerns and needs, interests and projects are no longer recognized. This is always the case when representative bodies do not deal with matters of importance, of general interest, but only of routine. Controversies of general interest at present include migration, climate change, the consequences of globalization and questions of redistribution. These findings are sobering, though. There is little empirical evidence to suggest that parliaments enjoy special trust or are considered capable of leadership in solving current social problems. This may also be due to the practice of outsourcing central issues from the institutionalized political process to the back rooms of parliaments and ministries, to committees, advisory councils and expert commissions, where they are worked on by lobby organizations or transnationally composed bodies. Anything but agonal is a political rhetoric that continually claims there are no alternatives to the solutions that are proposed or the measures that are taken, such as the bank rescue programme during the euro crisis in 2008–09, or the decrees and resolutions to contain and control the coronavirus pandemic.

It is therefore unsurprising that civic democracy initiatives – such as *Indignados* and *Democracia Real Ya!* or *Podemos* in Spain – have emerged to protest against austerity policies and increasing unemployment. In the name of the 'authentic' people and 'real' democracy and representation, radically nationalist organizations brought charges in Europe and elsewhere against the established democratic 'system' and its privileged elites. The promise of an alternative to the system and simple solutions is still gaining ground. This shows that democracy is undermined when people no longer believe that the

---

53 In detail on the normalization of conflicts: Frankenberg, G. (2016), *Comparative Law as Critique* (Cheltenham: Edward Elgar Publishing), Chapter 6.

official channels are open to them and that elections make a difference in their lives, and therefore do not see any way to influence politics; when a mood of pessimism has spread across the party spectrum; and when false prophets set out to preach a doctrine of aggressive intolerance.[54]

3.4 Expressive Democracy

The theatrical aspect also refers to the democratic 'theatre of passions'.[55] Here, the aesthetic-expressive sense of democracy unfolds in a 'dramaturgy of the visual'.[56] The script reduces the complexity of the political in order to achieve an effect of mobilization. According to the logic of what can be represented, the abovementioned topics and problems are brought up in a vivid way, moved on to the political stage and placed in the perception horizon of the political audience.[57] By the same token, the 'theatre of passions' makes controversies visible and comprehensible. However, the democratic script suffers when the political class runs out of ideas (although not of words) and is unable to translate the concerns of the population into the language of politics.[58]

Apart from the linguistic aspect, in order to be recognized as a 'theatre of passions', democracy requires adequate representation. Anyone who argues that democracy is suffering from the 'embarrassing weakness' of not having a 'concise aesthetic representation'[59] will conclude that a democratic theatre is impossible. This argument is not particularly convincing in view of the many examples of productive democratic imagination: the orchestration of presidential inaugurations; the spectacles at 'roundtables' and displays of unity through the choreography of parliamentary seating arrangements or 'democratic' architecture.[60] Democracy happens not only through the medium of discussion and

---

[54] Löwenthal, L. (2015), *False Prophets: Studies on Authoritarianism* (Milton Park: Taylor & Francis).

[55] Bossuet, J.B. (1999), *Politics Drawn From the Very Holy Scriptures* (Cambridge: Cambridge University Press).

[56] See Vorländer, H. (2003), '*Demokratie und Ästhetik. Zur Rehabilitierung eines problematischen Zusammenhangs*', in: *id* (ed), *Zur Ästhetik der Demokratie. Die Formen der politischen Selbstdarstellung* (Stuttgart: DVA), 11 ff./26.

[57] Vorländer (n 56).

[58] This is how I read Furedi's 'politics is lost for words', in: Furedi, F. (2005), *Politics of Fear* (New York/London: Continuum), 5; see also Vismann (n 52), 72 ff.

[59] Similarly Grasskamp, W. (1992), *Die unästhetische Demokratie: Kunst in der Marktgesellschaf* (Munich: C.H. Beck, 7 and 9).

[60] For example, the Westminster model, the Bourbon style or the dome of the German *Reichstag*. See Frankenberg, G. (2014), *Political Technology and the Erosion of the Rule of Law. Normalizing the State of Exception* (Cheltenham: Edward Elgar Publishing), Chapter 2; Geertz, C. (1985), 'Centers, Kings, and Charisma: Reflections on the Symbolics of Power', in: Wilentz, S. (ed), *Rites of Power. Symbolism, Ritual,*

deliberation as a cognitive and mental matter, but also as a performance and representation on the political stage. The question is whether these productions of politics are adequate, capture and channel the 'passions of the street', and give emotions a democratically appropriate venue and role.[61]

Enlightenment and liberalism have always placed an emphasis on controlling emotions. Their distance from the 'passions of the street' is probably due both to the rationalist premises of the Enlightenment project, which moved in the medium of the law, and to historical experience with political authoritarianism, which tapped into the irrational. Accordingly, liberal-democratic constitutionalism focuses on the sublimation (and suppression) of feelings. It guarantees political communication in the 'marketplace of ideas'; provides for party competition and elections; and, above all, establishes the sober script of law-rule that claims to keep its distance from the prejudices and emotions of everyday life.

This political practice and behavioural theory of coolness,[62] combined with liberal ideas of private, rational, market-oriented happiness in politics, has always found it difficult to tap the motivational resources of the citizenry. Adding patriotic feelings and virtues, as republicanism suggests,[63] does not really unlock the control of emotions, because here too democracy is not turned into a theatre of passions. Emotions are not released, but are rather purified in the cooling pond of virtues and brought down to the temperature of state-compatible patriotism. Admittedly, insofar as it is possible to win over the citizens to identify themselves as constitutional patriots[64] with the basic values, institutions and procedures of the republican constitution, the democratic Passion Play may very well remain closed – especially in socially calm situations.

---

and Politics since the Middle Ages (Philadelphia: University of Pennsylvania), 29; Manow, P. (2010), *In the King's Shadow* (Cambridge: Polity).

[61] Regarding the role of emotions in politics: Hirschman, A.O. (2013), *The Passions and the Interests* (Princeton: Princeton University Press); Heidenreich, F. and Schaal, G.S. (eds) (2012), *Politische Theorie und Emotionen* (Baden-Baden: Nomos).

[62] See Lethen, H. (1994), *Verhaltenslehren der Kälte – Lebensversuche zwischen den Kriegen* (Frankfurt am Main: Suhrkamp).

[63] Pocock, J.G.A. (1985), *Virtue, Commerce and History: Essays on Political Thought and History Chiefly in the Eighteenth Century* (Cambridge: Cambridge University Press); Rödel, U. *et al* (1989), *Die demokratische Frage* (Frankfurt am Main: Suhrkamp); Frankenberg, G. (1997), *Die Verfassung der Republik* (Frankfurt am Main: Suhrkamp), 208 ff.

[64] Habermas, J. (1996), *Between* Facts and Norms*: Contributions to a Discourse Theory of Law and Democracy* (Cambridge: MIT Press)); *id.* (1998), *The Inclusion of the Other: Studies in Political Theory* (Cambridge: MIT Press, 1998); Müller, J.W. (2007), *Constitutional Patriotism* (Princeton: Princeton University Press).

In times of crisis, however, the *triad* of republic, democracy and law-rule, girded by sedate liberal constitutionalism, leaves to its authoritarian opponents a domain in which politically explosive issues and emotionally charged topics are discussed and heated ideological battles are fought. What could have been achieved out of a passion for democracy or a democratic passion is yielded, after the liberals have capitulated, to those who mobilize prejudices against strangers and minorities; who unleash – under the guise of civic concern – resentment and discontent, reducing social problems to hate slogans.[65] Euro-crisis, refugees, Dieselgate, precarious working conditions, climate change: whatever the issue, indignation invariably takes the lead – if at all possible, combined with a hatred of elites and outsiders. Instead of passionately seeking democratic confrontation, this free-standing hatred – alienated from constitutional democracy as both a form of government and a form of life – pervades all topics: social disintegration (exclusion), political alienation (disenchantment with politics), loss of economic control (globalization), capitalist land grabs. It is justified with the help of dichotomous world views, fuelled by apocalyptic visions of a nation's downfall. This hatred is channelled by authoritarian demagogues, movements and parties that call on their followers to avert danger; to defend 'us' against 'them' – 'the foreigners':

> We have to close the borders and then endure the cruel images. We cannot allow ourselves to be blackmailed by the eyes of children.[66]

> It is becoming more and more obvious that the Radical Democrats are a Party of open borders and crime. They want nothing to do with the major Humanitarian Crisis on our Southern Border. #2020![67]

> The Syrian who comes to us, he still has his Syria. The Afghan who comes to us still has his Afghanistan. And the Senegalese who comes to us still has his Senegal. When we have lost our Germany, we have no home anymore! [68]

---

[65] Theodor W. Adorno refers to them as merchants of hatred ('*Hassverkäufer*'): 'Die Freudsche Theorie und die Struktur faschistischer Propaganda', in: 24 *Psyche. Zeitschrift für die Psychoanalyse,* (1970), 486 ff/487. See also, regarding the current propaganda: Levitsky and Ziblatt (n 33).

[66] Then vice-chairman of the *Alternative für Deutschland* (AfD) party and member of the Federal Diet, Alexander Gauland commenting on Germany's refugee policy, in: *ZEIT online,* 24 February 2016.

[67] @realDonaldTrump, 18 January 2019.

[68] Nationalist-extremist Björn Höcke (AfD), quoted by *Abendzeitung,* 4 June 2016, www.abendzeitung-muenchen.de/inhalt.lumpenproletariat-quotenneger-schiessbefehl-so-fremdenfeindlich-it-die-afd-eine-zitatesammlung.7608283f-6291-44bf-b4f0-16033928e83c.html/ (last accessed 18 November 2018).

Should this agreement [by the Christian-Democrats regarding transit centres for refugees] become the German government position, we will be forced to take action to avert disadvantages for Austria and its population.[69]

4. AUTHORITARIAN CONSTITUTIONALISM AND FORMS OF PARTICIPATION

While representative democracy operates in the mode of remote control, with the self-governing people absent – or at any rate, kept at a distance – authoritarian regimes build a network of direct and indirect controls; establish early warning systems to register moods and protests as promptly as possible and, if necessary, close them down; and co-opt opposition movements and parties or eliminate them repressively. These controls include peculiar forms of participation that do not endanger authoritarianism.

4.1 Petitions, Consultations, Elections

In the history of authoritarian constitutionalism, submissions and petitions have a long tradition that reaches far back into the pre-modern era. In imperial China, complaints (not bound to any specific form) were submitted to the emperor by the people 'humbly', and by the authorities 'respectfully'. In contrast, the *Cahiers de Doléances*,[70] in which the French population recorded their complaints, were initially addressed to the deputies as binding orders to act and were ultimately consigned to the king.[71] For the monarch, these *cahiers* had the inestimable advantage of registering at an early stage emerging moods and problems in the country.

Submissions and petitions fit seamlessly into a hierarchical governmental and administrative structure. Unlike, for example, a formal objection or administrative court procedure, they do not evoke a conflict of state and citizen interests. As they do not call into question the 'concurrence' (if not identity) of interests between state and citizens – the basic principle of a socialist society

---

69 Austrian Chancellor Kurz, quoted by *Die Welt*, 3 July 2018.

70 A practice that dates back to the fourteenth century; Grateau, P. (2001) *Les Cahiers de doléances: une relecture culturelle* (Rennes: Presses Universitaires).

71 When the king of France called for the election of deputies for the General Estates on 24 January 1789, he also called on his subjects to instruct these deputies as to what tasks they should perform in order to overcome the social and economic problems. The deputies thus had a kind of imperative mandate. In theory, therefore, there was a complaints booklet for each constituency. About 60 000 of them remained. Their importance to the French Revolution is controversial. For a detailed analysis, see Thamer, H.U. (2004), *Die Französische Revolution* (Munich: C.H. Beck).

– submissions (despite their imperial past) were also extremely popular in socialist states as a form of self-monitoring, reminiscent of the royal court, and a filter to pick up signals of popular discontent – albeit limited to a constructive right of appeal for the 'consolidation of revolutionary legality' or the construction of socialism:[72]

> Every citizen of the USSR has the right to submit proposals to state bodies and public organizations for improving their activity, and to criticize shortcomings in their work.
>
> Officials are obliged, within established time-limits, to examine citizens' proposals and requests, to reply to them, and to take appropriate action.
>
> Persecution for criticism is prohibited. Persons guilty of such persecution shall be called to account.[73]

Reflecting a certain sense of the involuntary irony of autocracies, in the German Democratic Republic, applications to marry were also registered as petitions, so that registry offices were not 'disadvantaged' in comparison with other authorities when their 'proximity to the citizens' was measured by counting the petitions they received.

The special quality of the petition as an informal legal remedy in autocracies of all kinds is evident in its structural features: deposited in the darkness of official self-control, the petition casually lends itself to constitutional opportunism. Its informality withdraws it from the light of the public and a controlling judiciary. Its individualization allows protest and dissatisfaction to be reduced to a small scale on a case-by-case basis, to prevent possible solidarity effects. In the absence of procedural provisions and intermediate institutions, it also accommodates the cult of immediacy, as will be shown in the next chapter.

Insofar as authoritarian regimes follow a (semi-)representative path – whether out of inevitable consideration for the constitution or out of constitutional opportunism – they make use of national consultations, referenda and even orchestrated elections as a covertly ironic, sometimes cynical imitation of representative democratic procedures. On the one hand, these act as warning mechanisms designed to detect and eradicate any clusters of oppositional

---

72 For example, '1. The citizen has the right to participate in the administration of the State and management of society, and to participate in the discussion and recommendation to the state organs on the issues of the community, the region, and the country. 2. The State shall create conditions for the citizen to participate in the administration of the State and management of society; the receipt and response to citizen's opinion and recommendation shall be public and transparent' (Article 28 of the 2013 Constitution of Vietnam); similarly, Article 63 of the 2002 Constitution of Cuba.

73 Article 49 of the 1977 Constitution of the Soviet Union.

thinking; on the other hand, they function as valves to deflate the pressure of conflict and thus help pacify society.

Miscalculation or narcissism – neither harmless – may persuade despots not only to manipulatively stimulate popular sentiment, but also to hear the public's unadulterated voice every once in a while. To this end, they loosen the tight, top-down control of participation and its manipulated results, and engage in referenda or competitive elections. The paradoxical desire to hear the *vox populi* can sometimes bring down autocracies and redirect authoritarian constitutionalism, however. The classic example of such a miscalculation was the convocation of the General Estates in France in October 1789, which marked the beginning of the end of the French monarchy.[74] Like his predecessors, Louis XVI had governed in absolutist style without consulting the Estates. However, he convened the representatives of the clergy, nobility and bourgeoisie in order to make them his accomplices, as it were – to help legitimize the imposition of new taxes in the face of the threat of national bankruptcy. He had wanted to include the Estates in the political decision-making process only formally. However, this inclusion became quite substantive when the Third Estate constituted itself with its historical oath as the National Assembly. In fact, the pre-constitutional absolutism of the old kind was thus buried. In 1791, the constitutional consequence followed: the king had to reluctantly squeeze himself into the all-too narrow framework of a constitutional monarchy.

Two centuries later, Chilean head of state Auguste Pinochet also learned the hard lesson – rare among dictators – that it is dangerous to take the basic democratic risk of losing. In accordance with the 1980 Constitution, a referendum was held in October 1988 as to whether Pinochet should once again be the only candidate in the 1989 presidential elections. Some 56 per cent of the voters said 'no', thus denying Pinochet a further extension of his term of office. This led to reasonably free elections a year later. The result of the 1988 referendum, which Pinochet had originally coordinated to confirm and legitimize his power, rather surprised the members of the junta and especially the dictator himself. It ended 16 years of brutal dictatorship and forced the despot to withdraw to the enclaves of autocratic rule: in accordance with the 1980 Constitution, Pinochet remained commander-in-chief of the army and senator for life, and could thus take refuge under the constitutional cloak of immunity.[75]

---

[74] This was a rare event; the last time it had previously taken place in a similar form was in 1614. See Furet, F. and Richet, D. (1999), *La Révolution française* (Paris: Hachette).

[75] *Instituto Nacional Democrata para Asuntos Internacionales* (1989), *La Transición Chilena Hacía la Democratica*, Washington, DC; Tagle, M.D. (ed) (1995), *Diálogos de Justicia y Democracia. N°1: El Plebiscito del 5 de octubre de 1988*

4.2 Attunement and Desublimated Ecstasy

Such democratic accidents are anything but common in autocracies. Participation in authoritarian constitutionalism aims – as far as possible and within the constitutional framework – at acclamation and acquiescence of the followers to the ruler, not at actual elections with an open outcome. Consequently, even elections – insofar as party or candidate competition can be restricted or excluded altogether – have the character of referendums or national consultations with a predisposed outcome. Autocratic regimes tend to produce feelings and moods, rather than counting votes. Authoritarianism is about performance and consent, not risky events of elective action. It assumes unity and proprietorship of the state, as was discussed before (Chapter 5). Consequently, it is neither fair nor constitutional in the strict sense, but quite logical, that the Hungarian government's campaign advertising and anti-Soros campaign were financed from the state budget.[76]

By definition, attuning the people is primarily a matter of governments and movements that claim to be close to the people (and that usually come with an authoritarian-nationalist agenda). In the beginning, they may promote participation and mobilize the population to their agenda. Their appeal to the people and their (presumed) will strengthen the relationship between charismatic leader and mobilized followers.[77] Early Peron in Argentina and early Chávez in Venezuela banked on their potentially democratic valence. Later, their politics illustrated the ambivalence of participation and the turn towards authoritarianism, unfortunately labelled 'populist'. While these governments and movements initially mobilize a programme of comprehensive and sustainable political participation, along with a social agenda, they eventually make a U-turn towards autocracy.[78]

As soon as participation becomes an illusion, the followers of such regimes eventually regress to a state of 'desublimated ecstasy'.[79] Mobilizing regimes and movements that promote participation must therefore be carefully observed in their evolution. The question is whether and when they switch from mobi-

---

(Santiago de Chile: Corporación Justicia y Democracia). Very illuminating: the movie about the referendum in Chile directed by Pablo Larraín, *No*, Chile, 2012.

[76] Quoted by *The Guardian,* 9 April 2018, www.theguardian.com/world/2018/apr/09/hungary-election-osce-monitors-deliver-damning-verdict/ (last accessed 19 January 2019).

[77] See Vorländer, H. (2011), 'The good, the bad, and the ugly', in: 8 SSOAR, 187 ff.

[78] Rein, R. (2012), 'From Juan Perón to Hugo Chávez and Back: Populism Reconsidered', in: Sznajder, M. *et al* (eds), *Shifting Frontiers of Citizenship: The Latin American Experience* (Boston: Brill), 289 ff.

[79] I borrow the term from Adorno, (n 65).

lization and emancipation to the establishment of a boundary between those who act and those who may only look on and applaud; whether and when a democratic awakening mutates into 'abolition of democracy through mass support against the democratic principle'.[80]

Experience shows that it is difficult to preserve the character of a movement once it has entered government, taken it over and, in particular, consolidated it into a regime. An initially democratic participatory strategy evolves into pure authoritarianism when the energies for activation are exhausted, political considerations for coalition (or trade) partners demand pragmatism or mobilized forces get out of hand and endanger the stability of the regime. In Peronist Argentina, the ecstasy and mobilization had already begun to end during Peron's first presidency (1946–58), as a result of his autocratic style of leadership; this was subsequently exacerbated by a political programme that pitted political rights – including the freedoms of political participation – against social rights. The last remaining democratic traces were finally demolished with brute force by the military junta (1976–83), which banned the Peronist party (*Partido Justicialista*), persecuted its functionaries and prohibited Peronist trade unions and grassroots organizations.

Not at all identical, but nevertheless comparable, was the evolution of Chávism in Venezuela: – the movement, which was initially democratic in style, became increasingly authoritarian over time. During Hugo Chávez's rise to power and his struggle against 'counter-revolutionary oligarchies' – by which he meant the anti-Christian majority in Parliament – the participation rate fell considerably; while at the same time, careful control of citizen participation and disempowerment of the judiciary, especially the Constitutional Court, intensified. From the outset, his successor, Nicholas Maduro – who was much less interested in mobilizing any group other than his followers – took at best selectively 'proactive' paths. The demobilization of the Venezuelan population has come at a high price, if recent reports of the UN Commission on Human Rights are to be believed: since 2016, some 18 000 'extra-judicial killings' in instances of alleged 'resistance to authority' were attributed to special actions forces set up by the Maduro regime.[81] Despite significant differences between Peronism and Chávism, in both cases participation morphed from democratic action and voting to (an increasingly failed) attunement of the population to the political leaders and their agendas.

---

80 *Ibid*, 486.

81 'U.N. Report Reveals "Shockingly High" Number of Extrajudicial Killings in Venezuela', in: *National Public Radio,* 5 July 2019, www.npr.org/2019/07/05/739051958/u-n-report-reveals-shockingly-high-number-of-extrajudicial-killings-in-venezuela/ (last accessed 10 March 2020).

In Nicaragua, former revolutionary hero and current despot President Daniel Ortega steered the country into another civil war against the majority of the population. In 2019, he had demonstrations bloodily suppressed in a move which saw more than 300 dead killed and more than 2000 injured.[82] From the opposite starting point – that is, a government that was neither revolutionary nor particularly geared towards participation, but simply liberal-conservative – Viktor Orbán's regime increasingly utilized the understanding and practice of political participation as a way to attune the Hungarian population to his nationalist, xenophobic agenda. Once he had secured a position of power, Orbán – co-founder and chairman of the *Fidesz* party (Hungarian Civic Association) and originally also vice president of Liberal International – pushed through his conservative anti-European platform, which extends deep into the extreme right. He won the 2010 elections and was re-elected in 2014. His rhetoric culminated in incendiary statements suggesting that Hungary is 'under siege' (from refugees) and migration is the 'Trojan horse of terrorism'.[83] Orbán mutated from a Parliament-elected, initially rather inconspicuous prime minister to an autocratic, radical nationalist. He could not avoid elections at the cost of openly breaching the constitution, but minimized the risks of such elections through rigorous control of the media and political intimidation of opposition members.[84]

5. PARTICIPATION AS COMPLICITY

In authoritarian regimes, I argue, popular participation is designed to provide legitimacy and to win accomplices for the regime. This argument mediates between the contrary positions either that the political voice and agency of the population are meaningless, irrelevant to the system or even considered dangerous and therefore discouraged and suppressed; or alternatively that authoritarian regimes are very much dependent on the active involvement of their citizens. Complicity here refers exclusively to forms of political engage-

---

[82] Vilchéz, D. (2019), 'One Year After Revolt Ortega Continues to Oppress Nicaraguans', in: *The Washington Post*, 18 April, www.washingtonpost.com/opinions/2019/04/17/one-year-after-revolt-ortega-continues-oppress-nicaraguans (last accessed 9 March 2020).

[83] Brunsden, J. (2017), 'European Refugee Policy is "Trojan Horse of terrorism"', in: *Financial Times*, 30 March.

[84] Ariès, Q. (2019), 'Europe's Failure to Protect Liberty in Hungary', in: *The Atlantic*, 29 December.

ment, and does not exclude other factors that are meant to stabilize autocratic systems, such as repression, patronage[85] and distributive measures.

5.1 Complicity as Public Presence and Support

Political complicity neither implies a strategic alliance with or active support (ideological, financial or other) of an autocracy, nor resembles the deliberate collaboration of perpetrators who jointly commit a crime. In contrast, *political accomplices* are *implicated* rather than *involved.* They are not sufficiently informed; nor do they play a role in the planning of politics. They get *entangled*[86] in the schemes and practices of an autocracy that wants them to be supportive and publicly attest to this support (see Figure 6.2) by attending parades, marches and rallies, and backing the regime. Accomplices demonstrate enthusiasm and cowardice, conjoined in the act of acclamation. The well-trained accomplice has learned to suppress shame about the infamy of a regime and its politics, such as the imprisonment of opposition members, the persecution and expulsion of minorities, censorship and war of aggression; and performs as *claqueur*, watchdog or informer.

When Propaganda Minister Joseph Goebbels asked those present at the Berlin Palace of Sports, 'Do you want total war?', he may have had all sorts of things in mind; but certainly not to engage anyone there – let alone the population at large – as consultants or decision-makers in the forthcoming war. When Turkish President Erdoğan, North Korean head of state Kim Jong-un and other autocrats and despots call or order their followers to join in mass marches, parades and other major events organized by the government, they do not mean to inform those people about or discuss the guidelines of their political agendas. Similarly, Viktor Orbán and his government have not set up national consultations to invite Hungarians to share their opinions and thereby influence decisions. These leaders rather appeal to their national constituency solely for public endorsement. To the same end, Bonapartists and their copycats of today organize referendums to attune the population and ascertain popular loyalty. Despite their acclamation and ovations, accomplices have no voice.

Quite differently from organizing crime, political complicity is secured in the full light of the (unreasonable) public. The necessary condition for people to become political accomplices is presence rather than representation; symbolic cooperation rather than instrumental involvement. The relationship of

---

[85] See Slater, D. (2010), *Ordering Power: Contentious Politics and Authoritarian Leviathans in Southeast Asia* (New York: Cambridge University Press).

[86] The concept of entanglement (*Verstrickung*) is reminiscent of Niklas Luhmann's theory of legitimation through procedure; *id* (1969), *Legitimation durch Verfahren* (Frankfurt am Main: Suhrkamp).

Source: © Bundesarchiv, Bild 183-C06292/Photo: Schwahn, Ernst. With friendly permission.

Figure 6.2 *Adolf Hitler enters the Olympic Stadium for the May Day celebrations in 1937*

complicity can be established only if the leader and the followers are present in the public space: directly at mass events such as military parades or national party congresses (eg, *Reichsparteitage*), or indirectly through media such as Twitter today or the *Volksempfänger* ('people's receiver') in Nazi Germany; through referendums or (arranged) consultations;[87] or through events such as China's National People's Congress, whose almost 3000 members – representing the Central Committee of the Communist Party of China – function as atypical accomplices when they meet once a year in Beijing (Article 61 of the 1982 Constitution) to approve the decisions of the leadership.

[87] This means that inclusiveness, fair competition and effectiveness are not guaranteed. See Merkel, W. *et al* (2003), *Defekte Demokratie* (Opladen: Leske & Budrich), 77. Magaloni, B. (2006), *Voting for Autocracy. Hegemonic Party Survival and its Demise in Mexico* (New York: Cambridge University Press), shows that hegemonic parties and regimes can quite successfully 'buy' elections.

5.2 Accomplices as Inactive Partners

Bereft of any actual power to shape the common affairs of society, the accomplice provides what authoritarian leaders need most: loyalty and conformity.[88] Across almost all regimes, leaders, cliques, clans and cadres have an insatiable desire to be supported, acclaimed or at least tolerated by the people (without audible protest). Accomplices are the silent shareholders or – better yet – the inactive partners of the regime.

In the long run, encouraging conformity usually comes cheaper than repression. It is therefore strategically astute and helps to boost the regime's legitimacy to entrap people as accomplices in government, and if necessary, to make them morally liable at a later hour of reckoning.[89] The advantage of this strategy, which varies from context to context, is obvious: despite the asymmetrical relationship between the population and the leadership, the accomplices cannot easily distance themselves from the policies and practices of the regime. Once co-opted, accomplices can hardly claim ignorance or resistance afterwards.

Complicity presupposes a political agenda, a plan of action, about which accomplices must be informed (however vaguely) in order to win their loyalty. All that is needed are general, catchy slogans, such as 'Good days are coming'; 'Total war'; 'Socialism or death'; 'Make America great again'; 'Never return to capitalism'; 'One people, one empire, one leader'; or 'One China'.[90] Especially popular and effective is the propaganda of fear: the demonization of enemies, organized crime, traitors, renegades, terrorists, Jews and Muslims, as well as campaigns against 'evil elites' or 'unwanted minorities', financial capital and more. Autocratic governments and movements see themselves as authorized by the people to defend the nation, the country, the people against external or internal threats.[91] In consequence, situations of (imagined) danger generate extraordinary powers that tend to dwarf the constitution: 'The well-being of the people is above the law' (Poland's Catholic-nationalist party PiS) or 'common good comes before self' (Adolf Hitler).

---

[88] See the research project 'Critical Junctures and the Survival of Dictatorship', pursued at the *Wissenschaftszentrum Berlin* by Wolfgang Merkel, Christoph Stefes, Alexander Schmotz, Dag Tanneberg and Johannes Gerschewski.

[89] This assumption cannot rely on evidence or plausibility, but must be empirically validated. See Art, D. (2012), 'What Do We Know About Authoritarianism After Ten Years?', in: *Comparative Politics*, 351 ff.

[90] See the preambles of the constitutions of authoritarian regimes, such as the People's Republic of China 1982; Cuba 2019.

[91] For an analysis of Viktor Orbán's rhetoric: Ozsváth, S. (2017), *Puszta-Populismus. Viktor Orbán – ein europäischer Störfall?* (Ulm: Danube Books).

To sum up: in the context of authoritarian constitutionalism, complicity is characterized by the fact that leaders or leadership cadres set the collective agenda, while their followers demonstrate their loyalty through presence and acclamation, and participation in constitutional rituals or quasi-constitutional events – such as the solemn 'swearing-in' of the supporters in lieu of President Chávez, who was absent due to illness. Complicity can also be confirmed by symbolic acts, such as offering the official Nazi salute ('*Hitlergruß*'),[92] reading Mao's *Red Book* or downloading *Xi Jinping Thought* to please the regime. Such demonstrative loyalty and legitimizing acclamation have an unintended secondary consequence: through support and acquiescence, they establish the collective moral responsibility of the accomplices for the regime's macro-crimes and its 'odious debt'. Accomplices assume this responsibility through public presence and compliance or, if you like, through implied passivity.

---

[92] See the fascinating analysis by Allert, T. (2016), *Der deutsche Gruß. Geschichte einer unheilvollen Geste* (Frankfurt am Main: S. Fischer); Buckley, C. (2017) 'China Enshrines "Xi Jinping Thought", Elevating Leader to Mao-Like Status', in: *The New York Times*, 24 October.

7. The cult of immediacy

El pueblo ya sabe de que se trata.[1]

The President… may have direct recourse to the expression of the will of the people… He may appeal directly to the Nation.[2]

1. THE ARGUMENT

Authoritarian leaders and regimes grind down, as far as possible, the distance established by representation and law-rule. They are bent on controlling the agonal dimension of democracy and playing out the theatrical dimension as per their script. They introduce a style of communication that brings politics, their charisma and their propaganda to bear without mediation by institutions and organizations. Their trademark is (phony) direct contact and communication with supporters and the population at large. Of course, this plan will work only if the leaders appear in public;[3] if forms and procedures of communication that are not controlled by the regime can be eliminated; and if their agents and institutions – above all, the media and parties, parliaments and courts – can be neutralized. Only then can the authoritarian theatre play out its repertoire of tragedy and farce. Immediacy prepares the stage for leaders to seduce their audiences to succumb to the authoritarian temptation and renounce their right to determine their own political existence. This script works if the totality of *direct* communications can disperse and condense into the cult of immediacy, which spreads – in word, writing and image – like a toxic fog over organizations, institutions and procedures of representative democracy.

1 'The people know what it's about!' Perón, J. (1973), *Discursos*, Instituto Perón (ed), *Recopilación de discursos del coronel Perón,* Buenos Aires, www.jdperon.gov.ar/1945/10/discursos/ (last accessed 10 March 2020).

2 Articles 8 IV and 84 of the 1989/2016 Algerian Constitution.

3 A counter-example is Algeria's President Bouteflika, who in 2019 was preparing to take up his fifth term of office at the age of 82, even though he had not made a public speech since 2012.

Once immediacy is consolidated and condensed as a cult,[4] disputes are transferred from parliaments and courts to the theatre of the authoritarian, attended by an acclamatory audience. United in complicity,[5] individuals and groups perform as supportive, tax-paying members of an imaginary disempowered community, who have nothing to decide; while their leaders assume the role of omnipotent, supreme communicators and targets of their veneration.[6]

What role do the constitutions of authoritarian regimes play in this setting? Do they function as scripts that are used or abused? Are they ultimately instrumentalized towards a cult of immediacy that encourages and guides the citizen public to enter the magical forum of theatrical action and participate in the national project, whatever that may be – a national uprising, the patriotic defence of the country, the repulsion of foreigners or a country-specific variation of 'America first', such as 'India first', 'Homeland first' or the somewhat foolish 'Austria first'?

2. DEMOCRATIC LAW-RULE AND DISTANCE

Political authoritarianism has a particularly visible impact on the form and practice of government. It has been shown that autocrats make use of certain techniques of governing (or certain instruments of political technology) to accomplish this task. Often, executive-informal action and constitutional opportunism take the lead. Authoritarianism cannot always express itself freely, but must sometimes wrap itself in a cloak of democracy and is sometimes fettered by the law-rule that complements the democratic form of government.

---

4 The term 'cult of immediacy' as it is used here was originally inspired by studies of the cult of the nation in the French Revolution and the *Loi le Chapelier*, which outlawed intermediate organizations in 1791. I came across the concept of the 'cult of immediacy' in 2016 in an essay analysing the influence of the Internet on the political process – Zehnpfennig, B. (2016), '*Der Kult der Unmittelbarkeit*', in: *Frankfurter Allgemeine Zeitung*, 22 October. While working on the German version of *Authoritarianism*, I found Jeffrey Librett's analysis of Trump's communicative style quite illuminating – Librett, J. (2017), 'Sovereignty and the Cult of Immediacy', in: IX *Konturen*, 7 ff. So the concept was already 'in the air' when I picked it up and used it to characterize mainly fascist and democracy-enhancing, nationalist versions of authoritarianism.

5 See Chapter 6, Section 7.

6 See Rancière, J. (2014), *The Emancipated Spectator* (London: Verso), 11 ff. As regards the religious connotations of immediacy: Leppin, V. (2015), *Transformation: Studien zu den Wandlungsprozessen in Theologie und Frömmigkeit zwischen Spätmittelalter und Reformation* (Tübingen: Mohr Siebeck).

The rule of law has been accepted as a distanced form of governing that is intrinsically linked to democracy. It provides governance with the contours of legality. First, decisions become predictable, because they can usually be traced back to a legal authority. Second, decisions are relatively transparent, because they are issued in the context of legal procedures. Third, decision makers can be called to account, because their decisions are subject to judicial (or parliamentary) review. At any rate, that is how things should be. Committed to the principle of legality, the executive should not intervene in the social sphere by personal order or arbitrary individual acts (as the Prince would have had it in the past), but should rather rule with a steady hand – lawfully and proportionately, as they say. To the extent that this practice is firmly established, the constitutional state is characterized by freedom from the fear of arbitrariness. Irrespective of their effectiveness in individual cases, mediating bodies such as representative institutions and the judiciary set up an institutional distance between the state and citizens. The state appears as the imaginary incarnation of the collective conscience of rules and functions ideally as the power to enforce these rules.[7]

Consequently, the autocratic transformation of a relatively stable law-rule/self-rule system must raze these barriers to the exercise of power. As discussed in the previous chapters, this can be done through several moves: by shifting political technology to the domain of the executive, buffered by opportunism and informality; by consigning power from public to private property; and by contriving political participation as complicity. Installing a cult of immediacy bridges the institutional divide between the leadership and its followers. More radically than the complicit co-opting of citizenship, this cult exploits the crisis of representation and repurposes both the democratic form of government and the democratic way of life towards authoritarian ends. The cult of immediacy is based on a double strategy: on the one hand, it eliminates mediating institutions and organizations at the level of experienced democracy; and on the other, it creates the phantasm of lived democracy through communicative shortcuts and the imaginary community of leaders and followers.

3. INAUGURATION OF THE CULT OF IMMEDIACY

Closing distance is the starting point for a variety of styles of political authoritarianism that operate according to the pattern of non-mediated communication – among them a conspicuously large number of regimes that are referred

---

[7] Frankenberg, *Political Technology and the Erosion of the Rule of Law*, Chapters V and VI. *Id*, (1977), 'Angst im Rechtsstaat', in: 10 *Kritische Justiz*, 353 ff.

to as 'fascist' or 'populist'. They aim to bridge the gap between leader and people and take a communicative hold on the 'people' or the 'community' by bypassing intermediary organizations, representative channels and law-rule procedures. This loss of distance becomes apparent once the omnipresence of the leader or regime has been established. Autocrats not only marshal presence and immediacy, but also are often so narcissistic as to revel in this intrusive style of forced conversation, and sufficiently ruthless and powerful to impose their ego-cult on the population.[8] Moreover, they have no qualms in exploiting the institutional and symbolic shortcomings of constitutional democracy, and will not hesitate to abandon the fragile style of constitutional democratic government. In the style of a cult, the leader presents himself as an object of idealization and worship, and at the same time mobilizes – and serves – the desire of his followers for community. In the 'national conversation' between leaders and followers – however monologic and asymmetric it may be – social cohesion is generated which is expressed in phantasms of a national community.

Strategies of immediacy are implemented through the fantasy of one-to-one connection – a 'direct line' – between leadership and followers, government and governed. This can work only if such a fantasy can be created, condensed into a cult and thus consolidated, however illusory it may be. Insofar as the imagination of such a connection can be created, it can trigger the citizenry's temptation to yield to the authoritarian. The perils are inadequately described through concepts such as charisma and demagogy, which do not capture the side-effects of the phantasm of a quasi-intimate relationship whose exclusivity calls for the exclusion of those who do not belong and submission to whatever violence the idolized autocrat may deem necessary.

3.1 Neutralizing Intermediary Organizations

In order to stop or control the risky free flow of public communication about controversial life plans, interests and demands, authoritarian regimes can take two pre-emptive tactical approaches: on the social side, as far as possible, the destruction or disempowerment of intermediate organizations and bodies – especially competing parties, unions, other associations and the media; and on the state side, the elimination or circumvention of the institutions and procedures mediating between the executive and the population – in particular, parliaments, other representative bodies and courts. Both tactics work to the detriment of constitutions, which usually enshrine these institutional,

---

8 See Stanley, J. (2017), *How Propaganda Works* (Princeton: Princeton University Press); and Dikötter, F. (2019), *How To Be A Dictator: The Cult of Personality in the Twentieth Century* (London: Bloomsbury).

procedural and functional mediations and open up forums of 'intermediate' communication. Traditionally, print and visual media have served as a conduit between the population and the government, among other tasks. For some time now, however, they have been supplemented and partly replaced by the Internet and social media. Autocrats who address 'their' population in direct 'conversation' are seldom interested in any kind of mediation in a non-state-regulated public sphere, because it tends to result in a loss of control and may erode the sense of intimacy between leader and followers.

In contrast, social media – especially Facebook, Instagram and Twitter – are particularly suited to creating the illusion of spontaneous closeness and urgency in the public sphere of cyberspace through 'digital demagogy'.[9] They bypass the traditional mediating instances and levels and extend the political theatre straight into our living rooms. And unlike traditional media, in the social media age they can reach us 24/7 via our constant companions from Apple, Samsung and so on. A few extracts from Donald Trump's Twitter feed[10] on the November 2018 elections are instructive in this regard:

> Just landed - will see everyone in Southport, Indiana shortly!
>
> Heading to Montana and Florida today! Everyone is excited about the Job Numbers - 250,000 new jobs in October. Also, wages rising. Wow!
>
> Scott Perry of Pennsylvania is fantastic. He is strong on the Border, Crime, the Military, our Vets and the Second Amendment. Scott has my Total Endorsement!
>
> [5.959 Answers, 14.445 Retweets, 58.809 Likes.]

As a rule, constitutions require that government – especially with regard to guarantees of political communication – not arbitrarily adopt a kind of *Loi le Chapelier*:[11] a law which, following the French model of 1791, prohibits any mediation by the media and intermediary organizations that could come between the individual and the nation/state, and punishes it as insurrection or high treason. The law introduced by Le Chapelier forbade masters, journeymen and workers to organize themselves in federations (coalitions). It confirmed the abolition of the guilds. Petitions drafted in the name of a profession and meetings held to fix wages were considered illegal. Accordingly, agreements to strike were also illegal and striking workers were prosecuted.

---

9 Fuchs, C. (2018), *Digital Demagogue: Authoritarian Capitalism in the Age of Trump and Twitter* (London: Pluto).

10 Jeffrey Librett illustrates the cult of immediacy using the style of communication of Donald Trump: Librett (n 4), 1.

11 See Jaurès, J. (1927), '*La Loi Chapelier*', in: *id*, *Histoire socialiste de la Révolution française*. II (Paris: Éditions de la Librairie de l'Humanité), 260–87.

The political logic of the *Loi le Chapelier* was to facilitate a non-mediated relationship between the French nation and its citizens, thus supporting the cult of the nation.

Quite a few autocratic constitutions, however, do not guarantee the freedoms of opinion, the press and information *per se* ('not subject to any limitation whatsoever'). Rather, they assign a purpose to these freedoms, such as serving the goals of socialist societies; or link them to a duty; or limit them by one or another public interest[12] – for example, 'national principles' or state religion;[13] or exclude certain topics and practices from rights protection.[14] Such restrictions on the freedom to communicate and demonstrate publicly make it easier for autocracies to mask themselves constitutionally and legitimize interventions to curb protests, as is shown by the following examples:

> *In accordance with the interests of the people* and *for the consolidation and development of the socialist order*, the citizens of the USSR are guaranteed freedom of speech, freedom of the press, freedom of assembly and demonstration, freedom to hold street parades and demonstrations.[15]
>
> Freedom of expression in publications and the press is guaranteed unless the foundations of Islam and the rights of the public are compromised.[16]

In this way, constitutions allow authoritarian regimes to engage in an extensive repertoire of harassment, intimidation and repression, and lower the threshold for measures such as censoring or banning the media, 'shutting down' and monitoring the Internet or – as has happened in Iran, North Korea and China – temporarily turning it into an intranet. In any case, media control and censor-

---

[12] 'No one shall exercise these rights to infringe upon the honor of others, or to affect the good customs of society, public order and national security.' Article 41 of the 2008 Constitution of Cambodia. Similarly, Article 24 of the 2004 Constitution of Afghanistan.

[13] Article 23 of the 2017 Constitution of Bahrain 2017 states: 'provided that the constitution and fundamental beliefs of Islamic doctrine are not infringed, the unity of the people is not prejudiced, and discord or sectarianism is not aroused.' National principles are registered in Article 50 of the 2016 Constitution of Algeria.

[14] 'Any form of religious fundamentalism [*intégrisme*] and intolerance is prohibited' – Article 10 of the 2016 Constitution of the Central-African Republic. 'Propaganda of or agitation for the forcible change of the constitutional system, violation of the integrity of the Republic, undermining of state security, and advocating war, social, racial, national, religious, class and clannish superiority as well as the cult of cruelty and violence shall not be allowed' – Article 20(3) of the 2017 Constitution of Kazakhstan.

[15] Article 50 of the 1977 Soviet Constitution – emphasis added.

[16] Article 24 of the 1979 Constitution of the Islamic Republic of Iran – emphasis added.

ship can be enforced more easily and above all more discreetly in the interests of the respective government.

3.2 Controlling the Media and the Internet

If regimes do not wish to violate the constitution too obviously, they must either use restrictions of this kind or take other paths, such as shutting down or deactivating the media and the Internet, intimidating their providers or nationalizing them altogether, so that information and communication technology – and even the Internet, depending on the situation – can function as an instrument of repression or 'reform', or at least of stabilizing power.[17] Where the constitutional situation is an obstacle to repressive media laws and censorship, or where the necessary political majorities are not at hand, autocrats who must rely on constitutional masquerade can still try to undermine the media through defamation ('lying press') or mockery ('fake news').

The media policy of the Orbán government in Hungary illustrates how television, radio and newspapers in the state have been gradually disempowered. Unimpressed by criticism from other EU member states and the European Commission, or by protests in the country, the regime relied on its two-thirds majority to push through a law in 2010 which, among other things, established the National Media and News Agency (NMHH) to monitor the media.[18] In the following years, the government effectively came to control a large part of the media and the advertising market; ordered the dismissal of journalists who were critical of the government and the closure of critical newspapers; sanctioned opposition media with warnings and fines; and censored press products and broadcasts. For this reason, a majority of the European Parliament voted in favour of initiating constitutional proceedings against Hungary under Article 7 of the Treaty on European Union for violation of democratic principles and the rule of law. It is now up to the European Council to determine the risk

---

[17] See Mughan, A. and Gunther, R. (2000), 'The Media in Democratic and Nondemocratic Regimes: A Multilevel Perspective', in: *id* (eds), *Democracy and the Media. A Comparative Perspective* (Cambridge: Cambridge University Press,) 1 ff; Rod, E.G. and Weidmann, N.B. (2015), 'Empowering activists or autocrats? The Internet in authoritarian regimes', in: 52 *Journal of Peace Research*, 338 ff; Stier, S. (2015), 'Democracy, Autocracy and the News: The Impact of Regime Type on Media Freedom', in: 22 *Democratization*, 1 ff; Deibert, R. *et al* (eds) (2008), *Access Denied. The Practice and Policy of Global Internet Filtering* (Cambridge: MIT Press); Deibert, R. *et al* (eds) (2010), *Access Controlled. The Shaping of Power, Rights in Cyberspace* (Cambridge: MIT Press).

[18] Formally based on Article IX (6) of the Basic Law of Hungary. Regarding censorship and freedom of the media in Hungary: www.metronaut.de/2010/12/zensur-ungarn-china/ (last accessed 13 March 2020).

of a serious breach of fundamental values under Article 2 of the Treaty on European Union. Notwithstanding this development, a 'government-related media giant' emerged in Hungary at the end of 2018 in the form of a foundation that unites numerous news channels, Internet portals and local newspapers under one roof. The foundation is managed by a newspaper publisher loyal to Orbán. And in 2019 a 'culture law' was passed by the *Fidesz*-controlled Parliament that allows for funds to be stripped from cultural productions that 'do not sit well with Fidesz'.[19]

Poland's ruling Law and Justice party (PiS) resembles in spirit Orbán's *Fidesz* and follows a similar strategy in its dealings with the media.[20] Since 2015, the conservative right-wing nationalist party leadership has been trying to create and enforce a Christian-Catholic Polish identity, to replace the allegedly corrupt 'post-communist elites' and to restore legitimacy to the institutions of the state. New media laws at the heart of this policy aim to serve this 'political mission' and the agenda to nationalize and 'repolonize' the press, radio and television. A National Media Council fills the management positions and supervisory boards of public television and radio companies, and of the Polish Press Agency. Even if PiS, like *Fidesz* in Hungary, has in mind the establishment of an illiberal democracy, this plan is likely to be more difficult to implement in view of media pluralism and the *Solidarność* tradition in Poland.

Italian Prime Minister Silvio Berlusconi favoured a different style, combining ego-cult and strategies of immediacy. Through his private television stations (Mediaset), he developed a complex network of relationships between the media and politics, which he exploited at will for his political purposes and power interests. Quite openly, he commissioned his media companies for his sultanate.[21] In doing so, the media mogul took advantage of a 14-year phase of legal non-regulation to build and expand his empire through clever entrepreneurial and advertising strategies. He rounded this off with a media law that was very much aligned with his interests. Thanks to a monopoly (in the private broadcasting sector), his channels were able to serve propaganda functions

---

19 In: *trtworld*, 16 December 2019, www.trtworld.com/magazine/hungary-passes-culture-law-prompting-fears-of-censorship-32231/ (last accessed 13 March 2020).

20 European Commission (2016) Commission Recommendation of 21 December 2016 regarding the rule of law in Poland, complementary to Commission Recommendation (EU) 2016/1374, C (2016) 8950 final, http://europa.eu/rapid/press-release_IP-16-4476_en.htm/ (last accessed 13 March 2020); Klimkiewicz, B. (2017), 'State, media and pluralism: tracing roots and consequences of media policy change in Poland', in: 62 *Publizistik*, 197 ff.

21 Hambückers, M. (2006), Arrivederci Berlusconi. Medienpolitische Verflechtungen in Italien seit 1945, (Konstanz: UVK-Verlag).

very effectively by combining humour with anti-communism. As a mediator and communicator, Berlusconi gathered his audience around a 'virtual campfire',[22] desensitized them through an endless loop of monotonous television shows and thus showcased – for considerable profit – his omnipresence and politics around the clock as entertainment.

Departing from the prevailing, one-sided perspective on China, which focuses on repression only, the media and the Internet can be recognized as having played a considerable and ambivalent role in stabilizing the regime there.[23] One study concludes that 400 million Internet users in China feel freer and less afraid of their government than ten years ago, even though the government is still making arrests for 'endangering national security' and monitoring the population so intensively – censoring and manipulating online conversations – that no significant opposition movement has been able to develop online.[24] Activists' hopes that the Internet, as a Trojan horse, could help to subvert China's autocracy from within have thus far proved to be little more than wishful thinking. While information technology has contributed to the development of a 'working-class network society'[25] in China, it has also furnished the leadership and management of companies with new tools to organize a class of 'programmable work'. Online activism does not necessarily lead to democratization or intensified state repression, because the Chinese government has long since recognized and is making full use of the opportunities to perfect its monitoring, to propagate 'positive ideology' and to secure its legitimacy with the help of supervised access to the Internet, programme controls (often designated as anti-terrorism measures) and 'compliance' rules.[26] In contrast to the nationalist-patriotic authoritarianism of Orbán in Hungary and the personalist style of Berlusconi in Italy or the party-based, nationalist-Catholic authoritarianism in Poland, China's media policy does not underscore, as an accompanying measure, the cult of immediacy, but rather combines a sophisticated system of censorship and monitoring on the one

---

22 I borrow the term from Drösser, C. (1995), *Fernsehen* (Reinbek bei Hamburg: Rowohlt).

23 See Stockmann, D. and Gallagher, M.E. (2011), 'Remote Control: How the Media Sustain Authoritarian Rule in China', in: 44 *Comparative Political Studies*, 436 ff; MacKinnon, R. (2011), 'China's Networked Authoritarianism', in: 22 *Journal of Democracy*, 32 ff with further references.

24 MacKinnon (n 23), 33.

25 Linchuan Qiu, J. (2009), *Working-Class Network Society: Communication Technology and the Information Have-Less in Urban China* (Cambridge: MIT Press), 243 ff; Cardoso, G. and Castells, M. (eds) (2006), *The Network Society: From Knowledge to Policy* (Washington DC: Center for Transatlantic Relations).

26 This applies also to other authoritarian regimes (eg, Russia, India, the United States and the states of the European Union); see Deibert (n 17), *Access Controlled.*

hand with strategic media use to make governance more effective and promote top-down social change on the other.[27]

4. THE IMMEDIACY OF LIES AND PROPAGANDA

Deception, disinformation and lies have always been tools of politics. Machiavelli ennobled them as political virtues and honoured them as indispensable if power was to be successfully acquired and maintained.[28] The sixteenth century political realist held that rulers must be 'fox and lion at the same time': 'The art of deception, as the prince educated by Machiavelli and the republican politician must master equally, and the purposeful distortion of historical facts are thus in the service of a higher truth.'[29] And the governmental technique of deliberately misleading the public is in turn at the service of the community: 'Through salutary deceit alone, the selfish natural being, man, is transformed into a functioning citizen, who uncomplainingly stands up for and sacrifices himself for the common good.'[30]

The lie of an alleged stockpile of weapons of mass destruction (WMD) in Iraq proved to be a brilliant marketing strategy of the Bush/Cheney government. The Armageddon scenario of nuclear attack was linked to a possible war with chemical weapons. The US population and the 'coalition of the willing' were mobilized for a war which, as few were aware, was directed not against Afghanistan – where Osama bin Laden, the mastermind behind the 9/11 terrorist attacks, was allegedly in hiding – but against Iraq.[31] The WMD lie provided the US government with legitimacy for the invasion of Iraq – a 'just war' to

[27] Stockmann and Gallagher (n 23), 437–39. See Chapter 6, Section 7.

[28] Machiavelli, N. (2014), *The Prince* [1513] (London: Penguin Classics). Concerning the difference between Machiavelli and Machiavellism: Münkler, H. (2004), *Die Begründung des politischen Denkens der Neuzeit aus der Krise der Republik Florenz* (Frankfurt am Main: S. Fischer); and Rudolph, E. (2017), *Wege der Macht* (Weilerswist: Velbrück), 2017.

[29] Reinhardt, V. (2017), *Gefälscht. Die Macht der Lüge*', in: *Magazin ZEIT Geschichte*, 3.

[30] *Ibid.* Concerning Machiavellian techniques of governing: Frankenberg (n 7), Chapter I.

[31] 'The term WMD was a brilliant marketing campaign by the Bush administration to conflate the Armageddon scenario of a nuclear weapon (something most experts believed Iraq didn't have the capability to produce) with the specter of chemical weapons, which, while horrific, are much more limited in scope. This wasn't simply a vague case of "fake news". It was subtle propaganda, with just enough of an air of plausibility to lull a nation into a war of choice' – Rather, R. and Kirschner, E. (2018), 'Why a Free Press Matters', *The Atlantic Monthly*, August, www.theatlantic.com/ideas/archive/2018/08/why-a-free-press-matters/567676/ (last accessed 30 September 2018).

save the world from disaster. Crucial questions of ethics[32] were traded in not only small coins, but false coins. And tragedy returned as farce – or as tragedy again.[33]

The WMD story ushered in the age of 'fake news' and post-truth. Donald Trump effortlessly continued it, vulgarized it and took it to extremes with his maxim: 'There is no proof of anything but there very well could be.'[34] On the surface, invented stories and 'fake news' can be read as the renaissance of a Machiavellian doctrine of governing. In the struggle for political dominance and world interpretation, Trump (and other politicians of his ilk) have made the arbitrariness of dealing with facts and truth an integral part of a post-factual media and marketing policy. This does not serve any higher purpose, but is rather based on the amalgam of ignorance, narcissism and power maintenance. Trump's 'fake news' talk and tweets are not so much geared towards making false claims resemble facts (for which secret services have always made far greater effort, and with greater success). Instead, he deliberately refrains from supporting his own arguments with scientifically verifiable or at least empirically reasonably plausible data. In the post-factual or fake news age, the argument is boldly disavowed, while the lie is shamelessly courted. While Trump alleges that China 'invented' climate change and the coronavirus pandemic, Viktor Orbán invokes an imaginary plan by billionaire George Soros to promote 'mass immigration' of (Muslim) refugees. Likewise, Brexiteers cite false asylum statistics and inaccurate figures about the United Kingdom's allegedly horrendous payments to the European Union. In this way, 'feelings' and the perceived reality can take the lead, untroubled by empirical findings, and win spectators and listeners over to the aims pursued by the government.[35]

'In post-factual society it is not the strong argument that wins, but the strong performance – the will to power.'[36] Instead of promoting controversies

---

32 Baggini, J. (2014), '*Was ist ein gerechter Krieg?*', in: *id, Die großen Fragen Ethik* (Berlin/Heidelberg: Springer Spektrum), 141 ff.

33 See Chapter 1 for an interpretation of Karl Marx's dictum in 'The Eighteenth Brumaire of Louis Bonaparte'.

34 Donald Trump's comment on whether the caravan of refugees in Mexico might contain 'Middle Easterners' – https://edition.cnn.com/videos/politics/2018/10/23/trump-caravan-middle-easterners-no-proof-collins-tapper-lead-vpx.cnn/ (last accessed 14 November 2018).

35 Rabin-Havt, A. and Media Matters for America (2016), Lies, Incorporated: The World of Post-Truth Politics (New York: Anchor), analysing the industry of organized disinformation.

36 Assheuer, T. (2016), 'Wahrheit ist die Krücke der Verlierer', in: *Die Zeit,* 1 October, www.zeit.de/2016/41/donald-trump-fakten-realitaetsverlust-rechtspopulismus/ (last accessed 17 August 2018).

about ideas and social projects, politics is reduced to marketing. Thus, the Counter-Enlightenment finally dawns in a tired modern age:

> I call my own shots, largely based on an accumulation of data, and everyone knows it. Some FAKE NEWS media, in order to marginalize, lies![37]
>
> Any negative polls are fake news, just like the CNN, ABC, NBC polls in the election. Sorry, people want border security and extreme vetting.[38]

While the term 'fake news' may have been coined by Trump, the 'lying press' (*Lügenpresse*) has been cited for almost 200 years as a *topos* in authoritarian friend-foe constellations. In this century, the slogan of the 'lying press' – especially in Germany – has primarily accompanied the propaganda of right-wing radically nationalist movements (Pegida) and organizations (Alternative for Germany) that pursue a xenophobic agenda. The fake news statements of the Trump government are a perfect fit for this. For it is only logical that both Trump and his colleague Erdoğan[39] are quick to defame the media as the 'enemy of the people' in order to mobilize the uncivilized community of their followers – a community that specializes in hate mail, insults, intimidation and the threat of violence.

Besides defaming the search for truth and manipulating the truth, allegations of fake news and of the 'lying press' draw on the arsenal of conspiracy theory to mobilize their followers. Those who make these accusations are seeking to agitate the people in a battle against elites and their media accomplices – in short, the enemies:

> When a country is no longer able to say who can, and who cannot, come in & out, especially for reasons of safety & security - big trouble![40]
>
> The Fake News Media, the true Enemy of the People, must stop the open & obvious hostility & report the news accurately & fairly. That will do much to put out the flame...[41]

---

37 @realDonald Trump, www.spiegel.de/netzwelt/web/donald-trump-die-top-ten-seiner-gruseligsten-tweets-kolumne-a-1133673.html/ (last accessed 30 September 2018)

38 @realDonaldTrump, 04:01 - 6 February 2017.

39 Concerning Erdoğan's media policy: www.waz.de/politik/so-abhaengig-sind-die-medien-in-der-tuerkei-von-erdogan-id210275413.html/ (last accessed 11 November 2018).

40 @realDonaldTrump, 14:59 – 4 February 2017.

41 Tweet by D. Trump, 29 October 2018: see Chua, A. and Rubenfeld, J. (2018), 'The Threat of Tribalism', in: *The Atlantic* 10 October; Chua, A. (2018), *Political Tribalism, Group Instincts and the Fate of Nations* (London: Penguin Press).

5. NEUTRALIZING INTERMEDIARY INSTITUTIONS AND PROCEDURES

On the state side, installing a cult of immediacy presupposes that institutions that guarantee distance are abolished or, where this is impossible, controlled or circumvented; and that the sober discourses of politics are engulfed by the passions of the street. Transforming representation into presence – that is, establishing or feigning immediacy – requires not only the appropriate propaganda, but also careful institutional preparation. Constitutions, as discussed, can get in the way. The choice of strategy – to grind down representative institutions and transform them into forums of stately self-representation, or to bypass them altogether – depends not least on the obstacles that a constitution presents and the viability of constitutional culture. Easier, because more inconspicuous, is the discursive change of track from the finely tuned parliamentary piano to the drums of presenteeism and irrationalism; from argument to the emotions and prejudices of everyday life. It is astonishing how similar the rhetoric of leaders drifting towards totalitarianism and authoritarian nationalists fighting for allegedly 'authentic' democracy becomes when they pose as speakers for 'the good people' and satisfy their thirst for acclamation. More difficult than cheap propaganda, however, are interventions in the institutional arrangement and their justification. Some of these different strategies will be briefly discussed here.

5.1 Enabling by Destroying Institutions

A textbook example of a strategy of immediacy realized through disestablishing or disempowering institutions is the transformation of the Weimar Republic into a dictatorship and its ultimate disablement by the Act of 23 March 1933 that 'enabled' Adolf Hitler. The latter, who had only recently assumed the office of chancellor of the *Reich*, pursued a plan of eliminating the *Reichstag* and *de facto* and *de jure* invalidated the Constitution in order to centralize power in his hands and unshackle it from parliamentary interventions. His plan succeeded, after the majority of National Socialists – supported by the German Nationalists (*Deutschnationale Volkspartei*) – had initially amended the rules of procedure to formally meet the requirements for presence in spite of the imprisonment and absence of Communist deputies. Under the threat of the threatening, illegal presence in the *Reichstag* of armed and uniformed combat units of the Nazi party, the Enabling Act was passed with the support of the deputies of the Centrists[42] and the Liberals – for the sake of the 'national cause' – pursuant to the new Rules of Procedure. It was passed against the votes of the Social Democratic faction, which had been reduced by arrests and intimidation, but not eliminated altogether. The truncated *Reichstag* endowed the chancellor (soon to be the *Führer*) with far-reaching dictatorial powers.[43]

The script of brutal regime change regularly references a traumatic event to cover up or justify a constitutional coup. In 1933 the (staged?) *Reichstag* fire was invoked to call for a 'national uprising'.[44] Consequently, the law that accompanied the transition from a democracy to a commissarial and later sovereign dictatorship, *à la* Carl Schmitt,[45] was fittingly and dramatically called the 'Law to Remedy the Distress of the People and the *Reich*'.[46]

At almost the same time, the Dollfuß government in Austria also opted for the model of direct rule based on an enabling act. It governed by means of emergency decrees on the basis of the War Economic Enabling Act without a parliament. The immediate executive intervention was triggered by an extraordinary session of the National Council (*Nationalrat*) held on 4 March 1933 in connection with a strike by railway workers organized by the unions, in which three presidents resigned after a controversial vote. Federal Chancellor

---

42 The chairman of the Centrist Parts, Ludwig Kaas, quite tellingly justified the approval – which was not uncontroversial within the parliamentary group – as follows: 'The present hour cannot be a time for words, its only law is that of a quick, constructive and rescue action. And this act can only be born in the rallying. The German Centrist Party, which for a long time and despite all temporary disappointments has been a strong and resolute advocate of the great idea of collecting, is consciously and out of a sense of national responsibility, at this hour when all small and narrow considerations must remain silent, overlooking all party-political and other thoughts… In the face of the burning need in which the people and the State are presently standing, in the face of the enormous tasks which German reconstruction is presenting to us, in the face of the storm clouds which are beginning to rise in and around Germany, we in the *Zentrum* Party are reaching out our hand to all, including former opponents, at this hour to ensure the continuation of the work of national advancement.' *Verhandlungen des Reichstags, VIII. Wahlperiode 1933*, vol 457, (Berlin 1933), S 37.

43 The Act was extended twice by the '*nationalsozialistische Reichstag*' – certainly anything but a democratic institution – and in 1943 once more by decree of the *Führer*.

44 Deiseroth, D. (2008), '*Die Legalitäts-Legende. Vom Reichstagsbrand zum NS-Regime*', in: *Blätter für deutsche und internationale Politik*, 91 ff.

45 See Hermanns, S. (2018), *Carl Schmitts Beitrag zur Machtkonsolidierung der Nationalsozialisten* (Wiesbaden: Springer).

46 See the *Holocaust Encyclopedia*, 'The Enabling Act', https://encyclopedia.ushmm.org/content/en/article/the-enabling-act/ (last accessed 14 March 2020); and Morsey, R. (1976), *Das 'Ermächtigungsgesetz' vom 24. März 1933*. Reihe: Historische Texte: Neuzeit, 4th reprint (Göttingen: Vandenhoeck & Ruprecht).

Dollfuß then declared that the National Council had 'switched itself off' and considered himself authorized to take emergency measures.[47]

Hitler's Enabling Act was preceded since 1914 by a series of letters of *carte blanche* for the enactment of statutory ordinances to suspend or restrict the parliamentary process.[48] As a vehicle for introducing an authoritarian regime – at least for governing by decree – it was never out of fashion. Numerous current constitutions have adapted the Enabling Act of 1933 to different contexts, with (sometimes considerable) modifications. Four enabling acts were approved during the government of Hugo Chávez.[49] His successor Nicholas Maduro continued this style of governing without parliamentary control. In Turkey, members of the opposition compared the 2017 constitutional amendment with Hitler's Enabling Act; and the Emergency Laws of 2016 authorized President Erdoğan to govern by decree and emergency ordinance.

Citing in particular the 'war on terror' and the 'war on organized crime', a number of governments resorted to governing by decree and related executive techniques to expedite decision-making procedures by bypassing parliamentary debates and decisions, and to establish a 'direct line' of communication between leaders and followers. Thus, the USA PATRIOT Act (whose full title – 'Uniting and Strengthening America by Providing Appropriate Tools Required to Intercept and Obstruct Terrorism' – George Orwell would have enjoyed) was passed as a federal law by Congress on 26 October 2001 as a salvo in the war on terror. The PATRIOT Act was an immediate response to the 9/11 terrorist attacks and imposed far-reaching restrictions on civil rights, such as wiretapping without a court order, house searches and other executive measures.[50] Without significant media attention, a directive was passed in the United States on 9 May 2007 giving the president the option of bypassing Congress in the event of an unspecified 'catastrophic emergency'[51] (as was

---

[47] Schausberger, F. (1993), *Letzte Chance für die Demokratie. Die Bildung der Regierung Dollfuß im Mai 1932. Bruch der österreichischen Proporzdemokratie* (Vienna: Böhlau).

[48] See Frankenberg, G. (2016), 'Im Ausnahmezustand', in: 49 *Kritische Justiz*, 4 ff.

[49] Under the Constitution of Venezuela (1999), laws empowering the executive require the approval of three-fifths of the National Assembly (Article 203); they must contain guidelines, a purpose and a framework for the matters delegated to the president with the force of law; and they are limited to a certain period of time.

[50] Michaels, W.C. (2005), *No Greater Threat: America since September 11 and the Rise of the National Security State* (New York: Algora Publishing).

[51] 'Catastrophic emergency' is defined as an event that, regardless of its location, results in an extraordinary amount of casualties, damage or disruption to the US population, infrastructure, environment, economy or governmental functions; www.heise.de/tp/features/Das-amerikanische-Ermaechtigungsgesetz-3414515.html/ (last accessed 21 September 2018)

most recently demonstrated by President Trump in February 2019) and immediately executing the presumed interests of the patriotic community. Likewise, invoking the narrative of WMD allegedly stockpiled in Iraq, the Bush/Cheney administration turned directly to the American nation in order to get people in the mood for the war against Saddam Hussein's regime in Iraq.[52]

In response to a dilettantish coup attempt in 2016, Turkey added to the Enabling Act model a version that could be called 'emergency defence excess', which Erdoğan must answer for.[53] It may also be adopted by other regimes that can make a plausible claim that they face exceptional situations, such as a coup, catastrophe or pandemic. After declaring a state of emergency, Erdoğan implemented sweeping constitutional changes; 'cleansed' the military, police, judiciary and public service, including schools; and ordered an unprecedented wave of arrests and draconian measures against the media. He thus prepared the ground for the introduction of an autocratic presidential system by means of a constitutional referendum, which – in light of his measures of intimidation and the previous wave of arrests – bore little risk for the autocrat.[54] On 18 July 2018, Erdoğan could afford to formally lift the state of emergency, which had been extended several times, because in the meantime he had consolidated his regime and now had at his disposal the special powers he needed. These had been 'normalized'[55] in the shadow of the Constitution by their transposition in anti-terror and other security laws.

Enabling acts of whichever brand have an obvious drawback: more or less conspicuously, they signal the authoritarian transformation of a regime by formally suspending the constitution or by hiding special powers in ordinary legislation. This transformation invariably damages or weakens the constitution.

5.2 Bypassing Representation, Faking Dialogue

Autocrats who are forced to subvert the representative system without the formal declaration of a state of emergency and without institutional changes choose a different path for their non-mediated communication. Their strategy aims to weaken intermediary powers and institutions, in particular by circum-

---

52 President G.W. Bush, 'The State of the Nation', in: *The White House,* News Archive, 25 January 2003.

53 Altınordu, A. (2017), 'A Midsummer Night's Coup: Performance and Power in Turkey's July 15 Coup Attempt', 40 Qualitative Sociology, 139 ff; Çalışkan, K. (2017), 'Explaining the end of military tutelary regime and the 15 July coup attempt in Turkey', in: 10 *Journal of Cultural Economy*, 97 ff.

54 Observers estimate that more than 100 000 state officials lost their jobs and more than 70 000 people were imprisoned.

55 The concept of normalization is developed in Frankenberg (n 7), Chapter 1 (1.4).

venting institutional procedures and cultivating (illusory) direct communication with 'the people', instead of their elected deputies. Traditionally, this is done through public mass meetings, rallies and marches; and more recently, through social media.

After the demise (or in fascist systems, the destruction) of the traditional intermediary organizations (political parties) and bodies (parliaments, courts),[56] and the vertical division of labour in federal systems, autocratic regimes with a Machiavellian leaning seize the opportunity to transform society into an amphitheatre for their self-representation. Charismatic tribunes of the people like to pose on this stage as 'one of us' and compete for the favour of the audience, who become followers and then accomplices.[57]

This strategy of establishing and cultivating immediacy also implies that the regime bypasses established channels of communication and decision making. Petitions, legal proceedings, voting, parliamentary debates and party meetings are sidestepped in favour of instant interchange between the autocratic leadership and the population (or at least, the followers). Where the leadership operates with a nationalist-xenophobic script, the affinity between National-Socialist and right-wing authoritarianism is particularly striking: the contours of what is happening politically disappear behind a smokescreen of emotion and rhetoric. The masses regress to a passive body of acclamation that submits to the will of the leader: '*Führer befiehl, wir folgen!*' ('Leader command, we follow!')[58] The autocrat takes the stage as the leading actor and operates according to a script that sharply distinguishes between members and outsiders, between friends and enemies ('Us against them'). In monologues, the leader solicits approval, loyalty and allegiance in accordance with a principle of leadership. Examples include the heads of state in hyper-presidential systems and the 'Supreme Religious Leader' elected for life in Iran.[59] In North

---

[56] Including the supreme or constitutional courts (eg, Venezuela, Poland and Hungary); see Bánkuti, M. (*et al*) (2012), 'Disabling the Constitution', in: 23 *Journal of Democracy*, 138 ff.

[57] Regarding the concept and conditions of political complicity, see Chapter 6, Section 7.

[58] 'The power of the leader is comprehensive and total; it embraces all means of political organization; it extends to all aspects of people's life; it embraces all the people who are obliged to be loyal and obedient to the leader.' Forsthoff, E. (1933), *Der totale Staat* (Hamburg: Hanseatische Verlagsanstalt). Against democracy, separation of powers, parliamentarianism and pluralism, Hitler set an unrestrained *Führerprinzip*, according to which all authority in party and state should emanate from an unelected, only by acclamation confirmed '*Führer* of the people'. See Frei, N. (2007), *Der Führerstaat. Nationalsozialistische Herrschaft 1933–1945*, 8th ed (Munich : Deutscher Taschenbuch-Verlag).

[59] Article 5 of the 1979 Constitution of Iran.

Korea, the term 'Supreme Leader' is reserved for the respective heads of the Kim dynasty. Because of his abundance of power, Chinese President Xi Jinping is likewise called 'Supreme Leader'.

The cult of immediacy has a price that the people must pay – in the theatre of the authoritarian, they are alienated from themselves:

> Mankind, once a showpiece for the Olympic gods in Homer's play, has now become one for itself. In authoritarian settings, self-alienation has reached that degree which allows the people to experience their own destruction as an aesthetic pleasure of the first order. This is the aesthetization of the politics pursued by fascism. Communism responds with the politicization of art.[60]

The people thus morph into the ornament of the regime. And they become a foreign purpose of that regime, even though it thrives on their acclamation and loyalty.[61] The *Führer* sent his messages directly to the people, primarily over the radio ('*Volksempfänger*') and at mass events, as well as through the press, which was brought into line with the regime and thus made more straightforward.[62] Indian Prime Minister Modi celebrates his image as a guru at public rallies, while delegating the dirty work of Hindu nationalism to members of his cabinet (Amit Shah) and *Akhil Bharatiya Vidya Parishad*, the youth wing of the *Rashtriya Swayamsevak Sangh*. Public appearances and speeches provided the platform for Juan Perón's rise to power – first as a key player in the military regime, then as president of Argentina. In the spirit of immediacy, his wife Eva, though fatally ill, drove with him in an open car to the *Casa Rosada* at the inauguration of his second term of office on 5 June 1952.

The consolidated, democratic institutional system and constitutional barriers have forced US President Trump to resort to another strategy of immediacy. Against all evidence, he cultivates the myth of his competence and ubiquity. Thus, in the manner of a gospel preacher, he ritually asks his audience to believe him: '[Coronavirus] is a flu… it's going to disappear like a miracle. Believe me!' He idealizes himself as an authentic leader (@realDonaldTrump) at party or election events, in television appearances and in tweets, always seeking to identify with his followers as 'one of them'.[63] In this manner, he

---

[60] Benjamin, W. (1969), *The Work of Art in the Age of Mechanical Reproduction* (New York: Schocken Books).

[61] Kracauer, S. (1977), *Das Ornament der Masse* (Frankfurt am Main: Suhrkamp/Insel), 50 ff.

[62] No doubt he would not have refrained from using the social media available today.

[63] Instructive: Lee, B.X. (ed) (2017), *The Dangerous Case of Donald Trump* (New York: Thomas Dunne Books).

keeps his supporters in a state of constant availability and emotional alarm, which can be triggered at any time. Excitement and permanent visibility, tweets and public statements present his fans with insight into his solipsistic worldview. His politics of spontaneous affect infiltrates society primarily with the help of Twitter and dominates the people through quasi-magical constant contact. Eschewing dialogue, the presidential tweets are one-way messages aimed at soliciting reflexively agreeing 'likes'. This kind of unilateral, incessant communication leaves no room for direct criticism; instead, this plays out through the exchange of verbal blows between supporters and opponents.[64] In the frosty global climate of neo-liberalism, Trump invites followers into the warm room of white America, which he continually heats up further by pointing a finger at enemies:

> This week alone, the news broke that the Trump administration was seeking to ethnically cleanse more than 193,000 American children of immigrants whose temporary protected status had been revoked by the administration, that the Department of Homeland Security had lied about creating a database of children that would make it possible to unite them with the families the Trump administration had arbitrarily destroyed, that the White House was considering a blanket ban on visas for Chinese students, and that it would deny visas to the same-sex partners of foreign officials.[65]

Despite considerable differences in other respects, Donald Trump – very much like Mussolini, Hitler and today's authoritarian nationalists – expresses his narcissism in speeches and tweets that are infused with the spirit of the nineteenth-century Counter-Enlightenment and twentieth-century irrationalisms.[66] The functional ideological equivalent of the Aryan myth is white tribalism – the unity and purity of the (superior) white race[67] – to which the majority of Trump supporters subscribe, according to plausible empirical data.[68] The exclusion of non-Americans fulfils an integrative function in

---

[64] For examples, see 'Donald Trump's Most Offensive Tweets', *Forbes* 2020, www.forbes.com/pictures/flji45elmm/donald-trumps-10-most-of/#70db2b9170df/ (last accessed 13 March 2020).

[65] In: *The Atlantic*, October 2018, www.theatlantic.com/ideas/archive/2018/10/the-cruelty-is-the-point/572104/ (last accessed 26 November 2018).

[66] As regards Hitler: Lukács, G. (1955), *Die Zerstörung der Vernunft: Der Weg des Irrationalismus von Schelling zu Hitler* (Berlin: Aufbau-Verlag). As regards Trump: Librett (n 4).

[67] For an analysis of ethnic, racist or religious tribalism: Chua and Rubenfeld (n 41) and Chua (n 41).

[68] Coates, T.N. (2017), 'The First White President', *The Atlantic Monthly,* 10 October; for a different perspective, see Kennedy, D. (2017), 'A Left of Liberal Interpretation of Trump's "Big" Win, Part One: Neoliberalism', in: 1 *Nevada Law Journal Forum*, 98 ff.

Donald Trump's right-wing propaganda. The xenophobic phantasm of a wall between Mexico and the United States is just as much to blame for this as the signing of the executive orders, conspicuously displayed on television, which prohibited members from six predominantly Muslim countries from entering the United States[69] and separated migrant children from their parents at the Mexican border.[70]

Trump's pattern of direct monologic communication is reflected, *mutatis mutandis*, in Viktor Orbán's 'Friday Prayers' – direct addresses to the people – and the 'national consultations' he has initiated. Each 'consultation' begins with leading questions or predetermined statements to which the only possible response is that sought by the government, such as the 'theses' on the imaginary 'Soros Plan' for mass immigration invented by the government in 2017:

1. George Soros wants to persuade Brussels to resettle at least one million immigrants from Africa and the Middle East onto the territory of the European Union, including Hungary.
2. George Soros, together with the officials in Brussels, also wants to achieve the dismantlement of the fences and the opening of borders to the migrants.
3. One part of the Soros Plan is the compulsory distribution by Brussels of immigrants who conglomerated in Western Europe, especially in respect to the East European countries. Hungary would have to take part in this.
4. According to the Soros Plan, Brussels should force all EU Member States, including Hungary, to pay each immigrant HUF 9 million [approximately 30,000 Euros] in welfare payments.[71]

By pre-structuring the themes, the vote in these consultations takes on the character of an expression of moods in the garb of a reflexively delivered collective response. As expected, 98 per cent of respondents agreed with the government and rejected the (non-existent) 'Soros Plan'. Their participation in the consultation made them accomplices in the barely concealed anti-Semitism practised by the government.

---

[69] Executive Order 13769 of 27 January 2017. See Gooyer, S. *et al* (2018), *Vom Recht, Rechte zu haben* (Hamburg: Hamburger Edition).

[70] *DIE ZEIT online,* 20 June 2018, www.zeit.de/politik/ausland/2018-06/einwanderung-usa-trump-familien-trennung/ (last accessed 26 November 2018).

[71] Four of the seven topics submitted for a referendum on the 'Soros Plan'. See 'The Truth About the Soros-Plan', https://hungarianspectrum.org/2017/10/03/the-truth-about-the-so-called-soros-plan/ (last accessed 30 March 2020).

6. PUBLIC PRIVACY ON THE AUTHORITARIAN STAGE

At mass events and in televised speeches, through theatrical performances of all kinds and nightly tweets, the protagonists of authoritarianism demonstrate their omnipresence as a provident, controlling or punishing authority. The visualization of power and the one-way communications between rulers and subjects are supplemented by demonstrations of the leader's vitality and orchestrated glimpses into his supposedly private sphere. The illusory or deceptive portrayal of authority as a private person positions the autocrat at the centre of 'his' community in order to facilitate identification ('he looks just like one of us'). Where necessary, it weakens the image of punitive authority and introduces a benevolent one. A more or less entertaining performance by, and the illusion of a quasi-personal relationship with, the ruler distracts from the loss of real freedom. This illusion, of course, can be successfully created only if supported by political iconography. The leader must be portrayed not only as a remote Leviathan, but also as an approachable neighbour. He and his spin doctors must bring him close to his followers as a quasi-private person – if possible, in familiar or at least comprehensible surroundings that spectators can relate to. Images of everyday behaviour such as hiking and swimming do the job nicely. Pets are welcome – autocrats seem to prefer dogs and horses as beastly incarnations of loyalty.

6.1 The Body Politic

Other crucial features of the quasi-private person are health and virility, thus introducing body politics to the theatre of authoritarianism. In the world of moods and attunements, authoritarian rulers place more importance on appearing in good health than their democratic counterparts. Virility and masculinity function as essential elements of autocratic sovereignty. Dictators, despots and more moderate rulers very much like to appear in good health. They display their own bodies as 'proof of sportive energy, patriarchal care and leadership' – as if they wanted to compensate for the deficient sanctity of their symbolic body in a secular environment with the exuberant robustness of their natural body.[72]

Depending on the person and the body, presentations of masculinity follow diverse scripts. They become tricky where they must conceal the leader's

[72] See the elaborate and very inspiring study by Bredekamp, H. (2014), *Der schwimmende Souverän. Karl der Große und die Bildpolitik des Körpers* (Berlin: Wagenbach), in particular 13 ff.

obvious physical imperfections and flaws. Donald Trump – overweight and not very athletic; spongy, rather – presents himself in the public spotlight as an egomaniacal 'robot on attack'.[73] He plays a vulgar, fast-food version of Machiavelli's Prince, who is habitually obscured from seeing any higher goal beyond his own popularity and power: 'There is only the great fear that the applause will fail.'[74]

Russian Leviathan Vladimir Putin – a former secret service agent of short, but muscular build – has developed two ways to compensate for his Napoleon complex: he strides – purposefully and alone – down the halls of government, past serried lines of the political lightweights of his regime, who dutifully applaud; or he ostentatiously flaunts his muscles in sporting pursuits. Opaque in his state practice, Vladimir Putin seeks to portray himself outside the Kremlin as a private individual and maintains a rather intrusive masculine style. He is frequently pictured as a judoka or on mountain tours, often shirtless on horseback – just like the macho guy next door on a Siberian vacation. Meanwhile, he is glorified on state television as a benevolent patriarch and even-handed ruler of the national community.[75] Through this double strategy, he paves the way for the combination of idealization – implying freedom from criticism – and identification as an expression of an emotional tie between leader and followers (Figure 7.1).

In contrast, Recep Tayyip Erdoğan and Nahendra Modi come across as unobtrusive patriarchs of their extended families (Turkish and Hindu respectively). Both hide their harshness, indeed brutality, towards the opposition and religious minorities (Kurds and Muslims), as well as their ruthless 'cleansing' of the civil service. Erdoğan hides behind a rather prissy, middle-class image and ensures he is photographed *en route* to the mosque. Modi – the guru of Hindu nationalism – appears in traditional garb. He is a spiritual person, so no one would expect to see his body. Both consistently put identity and religion at the centre of their nationalist script and rely on 'lived experience'.[76] While Modi appears to trust his charisma, Erdoğan does not. Why else would he have

---

[73] Nutt, H. (2016), 'Donald Trump *kann nicht anders*', in: *Frankfurter Rundschau*, 23 October.

[74] Luther, C. (2018), '*So kann keine Demokratie überleben*', www.zeit.de/politik/ausland/2018-01/donald-trump-praesident-bilanz-usa-wirtschaft/ (last accessed 30 September 2018).

[75] *FAZ net,* 06 September 2018, www.faz.net/aktuell/politik/ausland/putins-selbstdarstellung-in-russlands-staatsfernsehen-15773354.html?service=printP/ (last accessed 30 September 2018).

[76] See Charim, I. (2018), 'Erdoğan *als Patriarch, Herrscher und Wegweiser*', https://anfdeutsch.com/hintergrund/erdogan-als-patriarch-herrscher-und-wegweiser-1047/ (last accessed 30 September 2018); and Khokhar, A. (2019), 'Modi's Identity Politics in Post-Secular India: A Threat to South Asia', https://strafasia.com/modis

Source: © Max Frankenberg 2020.

Figure 7.1 Autocrats swimming (Mao, Mussolini and Putin afloat)

commissioned the construction of the Aksaray Palace – larger than any other palace built in the last century – thus betraying his guise of pious modesty? The architecture (probably unintentionally) compares to the palace of former Romanian dictator Nicolae Ceaucețcu. It displays political megalomania and a de-territorialized claim to power that extends to Turks of all countries.

Mao Zedong chose to swim the Yangtze River to dispel rumours of his poor health. The 72-year-old chairman joined 5000 other swimmers in Wuhan's 11th annual Cross-Yangtze Competition.[77] Like no other, Mao staged his swimming as an act of state and 'public performance'.[78] By contrast, Mussolini swam to flaunt his muscular body, impress women and motivate the Italian people 'to take the plunge'.[79] As 'swimming sovereigns', Mussolini and Mao

-identity-politics-in-post-secular-india-a-threat-to-peace-in-south-asia/ (last accessed 15 March 2020).

[77] Hudson, R. (1966), 'The Great Helmsman Goes Swimming', in: 62 *History Today*, 5 May, www.historytoday.com/archive/focus/great-helmsman-goes-swimming/ (last accessed 15 March 2020).

[78] Bredekamp, *Der schwimmende Souverän*, 14 f.

[79] Greenleese, N. (2009), 'Diving with the Duce', in: *DW*, www.dw.com/en/diving-with-the-duce/a-4520879/).

successfully demonstrated both virility and superiority: Mao would likely have particularly impressed the (majority of) non-swimmers in rural China. In a show of closeness to the people, he did what they either did or could not do. Mussolini paraded his masculinity to emphasize the importance of physical education in Italy.

6.2 Concealing the Uncivil Charisma

Autocrats who cannot show off their bodies must instead draw the public's attention to other features and work with a different iconography in order to sustain the cult of immediacy and the illusion of private appearance. Gurbanguly Berdimuhamedov, the evil despot in Turkmenistan, makes efforts to conceal the uncivilized side of his charisma:[80] brutal repression that violates all imaginable human and international law standards. He seamlessly connects the personality cult with the cult of immediacy through images of members of his family casually singing or playing music, voting *en famille* for himself and often riding horses. He cultivates the image of the 'Turkmenistor' – his symbolic body always on horseback. He once had to keep news of a fall from his horse at a horse race, after he had crossed the finishing line as winner, out of the public eye. Every once in a while, Recep Tayyip Erdoğan and Viktor Orbán – neither any beefcake – take part in physical activities and trivialize the body's image politics. They participate, less spectacularly, in celebrity football matches, demonstrating not so much virility than popularity and success: 'Our prime minister scored one dream goal after another.'

An ersatz body politic was depicted in Hitler's image politics. Photos showing him relaxing with friends at his *Berghof* residence, shaking the hands of innocent children or sitting in the grass with his German shepherd, Blondie (Figure 7.2) distracted from his unimpressive physicality, and even more so from his unapproachability and mercilessness as a punitive authority and ruthless dictator, creating the impression of a private person who likes to 'unwind after work', loves children, enjoys having a meal with ordinary people and going for a walk – like any decent person. Such impressions and images animate libidinal ties and trigger fantasies of an imaginary connection between the head of state and his people, which is liable to re-feudalize the concept of democratic loyalty. They suggest that both leaders and followers belong to the same household dominated by the leading (father) figure, within the national

---

[80] See Sennet, *The Fall of Public Man*, and Halloran, S.M. (1981), 'Public vs. private: Richard Sennett on public life and authority' in: 67 *Quarterly Journal of Speech*, 322ff.

Source: © Süddeutsche Zeitung SZ-Photo-h-00088859 (1935). With friendly permission.

Figure 7.2 Hitler with his German shepherd, Blondie

community; and that obedience and loyalty are personal duties owed to the leader, not abstract duties with regard to the office or law:

> The Law on the Head of State of the German Reich of August 1, 1934 and the Law on the Oath of the Officials and Soldiers of the Wehrmacht of August 20, 1934 have shaped the bond between the German civil service and the *Führer* and *Reich* Chancellor into a highly personal and indissoluble relationship of loyalty, to which the civil servants, employees and workers of the public administration are, I am convinced, willing to give a special form of German greeting.[81]

6.3 The Iconography of Innocence

Political iconography and the cult of immediacy took a peculiar turn in Myanmar, in a tale which could be titled 'The freedom fighter and the generals' or 'An autocracy's never-wilting flower'. Comparable to the representatives of immediacy exhibited thus far, Aung San Suu Kyi has held the

[81] '*Gesetz über das Staatsoberhaupt des deutschen Reiches*' and '*Gesetz über die Vereidigung der Beamten und Soldaten der Wehrmacht*', quoted in Allert, *Der deutsche Gruß. Geschichte einer unheilvollen Geste*, 45.

military-invented office of 'state counsellor' since the landslide victory of her party, the National League for Democracy, in 2015 after an election process that observers called 'credible'. *De facto*, she has been president since then; however, she has been deliberately prevented from holding the very same office *de jure* by a clause in the Constitution that the military regime introduced many years before as a precautionary measure.[82]

For her longstanding struggle against the military dictatorship, the iconized politician, diplomat and author was awarded the Nobel Peace Prize in 1991, followed by many other accolades. In the run-up to the election, the military had secured one-quarter of the parliamentary seats. Before her election victory, Aung San Suu Kyi had declared she would lead Myanmar even if another party member were to serve as head of state. From a freedom fighter, she mutated first to an intermediary between the opposition movement and the military, and then to the mouthpiece of the generals. This dramatic and disillusioning political change came to light during the genocide of the Rohingya, a Muslim ethnic group in the west of the country. As usual, 'Daw Suu' was regularly seen in public with the generals, but remained silent on the brutal repression, expulsion and mass murder ordered by the military. One may presume that she tried her best not to annoy the military and her predominantly Buddhist supporters. The shining light of the non-violent democratic liberation movement clearly bent over backwards to serve the *ancien régime.*[83] For good measure, she defended the regime against the charge of genocide before the International Court of Justice in The Hague.

Undeterred, she continues to cultivate her image as Myanmar's icon of freedom. Removed from the everyday and yet close to the people, she orchestrates her public appearances, always sporting fresh flowers in her hair. She innocently offers these flowers – and her reputation – to garland what might be called a demarcated democracy or dual state. In doing so, she risks being used as the tool of the generals, who may now tolerate a democratic zone, but have not given up on their political goals, albeit now pulling the strings more flexibly and in the background – in the prerogative state (Figure 7.3).

---

[82] Aung San Suu Kyi's husband and her children respectively hold British citizenship. Because of this, she was barred from the office of the president. Popham, P. (2016), *The Lady and the Generals: Aung San Suu Kyi and Burma's Struggle for Freedom* (London: Penguin Books).

[83] Taub, A. and Fisher, M. (2017), 'Did the World Get Aung San Suu Kyi Wrong?', in: *The New York Times*, 31 October.

Source: 127426341 picture alliance / REUTERS / Soe Zeya Tun. With friendly permission.

Figure 7.3 *Aung San Suu Kyi among her military advisers*

7. DELUSIONS OF COMMUNITY

Citizens who are bombarded by stage-managed images of their leaders designed to present them as men (or women) of the people are liable to succumb to the phantasm of a non-mediated, quasi-personal relationship with the ruler. In this way, the connection between ruler and subjects can help to establish the basic psychological trope of authoritarian constitutionalism: the imaginary, homogeneous community that excludes all those who do not belong – strangers, immigrants, asylum seekers and so on. As soon as intermediary organizations and institutions are eliminated, the stage is set for the authoritarian theatre of *community*. While political power is released from responsibility and set free to operate on the basis of an informal script, politics transforms into *performance*. The authoritarian *dispositif* now takes the lead and spreads ideas of affiliation based on a Manichaean egalitarianism,[84] which

[84] Adorno, T.W. (1970), 'Die Freudsche Theorie und die Struktur faschistischer Propaganda', in: 24 *Psyche – Zeitschrift für Psychoanalyse*, 486 ff, 494; see also Librett (n 4).

emphasizes the differences between insiders and outsiders – those who belong and those who don't – while simultaneously trying to cover up the political diversity and social disparity within the cohort: 'Us versus them.'[85] In this spirit, Turkish President Recep Tayyip Erdoğan addressed his critics in the country: 'We are the people. Who are you?'[86]

7.1 Phantasm of People and Nation

While constitutions of democracies and republics usually describe the collective as a 'nation' or a 'people' (in a federal system, 'union' would be a functional equivalent), authoritarian constitutionalism sometimes comes to Manichaean egalitarianism with clearly profiled offers of fellowship and belonging. To provide a few examples: the Basic Law of Hungary, revised by the Orbán regime, conjures up a national, Christian, political community with deep historical roots (Preamble and Article D).[87] Unsurprisingly, given the state religion of Islam and the regime's geopolitical intentions, Iran's Constitution sealing the Islamic Revolution refers to the religion-based community of all Muslims – the *Ummah* – in Article 11. The Polish Constitution, as revised in 2009, contains religious references to the country's Christian heritage, but keeps the community more on the track of the (Second) Republic; whereas the programme of the governing PiS party undertakes a Catholic-nationalist reinterpretation. China's 1982 Constitution constructs the community quite counterfactually as 'the Chinese people of all ethnic groups and nationalities' – the cohesion created by the Communist Party, one may assume. Similarly, the Socialist Republic of Vietnam is presented as a 'united nation of all nationalities'. The Cuban Constitution of 1976, in the good socialist tradition of class, refers to the socially constituted union of workers, peasants, students and intellectuals, writ large as the proletarian international community, open to the nations of Latin America and the Caribbean. Many constitutions, such as the charter of Kazakhstan (1995/2011), transform the population into a cohort

---

[85] Typical Trump statements and tweets include: 'When Mexico sends its people, they are not their best … They are sending people that have lots of problems, and they are bringing those problems with us (sic)!' Quoted by Gutsche Jr., R. (2018), *The Trump Presidency, Journalism, and Democracy* (New York: Routledge), Introduction.

[86] Müller, J.W. (2016), 'Trump, Erdoğan, Farage: The attractions of populism for politicians, the dangers for democracy', in: *The Guardian*, 2 September, www.theguardian.com/books/2016/sep/02/trump-erdogan-farage-the-attractions-of-populism-for-politicians-the-dangers-for-democracy (last accessed 30 March 2020).

[87] 'Bearing in mind that there is one single Hungarian nation that belongs together…' (Article D of the Hungarian Basic Law, 2016).

forged together by 'historical fate'. The community united by 'a common destiny' has the potential to act as a slogan to ward off strangers.

7.2 '*Volksgemeinschaft*' – a Unity Gimmick

Less committed to restraint and generality than constitutions, authoritarian movements and organizations make liberal reference to the *topos* of 'community' in pamphlets and speeches. Such associations – which according to conventional political geography are located on the extreme right – make little effort to conceal racist, xenophobic or supremacist charges of the term, especially since they are supposed to give meaning and sharpness of demarcation to the Manichean worldview and internal egalitarianism based on exclusion. This will be illustrated by three examples.

It was not only National Socialism that put the '*Volksgemeinschaft*'[88] at the service of its propaganda. During the First World War, this concept changed fundamentally, meaning less and less a specific social class or stratum (the 'simple' working people, as opposed to the nobility or the ruling class), and serving more and more to invoke an 'inner unity'[89] that spanned all social strata. This semantic *mélange* of national and military community played into the hands of the right-wing nationalism of the Weimar period. It linked the *Volksgemeinschaft* with the rejection of communism and liberalism, which Carl Schmitt reveals in his authoritarian-apocalyptic moments.[90] The National Socialists had only to recall the term and incorporate it into their propaganda for a 'racially pure' *Volksgemeinschaft* directed against 'foreign peoples' and 'foreigners of the community' – above all, the Jews.

After the violent strategy of immediacy achieved by means of *Gleichschaltung* (alignment) and the destruction of intermediary structures – for example, breaking up other political parties and trade unions, and streamlining the media – this 'unity gimmick'[91] worked and the *Volksgemeinschaft* was elevated to both a formula of mobilization and the goal of a new social order.[92]

---

[88] See Steber, M. and Gotto, B. (eds) (2014), *Visions of Community in Nazi Germany: Social Engineering and Private Lives* (Oxford: Oxford University Press).

[89] Reichardt, S. (2013), '*Triumph der Tat*', www.zeit.de/zeit-geschichte/2013/03/faschismus-propaganda-willensstaerke-entschlusskraft-weltkriege/ (last accessed 6 November 2018).

[90] See Frankenberg (n 7), Chapter 4.

[91] Adorno (n 84); see also Steber and Gotto, 'Volksgemeinschaft: Writing the Social History of the Nazi Regime', in: *id*, *Visions of Community in Nazi Germany,* 1 ff; Bajohr, F. and Wildt, M. (eds) (2009), *Volksgemeinschaft. Neue Forschungen zur Gesellschaft des Nationalsozialismus* (Frankfurt am Main: Fischer).

[92] Wildt, M. (2012), 'Volksgemeinschaft'*?, bpb* 29 October, www.bpb.de/izpb/137211/volksgemeinschaft?p=all/ (last accessed 9 November 2018); Howind, S.

As a result, political identification – alloyed with racism, instead of civic membership – became the decisive binding agent between the leader and his followers. According to T.W. Adorno, the fascist fantasy of an ethnic community corresponds exactly to Freud's definition of the masses as 'a number of individuals who have put one and the same object in the place of their ego ideal and have consequently identified themselves with one another in their ego'. 'On the other hand, the ancestral omnipotence of the *Führer* image is, so to speak, borrowed from the power of the collective.'[93] The latter submitted to the leader's authority in order to experience authority as (the delusion of) community (Figure 7.4).

Source: © Bundesarchiv, Bild 183-C06292/Photo: Schwahn, Ernst. With friendly permission.

Figure 7.4 *Adolf Hitler drives into the Berlin Olympic Stadium in 1937 during the National Socialist May Day celebrations*

(2011), 'Der faschistische Einheitstrick. Die Suggestion von Einheit und Gleichheit in der nationalsozialistischen "Volksgemeinschaft"', in: Brunner, M. *et al* (eds), *Volksgemeinschaft, Täterschaft und Antisemitismus* (Gießen: Psychosozial-Verlag), 111 ff.

[93] Adorno, (n 84), 496.

Beginning with the right-wing nationalism of the Weimar period and especially Nazi fascism, the concept of the *Volksgemeinschaft* in Germany has been associated with organizations and political parties that can be seen as their ideological successors and, like them, pretend to speak 'in the name of the existence of all' (Michel Foucault) and defend 'real' democracy. Right-wing nationalist movements such as the Alternative for Germany must therefore distance themselves from the term, if only for tactical reasons. The Hungarian 'freedom fighters' of the right-wing extremist *Jobbik* party or the Golden Dawn Party in Greece have it easier: circumstances – including history – allow them to openly declare their racism, anti-Semitism and homophobia.

Admittedly, the concept of the people as a 'natural' reality, as opposed to an 'artificial' system of society, is well suited to authoritarian purposes, given the appropriate interpretation. The constitutions of autocracies tend to link the protection of citizens living abroad to the concept of their people as a homogeneous unit. The Hungarian Basic Law goes out of its way to extend the nation in this way. Some constitutions also provide for state protection of the community's spiritual wellbeing, education and familiarity with the local culture.[94] Others limit their reach to the formal extension of protection inside and outside the country.[95]

The democratic connotations of the concept of the people help to mobilize supporters and conceal cultural-ethnic exclusion, xenophobia and racism – at least superficially.[96] This is why nationalist-authoritarian movements such as Alternative for Germany and Pegida do not refer to 'the people' by chance, but also claim 'the people' for themselves ('We are the people') and seek to save them: 'We will get our Germany and our people back step by step.'[97] In connection with claiming 'our country' and 'our people', Heinrich Detering

---

94 'Bearing in mind that there is one single Hungarian nation that belongs together, Hungary shall bear responsibility for the fate of Hungarians living beyond its borders, and shall facilitate the survival and development of their communities; it shall support their efforts to preserve their Hungarian identity, the assertion of their individual and collective rights, the establishment of their community self-governments, and their prosperity in their native lands, and shall promote their cooperation with each other and with Hungary' (Article D of the Basic Law, 2011/2016). Similarly, Article 62 of the 1982/2017 Constitution of Turkey: 'The State shall take the necessary measures to ensure family unity, the education of the children, the cultural needs, and the social security of Turkish citizens working abroad, and to safeguard their ties with the home country and to help them on their return home.'

95 For example, Article 61 of the Constitution of Russia; Article 6 of the Constitution of Poland (extended protection); Article 18 of the 2016 Constitution of Moldavia.

96 Detering, H. (2018), 'Der Redner befiehlt, die Zuhörer folgen', in: *Frankfurter Rundschau,* 28 November, 30 f.

97 For references, see Detering (n 96).

recalls the open letter that Thomas Mann wrote when he was denied an honorary doctorate by Bonn University: 'You have the incredible audacity to confuse yourself with Germany! When perhaps the moment is not far off when the German people will do everything in their power not to be confused with you.'[98]

7.3 Tribal Community and Racial Supremacy

The Weimar Constitution launched the Republic with a sigh of relief: 'The German people, united in their tribes.' In contrast, the concept of 'tribe' is widely frowned upon today, especially in the post-colonial constitutions of plurinational or ethnically fragmented states.[99] It is replaced by 'nation', 'community' or 'Indigenous people'. When I talk about tribalism or tribal thinking, I do not mean to invoke apologetically the language of colonialism,[100] but rather designate polemically a rhetoric that refers to the addressees of the cult of immediacy, covering (the whole) society – or more precisely, the political followers – as a politically and socially homogeneous population.

According to tribalist ideas, the members of a given tribe not only inhabit the country together, but also share a uniform culture and identity. The racist connotations are obvious. In an essay for *The New Yorker*, George Packer attributes Donald Trump's tribalism to an Orwellian brand of nationalism and characterizes it as 'the habit of identifying oneself with a single nation or other entity, placing it beyond good and evil and recognizing no obligation other than to promote its interests'.

With regard to the political style of Donald Trump, he adds: 'Our tribes are competing for power over the state, the media, public opinion, the verbal battleground. When politics becomes a perpetual tribal war, ends justify

---

[98] Detering (n 96).

[99] For example, the people of Bolivia are constituted by 'the native *indigenous nations and peoples*, and the *inter-cultural and Afro-Bolivian communities*' (Constitution of Bolivia 2009 – emphasis added). The citizenship of Ecuador explicitly recognizes the affiliation with 'any of the other indigenous nations that coexist in plurinational Ecuador' (Constitution of Ecuador 2015). The Constitution of Uganda extends the rules of citizenship to 'indigenous communities'. The Constitution of Portugal (2005) uses administrative terminology and denotes the Azores and Madeira as 'autonomous regions'.

[100] Southall, A.W. (1970), 'The Illusion of Tribe', in: Gutkind, P. (ed), *The Passing of Tribal Man* (Leiden: Brill), 28 ff; Lentz, C. (1995), '"Tribalismus" und Ethnizität in Afrika – ein Forschungsüberblick', in: 23 *Leviathan*, 115 ff.

almost any means and individuals are absolved from the constraints of normal decency.'[101]

Other authors associate tribalism *à la* Trump with hyper-partisanship, but above all with the renaissance of 'white supremacy',[102] and fear that the Constitution could fall by the wayside as cynical, racist supremacy advances. These fears may be based on the rhetoric and ideological approach of the US president during his election campaign and in his government practice. Adorno's interpretation of fascist propaganda in the light of Freudian theory can be read as an adequate commentary on the techniques of Trump's tribalism and its success:

> The *Führer* can guess right the emotional needs and desires of those susceptible to his propaganda because he is psychologically similar to them, and what distinguishes him from them is not any real superiority, but the ability to express without their inhibitions what is latent in them. Leaders are usually oral character types with a compulsion to talk and coax others incessantly. Their famous power over those being led seems to be based largely on their orality: language itself, emptied of rational meaning, functions magically with them, promoting archaic regressions that degrade individuals to mass members. Since this characteristic of uninhibited but largely associative speech presupposes an at least temporary lack of ego control, it is more a sign of weakness than of strength.[103]

Trump's incessant tweets, repetitive, simplistic rhetoric and stereotypical thinking correspond to the infantile desire of those susceptible to this propaganda for endless repetition and reaffirmation of their cohesion, based on their desire to belong to his group and submission, as well as their hostility towards those who do not belong in it. The immediacy, uniformity and repetitiveness of this propaganda[104] should not be misjudged as the results of a simple-minded protagonist: like hypnosis, they are the conditions for its success. Instead, Trump's limited vocabulary, incapacity for moderation and lack of emotional restraint[105] during his campaign and in office must be considered as a mobili-

---

[101] George Packer, G. (2018), 'A New Report Offers Insights into Tribalism in the Age of Trump', *The New Yorker*, 12 October, www.newyorker.com/news/daily-comment/a-new-report-offers-insights-into-tribalism-in-the-age-of-trump/ (last accessed 9 November 2018); see also Gordon, P.E. (2017), 'The Authoritarian Personality Revisited: Reading Adorno in the Age of Trump', in: 2 *boundary*, 44 ff.

[102] Coates (n 68).

[103] Adorno, (n 84), 502; see Freud, S. (1922), *Group Psychology and Ego Analysis* (London/Vienna: International Psychoanalytic Press), especially 102 ff.

[104] Howind, '*Der faschistische Einheitstrick*' (n 92), 118 f.

[105] Illustrated by his personal attacks especially against Hillary Clinton ('Lock her up'), other competitors and non-loyal members of his staff. See the remarkable analysis by Bump, P. (2019), 'The expansive, repetitive universe of Trump's Twitter insults', in: *The Washington Post*, 20 August, www.washingtonpost.com/politics/2019/08/20/

zation resource and trick to unify his supporters, which could help to explain why Donald Trump was elected president.

The cult of immediacy intertwines and brings to bear the essential characteristics of political authoritarianism. The executive political technology introduces its informality and opportunism. The concept of power, based on the spirit of ownership, keeps institutions and the public space occupied, and enables autocracies to deploy their practice of participation as generating complicity. At the same time, authoritarian power infiltrates this space through the commander-in-chief's perpetual presence and direct communication. All of this allows the leader (or clique, party, junta) to display and execute, depending on the context, his (or its) patriarchal, mythical, sovereign, benevolent, punitive or vindictive authority.

To sum up: the mechanism of identification functions as a link between leader and followers, heads of state and subjects. The cult of immediacy takes this connection one step further and works in the service of an imaginary community whose unity – be it patriotic, national, ethnic, religious or tribal – is based on a Manichean egalitarianism that includes only followers and excludes and rejects all non-members. The xenophobia of right-wing, radically nationalist regimes, parties and movements is therefore neither a historical coincidence nor dependent on the number of aliens who actually live in or wish to enter a country. Xenophobia is embedded in the very fabric of those imaginary communities that autocrats invoke to stabilize their regime and that supporters fantasize to assuage their desire to belong.

8. CONSTITUTIONS OF IMMEDIACY

It was previously mentioned in passing that the establishment of a non-mediated connection between a leader and people regularly comes at the expense of constitutions – especially those that install institutional, procedural and functional mechanisms of control, intervention and mediation precisely in order to establish the form of distanced rule and make democracy liveable and practicable through participation.[106] So what happens to constitutions when, on the society side, intermediary organizations and bodies – notably associations, parties and the media – are destroyed or disempowered; and when, on the state side, the institutions and procedures that intervene in the relationship between the

---

expansive-repetitive-universe-trumps-twitter-insults/ (last accessed 17 March 2020). See also the list of over 500 persons, media and institutions he insulted: *The New York Times*, 28 January 2018, www.nytimes.com/interactive/2016/01/28/upshot/donald-trump-twitter-insults.html/.

[106] Uwe Volkmann suggested adding considerations how the cult of immediacy plays out constitutionally. I have to thank him for this reminder.

executive and the population are eliminated or circumvented? Four different answers and strategies will be briefly outlined in conclusion: immediate constitution, parallel constitution, sub-constitution and bypass.

8.1 Immediate Constitution

An immediate relationship does not negatively affect constitutions that actually include structures of immediacy. The Algerian Constitution, for instance, provides for the president's right to appeal directly to the will of the people and to address the nation directly.[107] This at least lays the foundation stone for the constitutional enshrinement of immediacy. Another factor favouring immediacy in Algeria is the very strong position of the president as head of state (with no time limit on his term of office), guardian of the Constitution and holder of prerogatives[108] on the one hand, and of the people on the other, as the source of all authority and legitimacy and the seat of constituent power.[109] Nevertheless, in practice, the country has always been run as a semi-presidential system (with great influence of the military),[110] as the Constitution also furnishes structures of representation. Moreover, former President Bouteflika – who was steered into his fifth term of office by a clique of political advisers or by the actual power managers, despite his ill health – was anything but a charismatic figure and was seldom present in public. So, essential elements of a cult of immediacy were missing. The protests against the continuation of his 'chain-presidency' signalled that a relationship of authority, even if non-mediated, can be disrupted.

Ultimately, however, it is difficult to find other candidates that qualify as immediate constitutions. At best, they are hybrid constructions that arguably contain elements of immediacy. The Weimar Constitution, before its normative gutting in 1933, did indeed include an emergency clause (Article 48, Section 2), but still installed a representative system – however precarious – and allowed for vital party competition and an active media landscape. It took the Enabling Act to destroy the design of the Weimar Constitution and violently enforce immediacy. It was accompanied by a crackdown on and censorship of the media to facilitate conformity and monitoring, and by intimidation and prohibition of social organizations and parties. What remained after the Nazis had completed their work of destruction hardly deserves to be called a constitution.

---

107 Articles 8 IV and 84 of the 2016 Constitution of Algeria.

108 Articles 84, 91 and 143 of the 2016 Constitution of Algeria.

109 Articles 7, 8 I and 12 of the 2016 Constitution of Algeria.

110 See Schmid, B. (2005), *Algerien – Frontstaat im globalen Krieg? Neoliberalismus, soziale Bewegungen und islamistische Ideologie in einem nordafrikanischen Land* (Münster: Unrast Verlag).

Perhaps unnoticed by the regime, Chile's Pinochet Constitution of 1980[111] also lacked a clear immediacy structure. It centralized political power in the hands of the directly elected president as head of government and banned political parties, but also allowed for '*grupos intermedios*' (although nowhere defined) and did not abolish the Congress – although this could easily be controlled by the dictator and the military leadership in the National Security Council.

By the same token, Erdoğan's post-coup Constitution of 2017 reveals how directness is privileged only marginally through the instrument of the referendum, but more clearly through its practice and the principles which parties must observe (Article 69); and how constitutional threats may paralyze party competition. Likewise, Venezuela's Hugo Chávez included some strategies of immediacy in the constitutional revision he initiated, such as abolishing the Senate's veto authority, giving the president the right to hold referendums to dismiss members of Parliament, and dissolving Parliament.[112] However, the revision did not completely neutralize political parties and required that elections and referendums – albeit manipulated – be held (a remarkable 15 referendums were held over 17 years).

8.2 Parallel Constitution

The cult of immediacy is more likely to push forward a 'parallel constitution', in which the immediate relations unfold independently of the written constitutional text. Where necessary, the text is ignored, reinterpreted or openly violated and thus devalued. The way Venezuela's presidency was transferred from Hugo Chávez to Nicolas Maduro illustrates the chasm between the written document and the practised parallel constitution. Chávez was elected president of Venezuela for the fourth time in a row in October 2012, but was unable to take office because of his severe cancer, for which he was receiving treatment in Cuba. Nicholás Maduro, nominated by Chávez as vice president, took over government affairs, thus far still pursuant to Article 236, Number 3 of the Venezuelan Constitution. Had the 1999 Constitution further been observed as the authoritative script, Chávez would have had to be introduced into office and sworn in; and when it was clear that he could not continue as president permanently, Maduro would have had to resign and the president of the National Assembly step in to serve temporarily as president. However,

[111] Wühler, N. and Lorca, R.M. (1981), 'Die neue chilenische Verfassung von 1980', in: 41 *Zeitschrift für ausländisches öffentliches Recht*, 825ff.

[112] Corrales, J. (2013), 'The Authoritarian Resurgence: Venezuela's Succession Crisis', in: 112 *Current History*, 37 ff, 38 f.

neither this nor the swearing in happened (a violation of the Constitution that was continued in the constitutional conflict in 2018). With the approval of the Supreme Court – previously hand-picked by Chávez – the inauguration was transformed into a major event, at which the Chávez supporters present were 'sworn in' as a symbolic stand-in for the president. They were also turned into accomplices of the Chávez regime, one might add. And to secure the continuity of the regime, Chávez was politically beatified in anticipation of his imminent demise.[113] Without the connotations of a political religion, this strategy was extended by Nicholás Maduro.[114] He exacerbated the regime's communicative hegemony by privileging state media; massively disregarded and manipulated election results; staffed the courts with judges loyal to the regime; and obstructed all criticism and opposition to the best of his abilities. Not only democracy, but also the Constitution fell by the wayside.

8.3 Sub-constitution

Hugo Chavez – certainly one of the most accomplished and charismatic 'immediatists' – pursued yet another strategy to give the cult of immediacy a constitutional attire. He carried out the necessary operations at the level of a 'sub-constitution'. As a hallmark of this strategy, the Constitution remains largely unchanged, both externally and formally, and intermediate institutions – such as Parliament and courts – have not been removed. However, at the level of parliamentary acts, backed by the co-opted Supreme Court, Chávez eliminated institutional mediation and control bodies. Thus, the elements of autocratic legalism are hardly or not at all prominent in the Constitution, but they do appear in 'organic laws'.[115] In Venezuela, the Telecommunications Law of 2000 authorized the government to suspend or revoke the broadcasting licences of private operators in the interests of the nation. Since 2004 and 2005, respectively, 'legitimately constituted authorities' and government officials have been protected from incitement to public disobedience and disrespectful remarks, hatred and intolerance by the Social Responsibility Law and the reformed Penal Code. In 2010, the Organic Law of Popular Power set up municipal councils with an undefined (but regime-loyal) composition, which sometimes overrode elected mayors in the distribution of state funds and the exercise of their powers. Finally, since 2010, the Law for the Defence

[113] Corrales, 'The Authoritarian Resurgence: Autocratic Legalism in Venezuela'; and *id* (2013), 'Venezuela's Succession Crisis', in: 112 *Current History*, 56 ff.

[114] For references, see Corrales, J. and Romero, C.A. (2013), *U.S.-Venezuela Relations Since the 1990s: Coping with Midlevel Security Threats* (New York: Routledge).

[115] See Corrales (n 113), 38–40.

of Political Sovereignty and National Self-Determination has cut off all non-governmental organizations defending human rights and monitoring state practices from any financial support from abroad.

The Hungarian Constitution appears to give autocrat Viktor Orbán little elbowroom to grind down state institutions that might be in his way. However, the right to hold referendums – national consultations – is a suitable constitutional basis on which to establish a cult of immediacy. To secure this basis, Orbán – with different instruments from, but similar objectives to, Chávez and Maduro – pursued the goal of 'harmonizing' the media.[116] The Media Act of 2010 primarily obliged the public press, television and radio stations to ensure 'balanced reporting' and 'strengthen national identity'. Critical journalists and editors were intimidated, and some 3400 were dismissed. Since 2010, the NMHH – which of course is close to the government – has monitored the media sector. As the cornerstone of non-mediated structures, all private government-related media (broadcasting, print, online) recently had to join a single foundation, which is headed by government representatives. In December 2018 Orbán prevented the obvious antitrust review through a decree attesting to the foundation's national importance.[117]

8.4 Bypassing the Constitution

For some time now, the regime of Xi Jinping has bypassed the Chinese Constitution with the app 'Xue Xi Qiang Guo' ('Study Xi to make the country strong').[118] In many state-run businesses, schools, universities and hospitals, it is obligatory – especially for party members – to download the app and register with their name and phone number. The local Communist Party organizations check whether the app has been downloaded to all smartphones and how often it is actually accessed. The app contains Xi Jinping's thoughts, which have been dignified with constitutional status. The app measures how many texts each user reads per day and how many comments he or she posts. Quiz questions are inserted to check whether the texts are read carefully. Like the social scoring discussed in the previous chapter, users receive points for fulfilling

---

[116] See Simon, K. and Rácz, T. (2017), 'Hostile takeover: How Orbán is subjugating the media in Hungary', Heinricht-Böll-Foundation, (ed), 22 August, www.boell.de/en/2017/08/22/hostile-takeover-how-orban-subjugating-media-hungary/ (last accessed 17 March 2020).

[117] See Simon and Ràcz, 'Hostile Takeover'; Ariès, Q. (2019), 'Europe's Failure to Protect Liberty in Hungary', in: *The Atlantic*, 29 December.

[118] Li, J. (2019), 'An app to teach Xi Jinping thought can study the phones of its 100 million users', 14 October, https://qz.com/1727362/chinese-app-promoting-xi-jinping-thought-has-access-to-100-million-users-phones/ (last accessed 17 March 2020).

these tasks. If the minimum number of points is not achieved, sanctions are threatened or imposed, such as salary reductions or the suspension of bonus payments.[119] Sidestepping the Constitution, the app operates as a functional equivalent of Mao's 'Red Book'. It ensures political loyalty with the support of information technology. Unlike in Mao's days, the Internet has made it possible to tap into and control even those areas to which the individual was once able to retreat.

The election campaign and governing practice of US President Donald Trump reflect a different bypass version of a 'constitution of immediacy'. He does not take the path of constitutional amendment (hardly promising because of the qualified majorities required and the inevitable failure before the citadel of the sacrosanct First Amendment); nor does he devalue the Constitution at the level of simple law – apart from the unconstitutional and illegal declaration of a 'national emergency' which he freely admitted did not exist. He prefers to undermine the freedoms of vulnerable groups, misinform supporters, blast out Twitter volleys[120] and insults, slander his critics and opponents, and perform an unmediated style of politics and communication that disavows the Constitution's underlying concept and image of government information and public relations. Trump's 'state practice' gives the impression that the US Constitution does not have the normative power to defend a rule of distance against the force of immediacy, unless there is significant resistance to it in the political class or in civil society.

---

[119] Kuo, L. and Lyons, K. (2019), 'China's most popular app brings Xi Jinping to your pocket', in: *The Guardian*, 15 February.

[120] Tsur, O., Ognyanova, K. and Lazer, D. (2016), 'The Data Behind Trump's Twitter Takeover', in: *POLITICO*, 29 April.

8. Audience and purposes of authoritarian constitutions

What use are constitutions in advancing the cause of political authoritarianism? 'Zero,' the ideal-generalized liberal will answer, without being able to explain plausibly why authoritarian regimes nonetheless 'constitutionalize' themselves all the same. One might add, ironically: because constitutions distract from the work of repression, which is tiring and paralyzing in the long run (although this objection cannot really be taken seriously).

In the preceding chapters, practices and speeches, representations and ideas have been discussed in order to profile authoritarian constitutionalism and point out possible ways to make sense of it. This discussion should have made it quite clear that I do not consider the constitutions of autocracies to be trivial matters. That is why I will now attempt to link the four basic elements – executive-informal techniques of governing; political power as property; participation as complicity; and cult of immediacy and imaginary communality – to possible purposes and audiences of constitutions, in order to define their relationships more precisely and illustrate them in a diagram.

In a first step, the elements of authoritarianism are connected to form a network, which I introduce as an authoritarian *dispositif*[1] to map the heterogeneous ensemble of regimes and to emphasize the strategic roles that these elements may play in the construction and stabilization of autocracy. After some notes on the structure of authoritarian constitutions, I attempt in a second step to answer the constitutional question at least tentatively by distinguishing and assigning instrumental and symbolic purposes on the one hand, and internal and external audiences on the other.

---

[1] I borrow the term from Michel Foucault and cautiously apply it to political authoritarianism. Regarding the difficult concept and its diverse applications, see Larroche, V. (2019), The Dispositif: A Concept for Information and Communication Sciences (Hoboken: John Wiley & Sons); Bührmann, A.D. and Schneider, W. (2008), *Vom Diskurs zum Dispositiv. Eine Einführung in die Dispositivanalyse* (Bielefeld: transcript-Verlag). See also Chapter 4.

1. ONCE AGAIN: THE CONSTITUTIONAL QUESTION

So why did the Bolsheviks, after their successful October Revolution and at a rather difficult moment, have historical and dialectical materialism escorted by a constitution on their way towards the first Soviet republic?[2] What prompted Adolf Hitler to repeatedly extend the Enabling Act, which suspended the Weimar Constitution and transferred legislative power to him, even though he had long since established a barbarous dictatorship that operated 'lawlessly'?[3] What were the motives that led Bashar al-Assad to put the revised Syrian Constitution to the vote in 2012 amid civil war and bloodshed? Why did Myanmar's military government convene a National Congress after years in power to reconstitute the regime in the face of protests across the country? Why did President Erdoğan have 74 amendments added to the Turkish Constitution after he won the presidential election in 2017 which transferred more power to him, even though a lack of power did not seem to be a problem? What was Augusto Pinochet trying to prove when, at the height of his dictatorial power, he enacted a Constitution in 1980 and, eight years later, submitted to a referendum for another term in office, instead of just granting himself an unlimited term as a *fait accompli*?[4]

---

2 Basic Law of the Russian Socialist Federalist Republic of 10 July 1918. Praising this Constitution, Lenin said that it had 'not been thought up by any commission, not elaborated by lawyers, not copied from other constitutions'; rather, he argued, 'the experience of the organization and struggle of the proletarian masses against the exploiters both at home and throughout the world'; www.1000dokumente.de/index.html?c=dokument_ru&dokument=0005_ver&object=context&l=de/ (last accessed 8 July 2019).

3 The Enabling Law (Law to Eliminate the Plight of the People and the *Reich*) of 24 March 1933 had (as already quoted in extracts above) the following wording: 'The *Reichstag* [national assembly] has passed the following law, which is hereby promulgated with the consent of the *Reichsrat* [second chamber], after it has been established that the requirements of legislation amending the Constitution have been met: Art. 1: *Reichsgesetze* [national laws] may be passed by the Government of the *Reich* in addition to the procedure provided for in the [Weimar] Reichs Constitution – Art. 2: The *Reichsgesetze* adopted by the *Reichsregierung* [national government] may *deviate* from the Constitution insofar as they do not relate to the establishment of the *Reichstag* and the *Reichsrat* as such. The rights of the President of the *Reich* remain unaffected.'

4 On 5 October 1988, a majority of almost 56 per cent voted against a further term of office. After all, the Pinochet Constitution at the time of the change of government secured the influence of the *ancien régime* through numerous regulations during the democracy that followed. These clauses are known as 'authoritarian enclaves'. See Codoceo, F. (2007), *Democratic transition in Chile. Continuity or New Beginning?* (Berlin: wvb Wissenschaftlicher Verlag Berlin). The film *Nó!* on the referendum is definitely worth seeing; directed by Pablo Larrain, Chile, 2012 (with Gael García Bernal, Antonia Zegers and Alfredo Castro).

It is difficult to precisely determine the motives and strategies in these and other cases, as authoritarian leaders, clans and cadres are not inclined to reveal openly what they have in mind and where they are heading. As when considering their financial circumstances, one is to an extent dependent on conjecture and interpretation. The starting point for this remains the *prima facie* peculiar circumstance that autocrats take the time and trouble to draft or revise a constitution and then let the population vote on the result in a referendum.[5] One cannot rule out the possibility that they are blindly following a procedure that is practised worldwide; but this would overlook their fundamentally strategic mind set. Explaining this away as mere window-dressing is also probably too vague, unless one indicates which windows and which spectators autocrats have in mind.

In general, indeterminacy and ambivalence hide the political impregnation and subtext of constitutions, as well as the aims that rulers want to pursue. The structures of standardized constitutional design and the established, conventional vocabulary do not easily reveal the purposes and projects of autocrats; at least, they try to marginalize or silence them.[6] And yet authoritarian constitutionalism presupposes that there is some kind of connection between regimes and their constitutions, however tense and precarious that may be.[7] In consequence, it is not all that unreasonable to read the charters of autocracies as texts written for a purpose (more or less clearly defined) and addressed to an audience (more or less predictable). Accordingly, I try to determine these purposes and audiences through a heuristic that hopefully helps to reveal what the mere text of authoritarian constitutions cannot. This heuristic places such constitutions in the four fields of a grid formed by two axes of a continuum:

---

[5] It is easier to overlook limited constitutional manoeuvres, such as Xi Jinping's lifting of the term limit or Hugo Chávez's attempt in 2012 to remove the term limit; although Venezuela's president had already failed in a much more comprehensive constitutional referendum at the end of 2007. At that time, a narrow majority of voters rejected the revision of a total of 69 articles of the Constitution. Informative: Weyland, K. (2013), 'Latin America's Authoritarian Drift. The Populist Threat from the Left', in: 24 *Journal of Democracy*, 18 ff and Priester, K. (2012), 'Hugo Chávez, *Führer, Armee, Volk – Linker Populismus an der Macht*', in: *id, Rechter und linker Populismus: Annäherung an ein Chamäleon* (Frankfurt am Main: Campus), 114 ff.

[6] Loughlin, M. (2017), 'The Constitutional Silences', in: 16 *International Journal of Constitutional Law*, 922 ff.

[7] As discussed above, an authoritarian regime can very well coexist with a formally democratic, parliamentary system of constitutionalism. This is illustrated by the Fifth French Republic, for example. Authoritarianism can also develop in a reasonably democratic institutional setting, as illustrated by the metamorphosis of the Abe government in Japan. See the analysis by Yamamoto, H. (2019), 'An authorization of Japanese constitutionalism?', in: Alviar, H. and Frankenberg, G. (eds) (2019), *Authoritarian Constitutionalism* (Cheltenham: Edward Elgar Publishing), 338 ff.

one addresses and charts purposes, the other audiences. Moreover, constitutions are read as performative acts. I assume that authoritarian leaders and regimes predominantly act with a strategic intention and follow a purposive rationality (regardless of how strongly one may disapprove of those purposes) when they deal with constitutions.

2. ARCHETYPES OF AUTHORITARIAN CONSTITUTIONS

Four distinct archetypes – and countless hybrids and crossovers – have shaped the history of constitutions and constitutionalism.[8] Each is characterized by a recognizable style and comes with a specific register, informed by a constitutional grammar and vocabulary that depend on the respective historical-political constellations and other contextual conditions. Contract, manifesto, programme and (higher) law or code are constitutional speech acts that can be distinguished as archetypes. It remains to be seen which of them best accommodates the strategies of political authoritarianism.

2.1 Semantics and Structure of Authoritarian Constitutions

Seen from a distance, it would appear that the semantics and structure of authoritarian constitutions and the rhetoric of authoritarian constitutionalism have no particularly striking features and very much resemble those of their non-authoritarian counterparts. Conformism seems to shape their external form. But as always, appearances are deceptive. First, not all constitutions of autocracies fit within the same framework. They are quite open about their preference for the executive and its techniques of governing. With unsurpassed frankness, the Russian Constitution of 1918 transferred 'all state and local power' to the Soviets (Article 1); but in 'the present moment of transition' (Article 9), it assigned the leading role to the All-Russian Central Executive Committee of the Soviets, which functioned as a collective presidency for the 'all-round protection of the achievements of the great workers' and peasants' revolution' (Article 19). The Central Executive Committee elected the Council of People's Commissars for the management of administrative affairs. Behind the façade of fairly amorphous, overlapping institutionalizations of the Soviets, the Bolsheviks thus installed their monopoly of power. In contrast, authoritarian constitutionalism *à la* Putin adheres in form to the 1993 Constitution, but

[8] For a more detailed characterization of the archetypes, see Frankenberg, G. (2018), *Comparative Constitutional Studies – Between Magic and Deceit* (Cheltenham: Edward Elgar Publishing), Chapter II.

does not prevent the autocrat from establishing the structures and institutions of a vertical 'guided democracy' as a deep state according to his preferences.

Hitler's Enabling Act of 1933 disempowered the *Reichstag* and transferred legislative power to the *Reich* government, thus suspending the Weimar Constitution (Article 2) without further ado. On careful reading of the organizational part, Myanmar's democratically challenged Constitution of 2008 also reveals the extent to which local, regional and state institutions continue to be infiltrated by the military, despite the 'democratic reform'.[9] The Erdoğan regime took the opposite approach in its comprehensive constitutional reshuffling of powers in 2017. Among other things, the despot was keen to secure his position of power by subjugating the military, which previously played the role of 'guardian of the republic' – in particular, by abolishing military courts and military academies.[10]

Hence, charters of authoritarianism must be examined to find out whether, how and to what extent the text permits the centralization of executive power, abolishes the limitations on terms of office, lays the groundwork for complicity, favours the neutralization of intermediary institutions and organizations – or at least accepts it in state practice – or allocates emergency powers to the executive.

Depending on the context, autocracies always have, and sometimes exercise, the option to wrap themselves in a cloak of democracy. Thus, Syria's constitutional and legislative reforms in 2012, viewed in isolation, are not only meaningless, but also misleading. On 25 July, the Syrian government passed a draft law allowing the establishment of political parties. In the new Constitution, the Ba'ath Party's claim to leadership (laid down in Article 8 of the previous Constitution) was revised – in theory. In practice, however, this revision was largely meaningless, given the Assad clan's hold on power and the absence of an institution that might control compliance. Furthermore, the commitment to 'political pluralism' proclaimed in the new version of Article 8 should not be read too enthusiastically – for instance, as decentralizing power[11] – because political parties are still required to obtain explicit approval

---

[9] Notably the representative bodies: 'The Pyidaungsu Hluttaw, the Region Hluttaws and the State Hluttaws include the Defence Services personnel as Hluttaw representatives nominated by the Commander-in-Chief of the Defence Services' (Section 14).

[10] See Karabelıas, G. (2009), 'The Military Institution, Atatürk's Principles, and Turkey's Sisyphean Quest for Democracy', in: 45 *Middle Eastern Studies*, 57 ff; Platter, J. and Çalışkan, B. (2008), 'Das türkische Verfassungsgericht auf dem Weg zum "Hüter der Verfassung"', in: 39 *Zeitschrift für Parlamentsfragen*, 832 ff.

[11] See El Manfalouty, O. (2019), 'Authoritarian Constitutionalism in the Islamic World – Theoretical Considerations and Comparative Observations on Syria & Turkey', in: Alviar and Frankenberg (n 7), 95 ff.

(from the government) and are further prohibited from organizing on the basis of a regional or religious programme. So the danger of excessive participation of Kurds and Sunnis is averted.[12]

2.2 Authoritarian Manifesto

Authoritarian constitutions reveal their dark side, if at all, in elusive moments and marginal remarks. It is these which reveal them as variants of the political manifesto (and in turn expose authoritarian features of this archetype in liberal settings).

In the allegorical passages, where purposes tend to lean towards the symbolic side, the authoritarian archetype comes across as a political manifesto. Authoritarian constitutionalism favours unilateral declarations made by a (self-appointed) elite on its own initiative or on behalf of a leader, such as the Central Executive Committee of the Soviet Union (1924), Iran's Assembly of Experts (1979), the Communist Party of China (1982) or the State Peace and Development Council that convened the National Assembly in Myanmar (1993). Following the structure of the manifesto, the authors present the result of this performative act – namely, the creation of a symbolic system; the constitutional 'world-making'[13] – as something that the addressees have learned and already know and recognize beyond doubt. The American Declaration of Independence, authored also by slaveholders, provides the frequently copied model: 'We hold these truths to be self-evident, that all men are created equal, that they are endowed by their Creator with certain unalienable Rights that among these are Life, Liberty and the pursuit of Happiness...'[14]

---

[12] Article 8 of the 2012 Constitution of the Syrian-Arab Republic: '1. The political system of the state shall be based on the principle of political pluralism, and exercising power democratically through the ballot box; - 2. Licensed political parties and constituencies shall contribute to the national political life, and shall respect the principles of national sovereignty and democracy; - 3. The law shall regulate the provisions and procedures related to the formation of political parties; - 4. Carrying out any political activity or forming any political parties or groupings on the basis of religious, sectarian, tribal, regional, class-based, professional, or on discrimination based on gender, origin, race or color may not be undertaken...'.

[13] Goodman, N. (1978), *Ways of World Making* (London: Hackett).

[14] US Declaration of Independence, 4 July 1776.

'These truths' are founded as common experiences, learning processes and prejudices from collective struggles:

> After experiencing the anti-despotic constitutional movement and the anti-colonialist movement centered on the nationalization of the oil industry, the Muslim people of Iran *learned*...[15]

> [T]his Constitution *affirms* the achievements of the struggles of the Chinese people of all nationalities.[16]

> Invoking the memory of our ancestors and calling upon the wisdom of the *lessons* of our *shared history*...[17]

Algeria's 1989 Constitution refers to itself, in this very sense, as 'the result of its long resistance to the culture, values and fundamental components of its identity'. Hungary's 2011 Constitution, orchestrated by Viktor Orbán, evokes a quasi-millennial history of Hungary that insists on the sublimity of the 'Magyar nation'. It emphasizes the 'pride in our ancestors who fought for the survival, freedom and independence of our country'. Different country, same timespan: Vietnam's cadres deduce from its thousand-year history, and especially from its struggles for liberation, a mission to 'lead the nation to socialism' (Constitution of 1992/2013).

The documents of authoritarian constitutionalism also follow the logic of the manifesto, in that they make use of the normative register of necessity to justify autocratic forms of state or measures of state practice. In this vein, the Soviet Central Executive Committee found that the reconstruction of the national economy, the uncertainty of the international situation and the building of Soviet power 'imperatively demand the unification of the Soviet Republics in a federal state capable of guaranteeing external security and internal economic prosperity and the freedom of national development of peoples'.[18] The Fathers of the Constitution of the Islamic Republic of Iran (1979) conjured up the awakened consciousness of the nation under the leadership of Imam Khomeini, which had 'recognized the need to pursue a genuine Islamic

---

[15] 1979 Constitution of the Islamic Republic of Iran, emphasis added.

[16] 1982 Constitution of the People's Republic of China, emphasis added. See also the 1972 Constitution of Cameroon, Article 1(2) and the 2005 Constitution of the Democratic Republic of the Congo, Articles 42 ff.

[17] 'Invoking the memory of our ancestors and calling upon the wisdom of the *lessons* of our *shared history*...' 2010 Constitution of Angola – emphasis added.

[18] Soviet Constitution of 1924. 'Being guided by the interests of the working class as a whole, the Russian Socialist Federated Soviet Republic deprives all individuals and groups of rights which could be utilized by them to the detriment of the socialist revolution' (Basic Law of the Russian Socialist Federative Soviet Republic of 1918, Article II, No 23).

and ideological line in its struggles'. The Constitution of Rwanda, which allowed President Paul Kagame to morph from peacemaker to autocrat,[19] also stresses 'the need to strengthen and promote national unity and reconciliation, which was seriously shaken by the genocide against the Tutsis'.

More clearly than the classic manifestos that deal less with criteria of membership than with shared values, authoritarian constitutions sometimes reveal which persons, groups and ideas should be excluded from the community thus constituted. In this respect, Russia's Constitution of 1918 provides what might be called a model of 'corporate honesty': in 'unshakable determination... to snatch humanity from the clutches of finance capital and imperialism' and to affirm the 'alliance of the working classes', the 'dictatorship of the urban and rural proletariat and the poorest peasantry' was established, for the 'complete suppression of the bourgeoisie' and 'elimination of the parasitic strata of society'. Hardly less clearly, all (presumed) opponents of the socialist revolution were *a priori* excluded from the use – actually, from the presumed abuse – of constitutionally guaranteed rights. Likewise, members of the higher classes and supporters of the White Armies were barred from gaining access to political power during the civil war.

Some authoritarian constitutions of more recent provenance follow this example and take all keys to power out of the hands of the partisans of the replaced political system:

> [N]o protection shall be accorded to an activity contrary to Turkish national interests, Turkish existence and the principle of its indivisibility with its State and territory, historical and moral values of Turkishness; the nationalism, principles, reforms and civilizationism of Atatürk and that sacred religious feelings shall absolutely not be involved in state affairs and politics as required by the principle of secularism...[20]

Following this logic, the Iraqi Constitution of 2005 prohibited the Saddamist Baath Party, as well as any organization or programme that promotes or justifies racism, terrorism or ethnic cleansing (Article 7). With almost noble reserve, the Constitution of the Kingdom of Bhutan reserves basic rights

---

[19] Beaumont, P. (2010), 'Paul Kagame: A tarnished African hero', in: *The Guardian*, 18 July, www.theguardian.com/theobserver/2010/jul/18/paul-kagame-rwanda-profile/ (last accessed 20 January 2020).

[20] Preamble, 1982 Constitution of Turkey. See also Article 301 of the Penal Code of Turkey: 'A person who publicly denigrates the Turkish Nation, the State of the Turkish Republic or the Grand National Assembly of Turkey and the judicial institutions of the State shall be punishable by imprisonment from 6 months to 2 years.' Italy's post-fascist Constitution (1947) prohibited the reorganization of 'the dissolved fascist party in whatever form' (Article XII, Transitional and Final Provisions).

(including duties), party membership and eligibility for political office for nationals, and excludes only – unnamed – foreigners.

If enemies and opponents of a regime are marked, and persons, groups, ideas and opinions are excluded from protection, constitutions give up the noble style and appearance of formal equality. Instead, they act as the mouthpiece of a dictatorial agenda, which is reinforced by the autocratic preference for one-way communication (see above). The lack of tolerance that characterizes political authoritarianism with regard to surprises and risks, dissent and opposition or even diversity is thus also expressed in the enemy and prohibition clauses of constitutions.

3. *DISPOSITIF* OF AUTHORITARIAN CONSTITUTIONS

To the extent that constitutionalism – that is, constitutions, their theory and practice, culture and ideology – in authoritarian regimes is not expected to yield a significant normative dividend in liberal terms, authoritarian constitutionalism can be taken analytically seriously and can indeed be criticized as such. In the following, I try to do this by placing the constitutions of autocracies on a heuristic grid and examining their (possible) purposes and audiences. This heuristic distinguishes between two internally related dimensions and thus facilitates the development of a four-field matrix. Horizontally, I depict the tension between instrumental and symbolic purposes; and vertically, the variation between internal (local, national) and external (regional, international) addressees (see Figure 8.1).

3.1 Audience and Interests

Insofar as the audience is concerned, I assume that it makes a difference whether a constitution is essentially internally or externally oriented, or whether constitutional events and issues are likely to affect those living in the domestic arena or abroad. While one can distinguish diverse fields or horizons of attention for the respective audience, these do not enclose a uniform group of addressees within the respective zone.

The domestic horizon primarily comprises the population (this orientation is usually not very revealing) and the general public (insofar as they are interested in constitutional issues). However, it may also include specific target groups – such as the regime's supporters, to be mobilized or appeased; or its opponents, to be deterred or given a last chance to join; as well as the ruling (party) elites, including possible rivals for power, such as parties in a coalition government or members of a junta.

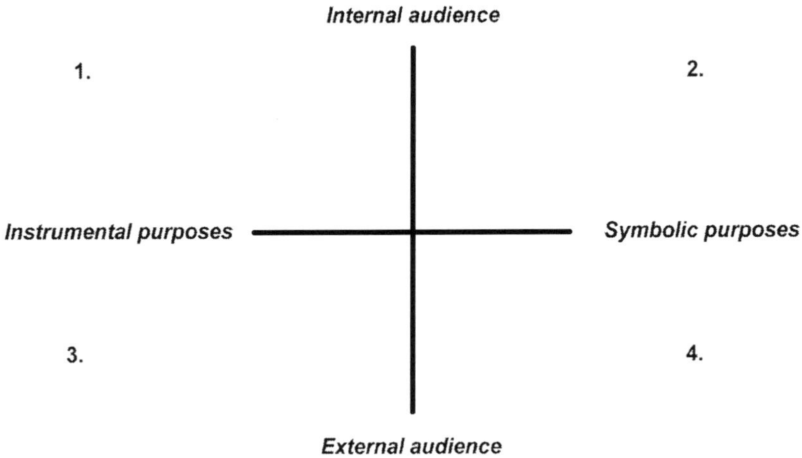

Figure 8.1 *Basic matrix of audiences and purposes*

Once national borders are crossed, it becomes more difficult to mark and map the persons and groups who might count as an 'audience'. Beyond the national (or supranational) arena, attention to and interest in another country's constitutional matters are likely to decline significantly. Often, constitutions do not even domestically qualify as primary or secondary objects of interest, so framers have *a fortiori* a much harder time reaching audiences beyond the national sphere. Neighbours' constitutions will be of interest, though, if they address a relevant political or economic issue, such as border claims or investment protection.

In general, the *populations* of other states can regularly be discounted as significant audiences, due to a lack of information and interest. Likewise, *governments* of neighbouring states, unless politically affected, are likely to be unconcerned about constitutional business as usual in other countries. However, *global actors* (companies, corporations, consultants) may be expected to pay attention at least selectively, insofar as they are or may be concerned by the constitutional affairs of neighbouring countries. In particular, *consultants*[21] – the brokers of globality, who sell legal expertise and are the midwives of legal transfer – are always on the lookout for the need for (con-

---

[21] Dezalay, Y. and Garth, B.G. (2016), '"Lords of the Dance" as Double Agents: Elite Actors in and Around the Legal Field", in: 3 *Journal of Professions & Organisations*, 188 ff; *id* (2002), *The Internationalization of Palace Wars Lawyers, Economists, and the Contest to Transform Latin American States* (Chicago: Chicago University Press).

stitutional) advice; and corporations evaluate (constitutional) conditions for investment, property and protection.

Examples of the asymmetry of interests are events or decisions that have transnational impact. The Modi regime's move to revoke Article 370 of the Indian Constitution and severely limit the autonomy of Jammu and Kashmir[22] received considerable attention in neighbouring Pakistan and Bangladesh. The political class and the media were likewise stirred up by Putin's recent announcement of a constitutional revision, keen to know how he planned to revise his power scheme so as to preserve his power or reinvent himself at the end of his latest term.[23] Vietnam's decision in 1992 to grant foreign private property constitutional protection was registered by potential investors. Erdoğan's post-coup constitutional turn to autocracy was noted by Turks living in other countries – notably Germany – as well as observers who were concerned about increased volatility in an already highly destabilized Middle East. The institutions of the European Union (the European Parliament, Council and Commission, first and foremost) can be expected to closely monitor constitutional events in Hungary and Poland.

3.2 Purposes of Constitutions

According to the nature of the dominant purposes and practices in each regime, the grid allows us to distinguish, at least analytically, the instrumental purposes of authoritarianism – such as creating order or disciplining rival elites – from the symbolic ones, such as mobilizing society for a collective agenda. Both instrumental and symbolic purposes provide important services for autocratic rule. Together, they form the horizontal axis of the grid, which charts the purposive elements[24] of an authoritarian regime. At one pole, the matrix maps forms of knowledge, practices, strategies and tactics that determine and are enforced as 'order' in constituted institutional arrangements; at the other, the grid buttons down, in particular, 'soft' concepts, such as collective identity,

---

[22] 'Modi's revocation of Kashmir's autonomy', in: *The Economist,* 10 August 2019, www.economist.com/leaders/2019/08/10/modis-revocation-of-kashmirs-autonomy (last accessed 31 January 2020).

[23] Miller, C. (2020), 'Succession and Punishment', in: *Foreign Policy* 21 January, https://foreignpolicy.com/2020/01/21/succession-and-punishment/ (last accessed 31 January 2020).

[24] To repeat: for a regime to be qualified as authoritarian, not all elements must be present. Rather, the various combinations lead to different types of regimes, such as authoritarian nationalism, unitary state, kleptocracy, competitive authoritarianism or dictatorship.

representations of society and nation, rule and state, as well as programmatic ideas and common goals.

3.2.1 Instrumental purposes

In accordance with the elements of authoritarian techniques of governing and conceptions of power, the autocratic notion of participation as complicity and the creation of an imaginary community, discussed in the previous chapters, I assign on the horizontal axis of constitutional purposes either the *instrumental* pole (in Figure 8.2, the pole of *coordination*) or to the *symbolic* pole (in Figure 8.2, the pole of *cooperation*). 'Instrumental' comprises those purposes that are (or should be) realized through planned and calculated measures of government and administration, when these intervene in social processes in order to coordinate actions and the consequences thereof.[25] Instrumental objectives are regularly implemented in a (purposive-) rational way by means of institutions and procedures.

As far as governance is concerned, standard constitutional *instruments* include the allocation of power by means of a system of competences and, as far as the citizenry is concerned, the controlled allocation and distribution of freedom (voice) and power to act (agency). Insofar as authoritarian regimes do not develop an informal auxiliary (or 'deep state') constitution, the instrumentality of their formal constitution is illustrated, for example, by norms that regulate the responsibilities and powers of the executive, such as the right to initiate laws and rule by decree; and that determine structures of command (notably of the armed forces, police and secret services) and authorize the declaration and execution of a state of emergency.[26] Moreover, the ensemble of authoritarian instrumental purposes includes rules that limit the use of freedom and link it to systemic imperatives – for instance, what socialist legality or the

---

[25] See Habermas, J. (1991), '*Die andere Zerstörung der Vernunft*', in: *Zeit Online*, 10 May, www.zeit.de/1991/20/die-andere-zerstoerung-der-vernunft/ (last accessed 22 December 2018); concerning the concept of coordination: Frankenberg, G. (n 8), Chapter 6 with further references.

[26] For example: 'Whenever the country is threatened by an imminent danger to its institutions, its independence or its territorial integrity, the President of the Republic shall decree the state of emergency' (1989/2016 Constitution of Algeria, Article 107). For a more elaborate discussion, see Frankenberg (n 25).

defence of the achievements of the revolution may require,[27] or what is owed to the hierarchical order and the integrity of the head of state.[28]

3.2.2 Symbolic purposes

Constitutional symbolism is not meant to express the 'palpable' reality of practices and institutions, but rather the emblematic dimension of a political order – its sign language, so to speak. As is well known, political authoritarianism withdraws the imposition of democratic symbolism and replaces it with iconography (as was shown in the previous chapter), and a language of images and mobilization, which is also designed to give orientation to social actions and create a collective identity.[29] However, this is regressively oriented towards (forced or manipulated) cooperation for common goals and the creation of an imaginary community. The authoritarian symbolism deploys the arsenal of the *ancien régime* for this or that purpose and, as far as possible, falls back on embodiment as a representation mechanism. Societies or nations appear as homogeneous units 'embodied' by the head of state.[30] In this sense, the absolutist monarchy informed a principle that some autocratic constitutional framers have adopted even today: 'the person of the President of the Republic … is inviolable.'[31]

---

27 1918 Constitution of the Russian Socialist Federative Soviet Republic: 'Article 23. Guided by the interests of the working class as a whole, the Russian Socialist Federative Soviet Republic shall deprive individuals and individual groups of the rights which are exploited by them to the detriment of the interests of the socialist revolution.'

28 The Thai Constitution grants the king and head of state a position of veneration that removes him from any accusation or criticism: 'The King shall be enthroned in a position of revered worship and shall not be violated. No person shall expose the King to any sort of accusation or action' (Section 6, 2017 Constitution of Thailand).

29 The symbolic dimension of the theory of democratic representation is discussed by Diehl, P. (2015), *Das Symbolische, das Imaginäre und die Demokratie* (Baden-Baden: Nomos), 26 ff with reference to Lefort, C. (1994), *L'invention démocratique: Les limites de la domination totalitaire* (Paris: Fayard); *id* (1990), 'Die Frage der Demokratie', in: Rödel. U. (ed), *Autonome Gesellschaft und libertäre Demokratie* (Frankfurt am Main: Suhrkamp), 281 ff. See also Rödel, U. *et al* (1989), *Die demokratische Frage* (Frankfurt am Main: Suhrkamp); and Manow, P. (2010), *In the King's Shadow* (Cambridge: Polity).

30 'The Syrian Arab Republic is proud of its Arab identity and the fact that its people are an integral part of the Arab nation. The Syrian Arab Republic *embodies* this belonging in its national and pan-Arab project and the work to support Arab cooperation in order to promote integration and achieve the unity of the Arab nation.' Preamble of the 2012 Constitution of the Syrian-Arab Republic (emphasis added).

31 Basic Law of Hungary, 2011, Article 12. Similarly: 'The King is Head of State, and its nominal representative, and his person is inviolate. He is the loyal protector of the religion and the homeland, and the symbol of national unity' (2012 Constitution of

4. VARIANTS OF AUTHORITARIAN CONSTITUTIONALISM

The analytical distinction between instrumentality and symbolism, as well as of internal and external audiences, has a predominantly heuristic meaning here. I do not mean to suggest that constitutions correspond to only *one* type and are located on the horizontal axis at only *one* pole, and on the vertical axis only *one* group at a time. On the contrary, coordination for the purpose of constructing an authoritarian order or disciplining competing elites or opponents can also be combined with symbolic politics – whether in the form of mobilizing for a joint project (eg, revolution, liberation) or promoting security and unity. At best, gradations can be made or priorities set: in particular, that a constitution should primarily address its own supporters with the construction of a normative order or convince undecided parties that state identity, as seen by the international community of states, is a constitutional issue – especially in divided nations.[32]

The hybrid character of many constitutions of autocracies, the diversity of purposes that they pursue and the difficulties in determining their audience and purposes in a reasonably plausible way are illustrated by the Syrian Constitution of 2012.[33] Internally, the despot seemed hardly in need of an additional layer of legitimation. His opponents could not be expected to grant him any legitimacy – especially since they saw through its manipulated production and boycotted the referendum. To the extent that opposition members expressed themselves publicly about the referendum at all, they disqualified it as a farce amid the unfolding Syrian tragedy. Loyal regime supporters could be expected to react quite differently. Regardless of what the Constitution might have to say to them, they would remain loyal to al-Assad in his scorched-earth war. It would appear that his primary aim in revising the Constitution was to impress and discipline the competing elites, to show them that despite the chaos, he was in charge of constitutional matters. Possibly al-Assad also wanted to force his opponents to recognize his power through a constitutional

---

Bahrain, Article 33). Cambodia follows the same path: 'The King shall be the Head of State for life. The King shall be inviolable' (Constitution of 1993, Article 7).

32 Instructive: the two-states theory concerning the legal existence of the Federal Republic of Germany and the German Democratic Republic (GDR). See the decision of the German Constitutional Court – BVerfGE 36, 1; also the one-China doctrine: 'Taiwan is part of the sacred territory of the People's Republic of China. It is the lofty duty of the entire Chinese people, including our compatriots in Taiwan, to accomplish the great task of reunifying the motherland' (Preamble of the 1982 Constitution of the People's Republic of China).

33 Yassin-Kassab, R. (2016), *Burning Country* (London: Pluto Press), ix and 108 ff.

act and the projection of order amid a civil war. The constitutional revision and referendum may have been intended to convey the image of a strong president who – despite war and chaos – had matters under control and had mastered the autocratic monster constitutionally, and not just with the help of the military and secret police. These purposes and addressees suggest that al-Assad's project should be located in the first grid field. Another aim of the constitutional revision may have been to send a signal to the undecided – the non-organized opposition – to get them to support the regime: 'Enter the constitutional circle; it will be of advantage to you.' Likewise, in the second quadrant falls the elevation of martyrdom to the highest constitutional value – the realization of which, after all, entails state support.[34]

Whether the revised Syrian Constitution was designed to influence (and excite) an external audience is doubtful. The official legal recognition of Syria by the community of (un)civilized states was at no point endangered. However, al-Assad's reshuffle might have been an attempt to demonstrate to the outside world that the regime was still in charge and sufficiently powerful to reorganize the country in times of civil war. This message would place the new Constitution as a show of force in the fourth sector of the grid. Finally, one may consider whether al-Assad wanted to reach an external audience. Syria's 'constitutional moment' was barely noticed by the populations of neighbouring countries. It is rather unlikely that this elaborate, redundant affirmation of democracy and popular sovereignty would have impressed anyone abroad.[35] Yet it is notable that the new Constitution makes express reference to the interventionist power of the United States through the wording 'the rule of the people by the people and for the people' – a quotation from one of the cherished legends of US constitutional history, Abraham Lincoln.[36] Al-Assad may have been making a (probably unsuccessful) attempt to win the trust of the Obama administration and/or to rehabilitate its image of brutal authoritarianism (Figure 8.2).

---

[34] 'Martyrdom for the sake of the homeland shall be a supreme value, and the State shall guarantee the families of the martyrs in accordance with the law' (2012 Constitution of Syria, Preamble).

[35] 'The system of governance in the state shall be a republican system; Sovereignty is an attribute of the people; and no individual or group may claim sovereignty. Sovereignty shall be based on the principle of the rule of the people by the people and for the people; The People shall exercise their sovereignty within the aspects and limits prescribed in the Constitution' (2012 Constitution of Syria, Article 2).

[36] Conant, S., (ed) (2015), *The Gettysburg Address: Perspectives on Lincoln's Greatest Speech* (New York: Oxford University Press); Haney, J.L. (1944), 'Of the People, by the People, for the People', in: 88 *Proceedings of the American Philosophical Society*, 359 ff.

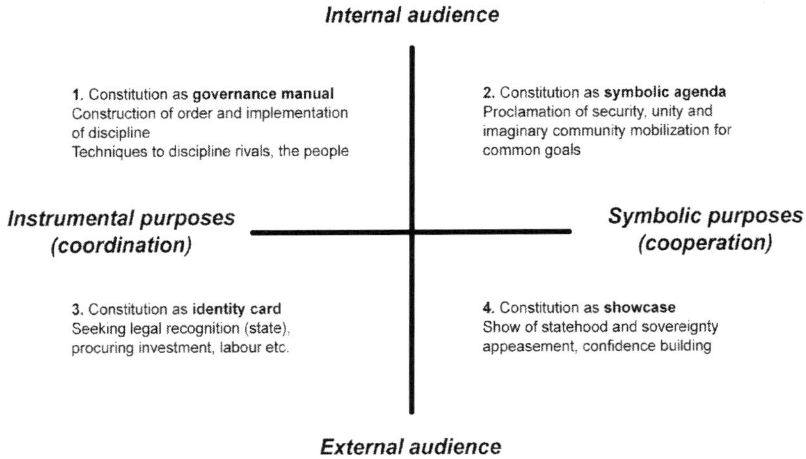

Figure 8.2 *Variants of authoritarian constitutionalism*

4.1 Authoritarian Constitutions as Governance Manuals

In the local or national terrain, the focus – according to the grid presented in Figure 8.2 – is on the coordination of actions and the consequences thereof. The first variant of authoritarian constitutionalism stresses its instrumental character as a script instructing autocratic governance. It focuses on the construction, stabilization and enforcement of an order, and functions as a kind of instruction manual. As discussed in the previous chapters,[37] scripts of authoritarianism oscillate permanently between normalcy and states of exception. Authoritarian political orders are generally characterized by a structure that provides more or less modest elements of normativity within a general situation of lawlessness – either for reasons of reputation or because the transition from democracy to autocracy is not yet complete and requires a veneer of democracy, such as elections. The flexible, institutional *dispositif* of authoritarianism covers a considerable diversity of regimes: according to the criterion of legality, 'dual states' combine varieties of the prerogative state with the law/normative state. For the stability of an authoritarian order, dual-state constructions have the inestimable advantage of wrapping some coercive measures in the cloak of legality[38] with the help of (constitutional) special powers, martial law or exceptional law, while preserving legitimacy.

[37] See Chapters 2 and 4–7 discussing the elements of authoritarianism.
[38] For references, see Frankenberg (n 8), Chapter VIII.

In contrast, the institutional dimension of the authoritarian *dispositif* also qualifies as a 'deep state',[39] according to the criterion of publicity, insofar as it links the constituted governmental institutions to a 'state within the state' that has developed in the background or been constructed quite deliberately in violation of or by bypassing the constitution. It lends itself to conspiracy theories that intertwine the security apparatus (military, secret services, the police) with the state apparatus (government, administration, judiciary), because it largely operates in the arcane sphere and thus eludes democratic or judicial control.[40]

The Constitutions of the United States and Turkey give no indication that the structures of a deep state have long since developed in those countries. Yet it is a foregone conclusion that a powerful covert conglomerate of interests of its own kind has established itself in the United States in recent decades, sidestepping the Constitution and democratically elected governments.[41] It comprises lobbyists, Wall Street, Silicon Valley, the secret services, the military and its supply industry, parts of the media and the judiciary. Unfortunately, the analytical potency of the deep state theory is undermined by the fact that it is sometimes indiscriminately linked to other theorems, such as that of the 'military-industrial complex', or to conspiracy theories and right-wing populist jargon that reveal defamatory connotations of a 'system' or 'establishment'.

Turkey has also been home to a deep state for decades.[42] Naturally, this state is even further removed from the constitutional text than Fraenkel's prerogative-state. The established and exercised network consists of members of the armed forces and the secret services, (former?) Kemalist organizations and organized crime. It is suspected that the Turkish deep state had a hand in the country's repeated coups, including the failed attempt in 2016. The same applies to the 'dirty war' against the Kurdistan Workers' Party in the 1980s and 1990s.[43] It may be no coincidence that most of the crimes committed against journalists and politicians from the political left have remained unsolved.

---

[39] Such as the deep state in Thailand, which includes the monarchy: Mérieau, E. (2015), 'Thailand's Deep State, Royal Power and the Constitutional Court (1997–2015)', in: 46 *Journal of Contemporary Asia,* 445 ff.

[40] See Lofgren, M. (2016), *The Deep State: The Fall of the Constitution and the Rise of a Shadow Government* (New York: Penguin).

[41] Lofgren, M. (2017), 'The Deep State', in: *Der Tagesspiegel* 17 February, www.tagesspiegel.de/politik/pressekonferenz-von-donald-trump-droht-in-den-usa-ein-krieg-zwischen-der-regierung-und-dem-tiefen-staat/19407558.html/ (last accessed 25 December 2018).

[42] Heinrich-Böll-Stiftung (ed) (2012), '*Auf den Spuren des tiefen Staats*', 19 July, www.boell.de/de/navigation/europa-nordamerika-auf-den-spuren-des-tiefen-staates-15152.html (last accessed 20 February 2020).

[43] *Foreign Policy,* 25 February 2010, https://foreignpolicy.com/2010/02/25/whats-really-behind-turkeys-coup-arrests/ (last accessed 28 December 2018).

The instrumental characteristics of authoritarian constitutionalism initially orient the construction of order towards the presumed and actual behaviour of the population. However, very few charters of autocracies offer a matrix that allows for a distinction to be drawn between legitimate and illegitimate expectations. Nor do they define zones of permitted opposition and tolerated dissent. They impose on the population the risk of disloyalty and contradiction – above all, by failing to protect the certainty of expectations and guarantee predictability of state action. Some constitutions may be exempted from this verdict. Soviet constitutionalism reduces the dangers of expecting too much from rights by basically identifying them as programmatic and not justiciable. Moreover, the Constitution's normative 'purchasing power' is linked in advance to the conditions of socialist legality[44] and its use is bound to serve the working population and the interests of society.[45]

Post-Soviet Russia – or more precisely, the Putin regime – tends to follow a different, but ultimately similar maxim, embracing a Machiavellian approach to the acquisition and retention of power. Since Putin's networks of vertically directed authoritarianism dictate order, no protection can be expected from (fundamental) rights and no information can be derived from the constitutional allocation of competences.[46] Reports of arbitrary detentions, systematic torture of detainees by the police, murders of opponents of the regime, extrajudicial executions, intimidation and killing of journalists, neglect and cruelty in orphanages, violations of children's rights, discrimination, racism and assassinations of members of ethnic minorities speak a particularly brutal language of authoritarianism. With alarmingly strong approval from the Russian population, its instrumental dimension is (still) not doing what is expected of it, even in imitated democracies that are somehow related to the rule of law. The transformation of a mafia state into a government has yet to happen.[47] As was discussed previously, during his terms of office Putin has systematically

[44] See Newton, S. (2017), *The Constitutional Systems of the Independent Central Asian States. A Contextual Analysis* (London: Bloomsbury Publishing).

[45] '...the press, radio, television, movies and other organs of the mass media are State or social property and can never be private property. This assures their use at the exclusive service of the working people and in the interest of society' (Article 53 of the 1976/2002 Constitution of Cuba).

[46] For a look at the dark side, see Satter, D. (2003), *Darkness at Dawn: The Rise of the Russian Criminal State* (New Haven: Yale University Press); and Weiler, J. (2004), *Human Rights in Russia: A Darker Side of Reform* (Boulder: Lynne Rienner Publishers); Politkovskaya, A. (2001) *A Dirty War: A Russian Reporter in Chechnya* (London: Harvill Secker).

[47] '*Die Grundform der Herrschaft ist das Racket*' ('The basic form of rule is the racket'). Horkheimer, M. (1985), 'Zur Soziologie der Klassenverhältnisse', in: *id*, *Gesammelte Schriften XII* (Frankfurt am Main: Fischer), 75 ff.

built up a 'vertical of power' alongside the constitutional institutions, under his control, that allows him to eliminate all residual forms of democracy and separation of powers.[48]

Against the backdrop of less drastic state practices, numerous constitutions signal on the citizen-oriented side that fundamental rights of political communication are inherently limited, or that their use is fraught with considerable risk. On the gradually ascending scale of the validity of those rights in the context of political authoritarianism, the former British protectorate and now sultanate of Brunei Darussalam refrains most clearly from making any concessions towards democracy. The Constitution is designed as a purely organizational statute of absolutist rule, which denies its subjects any basic rights, without offering any compensations for this deficit, such as socialist constitutions do by granting social protection.

It is generally characteristic of the constitutions of autocracies (which follow the rhetoric of guaranteeing fundamental rights) that: (1) freedoms are linked to both obligations and reservations in favour of the security and stability of the public order;[49] (2) they contain clauses prohibiting abuse of rights; (3) they provide for restrictions on or the lifting of restrictions in exceptional situations, such as riots, war or disasters;[50] and/or (4) they are subject to a general legal reservation.[51] Thus, the repressive state practice in Turkey towards the political opposition can already be seen in the text of the Constitution, inscribing itself in the barriers against freedom of assembly and association.[52]

It may be inferred from fundamental rights and their manifold barriers in the Turkish Constitution that, although authoritarian constitutionalism would allow for the meticulous observance of forms of a constitution, its terminology subjects civil liberties – above all, the freedom of opinion, assembly and the press (Articles 26, 28 and 33) – to a repressive conception of public order and

---

48 Mommsen, M. (2007), 'Putins *"gelenkte Demokratie": "Vertikale der Macht" statt Gewaltenteilung*', in: Buhbe, M. and Gorzka, G. (eds), *Russland heute – Rezentralisierung des Staates unter Putin* (Wiesbaden: VS Springer), 235 ff.

49 For a rather elaborate version, see the limitation of the freedom of occupation in the Thai Constitution: 'The restriction of such liberty under paragraph one shall not be imposed except by virtue of a provision of law enacted for the purpose of protecting public interest, for maintaining public order or good morals, or for preventing or eliminating barriers or monopoly' (Article 40).

50 The Constitution of Thailand permits censorship in times of war: 'Censorship by a competent official of any news or statements made by a media professional before the publication in a newspaper or any media shall not be permitted, except during the time when the country is in a state of war' (Article 35).

51 For example, the Constitutions of Singapore of 1963/2016 and Vietnam 1992/2013.

52 1982/2017 Constitution of Turkey, Articles 68–69.

security, public morality and economic interests, and practically places them in a system of averting political dangers.[53]

Often, the wording of the constitutions of authoritarian regimes cannot be trusted, because they not only conceal important elements of the instrumentality of the authoritarian *dispositif*, but also clearly misinform the readers. This applies (if one does not treat them as irony) to the explicit prohibitions on usurping power[54] that are particularly common in post-Soviet documents, as well as to the silence on the transformation of a democratic constitution into an authoritarian one – as exemplified in Russia's 'Putinstate' and Hungary's 'Frankenstate';[55] in the Central Asian '-stans'; and – albeit currently with less dramatic consequences – in Poland.

Finally, the instrumentality of authoritarian constitutions also includes – to no small extent – the ability to anticipate and control the reactions of competing elites, members of the regime's cadres or the political opposition. Stalin's Constitution of 1936, al-Assad's constitutional revision of 2012 and Erdoğan's constitutional amendments of 2016 are different examples of how constitutions can be designed to function as a disciplinary instrument. Pre-emptively, following the logic of mitigating political dangers, they send a message to all those who compete with the leader or the leadership clique for political power that – even in crisis situations, such as the escalation of the economic crisis in the Soviet Union, the civil war in Syria and the recent coup in Turkey – the tentacles of the autocratic monster are under control at all times, and neither dissent nor disloyalty will be tolerated. The Constitution of Myanmar (2008) serves as another example. In several places – in the National Security Council (No 201) and in the singular task of the defence forces to protect the Constitution (No 20) – the military regime is positioned in the text of the Constitution as a ruler and a force of order.

---

53 Isiksel, T. (2013), 'Between Text and Context: Turkey's Tradition of Authoritarian Constitutionalism' in: 11 *International Journal of Constitutional Law*, 702 ff; Thio, L.A. (2012), 'Constitutionalism in Illiberal Polities', in: Rosenfeld, M. and Sajó, A. (eds), *Oxford Handbook of Comparative Constitutional Law* (Oxford: Oxford University Press), 134 ff.

54 The Constitution of the Russian Federation of 1993 proclaims: 'Nobody may usurp power in the Russian Federation.' Moldavia's 1994/2016 Constitution calls the usurpation of power 'the most serious crime against the people' (Article 2). The GDR Constitution ordained in 'Soviet times': 'under no circumstances shall other than the constitutionally determined organs exercise state power.' See also Article 138 of the Constitution of Venezuela.

55 Scheppele, K.L. (2013), 'The Rule of Law and the Frankenstate: Why Governance Checklists Do Not Work', in: 2 *International Journal of Policy Administration and Institutions*, 559 ff.

Discipline and loyalty could also at least partially explain why Hitler did not completely cut the already strained umbilical cord of his totalitarian regime to the Weimar Constitution. In 1937 and 1939 he had the Enabling Act extended twice without any external need to do so; and in 1943 he extended its validity indefinitely by '*Führer* decree'. Since the resolution of the Law against the Formation of New Political Parties of 14 July 1933 was issued, the Nazi Party was the sole ruling state party, thus also eliminating the role of the *Reichstag* in this regard. The Weimar Constitution had been *de facto* suspended since 23 March 1933. In view of the normative power of the factual, especially the terror of Nazi state practice, the extensions could at best have been instrumental in disciplining the monster of totalitarian dictatorship. Incidentally, it is reasonable to assume that Hitler was interested in preserving the legality of the document to the outside world. We will return to this in a moment.

4.2 Authoritarian Constitutions as Symbolic Politics

Autocrats also play on the keyboard of symbolic politics. Just as they strive to eliminate their opponents, they also try to flaunt constitutional moments: in Stalin's case, the reconstitution in 1936; in al-Assad's case, the demonstration of order during the civil war in 2012; in Erdoğan's case, a show of power through the rededication of the Constitution through a referendum in 2017; in the case of Orbán, an authoritarian-nationalist, invocation of the spirit of a long-dead king to conceal his autocracy; in the case of Chávez, the introduction of a left-wing populist manifesto; and more. Through extending the Law for the Elimination of the Plight of the People and the Reich, Hitler revived the myth of empowerment to address an emergency situation and tried to use this opportunity to ostentatiously stage the farce of constitutional continuity.

In the second grid field, the accent of the dispositive shifts from the technique of legal coordination and discipline to the normatively more demanding mobilization of people to cooperate in the pursuit of common values in an (imaginary) community. Moreover, the second grid represents concepts of collective identity and commits people to loyalty to the regime.[56]

Cooperative projects that address the citizenry are often launched in situations of radical upheaval, such as after a revolution or liberation, or after catastrophic events. However, they also come in handy for the everyday support of an autocracy. Manifesto-style constitutions help to mobilize people towards

---

[56] Such as Saudi Arabia's Basic Law of 1992/2013, Article 11: 'The Saudi society shall hold fast to the Divine Rope. Its citizens shall work together to foster benevolence, piety and mutual assistance; and it avoids dissension.' And Article 34: 'Defending the Islamic faith, the society and the homeland shall be the duty of each and every citizen.'

collective values, such as freedom, progress, unity, social justice, prosperity or security.[57] The same logic – that is, to defend values – guides calls to prevent a return the dark epoch of foreign rule,[58] barbarism, exploitation[59] or genocide;[60] or to fight for or 'adher[e] to the (eternal) values of humanity'[61] – if needs be, by means of a 'militant democracy'.[62] The emphasis on (inner) peace in the Constitution of Bhutan, which admittedly fits the goal of 'Gross National Happiness' propagated therein, falls outside the standard framework of authoritarian value politics (Article 9).

As an example of cooperation-oriented symbolism, Article 27 of the Chinese Constitution – which provides that 'The state must rely on the support of the people' – clearly attends to political authoritarianism, insofar as it does not transform the masses into sovereign people, but represents them

---

57 The authors of the Constitution of Angola (2010) feel obliged by 'the commitment to the values and fundamental principles of the independence, sovereignty and the unity of a democratic state based on the rule of law, pluralism of political expression and organization, the separation and balance between the powers of bodies that exercise sovereign power, the market economy and respect and guarantees for fundamental human rights and freedoms, which constitute the essential pillars supporting and structuring this Constitution'. Similarly, the Constitution of Myanmar (2008) propagates a catalogue of 'eternal values', among them 'justice, freedom, equality, wealth, equality of races, patriotism'. The duty to strive for reunification is laid down in the constitutions of partitioned nations (China; North Korea; the original version of the German Basic Law), whereas the GDR Constitutions sported a two-state theory (nevertheless, the first Constitution of 1949 followed the example of the one-China principle: 'Deutschland is an indivisible democratic republic' (Article 1) and 'There is only one German nationality'.

58 See the Constitutions of Egypt (1956); Iran (1979); Algeria (1989); and Hungary (2016).

59 'The first Russian Constitution after the October Revolution promised to pursue the goal to end the exploitation of man by man and introduce socialism where there would be no social classes' (Article II, No 9 Russia 1918).

60 See the 2003 Constitution of Rwanda.

61 Examples are the 1976 Constitution of Cuba; the Constitutions of Belarus (1994), Bahrain (2012) and Myanmar (2008). The Constitution of Turkey invokes 'the eternal existence of the Turkish Motherland and Nation and the indivisible unity of the Sublime Turkish State'.

62 See Müller, J.W. (2012), 'Militant Democracy', in: Rosenfeld, M. and Sájo, A. (n 53).

as a unified body[63] through regressive symbolism;[64,65] promotes integration (through values) from the top down; and propagates unity as homogeneity and togetherness to keep out all kinds of enemies.[66] The authors of the first two Soviet Constitutions of 1918 and 1924 likely set themselves the task of providing the addressees with a register of (constitutionalized) ideology, interpreting the post-revolutionary world of the Soviet state and adapting it to the new legitimacy. In 1924, the focus shifted to reaffirming the competencies of the (Soviet) 'supreme organs of power' and limiting the rights of the republics.

It is striking that Soviet constitutions[67] have both internal and external targets. Internally, they reached out to those who participated in the revolutionary project in the socialist camp of 'mutual trust and peace, national freedom and equality', and to potentially reactionary forces and organizations. Externally, they promised allies 'peaceful coexistence and fraternal cooperation among peoples', and threatened the reactionary forces – the enemies in the capitalist camp:

> There, in the camp of capitalism, there is national enmity and inequality, colonial slavery and chauvinism, national oppression and pogroms, imperialist cruelties and wars.
>
> Here, in the camp of socialism, mutual trust and peace, national freedom and equality, peaceful coexistence and fraternal cooperation of peoples prevail.[68]

Leaders and ruling clans and cliques which, unlike the Bolsheviks, cannot present a compact ideology will seek other ways to demonstrate their legitimacy, one of them being collective goals laid down in the constitution. To make a repressive regime look better, raise expectations of a bright future and, if necessary, appease opponents, constitutional elites can seek to mobilize the

63 As regards the body metaphor, see the examples mentioned before: 'We honor the achievements of our historical constitution and we honor the Holy Crown, which *embodies* the constitutional continuity of Hungary's statehood and the unity of the nation' (emphasis added). Ulrich K. Preuß pointed out to me the constitutional transformation of the population and masses into a 'people'.

64 In constitutional monarchies, this symbolization corresponds to the pre-democratic tradition – for example, Cambodia: 'Nation, Religion, King'; and Morocco: 'God, the Land, the King'.

65 Similar to the reference in the Nazi regime to 'One People, One Reich, One Leader', or '*Volksgemeinschaft*'.

66 Similar to how Trump refers to immigrants as 'poison'.

67 After 1924 followed the (Stalin) Constitution in 1936 and the Brezhnev Constitution in 1977.

68 Constitution of 1924: declaration concerning the formation of the union of Socialist Soviet Republics.

people towards a collective agenda – such as nationalism[69] or socialism[70] – or against (imaginary) enemies. There are quite a few examples of these: the American conspiracy against Iran, the 'Islamization' of Hungary, the Jewish conspiracy and more. So a set of collective values always comes in handy.[71]

Meanwhile, societies are also presented as a homogenous unit and given a collective identity. In this way, Hungary's Basic Law, masterminded by the Orbán regime, seeks to restore 'the spiritual and mental unity of our nation torn to pieces by the storms of the past century'. Algeria's Constitution defines Islam, its membership of the Arab community and *Amazighité*[72] as 'fundamental components' of collective identity. Members of the Syrian Islamic-Arab community must recognize martyrdom as the supreme value. Morocco went down a different constitutional path towards unity and, to this end, laid down general values and forbade political parties to organize themselves on a religious, ethnic, linguistic, ethnic or regional basis, so as not to endanger unity. More generally, human rights are protected from party programmes that could provide a basis for discrimination that is contrary to human rights.[73]

Values and duties fit particularly well into the constitutions of authoritarian regimes, for two reasons. On the one hand, values *can do* anything, while obliging a government to do virtually nothing. Bhutan's 'Gross National Happiness' target, to cite a particularly striking example, cannot be invoked and does not allow citizens to bring action to enforce it. Therefore, it has no influence on government policy; it simply sounds good. In any case, happiness is obviously not benefiting the Nepalese part of the population, which has been subject to discrimination and persecution for years.[74] On the other hand, values and duties have an inherently authoritarian tendency. They must be implemented top-down. Since they have no civil society support, they are ideally suited to implementation through government programmes aimed at securing general support or loyalty.

---

69 The 1956 Constitution of Egypt; the Constitutions of Hungary and Poland today.

70 See the 1949 GDR Constitution, Article 6.

71 See above. Also the value catalogues of the Constitutions of Myanmar 2008, Iran 1979, Vietnam 1992, and China 1982.

72 Berbers understand *Amazighe* as the complex of their culture, language and identity. See Article 84 of the 1989/2016 Constitution of Algeria. Morocco's 2011 Constitution speaks with a sense of diversity of the 'convergence of its Arab-Islamic, Berber [*amazighe*] and Saharan-Hassan components, complemented and enriched by its African, Andalusian, Hebrew and Mediterranean influences'.

73 Article 7 of the 2011 Constitution of the Kingdom of Morocco 2011.

74 De Varennes, F. (2008), 'Constitutionalizing Discrimination in Bhutan: The Emasculation of Human Rights in the Land of the Dragon', in: 2 *Asia-Pacific Journal on Human Rights*, 47 ff with further references.

The effects of constitutional symbolism on interested 'circles', competing elites, indifferent groups and even supporters are more difficult to assess. Whether people are enthusiastic about cooperative projects or can be won over to an imaginary community is unlikely to depend solely on constitutional imagery and rhetoric, but rather on whether they are promised compensation for discipline, toleration and loyalty, or can expect significant legal or material premiums (social benefits).

Russia's 1918 Constitution may have been less important as a document that convinced the working class of the legitimacy of the newly established Bolshevik rule and called on it to defend workers' interests than as a demonstrative message addressed to opposition cadres and organizations that a revolutionary order and state power had now been established: the 'dictatorship of the urban and rural proletariat and the poorest peasantry in the form of a powerful All-Russian Soviet authority', the Bolsheviks. This new authority was given sharp contours and threatening potential by the Schmittian enumeration of political enemies who were excluded from the right to vote and from participation in any discussion of political legitimacy:

> The following persons enjoy neither the right to vote nor the right to be voted for…: (a) Persons who employ hired labor in order to obtain from it an increase in profits; (b) Persons who have an income without doing any work, such as interest from capital, receipts from property, etc.; (c) Private merchants, trade and commercial brokers; (d) Monks and clergy of all denominations; (e) Employees and agents of the former police, the gendarme corps, and the Okhrana [the Tsars' secret police – G.F.], also members of the former reigning dynasty; ..... (g) Persons who have been deprived by a soviet of their rights of citizenship because of selfish or dishonorable offenses, for the period fixed by the sentence.[75]

Hungary's constitutional father, Viktor Orbán – who is very keen on erasing the prehistory of Soviet state socialism[76] – is perhaps unwittingly perpetuating it in the fight against Hungary's enemies, using a political concept also informed by Schmitt's recipe:[77]

> Traitors and internal enemies of the nation had made deals with hostile foreigners in order to hand over the country and its people to the bureaucrats of the European Union, speculators and the international financial industry. But the nation decided to

---

[75] 1918 Constitution of Russia, Article 4, No 65.

[76] Article U of the Basic Law of Hungary 2011/2016.

[77] Schmitt, C. (2007), *The Concept of the Political* (Chicago: University of Chicago Press).

no longer live in the captivity of foreigners, it would fight against colonization and for its self-determination. Let's get our troops in place![78]

4.3 Constitution as Identity Card

If spectators and readers beyond national borders are likely to pay any attention to authoritarian constitutions, this will generally relate to the tools that they display – that is, their functions as a manual for governing and a form of 'identity card'. These are of interest to neighbouring governments, international organizations and legal experts that may need convincing that the state is constituted and constitutional. Quite a few regimes – including, without exception, the post-Soviet ones – emphatically affirm their 'stately' order.[79] Others, after foreign rule or other forms of deficient sovereignty, may have reason to seek recognition as a state and shake off colonial or other subalternity.[80] A constitution thus complements the traditional three elements: a politically and legally organized association of persons (the people) that has given itself its own order (state) in a delimited space (national territory). These elements are still the essential aspects for a state to be recognized under international law. This is also evident from the fact that a state can be recognized as soon as governmental authority has been established, even if it does not yet have any fixed institutional structures. In the concert of the international community of states, a constitution can also help to dispel doubts about the willingness of an autocracy to act in conformity with international law,[81] notably by transforming human rights pacts into national law.[82] Admittedly, however, the manifesto

---

78 '*Ungarn: Feldzug gegen die EU*'. Viktor Orbán quoted by *Bundeszentrale für politische Bildung* (bdp.de), 27 February 2014, www.bpb.de/179664/ungarn-feldzug-gegen-die-eu/ (last accessed 30 June 2019).

79 See the preamble and Article B of Hungary's Basic Law. Kazakhstan's Constitution (1995/2017) adopts the formula of the 'unitary state'; similarly Moldavia 1994/2016. Kyrgyzstan's Constitution (2010/2016) corroborates the 'plenitude of state power' (Article 1).

80 For example, the Constitutions of Egypt (1953); Democratic Republic of Congo (2005/2011); Djibouti (1992); Eritrea (1997) (Preamble and Article 1). As regards the subalternity of states: Mamdani, M. (1996), *Citizen and Subject: Contemporary Africa and the Legacy of Late Colonialism* (Princeton: Princeton University Press).

81 Whether it works or not depends on context and constellations; see the 2003 Constitution of Qatar: 'The State respects the international charters and treaties and works on executing all international agreements, charters and treaties to which it is a party.'

82 The 1993 Russian Constitution confirms the validity of human rights (which does not mean they mean much in Putin's governmental practice): 'The recognition, observance and protection of human and civil rights and freedoms shall be an obligation of the State' (Article 2). More restrained, the Constitution of Turkey: 'The fundamental

statements provide little information about actual state practice in terms of affirmation of the separation of powers, the rule of law, international human rights and so on.[83]

While state diplomacy may be able to gloss over a blatant divergence between constitutional law and constitutional reality, this is not necessarily true of economic actors. Egyptian President Sadat experienced this with his rule of law agenda based on the Constitution of 1971 and the tax incentives he offered foreign companies. This message all to clearly contradicted his arbitrary rule, the re-Islamization of Egypt based on *Shari'ah* and an obviously manipulated referendum, the result of which invalidated Egypt's constitutional identity card.[84]

Autocrats are sometimes keen to persuade foreign companies to invest in their countries. In such cases they may also use constitutions to provide explicitly for the protection of the 'legitimate interests of foreign companies'.[85] Vietnam went further than other 'closed societies' by opening up its economy as laid down in the Constitution of 1992. The government at least partially succeeded in changing its economic identity by combining planned economy, family economy and the private sector on a constitutional basis. In order to legitimize one-party rule – which had been criticized for its lack of effectiveness – by increased economic growth, the Communist Party of Vietnam accompanied its controlled (and internally not uncontroversial) open-door policy with constitutional guarantees for foreign companies – in particular, protection against nationalization and the possibility of resorting to arbitration courts.[86]

---

rights and freedoms in respect to aliens may be restricted by law compatible with international law' (Article 16).

83 Morocco's Constitution (2011) is quite explicit: 'The constitutional regime of the Kingdom is founded on the separation, the balance and the collaboration of the powers, as well as on participative democracy of [the] citizen, and the principles of good governance and of the correlation between the responsibility for and the rendering of accounts.' Exaggerated or not, the statement was at least put into practice by reforms.

84 The referendum was officially accepted by 99.98 per cent. See generally Ginsburg, T. and Moustafa, T. (eds) (2008), *Rule by Law* (Cambridge: Cambridge University Press).

85 China's 1982/2004 Constitution, Article 18: China 'permits foreign enterprises, other foreign organizations and individual foreigners to invest in China…'

86 'The State encourages, provides favorable conditions for entrepreneurs, enterprises and individuals, and other organizations to invest, produce, and do business, contributing to the stable development of the economic branches and national construction. Private possessions of individuals, organizations of investment, production, and business are protected by the law and are not subjected to nationalization' (Vietnam 1992).

4.4 Constitution as Showcase

In the fourth sector of the grid, constitutional symbolism addresses an international or supranational audience – primarily the governments of other states, international organizations and probably also global economic actors. Complementary to the legal identification of statehood and investment protection schemes, constitutions of autocratic regimes operate on the transnational stage as media for the propagation of trust, reliability and predictable cooperation.[87] Such confidence-building measures are in demand above all from potential partners in political alliances and economic treaties. Authoritarian constitutionalism can contribute, or at least try to lend seriousness, to the solicitation of partners or the application for membership of an alliance. This will be briefly illustrated below with a few examples and 'basic forms' of personal, military and party-based authoritarianism.

A sober hermeneutic is needed to prevent the final chord of Haiti's Constitution of 1805 from being written off as wishful thinking or empty rhetoric, and instead to decipher in this brief statement a reference to the dangers of the (renewed) fight against slavery directed at the neighbours and (former) colonial powers:

> We commend [the Constitution] to our descendants and, in homage to the friends of freedom and the people of all countries, as a sign of divine goodness that, as a result of His Immortal Judgements, has given us the opportunity to break our chains and to constitute ourselves as a free, civilized and independent people.

In 1805, Haiti's constitutional elite gave political significance to racial distinctions based on skin colour. They demonstratively held up a black universalism against the colonial slave-owning societies surrounding them. As the governors set out to reverse the liberation of slaves in Haiti, this small island empire in the Caribbean and close to the United States dared to confront Franco-American constitutionalism with a normative revolt that was actually riskier and more radical than the Declarations of Philadelphia 1776 and Paris 1789:

> Calling all Haitians, regardless of skin color, black is a gesture like calling all people, regardless of the sex, women: it both asserts egalitarian and universalist intuitions and puts them to a test by using the previously subordinated term of the opposition as the universal term.[88]

---

[87] Examples of such cooperation include the Constitutions of Morocco (2011) and Oman (1996/2011). See also above Vietnam 1992.

[88] Fischer, S. (2004), *Modernity Disavowed – Haiti and the Cultures of Slavery in the Age of Revolution* (Durham: Duke University Press, 227–28 and 233).

If one reads the Constitution of the quite authoritarian *Empire d'Haïti* as a text written for specific purposes, this political manifesto also reveals itself as an address to slaveholders that turns their world upside down. In a society of overwhelmingly illiterate people, it had important symbolic and also educational significance. Former slaves were mobilized as actors for liberation and recognized on the constitutional stage as a generically 'black' composite of Lafayette, Madison and Abbé Sieyes.

In terms of constitutional window dressing, the strategy of King Mohammed VI of Morocco since 2011 has been quite astute. Whereas the absolutist style of his father, Hassan II, ruined the reputation of the country and the royal house, Mohammed VI styled himself as a reformer. Apart from the political necessity in 2011 to cautiously respond to the Arab Spring, to cool down tensions and contain protests, Mohammed VI presented to the world – and in particular, to the region and to companies willing to invest – in the guise of a revised constitution, a moderately reformist, monarchical authoritarianism that was suitable for 'consolidating and strengthening the institutions of a modern state'.[89] As Mohammed VI was willing to make some democratic concessions, he was able to dismantle the absolutism and feudalism of his father's regime in a controlled manner. This gave him space to modernize the school system and family law (within limits), initiate infrastructure projects, promote foreign trade and address the crimes of the *ancien régime*, among other things. In doing so, he did not have to give up his commitment to traditional values, Islam as the state religion, his dual role as head of state and head of the faithful (*Amir Al Mouminine*) or his considerable financial entanglements (see Chapter 5).

Military regimes naturally find it difficult to rehabilitate their external image or advertise themselves positively on the global stage. The forced assertion of their instrumental mind set and ideas of order and discipline is too deeply rooted in their DNA. Burma/Myanmar has been the home of military authoritarianism since 1962. In Myanmar, it took constant, massive public protests – which the regime initially tried to crush – to bring about change. After the failure of this strategy, and in response to international criticism, the military attempted to intercept the protests through a constitutional project. However, the chosen path of 'disciplined democratization' (rather than direct military rule) left the military's controlling leadership role untouched.[90] The icon of the opposition, Aung San Suu Kyi, became the symbolic figure of a military regime liberalized and superficially democratized only as a constitutional shell, to which she

---

89 Preamble of the Constitution of the Kingdom of Morocco 2011.

90 Bünte, M. (2011), 'Burma's Transition to "Disciplined Democracy"', www.giga-hamburg.de/de/system/files/publications/wp177_buente.pdf (last accessed 21 February 2020).

gave a human face. The strategy supported by the new Constitution seemed to work at first. Admittedly, the symbolic head of government has lately lost much of her reputation as an 'ambassador of good conscience' (and a number of honorary titles bestowed on her have been withdrawn) due to her silence on the military's massacre and expulsion of the Rohingya.[91]

Constitutional window-dressing, however, is likely to succeed only if it is tailored to the recipients. In this respect, the programmatic opening of Vietnam and its economy, which has been underway since 1986, must be judged ambivalently. On the one hand, the (constitutional) legal instruments provided were sensible and economically efficient: a reduction in inflation, balance of payments under control, steady growth.[92] On the other hand, Vietnam's self-portrayal too closely resembles the prose of a kind of reform socialism that certifies its own compliance with the law.[93] The enumeration of state virtues alone – not matched by state practice – is unlikely to prove externally effective as advertising.[94]

Hungary provides an unusual example in this regard. In its conflict with the European Union, it has neither demonstrated its loyalty to the Union in the legal sense (Quadrant 3) nor shown to the outside world that it is a reliable partner (Quadrant 4). On the contrary, at every opportunity – including the constitutional revision of 2011 – the government conspicuously behaved as an executor of the interests of the crown (adorning Orbán's head). While King Saint Stephen survives only in myth today, his autocratic revenant waves the flag of a historically stretched, nationalist authoritarianism: 'The EU is 65

---

[91] 'Aung San Suu Kyi: Myanmar democracy icon who fell from grace', BBC, 23 January 2020, www.bbc.com/news/world-asia-pacific-11685977/ (accessed 21 February 2020). See also Chapter 7.

[92] Boothroyd, P. and Xuan Nam, P. (eds) (2000), Socioeconomic Renovation in Viet Nam. *The Origin, Evolution, and Impact of Doi Moi* (Ottawa: International Development Research Centre).

[93] 'The Socialist Republic of Vietnam consistently carries out a diplomatic policy of independence, autonomy, peace and friendship, cooperation, and development; seeks to multilateral and diversified relations, and actively seek to international integration and cooperation on the basis of respect for each other's independence, sovereignty and territorial integrity, non-interference in each other's internal affairs, equality, and mutual interest; conforms to the Charter of the United Nation and international treaties in which Vietnam is a member; is a friend, trust partner, and responsible member in international community for national interests and the contribution to the world for peace, national independence, democracy, and social progress' (Constitution of Vietnam 1992, Article 12).

[94] That is why Sadat's invitation to foreign investors was generally not considered 'inviting'.

years old, the IMF 67 years, the United States 236 years, but Hungary is 1116 years old.'[95]

[95] 'Ungarn – *von der* Krisenbewältigung *zum* Aufstand gegen *das* EU-Regime', in: 4 *GegenStandpunkt. Politische Vierteljahreszeitschrift* 14 (2014), https://de.gegenstandpunkt.com/artikel/ungarn-krisenbewaeltigung-zum-aufstand-gegen-eu-regime/ (last accessed 30 June 2019).

9. Notes on the pandemic of authoritarianism

1. UNCERTAINTY AND EXPERTISE

Law does not tolerate doubt. Rulings must convince in order to be accepted as authoritative. Interpretations are meant to provide determinate – or at least plausible – results. Legal education and practice are geared towards certainty. And the opinions of legal experts often cloak the interests of the client behind a screen of definite assumptions and conclusions. Uncertainty, it seems certain, is not a matter for the legal profession.

The lesson that lawyers should learn from the coronavirus crisis is not to complacently issue coercive decrees or make gutsy judgement calls, but rather to learn what the pandemic is all about. Legal consultants must find their place in the debate between the disciplines – virology, epidemiology, medicine and so on. They have yet to define their role as advisers while operating in a nebulous terrain that offers little factual certainty, leaves many questions open and requires experts to continually check and revise their tentative prognoses, to process new data and adapt to changing criteria. The pandemic is spreading throughout all societies, and with it the uncertainty of how – and with which legal means and measures – to contain and control it. Thus far, lawyers are assiduously following the diverse and evolving assessments from the intellectual laboratories of virology, epidemiology and medicine. They find comfort in following epidemiologists and their imperatives of 'flattening the curve', reducing the 'rate of the reproduction of infections', limiting hotspots and more. In general, they are satisfied merely with helping to prevent intensive care facilities from becoming overwhelmed. But what exactly have they contributed?

At this point, some aspects of the pandemic are – or at least appear to be – certain. Coronavirus is highly infectious; comparisons with earlier influenza viruses are wildly inaccurate; for many, the virus is asymptomatic, it but selectively threatens especially the old and those with underlying health conditions. Then there are approximate estimates with only temporary validity: on the various courses of the COVID-19 disease, mortality rates, reproduction rates and infection chains. Little is known about the average duration of intensive care treatment; and even the benefits of protective masks are controversial. Politicians and the media have repeated concepts such as flat infection curves and infection rates below 1 like mantras. The number of people who have recovered is invoked daily, even though this means very little while the cohort of those who are and have been infected has not been thoroughly tested.

In the debate between the disciplines over these post-Kantian weeks and months, voices from the natural sciences have consistently been heard first, followed by economics; by contrast, law has been a mere also-ran. Even psychologists – who have warned about the effects of lockdowns, social distancing and isolation – and social workers, who have reported an increase in domestic violence and suicides, have received more attention in this debate. But legal experts – who should 'rule by argument and assertion'[1] – do not seem to have much purchase in this crisis. Politicians have been slow to consult jurists in deciding how to tackle the pandemic. To be frank, legal expertise is generally traded in very small coins, and rarely in large bills. Lawyers generally focus on what is unconstitutional or illegal, or at least disproportionate. Legal advisers should exercise caution rather than poring over the relevant legal norms to examine whether they justify what has been imposed on us.[2] If everything is or could be different, law must learn and adapt to conditions of uncertainty as quickly as possible – especially since the profession missed the chance to prepare for the pandemic in the early months of 2020 or even before any appreciation that a pandemic was imminent.

2. CONVENTIONAL LEGAL LEARNING

For selective, case-by-case learning, the security laws of many countries traditionally work with, and process information according to, the scheme whereby threats to safety trigger measures to defuse threatening situations. To alleviate the consequences of hazardous technologies, Ulrich Beck's study on the 'risk society'[3] – which reads like a commentary on Chernobyl (1986) – generalized the concept of danger and replaced it with 'risk' as a more abstract, statistical category to comprehend, measure and defuse disaster. Under the banner of what was officially called the 'war on terror' and the 'war on organized crime', the rule-of-law matrix – in which threats to security justify proportionate measures – morphed into a pattern for averting risk. As the dynamic and

---

1 Kennedy, D. (2016), *A World of Struggle. How Power, Law, and Expertise Shape Global Political Economy* (Princeton: Princeton University Press), 135.

2 Lübbe-Wolff, G. (2020), 'Geschlossene Gesellschaft', in: *Frankfurter Allgemeine Zeitung*, 24 March.

3 Beck, U. (1987), 'The Anthropological Shock: Chernobyl and the Contours of the Risk Society', in: 32 *Berkeley Journal of Sociology*, 153 ff.

attractive (because more hypothetical) category of risk took the lead, danger receded into the background. In consequence, the threshold for police action was significantly reduced. In turn, the 'good, old' police laws assumed the nature of flexible, hyper-preventive security regulations; data was insatiably collected and hoarded, and brought to bear in the face of imperceptible, information-dependent, cross-border threats. Monitoring and surveillance measures – that is, interventions with a broad scope that extend far beyond any clear and present danger zone – signal a transition to a special police law, in which 'clues', 'situation assessments' and 'experiences' furnished by the police guide their interventions.[4] This security law does not allow for more 'learning' – that is, the collection and processing of information; it is rather a 'danger invention law' that self-reflexively produces its own information and is impervious to (unsettling) data from the outside. While conventional police laws learn from case to case, firmly entrenched in their law-rule categories, the new type of security law assumes an emergency everywhere and constantly risks seeing the world in a state of exception.

In many democracies, the containment of epidemics either comes under emergency law or follows the regulatory pattern of conventional police law. The most common measures include lockdowns, shutdowns, closed borders, travel bans, social distancing and mandatory face masks. In some countries these are distinguished as extraordinary (emergency) measures; in others they are camouflaged as normalized emergency provisions or ordinary police regulations. All of the coronavirus laws allow or limit learning processes according to their regulatory schemes. Usually, these laws have a friendly title, such as the Consolidated Health Laws in Italy[5] or the German Infection Protection Act;[6] however, they take a tough approach underpinned by the collective traumas of past epidemics, such as the plague, cholera, typhoid fever and Spanish influenza; and leave little room to adapt the law to the new

---

[4] For a detailed analysis, see Frankenberg, G. (2013), *Political Technology and the Erosion of the Rule of Law. Normalizing the State of Exception* (Cheltenham: Edward Elgar Publishing), Chapters I, V–VI.

[5] See the report 'Italy: Legal Responses to Health Emergencies', www.loc.gov/law/help/health-emergencies/italy.php/ (last accessed 30 May 2020).

[6] In 2001 the Infection Protection Act updated rather than modernized the 1961 statute regulating contagious diseases.

challenges.[7] As a rule, they normalize the state of exception by introducing extraordinary measures into law as if they were ordinary regulations.[8]

Italy's Consolidated Health Laws empower the minister of health to issue a list of infectious and communicable diseases that are subject to special procedures and measures. They establish a system of reporting and provide for preventative measures, necessary assistance, mandatory medical treatment and disinfection interventions. In the case of epidemics or pandemics, they authorize the minister of health to issue special orders for the inspection and disinfection of premises, the organization of special services and medical assistance, and the adoption of protective measures against the spread of such diseases. Lockdown, shutdown and travel bans come under the state of exception (see below).

The German Infection Protection Act (IPA) adopts a danger prevention design that is similar to the Italian Consolidated Health Laws, but complements and intensifies it by licensing the public health authorities to take emergency measures that are normalized – that is, treated as the standard *modus operandi*. Taking this tendency towards the state of emergency even further, the recent revisions in response to the coronavirus crisis quite openly introduced extraordinary measures. Notably, they empower the federal minister of health[9] to sidestep standard legal procedures and rule by decree if the Federal Diet has declared an 'epidemic situation of national importance' (Section 5(2) of the IPA). This regime is reminiscent of the infamous emergency ordinances which contributed to the decline of the Weimar Republic and the erosion of its Constitution.[10] Furthermore, the coronavirus ordinances and general decrees of the *Länder* (the member states of the Federal Republic) extensively interpret and apply the authorization framework offered by the IPA. They authorize all 'necessary protective measures' 'to the extent and for as long as necessary to prevent the spread of communicable diseases'. In addition to reporting

---

[7] From the fascinating literature on the history of epidemics and pandemics, see McNeill, W.H. (1976), *Plagues and Peoples* (New York: Anchor Press); Ruffié, J., Sournia, J.-C. (1984), *Les Épidémies dans l'histoire de l'homme* (Paris: Flammarion); Vasold, M. (2008), *Grippe, Pest und Cholera. Eine Geschichte der Seuchen in Europa* (Stuttgart: Franz Steiner Verlag); Attali, J. (1979), *L'ordre cannibale* (Paris: Glénat).

[8] See above Chapter IV and for a detailed discussion of 'normalization': Frankenberg (n 4), Chapter 1.

[9] Section 5, para 2 of the Infection Protection Act.

[10] See Article 48, para 2 of the Weimar Constitution (1919): 'If public security and order are seriously disturbed or endangered within the German Reich, the President of the Reich may take measures necessary for their restoration, intervening if need be with the assistance of the armed forces. For this purpose he may suspend for a while, in whole or in part, the fundamental rights provided in Articles 114, 115, 117, 118, 123, 124 and 153.'

obligations, surveillance, bans on activities and the closure of communal facilities, the Infection Protection Act prohibits sick or dangerous persons from 'leav[ing] the place where they are located' or entering 'certain places'. If necessary, compulsory quarantine can also be imposed. The sentences that may be imposed for violations are more draconian than those provided under standard health legislation:[11] they include a fine of up to €5000 and imprisonment for up to five years. Federal and state governments agreed on extremely strict measures that have since been gradually eased. However, other measures – such as mobile phone tracking and drone surveillance – are on the horizon.

3. CORONAVIRUS STATES OF EXCEPTION

Thus far, those drafting or implementing schemes of national infection prevention have shown no signs that they are disturbed by the uncertainties surrounding coronavirus or are willing to learn more about its peculiar features. In her first speeches to the nation, Chancellor Merkel seemed to pursue a different strategy regarding measures regulating behaviour. Rather than clearly framing social distancing and staying at home as decrees, ordinances or administrative acts, with a touch of vagueness she referred to 'guidelines', 'instructions for action', 'rules' and most recently 'standards'. Perhaps also because of the vertical separation of powers in public health, Merkel avoided imposing definitive 'directives', while also stressing that the coronavirus rules were not mere 'recommendations'. Throughout the first four months of the crisis, she relied on the semantics of approximation. It may very well be that such vagueness is a virtue which appropriately reflects the uncertainty surrounding the pandemic. Admittedly, in the decrees and ordinances subsequently issued by German states and local authorities, infection protection has stepped out of this shadow of a gentle prerogative and shown its teeth.

Or should the chancellor, in conjunction with other decision makers at state level, have declared a state of exception, if only for reasons of clarity? In fact, a state of emergency could have distracted from the question of whether the enabling norms of the German IPA or the measures they provide for – such as a nationwide lockdown (for the whole or parts of the population), the closure of plants and above all the sweeping special powers of the federal minister of health – are compatible with the Basic Law.

But what state of exception could the chancellor have possibly declared? An 'epidemiological situation of national importance' pursuant to Section 5(1) of the IPA had to be (and was) announced by Parliament. This appears to be a kind of spurious state of emergency, which let the minister of health off the hook,

---

[11] See Sections 28–30 of the Infection Protection Act.

inadvertently following the unfortunate example of the Weimar Constitution. The wording carefully avoided the terms 'exception' and 'emergency', though. At first glance, one might consider this unconstitutional, insofar as it may be assumed that this 'situation' departs from the typical states of exception enumerated in the Basic Law. Admittedly, the typical states of emergency listed in the Basic Law do not encompass a pandemic, and it is difficult to imagine those states of emergency arising in a pandemic situation. The suppression of armed insurgents (perhaps who break out of lockdown or protest against the coronavirus measures?) is not a real concern; nor is it likely that cross-border battles (over protective clothing, test kits or respiratory equipment?) will amount to a 'case of tension' or 'defence' under the Basic Law. Article 35(3) of the Basic Law provides for the inter-state deployment and cooperation of police and armed forces in case of disasters and catastrophes. One might infer that the Basic Law is informed above all by history – or, more precisely, by the dangers associated with an executive branch cut loose and military operations within the country.

By the same token, a decent democratic governor, such as the German chancellor, certainly would not want authoritarian leaders to pressure her into declaring a state of exception. At any rate, most autocrats launched their anti-coronavirus measures after declaring a state of exception because they habitually operate in this mode in order to shore up their power. To list a few examples: President Rodrigo Duterte of the Philippines ordered the shooting of quarantine violators. Indian Prime Minister Modi initially recommended Ayurveda and homeopathic treatment to manage the virus, and subsequently ordered – with barely sufficient advance warning – a national lockdown and shutdown, and the government condoned police brutality against suspected quarantine violators. Poland's Jarosław Kaczynski would ordinarily have no qualms in declaring a state of emergency, as he has repeatedly demonstrated his willingness to normalize extraordinary powers; but at present, he and his government have avoided declaring a state of exception to avoid endangering the presidential elections (his party's candidate won) in May 2020.

Some autocrats have used the coronavirus crisis as a Machiavellian moment to consolidate their power especially by relaxing parliamentary controls and attacking the opposition.[12] Until mid-March 2020, neither 'comprehensive restrictive steps' nor additional powers were on the agenda of President Erdoğan's anti-coronavirus policy. The Turkish president did not need to grant himself emergency powers, as he had already accomplished that after the attempted coup in 2016. Journalists and members of the opposition continue

---

[12] 'Would-be autocrats are using covid-19 as an excuse to grab more power', in: *The Economist*, 23 April 2020.

to be targeted. In Hungary, Viktor Orbán took a significant step on 30 March to consolidate his autocracy by removing parliamentary control of his decrees and turning criminal law against the opposition with a statute that imposes a prison sentence of up to five years for spreading 'false information' about coronavirus.[13] After two and a half months and more than 100 decrees, which will remain in effect, Orbán's parliamentary majority suspended the emergency law – but passed a new law that authorized the prime minister to 'declare a medical crisis emergency'.[14]

The crisis hit Algeria at a very unfortunate moment: with oil prices falling and tourism suffering, it had no convincing arguments to contain the lively protest movement which has continued undaunted by coronavirus. By proxy, Xi Jinping cracked down on protests in Hong Kong.[15] In contrast, the government of Bhutan went down a different path, adopting a middle ground between denial and a state of exception. It ordered quarantine and surveillance of its closely controlled borders, without declaring a state of emergency.

After trivializing the virus, Brazilian President Jair Bolsonaro appeared to follow the lead of municipal and state authorities and finally asked Congress to approve a government decree declaring a public calamity so as to be able to spend beyond the limits of the Fiscal Responsibility Law and address the emergency situation.[16] His erratic, chauvinistic approach cannot be trusted, though. The question remains as to whether he will be held responsible for the increasing death rates in Brazil. Not to forget 'Europe's last dictator' (his own words): Alexander Lukashenko is one of the last outliers who remain in denial and shun any serious anti-coronavirus measures, insisting that keeping in good spirits and doing rural work ('tractor therapy') will keep people safe.[17]

In the time of coronavirus, some more or less democratically elected heads of state appear to be bent on joining the phalanx of their openly authoritarian colleagues. In India, the Philippines, Brazil, Hungary and elsewhere, the executivist practices of governing illustrate that states of emergency are tailored not to promote legal learning experiences, but rather to reward authoritarian ges-

---

[13] 'Hungary: Law to fight coronavirus creates "uncertainty" for journalists', in: *Deutsche Welle*, www.dw.com/en/hungary-law-to-fight-coronavirus-creates-uncertainty-for-journalists/a-53027631/ (last accessed 30 March 2020).

[14] *'Ungarn hebt Notstandsgesetze auf'*, *Deutsche Welle*, 16 June 2020, www.dw.com/de/ungarn-hebt-corona-notstandsgesetz-auf/a-53826802/ (last accessed 22 July 2020).

[15] Ramzy, A. and Yu, E. (2020), 'Under Cover of Coronavirus, Hong Kong Cracks Down on Protests Movement', in: *The New York Times*, 21 April.

[16] Grillo, B. (2020), 'Municipal, state-level authorities declare a state of emergency', in: *The Brazilian Report*, 17 March.

[17] Simmons, A. (2020), 'In Belarus, Everyday Life is Much the Same as Coronavirus Spreads', in: *The Wall Street Journal*, 27 April.

tures and stabilize autocratic structures. Emmanuel Macron – narcissistically offended by the fear he might not be re-elected – vainly and foolishly declared war on the virus: '*Nous sommes en guerre*.'[18]

Donald Trump has fluctuated erratically between denial, idiotic statements that reveal ignorance and lack of concern, and dramatization as the November election approaches.[19] Finally, after the situation had become exceptionally grave in the United States, he also adopted the rhetoric of war and declared a state of emergency, while simultaneously suggesting that 'things got better' and the economy would be 'opened again' soon, as well as holding China and the World Health Organization responsible for the pandemic.[20]

The Italian practice has been different, but again is suitable for neither imitation nor learning. The state of emergency and hard lockdown imposed on the country reflect the despair felt over a disaster that the government proved unable to control, especially in Lombardy.[21] The cascade of measures released in response to the crisis cut deeply into civil liberties.[22] Certainly, Article 77 of the Italian Constitution entitles the government to take extraordinary action on its own initiative in case of urgency and necessity. For a national curfew, however, this cloak of legality seemed somewhat short. But who questions the law when death is on the doorstep?

4. BALANCING ENDS AND MEANS?

Lawyers will probably have to do just that: question the law and apply it, even if the world is ending. However, they must prepare for uncertainty on a global and hitherto unknown scale. It is quite inadequate to continue what ministers of public health have been doing thus far, and what may account for the irrelevance of legal arguments in the dispute between the disciplines: that is, using conventional legal tools to handle the law on epidemics and check whether its present use is proportionate, and rushing to balance anti-coronavirus means with anti-coronavirus ends. The extent to which legal analyses have avoided questioning the proportionality of social distancing, lockdowns, shutdowns,

---

18 French President Emmanuel Macron, addressing the nation and calling for a 'general mobilization', in: *Le Monde*, 17 March 2020.

19 Stevens, H. and Tan, S. (2020), 'From "It's going to disappear" to "We Will Win this War"', in: *The Washington Post*, 31 March.

20 www.merkur.de/welt/coronavirus-usa-donald-trump-zahlen-infizierte-lockerung-china-tote-covid-19-twitter-zr-13775220.html/ (last accessed 30 May 2020).

21 See the detailed analysis in *Il Post*, www.ilpost.it/2020/05/07/two-months-that-shook-lombardy-to-the-core-coronavirus/ (last accessed 30 May 2020).

22 'Italy announces fines of up to 3000 € for breaking quarantine rules', in: *The Local*, 24 March 2020.

closed borders, travel bans and other interventions is almost tragic, given the far-reaching consequences of such measures for society, the economy, politics, mental health, women's burden and children's hearts and minds. And the legal discourse has barely strayed beyond the standard ideas and tools applied to avert danger. Few, if any lawyers questioned the infection protection schemes and emergency laws. They seem not to realize that anti-coronavirus decrees and regulations not only infringe freedoms, but transform everyday lives and disrupt the fabric of society.

First, the principle of proportionality had already been weakened and undermined through the aforementioned conversion of police laws into a generalized security (risk) matrix. With the reduced density of judicial controls, the judicial examination of police interventions thinned out the principle of proportionality. Second, balancing ends and means to guarantee that legal interventions are necessary and adequate is – and has always been – an open-ended, unpredictable process – more a metaphor than a stringent method of assessment. Third, in the wake of the pandemic, the prevailing social conditions have been completely disrupted; and there is no end to this disruption in sight. How and for what purposes can such desolate relations provide a measure? Flattened curves of new infections, national herd immunity, low reproduction rates of the virus and a ceiling of new infections for regional hotspots are likely candidates as legitimate epidemic-hygienic *ends*. Lawyers and judges have dutifully complied with the ever-changing virological and epidemiological prognoses and moving targets, and have fitted them within the schema of proportionality, often taking them as raw materials and not even translating them into legal categories and criteria of proportionality.

Meanwhile, the pandemic has globalized the *goals* and *means* that are being used to control and contain infections. Flattened curves, herd immunity and declining reproduction rates must be assessed and weighed against the consequences of social distancing and isolation; of lockdowns of cities and shutdowns of factories and businesses, schools and day-care facilities. Balancing must weigh an endless number of factors – from bankruptcy and unemployment to domestic violence, depression, disrupted education, social isolation, the cumulative negative impact on women working under precarious conditions, deprivation of children from opportunities, Kawasaki syndrome and more. Balancing faces the obvious dilemma of identifying and properly weighing all aspects of an overly complex situation. To reduce this complexity, some authors opt for one or the other highest value – life, health, dignity (including dignity in death) – rather than the protection of 'mere' health or 'naked life'.[23] They thus escape the demands of an exigent balancing process and avoid the mechanics of proportionality that have ossified in routine and amount to little more, during a pandemic, than testing the evident rationality of infection protection. Hence, balancing is barely worth the name – indeed, a metaphor rather than a rigorous legal method.

5. LAW, SECURITY, EXPERIMENTS

The coronavirus crisis calls for a law with a more flexible, open texture that allows for the integration of new ideas and perspectives, and for experimentation and learning, rather than relying on more or less centralized command and control structures. Co-determination and voluntariness must be introduced as (new) principles, without which even the prohibition-supported and compulsively enforced imperative against infection ultimately cannot work. Washing hands, staying at home and social distancing in workplaces, public spaces and educational institutions cannot be reliably supervised and enforced by an authoritarian regulatory model as maintained by standard police laws, exacerbated by the normalized state of exception or, in particular, its crude version. In contrast to conventional and extraordinary schemes of infection protection, the current uncertainty demands that other sources of information be tapped. There is no good reason to assume that individuals who want to protect themselves and their families, workplaces and businesses have nothing to contribute towards containing the pandemic, if properly supervised by public health authorities. On the contrary, groups have already proved themselves capable of organizing public assemblies with strict adherence to the rules of social distancing. Shop owners that want to do business during the pandemic can devise practical ways to protect customers and staff. Supermarkets have demonstrated how they can likewise meet this expectation. Schools and universities have organized new learning processes, so they might also organize new ways and means of protecting people. Societies do not need law's present coronavirus autocracy, but can instead be trusted – like markets, doctor's offices, bakeries, repair shops and others – to participate in the social coronavirus laboratory, where they learn how to work out rules and develop plans to prevent contagion.

According to practical reason, laws that are intended to protect against infection will have to change their modality: from coercion (which chafes with time) to incentives; from penalties (which might lose their edge once people die by the thousands) to trial and error; and from infection paternalism to

---

[23] Volkmann, U. (2020), 'Das höchste Gut', in: *Frankfurter Allgemeine Zeitung*, 1 April.

co-determination and a modicum of solidarity.[24] Through 'rules' that instruct (how to work out protection plans) and recommend rather than prohibit, and through (legal) education and consultation instead of deterrence, experimental approaches towards the crisis may yield a supply-oriented law – not a law that condones violence, but rather one that is geared towards the participation of all those affected and their voluntary contributions. As previously, the new law on how to cope with the pandemic as a societal experiment would advise everyone – especially the most vulnerable – to protect themselves. (Public funds which no longer need to be called upon to support ailing businesses could be used for this.) The law could focus on supporting those who need special assistance by offering social services. Volunteers can be an invaluable resource, as the willingness to help refugees in 2015 bears out – provided that civil society is no longer placed under house arrest and demobilized by ordinances and decrees, but is rather involved in the discussions on what the pandemic requires and in the actual delivery of that. This is another component of Sweden's and Uruguay's strategic mix of recommendations, legal requirements and adjustments to cope with coronavirus.[25]

But what if this experiment founders because many people do not 'play along'? In that case, the state may admittedly lose some time; but it will gain valuable practical knowledge about people's behaviour (far beyond what abstract models can provide), and could concentrate in the meantime on procuring protective clothing and respiratory equipment, supplying tests kits, promoting the search for vaccines and treatments, and actively supporting medical and healthcare services. Society will learn painfully that a pandemic requires all of its members to cooperate and participate in developing protective measures; unless people are happy for their countries to be run like leprosy wards, with citizens as inmates – disoriented by coronaphobia, acquiescent in states of exception and accepting of nationwide lockdowns and shutdowns and bans as 'proportionate'.

And as for the law? It is rarely any wiser than the society whose collective behaviour it regulates. Where it is to be applied in a situation of uncertainty, there is no choice: it simply must learn. One might hope that its theoreticians and practitioners have already learned: sovereign is she who does *not* declare

---

[24] Which might be the components of Chancellor Merkel's programme and seem to be a guiding principle of Sweden's and Uruguay's COVID-19 approach. See Tharoor, I. (2020), 'Sweden's coronavirus strategy is not what it seems', in: *The Washington Post*, 12 May, www.washingtonpost.com/world/2020/05/12/swedens-coronavirus-strategy-is-not-what-it-seems/ (last accessed 30 May)

[25] Government of Sweden, www.government.se/government-policy/the-governments-work-in-response-to-the-virus-responsible-for-covid-19/ (last accessed 22 July 2020); see '*Paradebeispiel* Uruguay', in: *Frankfurter Rundschau*, 22 July 2020.

a state of exception; and who does *not* normalize it under the flag of epidemic control.

10. Epilogue

What are all these people in line for? Is there free darkness here? But it never feeds anyone.[1]

Algeria is going through a sensitive period in its history.[2]

Authoritarianism has no expiry date; but nor is its longevity guaranteed. There is no reason to view autocracies as inevitable and their constitutions as necessarily enduring. Dictators, despots, sultans and autocrats operate according to the rules of a grammar that is tailored to their techniques of governing and concepts of power, which are not intended to be citizen-friendly or law-abiding. Whenever autocracies afford opportunities to participate, their ulterior motive is often to win accomplices. Whenever despots ostensibly enter into a direct 'conversation' with the people, they actually deliver monologues and seek approval, ignoring critical questions or opposing views. They also disregard the high price that people have to pay for the regime: a toothless media, ideologically streamlined parties, imprisoned opposition, rigged elections and delegates with neither voice nor vote. And what do people get in return? The phantasm of an imaginary community, as long as they believe and obey.

To give authoritarianism a profile – to examine it as closely as possible while at the same time keeping it far away at a critical distance – was one of the methodological tasks that this study set itself. Another was to analyse the constitutions of autocracies across the matrix of purposes and audiences. Above all, attention focused on the points at which the practices of authoritarian regimes, their rhetoric and constitutions lose their secure footing: in fleeting marginal notes and imprudent remarks, thoughtless drifts and concealed premises. These analytical efforts and interpretations aimed to explore that fateful fascination which (mis)leads many to succumb to the authoritarian

1 '*Wonach stehen all diese Leute an? Gibt es hier Dunkelheit umsonst? Aber davon wird doch keiner satt.*' Erpenbeck, J. (2014), *Aller Tage Abend* (Munich: Random House), 229.

2 This what Algerian President Bouteflika said when finally announcing his decision not to stand for election for a fifth time, in view of sustained protests throughout the country (quoted in *Frankfurter Rundschau,* 12 March 2019).

temptation.[3] A further aim was to determine what autocratic rulers expect from constitutions. Where possible, these reflections aimed to penetrate the heart of darkness, where authoritarian regimes hide their crimes – and their weaknesses.

Authoritarianism has an Achilles heel: authority. It is not enough to apply force and decide, enforce or repress. 'It's about authority, stupid!'[4] And authority ultimately depends on the willingness of others to lend it to the person who exercises it. Someone is 'only king because other people behave with regard to him as subjects'; and they are subjects because he is king.[5] Constitutions can be weak or can serve as a linchpin for authority. They can convey conformism or provide ways to challenge and reclaim authority.

It is therefore not surprising that a despot's power declines once his authority is challenged, as happened in the following constitutional settings.

Autocrats are seldom asked to apologize for anti-Semitic slanders; but this is exactly what the European People's Party demanded of Viktor Orbán's European People's Party. That could at least be a start.

Even for Recep Tayyip Erdoğan, the tree of authority does not grow unbounded into the sky. In the local elections of Spring 2019, his AKP party had to surrender the Turkish metropolises to the opposition.

In Slovakia, right-wing nationalism also suffered a bitter defeat in 2019, when civil rights lawyer Zuzana Čaputová challenged the authority of the old regime and won the presidential election.[6]

Myanmar's military junta was dealt a serious blow to its authority in 2008, when the generals were forced to leave their dictatorial comfort zone and pacify protesters with a new Constitution. Matters got worse in 2015, when they had to recognize the landslide victory of Aung San Suu Kyi's National League for Democracy and accept '*Daw* Suu' (Aunt Suu) as the *de facto* president.

---

[3] Chenoweth, E. (2016), 'The Authoritarian Temptation', https://idee-us.org/wp-content/uploads/2016/06/The-Authoritarian-Temptation_Eric-Chenoweth-1.pdf/ (last accessed 22 July 2020); Krauthammer, C. (2018), 'The Authoritarian Temptation', in: *id*, *The Point of It All* (New York: Random House); Cofre, L. (2020), 'Chile and COVID-19: A Constitutional Authoritarian Temptation', VerfBlog, 19 May 2020, https://verfassungsblog.de/chile-and-covid-19-a-constitutional-authoritarian-temptation/ (last accessed 22 July 2020).

[4] Ringen, S. (2011), 'It's about authority, stupid! Having power is not enough to get things done', in: 133 *WZB-Mitteilungen*, 7 ff.

[5] Marx, K. and Engels, F. (1972), *Das Kapital. Kritik der politischen Ökonomie*, *MEW* 23 (Berlin: Dietz-Verlag), 72 (fn.).

[6] Turp, C. (2019), 'Humanist lawyer becomes Slovakia's first female president', in: *Emerging Europe*, 31 March, https://emerging-europe.com/news/humanist-lawyer-becomes-slovakias-first-female-preside (last accessed 18 March 2020).

Stalinism – deep-frozen in the Cold War – was destined to rule forever, so its cadres believed. In the German Democratic Republic, one of its testing grounds, it assumed the form and rhetoric of 'the people's rule'. In 1989, those same people refused obedience and terminated the regime's authority. They took to the streets with the anti-authoritarian (not nationalist) slogan: 'We are the people.'[7] Stalinism collapsed across Central and Eastern Europe, one country after another, once Mikhail Gorbachev pulled the plug on the hegemonic authority of the Communist Party.

In 1990, the apartheid government of South Africa had to lift the ban on the African National Congress. After 27 years of imprisonment, one of the most famous anti-apartheid fighters, Nelson Mandela, was finally released from prison. Strikes, protest marches, terrorist attacks, acts of sabotage, international movements and sanctions had finally eroded the authority of the most vicious racist despotism and created space for transformative constitutionalism.[8]

From December 2010 onwards, first Tunisia and then other societies in the Maghreb and the Middle East destroyed the Western myth that the Arab world is culturally disposed to accept despotism because of religious orientations and the rule of favour.[9] In Tunisia, self-immolation became the signal for the all-too-brief 'Arab Spring',[10] which brought down an autocrat who had relied on a combination of repression, corruption and modest prosperity.[11]

The *ancien régimes* seem to be recovering, though. Algeria's autocratic power cartel – which in 2011 sacrificed a trivial state of emergency to the 'Spring' – experienced a 'sensitive phase' in Spring 2019, when the powers

---

7 See Hirschman, A.O. (1992), '*Abwanderung, Widerspruch und das Schicksal der Deutschen Demokratischen Republik. Ein Essay zur konzeptionellen Geschichte*', in: 20 *Leviathan*, 330 ff; Dalos, G. (2009), *Der Vorhang geht auf. Das Ende der Diktaturen in Osteuropa* (Munich: Beck).

8 Klug, H (2016), 'Towards a Sociology of Constitutional Transformation: Understanding South Africa's Post-Apartheid Constitutional Order', *University of Wisconsin Legal Studies Research Paper* No 1373, 8 February.

9 For moderate critiques of stereotypes and myths: Elbadawi, I. and Makdisi, S. (eds) (2017), *Democracy in the Arab World. Explaining the Deficit* (London: Routledge); and Tessler, M. (2002), 'Islam and Democracy in the Middle East', in: 34 *Comparative Politics*, 337 ff.

10 'Arab Spring' is a misleading term and also a misnomer with orientalist connotations: Susser, A. (2012), 'The "Arab Spring": The Origins of a Misnomer', in: *Foreign Policy*, 27 April, www.fpri.org/article/2012/04/the-arab-spring-the-origins-of-a-misnomer/ (last accessed 18 March 2020); see the thorough and critical analysis by Sultany, N. (2017), *Law and Revolution: Legitimacy and Constitutionalism After the Arab Spring* (Oxford: Oxford University Press).

11 Willis, M.J. (2016), 'Revolt for Dignity. Tunisia's Revolution and Civil Resistance', in: Roberts, A. *et al* (eds), *Resistance in the Arab Spring: Triumphs and Disasters* (Oxford: Oxford University Press).

that be had to make concessions, and then attempted to regroup. They had to wait, however, because protesters prevented President Bouteflika from standing again – for the first time in the *longue durée* of his presidency, which had been repeatedly interrupted by unrest, but seldom shaken to its foundations.[12] It appears that today, the Algerian people are persistently challenging the authority of those in power and questioning the relationship between chiefs and subjects. They neither believed nor feared the despotic behaviour of whoever was pulling the strings behind the scenes. 'Algerian conditions' determine what passes for authority there. These 'conditions' bring to mind Ferdinand Lassalle's definition of the concept of an 'actual constitution': 'The actual power relations that exist in every society are the actively acting force that determines all laws and legal institutions of this society in such a way that they cannot essentially be different from what they are.'[13]

And – for the time being at least[14] – the conditions are determined by those who have found their voice again. After years of patience, fear and suffering, Algeria's people have rediscovered their authority in protest against the regime: 'I am revolting, therefore we are.'[15]

In Algeria, an absurd theatre of authoritarian constitutionalism, if nothing else, has been successfully removed: the electoral appearance of a puppet of the military and secret services who wanted to remain in control and therefore dictated the narrative. But a different narrative was written in the streets. The power cartel responded with all due haste and faced up to the protesters with a new Constitution and a referendum. It remains to be seen what will become of the opposition, the regime and Algeria.

By the same token, we will also have to wait and see what will happen in Sudan after its surprising turn against despotism in 2019. Sustained public protests led to the overthrow of despot Omar al-Bashir, who had ruled 'with a hard hand' for 30 years and is now on trial for crimes against humanity. Even the chairman of the military council and former confidant of the ousted al-Bashir, who wanted to bring 'order' quickly, held office for only one day.[16]

---

[12] See Schmid, B. (2005), *Algerien – Frontstaat im globalen Krieg? Neoliberalismus, soziale Bewegungen und islamistische Ideologie in einem nordafrikanischen Land* (Münster: Unrast).

[13] Lassalle, F. (1993), Über Verfassungswesen, *Rede am 16. April 1862* (Hamburg: Europäische Verlagsanstalt), 1993.

[14] Cheref, A. (2019), 'After six months of protest, Algerians fear the old regime still prevails', in: *The National*, 18 August.

[15] Camus, A. (1951), *L'Homme révolté* (Paris: Gallimard), 1951, 36; [English] (1992) *The Rebel* (London: Vintage).

[16] Regarding the role of the military in Sudan: Battahani, A. (2016), 'The Sudan Armed Forces and Prospects of Change', in: *CMI Insight*, Number 3, April.

In Algeria, Sudan and elsewhere, the ultimate question is whether or to what extent the constitutions of authoritarian regimes can contribute to their transformation or even their end. The answer still lies in the stars. Test cases include Syria, where al-Assad has made a constitutional promise to withdraw from power in 2021; and Cambodia, where Hun Sen has done likewise. As too did Vladimir Putin for 2024; although we have just learned (which in truth, we knew all along) that he has changed his mind. Reconstituting Sudan or Algeria will be rather difficult. Reversing autocratic constitutionalism in Hungary, Poland and India will be a daunting task. Restoring constitutional culture in Brazil, Venezuela and the United States demands that the people pull themselves up by their bootstraps.

On all these constitutional construction sites and in these different contexts, it remains an open question whether the respective constitutions correspond to and correct the actual power relations. To quote Ferdinand Lassalle's famous lecture on constitutions:

> If you have an apple tree in your garden and now attach a note to it on which you write: this is a fig tree, has the tree become a fig tree as a result? No, and if you were to gather all your household servants, indeed all the inhabitants of the country, together and make a loud and solemn oath: this is a fig tree – the tree remains what it was, and the next year it will show itself to be what it was, it will bear apples and not figs. Just as we have seen with the Constitution. It does not matter what is written on that piece of paper if it contradicts the real situation, the real balance of power.'[17]

Can autocratic constitutions be more than the metaphorical note attached to an apple tree which says: 'This is a fig tree'? Maybe – if the spectators become the people.

17 Lassalle (n 13).

Selected bibliography

This selection concentrates on publications covering authority, authoritarianism, democracy and constitutionalism.

Abbott, E. (1988), *Haiti: The Duvaliers and Their Legacy*, New York: McGraw-Hill

Ackerman, B.A. (2007), *Before the Next Attack: Preserving Civil Liberties in an Age of Terrorism*, New Haven: Yale University Press

Adorno, T.W. *et al* (1950), *The Authoritarian Personality*, New York: Harper and Brothers

Adorno, T.W. (1970), 'Die Freudsche Theorie und die Struktur der Faschistischen Propaganda', in: 24 *Psyche*, 486 ff

Al-Azm, S.J. (2004), 'Islam, Terrorism and the West Today', in: 44 *Die Welt des Islams*, 114 ff

Albrecht, H. and Frankenberg, R. (eds) (2010), *Autoritarismus Reloaded – Neuere Ansätze und Erkenntnisse der Autokratieforschung*, Baden-Baden: Nomos

Alexander, M. (2012), *The New Jim Crow*, New York: The New Press

Ali, T. (2006), *Die Nehrus und die Gandhis. Eine indische Dynastie,* Munich: Heyne

Allert, T. (2016), 'Der deutsche Gruß. Geschichte einer unheilvollen Geste', Frankfurt am Main: Fischer

Altemeyer, R. (1988), *Enemies of Freedom: Understanding Right-Wing Authoritarianism*, San Francisco: Jossey-Bass

Alterio, A.M. and Niembro Ortega, R. (2018), 'Constitutional Culture and Democracy in Mexico – A Critical View of the 100-Year-Old Mexican Constitution', in: Graber, M. *et al* (eds), *Constitutional Democracies in Crisis?*, Oxford: Oxford University Press, 139 ff

Altınordu, A. (2017), 'A Midsummer Night's Coup: Performance and Power in Turkey's July 15 Coup Attempt', 40 *Qualitative Sociology*, 139 ff

Alviar Garcia, H. and Frankenberg, G. (eds) (2019), *Authoritarian Constitutionalism: Comparative Analysis and Critique*, Cheltenham: Edward Elgar Publishing

Alviar Garcia, H. (2019), 'Neoliberalism as a Form of Authoritarian Constitutionalism', in Alviar Garcia and Frankenberg, *Authoritarian Constitutionalism,* 37 ff

Anderson, B. (1983), *Imagined Communities. Reflections on the Origin and Spread of Nationalism,* London: Verso

Anscombe, G.E.M. (1981), 'One the Source of Authority of the State', in: *Ethics, Religion, and Politics* (Collected Philosophical Papers: Vol 3), Oxford: Blackwell, 130 ff

Applebaum, A. (2013), *Der Eiserne Vorhang: Die Unterdrückung Osteuropas 1944–1956*, Munich: Siedler

Arendt, H. (1976), *The Origins of Totalitarianism* [1951], New York: Schocken

Arendt, H. (2016), *On Revolution* [1963], London: Faber & Faber

Aron, R. (1985), '*L'avenier des religions séculières*', in: Nr 28–29 *Commentaire*, 369 ff

Art, D. (2012), 'What Do We Know About Authoritarianism After Ten Years?', in: *Comparative Politics*, 351 ff

Bajohr, F. and Wildt, M. (eds) (2009), *Volksgemeinschaft. Neue Forschungen zur Gesellschaft des Nationalsozialismus*, Frankfurt am Main: Fischer

Bank, A. (2009), 'Die Renaissance des Autoritarismus. Erkenntnisse und Grenzen neuerer Beiträge der Comparative Politics und Nahostforschung', 4 *Hamburg Review of Social Sciences*, 10 ff

Bánkuti, M. *et al*, (2012) 'Disabling the Constitution', 23 *Journal of Democracy*, 138 ff

Bánkuti, M. *et al* (2012), 'Hungary's Illiberal Turn: Disabling the Constitution', 23 *Journal of Democracy*, 138 ff

Baxi, U. (2003) 'The Colonial Heritage', in: Legrand, P. and Munday, R. (eds), *Comparative Legal Studies: Traditions and Transitions*, Cambridge: Cambridge University Press, 50 ff

Benjamin, W. (2003), 'Critique of Violence', in: *id*, *Reflections, Essays, Aphorisms and Autobiographical Writings*, Demetz, P (ed), New York: Schocken Books, 277 ff

Benni, S., Camilleri and Eco, U. (2002), *Berlusconis Italien – Italien gegen Berlusconi*, Berlin: Verlag Klaus Wagenbach

Berlin, I. (2003), *Generations of Captivity: A History of African-American Slaves*, Cambridge/London: The Belknap Press of Harvard University Press

Blum, W. (2003), *Killing Hope: US Military and CIA Interventions Since World War II*, London: Zed Books

Bogaards, M. and Elischer, S. (2016), 'Competitive Authoritarianism in Africa Revisited', in: 10 *Zeitschrift für Vergleichende Politikwissenschaft*, 5 ff

Boger, H.W. (2004), 'Bürger & Staat: Nomokratie Demokratie Bürokratie KLEPTOKRATIE', in: *HUMONDE. Zeitschrift für eine humane Welt und Wirtschaft*, No 02, 613 ff

Borejsza, J.W. *et al* (eds) (2006), *Totalitarian and Authoritarian Regimes in Europe*, Oxford/New York: Berghahn Books

Bos, E. (2004), *Verfassungsgebung und Systemwechsel: Die Institutionalisierung von Demokratie im postsozialistischen Europa*, Wiesbaden: Springer VS

Bourdieu, P. (1983), '*Ökonomisches Kapital – Kulturelles Kapital – Soziales Kapital*', in: Kreckel, R. (ed), *Soziale Ungleichheiten*, Göttingen: Vandenhoeck & Ruprecht, 183 ff

Bracher, K.D. (1993), *Die deutsche Diktatur. Entstehung, Struktur, Folgen des Nationalsozialismus*. Cologne: Kiepenheuer & Witsch

Braehler, E. and Decker, O. (2018), *Flucht ins Autoritäre: Rechtsextreme Dynamiken in der Mitte der Gesellschaft*, Gießen: Psychosozial Verlag

Brandt, M.J. and Henry, P.J. (2012), 'Gender Inequality and Gender Differences in Authoritarianism', in: 38 *Personality and Social Psychology Bulletin*, 1301ff.

Bratton, M. and van de Walle, N. (1994), 'Neopatrimonialism and Political Transitions in Africa', in: 46 *World Politics*, 453 ff

Bratton, M. and van de Walle, N. (1997), *Democratic Experiments in Africa. Regime Transitions in Comparative Perspective,* Cambridge: Cambridge University Press

Bredekamp, H. (2014), *Der schwimmende Souverän. Karl der Große und die Bildpolitik des Körpers*, Berlin: Wagenbach

Bredies, I. (2011), 'Verfassungen ohne Konstitutionalismus: quasikonstitutionelle Institutionalisierung des Autoritarismus in Osteuropa', in: 8 *Totalitarismus und Demokratie*, 133 ff

Breede, H.C. (2017), *The Idea of Failed States*, New York: Routledge

Brezhnev, L. (1977), *On the Draft Constitution of the Union of Soviet Republics*, Moscow: Foreign Languages Publishing House

Bröckling, U. *et al* (2011), *Governmentality – Current Issues and Future Challenges*, New York/London: Routledge

Brooker, P. (2009), *Non-democratic Regimes: Theory, Government, and Politics*, New York: St. Martin's Press, 2nd ed, New York: Palgrave

Brown, N.J. (2002), *Constitutions in a Nonconstitutional World*, Albany: State University of New York Press

Brown, W. *et al* (2018), *Authoritarianism. Three Inquiries in Critical Theory*, Chicago: University of Chicago Press

Bruff, I. (2016), 'The Rise of Authoritarian Neoliberalism', 26 *Rethinking Marxism: A Journal of Economics, Culture & Society*, 115 ff

Buck-Morss, S. (2009), *Hegel, Haiti, and Universal History*, Pittsburgh: University of Pittsburgh Press

Bui, T.H. (2013), 'Liberal Constitutionalism and the Socialist State in an Era of Globalisation: An Inquiry into Vietnam's Constitutional Discourse and Power Structures', 5 *Global Studies Journal*, 43 ff

Burke, E. (1992), 'The Fabrication of Louis XIV', in: 42 *History Today*, 24 ff

Burke, E. (2001), *Reflections on the Revolution in France* [1790], Clark, J.C.D. (ed), Stanford: Stanford University Press

Butterwegge, C. (2006), 'Globalisierung, Neoliberalismus und Rechtsextremismus', in: P. Bahtke and S. Spindler (eds), *Neoliberalismus und Rechtsextremismus in Europa. Zusammenhänge – Widersprüche – Gegenstrategien*, Berlin: Karl Dietz-Verlag, 15 ff

Çalışkan, K. (2017), 'Explaining the end of military tutelary regime and the July 15 coup attempt in Turkey', in: 10 *Journal of Cultural Economy*, 97 ff

Canovan, M. (1981), *Populism*, New York: Harcourt Brace Jovanovich

Canovan, M. (1999), 'Trust the People! Populism and the Two Faces of Democracy', in: 47 *Political Studies*, 2 ff

Canovan, M. (2002), 'Taking Politics to the People: Populism and the Ideology of Democracy', in: Mény, Y. and Surel, Y. (eds), *Democracies and the Populist Challenge*, Basingstoke: Palgrave, 25 ff

Chapman, P. (2007), *Bananas: How the United Fruit Company Shaped the World*, Edinburgh: Canongate Books

Chen, A.H.Y. (2014), 'The achievement of constitutionalism in Asia – moving beyond "constitutions without constitutionalism"', in: Chen (ed), *Constitutionalism in Asia in the Early Twenty-First Century*, Cambridge: Cambridge University Press, 4 ff

Chomsky, N. (2006), *Failed States: The Abuse of Power and the Assault of Democracy*, New York: Henry Holt & Co.

Chua, A. and Rubenfeld, J. (2018), 'The Threat of Tribalism', in: *The Atlantic Monthly*, No 10 October

Çıpa, H.E. (2017), *The Making of Selim: Succession, Legitimacy and Memory in the Early Modern Ottoman World*, Bloomington: Indiana University Press

Coates, T.N. (2017), 'The First White President', in: *The Atlantic Monthly*, No 10 October

Codoceo, F. (2007), *Demokratische Transition in Chile. Kontinuität oder Neubeginn?*, Berlin: wvb Wissenschaftlicher Verlag Berlin

Collinson, D. and Hearns, J. (1996), *Men as Managers, Managers as Men. Critical Perspectives on Men, Masculinities and Managements*, London: Sage

Corrales, J. (2013), 'Venezuela's Succession Crisis', in: 112 *Current History*, 56 ff
Corrales, J. (2015), 'The Authoritarian Resurgence: Autocratic Legalism in Venezuela', in: 26 *Journal of Democracy*, 37 ff
Cortés, J.D. (1854), *Obras* I, Madrid: Tejado
Cortés, J.D. *Über die Diktatur: Drei Reden aus den Jahren 1849/50, hrsg. v Günter Maschke*, Vienna: Karolinger Verlag 1996
Crouch, C. (2004), *Post-Democracy*, Cambridge: Polity
Crouch, C. *The Strange Non-Death of Neoliberalism*, Cambridge: Polity
Dahrendorf, R. (2006), *Versuchungen der Unfreiheit. Die Intellektuellen in Zeiten der Prüfung*, Munich: CH Beck
Davis, D. (2019), 'Authoritarian Constitutionalism: The South African Experience', in: Alviar and Frankenberg, *Authoritarian Constitutionalism*, 57 ff
Dawisha, K. (2014), *Putin's Kleptocracy: Who Owns Russia?*, New York: Simon & Schuster
Decker, O. *et al* (2012), 'Das Veralten des autoritären Charakters', in: Friedrich-Ebert-Stiftung (ed), *Die Mitte in der Krise. Rechtsextreme Einstellungen in Deutschland 2010*, Berlin: zu Klampen, S. 29 ff.
Deibert, R. *et al* (eds) (2008), *Access Denied. The Practice and Policy of Global Internet Filtering*, Cambridge: MIT Press
Deibert, R. *et al* (eds) (2010), *Access Controlled. The Shaping of Power, Rights in Cyberspace*, Cambridge MA: MIT Press
Deneen, P. (2018), *Why Liberalism Failed*, New Haven: Yale University Press
Denninger, E. (1990), *Der gebändigte Leviathan*, Baden-Baden: Nomos
Derrida, J. (1990), 'Force of Law: "Mystical" Foundation of Justice', in: 11 *Cardozo Law Review*, 921 ff
Derrida, J. (2002), 'Declarations of Independence', in: *Negotiations: Interventions and Interviews, 1971–2001*, Stanford: Stanford University Press, 46 ff
Diamond, L. and Plattner, M. (eds) (2015), *Democracy in Decline?*, Baltimore: Johns Hopkins University Press
Diamond, L. *et al* (eds) (2016), *Authoritarianism Goes Global: The Challenge to Democracy*, Baltimore: Johns Hopkins University Press
Diehl, P. (2015), *Der politische Repräsentant und der leere Ort der Macht'. Das Symbolische, das Imaginäre und die Demokratie. Eine Theorie politischer Repräsentation*, Baden-Baden: Nomos Verlag
Dikötter, F. (2019), *How To Be A Dictator: The Cult of Personality in the Twentieth Century*, London: Bloomsbury
Dirks, N. (2006), *The Scandal of Empire: India and the Creation of Imperial Britain*, Cambridge: The Belknap Press of Harvard University Press
Duverger, Maurice, *Les constitutions de la France*, Paris: Presses Universitaires de France 1944
Eisenstadt, S.N. (1973), *Traditional Patrimonialism and Modern Neopatrimonialism*, Beverly Hills: Sage
Elias, N. (2010), *The Society of Individuals*, Dublin: UCD Press
Esena, B. and Gumuscu, S. (2016), 'Rising Competitive Authoritarianism in Turkey', in: *Third World Quarterly*, 1581 ff
Estlund, D. (2008), *Democratic Authority*, Princeton: Princeton University Press
Figes, O. (2008), *Die Flüsterer. Leben in Stalins Russland*, Berlin: Berlin Verlag
Finaldi, G. (2008), *Mussolini and Italian Fascism*, Harlow: Routledge
Fischer, S. (2004), *Modernity Disavowed. Haiti and the Cultures of Slavery in the Age of Revolution*, Durham: Duke University Press

Foucault, M. (1977), *Discipline and Punish. The Birth of the Prison*, New York: Pantheon Books

Foucault, M. (1980), 'Truth and Power', in: *Power/Knowledge. Selected Interviews and other Writings 1972–1977*, Gordon, C. (ed), New York: Pantheon Books, 109 ff

Foucault, M. (1991), 'Governmentality', in: Burchell, G. *et al* (eds), *Studies in Governmentality*, Hemel Hampstead: Harvester Wheatsheaf, 87 ff

Foucault, M. (2008), *The Birth of Bio-Politics: Lectures at the Collège de France 1978–1979*, London: Palgrave Macmillan

Foucault, M. (2008), *Security, Territory, Population: Lectures at the Collège de France, 1977–1978*, New York: St. Martin's Press

Fraenkel, E. (2010), *The Dual State: A Contribution to the Theory of Dictatorship*, Clark: The Law Book Exchange, Ltd

Frankenberg, G. (2014), *Political Technology and the Erosion of the Rule of Law – Normalizing the State of Exception*, Cheltenham: Edward Elgar Publishing, 2014

Frankenberg, G. (2018), *Comparative Constitutional Studies – Between Magic and Deceit*, Cheltenham: Edward Elgar Publishing

Fraser, A. (2005), 'Architecture of a broken dream: The CIA and Guatemala, 1952–54', in: 20 *Intelligence and National Security*, 486 ff

Frederickson, G.M. (1981), *White Supremacy: A Comparative Study in American and South African History*, Oxford: Oxford University Press

Frei, N. (2007), *Der Führerstaat. Nationalsozialistische Herrschaft 1933–1945. 8. Auflage*, Munich: Deutscher Taschenbuch-Verlag

Frei, N. *et al* (2019), *Zur rechten Zeit. Wider die Rückkehr des Nationalismus*, Berlin: Ullstein

Freud, S. (1922), *Group Psychology and Ego Analysis*, London/Vienna: International Psychoanalytic Press.

Friedrich, D. (2016), *Salazars Estado Novo. Vom Leben und Überleben eines autoritären Regimes 1930–1974*, Bonn: Minifanal

Fuchs, C. (2018), *Digital Demagogue: Authoritarian Capitalism in the Age of Trump and Twitter*, London: Pluto

Gargarella, R. (2013), *Latin American Constitutionalism 1810–2010. The Engine Room of the Constitution*, Oxford: Oxford University Press

Gargarella, R. (2018), 'Latin America: Constitutions in Trouble', in: Graber, M.A. *et al*, *Constitutional Democracy in Crisis?*, Oxford: Oxford University Press, 177 ff

Gauchet, M. (2010), *L'avènement de la démocratie*, vol iii: *À l'épreuve des totalitarismes, 1914–1974*, Paris: Gallimard

Gauchet, M. (1990), '*Pacification démocratique, desertion civique*', in: 60 *Le débat*, 87ff.

Geddes, B. (1999), 'What Do We Know About Democratization After Twenty Years', in: 2 *Annual Review of Political Science*, 115 ff

Geertz, C. (1983), 'Local Knowledge: Fact and Law in Comparative Perspective', in: (*id*), *Local Knowledge. Further Essays in Interpretive Anthropology*, New York: Basic Books, 167 ff

Germani, G. (1978), *Authoritarianism, Fascism, and National Populism*, New Brunswick: Transaction Books

Gill, S. (1985), 'European Governance and New Constitutionalism: Economic and Monetary Union and Alternatives to Disciplinary Neoliberalism in Europe', 1 *New Political Economy*, 5 ff

Ginsborg, P. (2005), *Silvio Berlusconi: Television, Power and Patrimony*, London: Verso Books

Ginsburg, T. and Simpser, A. (eds) (2013), *Constitutions in Authoritarian Regimes*, Cambridge: Cambridge University Press

Ginsburg, T., Huq, A.H. and Versteeg, M. (2018), 'The Coming Demise of Liberal Constitutionalism?', in: 85 *The University of Chicago Law Review*, 239 ff

Gliech, O. (2010), *Der Sklavenaufstand von Saint-Domingue und die Französische Revolution (1789–1795)*, Cologne: Böhlau

Görgens, M. (2017), Die Präsidentialismus-Falle, Saarbrücken: AV Akademikerverlag

Gonzalez-Jácome, J. (2019), 'Authoritarianism and the Narrative Power of Constitutionalism in Venezuela', in: Alviar and Frankenberg, *Authoritarian Constitutionalism*, 136 ff

Gooyer, S. *et al* (2018), *Vom Recht, Rechte zu haben*, Hamburg: Hamburger Edition

Gordon, P.E. (2016), 'The Authoritarian Personality Revisited: Reading Adorno in the Age of Trump', in: *boundary*, 15 June

Gotanda, N. (1991), 'A Critique of "Our Constitution is Color-Blind"', in: 44 *Stanford Law Review*, 1 ff

Graber, M.A., Levinson, S. and Tushnet, T. (eds) (2018), *Constitutional Democracy in Crisis?*, Oxford: Oxford University Press

Graciel, C. and Laurent, E. (2012), *Le Roi Prédateur*, Paris: Seuil

Greenberg, D. *et al* (eds) (1993), *Constitutionalism and Democracy, Transitions in the Contemporary World*, New York: Oxford University Press

Grimm, D. (2016), *Constitutionalism – Past, Present and Future*, Oxford: Oxford University Press

Gross, O. (2003), 'Chaos and Rules: Should Responses to Violent Crises Always be Constitutional?', in: 112 *Yale Law Journal*, 1014 ff

Goodin, R.E. (2008), *Innovating Democracy. Democratic Theory and Practice after the Deliberative Turn*, Oxford: Oxford University Press

Gulick, A. (2008), 'We Are Not the People: the 1805 Haitian Constitution's Challenge to Political Legibility in the Age of Revolution', in: 78 *American Literature*, 802 ff

Habermas, J. (1992), 'Drei normative Modelle der Demokratie: Zum Begriff der deliberativen Demokratie', in: Münkler, H. (ed), *Die Chancen der Freiheit: Grundprobleme der Demokratie,* Munich/Zürich, 11ff.

Habermas, J. (1994), 'Hannah Arendt's Communication Concept of Power', in: Hinchman and Hinchman (eds), *Hannah Arendt. Critical Essays*, New York: SUNY Press

Habermas, J. (1996), *Between Facts and Norms*, Cambridge: MIT Press

Habermas, J. (1998), *The Inclusion of the Other: Studies in Political Theory*, Cambridge: MIT Press

Habermas, J. (2011), 'Wie demokratisch ist die europäische Union?', in: 8 *Blätter für deutsche und internationale Politik*, 37 ff

Hall, S. (1979), 'The Great Moving Right Show', in: *Marxism Today*, 14 ff

Hall, S. (2017), *The Fateful Triangle: Race Ethnicity Nation*, Cambridge: Harvard University Press

Hambückers, M. (2006), *Arrivederci Berlusconi. Medienpolitische Verflechtungen in Italien seit 1945*, Konstanz: UVK-Verlag

Hamilton, A., Madison, J. and Jay, J. (2009). *The Federalist Papers* [1787/88], London: Palgrave Macmillan

Harrington, J. (1992), *The Commonwealth of Oceana and A System of Politics* [1656], Pocock, J.G.A. (ed) Cambridge: Cambridge University Press

Harvey, D. (2006), *The Limits to Capital*, London: Verso;

Heidenreich, F. and Schaal, G.S. (eds) (2012), *Politische Theorie und Emotionen*, Baden-Baden, Nomos

Heitmeyer, W. (2018), *Autoritäre Versuchungen*, Berlin: Suhrkamp

Hellfeld, Matthias von, *Das lange 19. Jahrhundert – Zwischen Revolution und Krieg 1776–1914*, Berlin: Dietz, 2015

Hendricks, V.F. and Vestergaard, M. '*Verlorene Wirklichkeit? An der Schwelle zur postfaktischen Demokratie*', in: 67 *Aus Politik und Zeitgeschichte* (2017), 4 ff

Hill, C. and Menzel, J. (ed), *Constitutionalism in Southeast Asia*, Singapore: Konrad-Adenauer-Stiftung, 2008

Hillebrand, E. (ed) (2015), *Rechtspopulismus in Europa: Gefahr für die Demokratie?* Bonn: Dietz

Hirschman, A.O. (2015), *The Passions and the Interests*, Princeton: Princeton University Press

Hobbes, T. (1958), *Leviathan* [1651], Indianapolis/New York: Bobbs-Merrill

Hobbes, T. (2008), *The Elements of Law, Natural and Politic* [1640], Oxford: Oxford University Press,

Hofstetter, Y. (2016), *Das Ende der Demokratie*, Munich: Bertelsmann Verlag

Holliday, I. *et al* (2015), 'Institution Building in Myanmar: The Establishment of Regional and State Assemblies', 55 *Asian Survey*, 641 ff

Holmes, S. (2012), 'Constitutions and Constitutionalism', in: Rosenfeld, M. and Sajó, A. (eds), *The Oxford Handbook of Comparative Constitutional Law*, Oxford: Oxford University Press, 198 ff

Horcicka, F. (2015), *Das schmutzige Geld der Diktatoren*, Vienna: Knemayr & Scheriau, 2015

Horn, E. (2013), *The Secret War: Treason, Espionage and Modern Fiction*, Evanston: Northwestern University Press

Howind, S. (2011), 'Der faschistische Einheitstrick. Die Suggestion von Einheit und Gleichheit in der nationalsozialistischen "Volksgemeinschaft"', in: Markus Brunner *et al* (eds), *Volksgemeinschaft, Täterschaft und Antisemitismus*, Gießen: Psychosozial-Verlag, 111 ff

Huq, A.Z. and Ginsburg, T. (2018), 'How to Lose a Constitutional Democracy', 65 *UCLA Law Review*, 13 ff

Hunter, W. and Power, T.J. (2019), 'Bolsonaro and Brazil's Illiberal Backlash', in: 30 *Journal of Democracy*, 68 ff

International Crisis Group Working to Prevent Conflict Worldwide (2011), 'Popular Protest in North Africa and the Middle East (VII): The Syrian Regime's Slow-Motion Suicide', *Middle East/North Africa Report*, No 109, 13 July

Isiksel, T. (2013), 'Between Text and Context: Turkey's Tradition of Authoritarian Constitutionalism', in: 11 *International Journal of Constitutional Law*, 702 ff

Jackson, V.C. and Tushnet, M. (2014), *Comparative Constitutional Law*, 3rd ed, New York: Foundation Press

James, C.L.R. (1938), *The Black Jacobins: Toussaint L'Ouverture and the San Domingo Revolution*, London: Secker & Warburg Ltd.

James, D. (1988), *Resistance and Integration: Peronism and the Argentine Working Class, 1946–1979*, New York/Cambridge: Cambridge University Press

Keane, J. (2009), *The Life and Death of Democracy*, New York: Simon & Schuster

Kelsen, H. (2005), *General Theory of Law and State*, Piscataway Township: Transaction Publishers

Kennedy, D. (2006), *Of War and Law*, Princeton: Princeton University Press

Kennedy, D. (2016), *A World of Struggle – How Power, Law, and Expertise Shape Global Political Economy*, Princeton: Princeton University Press
Kennedy, D. (2001), 'Legal Formalism', in: Neil Smelser & Paul Baltes eds, 13 *Encyclopedia of the Social Sciences*, Amsterdam: Elsevier, Sp. 8634-5
Kennedy, D. (2017), 'A Left of Liberal Interpretation of Trump's "Big" Win, Part One 1', in: *Nevada Law Journal Forum*, 98 ff
Kennedy, D. (2019), 'Authoritarian Constitutionalism in Liberal Democracy', in: Alviar and Frankenberg, *Authoritarian Constitutionalism*, Cheltenham: Edward Elgar Publishing, 161 ff
Kibet, E. and Fombad, C. (2017), 'Transformative Constitutionalism and the Adjudication of Constitutional Rights in Africa', *17 African Human Rights Journal*, 340 ff
Kiernan, B. (2002), *The Pol Pot Regime. Race, Power and Genocide in Cambodia under the Khmer Rouge, 1975–79*, 2nd ed, New Haven: Yale University Press
King, S.J. (2009), *The New Authoritarianism in the Middle East and North Africa*, Bloomington: Indiana University Press
Kirchheimer, O. (1972), '*Die Rechtsordnung des Nationalsozialismus*', in: ders, *Funktionen des Staats und der Verfassung. 10 Analysen*, Frankfurt am Main: Suhrkamp, 115 ff
Klarman, M.J. (2016), *The Framers' Coup: The Making if the United States Constitution*, Oxford: Oxford University Press
Klug, H. (2016), 'Towards a Sociology of Constitutional Transformation: Understanding South Africa's Post-Apartheid Constitutional Order', *University of Wisconsin Legal Studies Research Paper* No 1373 (8 February)
Köllner, P. (2008), 'Autoritäre Regime – Ein Überblick über die jüngere Literatur', in: 2 *Zeitschrift für Vergleichende Politikwissenschaft*, 351 ff
Kojève, A. (2014), *The Notion of Authority. A Brief Presentation*, Verso
Konitzer, W. and Palme, D. (eds) (2016), *'Arbeit', 'Volk', 'Gemeinschaft': Ethik und Ethiken im Nationalsozialismus*, Frankfurt am Main: Campus
Klare, K. (1998), 'Legal culture and transformative constitutionalism', 14 *South African Journal on Human Rights*, 146ff.
Klug, H. (2000), *Constituting Democracy: Law, Globalism and South Africa's Political Reconstruction,* Cambridge: Cambridge University Press
Laclau, E. (1977), *Politics and Ideology in Marxist Theory: Capitalism, Fascism, Populism*, London: NLB/Atlantic Highlands Humanities Press
Law, D.S. and Versteeg, M. (2013), 'Sham Constitutions', 101 *California Law Review*, 863 ff
Lefort, C. (1986), *The Political Forms of Modern Society: Bureaucracy, Democracy and Totalitarianism*, Cambridge MA: MIT Press
Lefort, C. (1986), *Essais sur le politique*, Paris: Seuil
Lefort, C. (2007), 'The Concept of Totalitarianism' [1988], in: *Papers in Social Theory*, Coventry: Warwick Social Theory Centre, 22 ff
Lemke, T. (2019), *Critique of Political Reason. Foucault's Analysis of Modern Governmentality*, London: Verso
Lemke, M. (ed) (2017), *Ausnahmezustand – Theoriegeschichte, Anwendungen, Perspektiven*, Wiesbaden: Springer VS
Lemke, M. (2017), *Demokratie im Ausnahmezustand: Wie Regierungen ihre Macht ausweiten*, Frankfurt am Main: Campus
Lendvai, P. (2016), *Orbáns Ungarn*, Vienna: Kremayr & Scheriau

Levitsky, S. and Way, L.A. (2010), *Competitive Authoritarianism – Hybrid Regimes After the Cold War*, Cambridge: Cambridge University Press

Levitsky, S. and Ziblatt, D. (2018), *How Democracies Die*, New York: Broadway Books

Librett, J. (2017), 'Sovereignty and the Cult of Immediacy', in: IX *Konturen*, 1 ff

Lindsay, J.R. (2013), *The Concealment of the State*, London: Bloomsbury

Linz, J.J. and Stepan, A. (1996), *Problems of Democratic Transition and Consolidation. Southern Europe, South America, and Post-Communist Europe*, Baltimore: Johns Hopkins University Press

Linz, J.J. (1994), *The Failure of Presidential Democracy*, Baltimore: The Johns Hopkins University Press

Linz, J.J. (2000), *Totalitarian and Authoritarian Regimes*, Boulder CO: Lynne Rienner

Locke, J. (1988), *Two Treatises of Government* [1689], Laslett, P. (ed), Cambridge: Cambridge University Press

Loewenstein, K. (1937), 'Militant Democracy and Fundamental Rights', 31 *American Political Science Review*, 417 ff and 638 ff

Lofgren, M. (2016), *The Deep State: The Fall of the Constitution and the Rise of a Shadow Government*, London: Penguin

López, E. (2009), *El primer Perón. El militar antes que el politico*, Buenos Aires: Capital Intelectual

Loughlin, M. (2010), *Foundations of Public Law*, Oxford: Oxford University Press

Luce, E. (2017), *The Retreat of Western Liberalism*, New York: Abacus

Lukács, Georg, *Die Zerstörung der Vernunft: Der Weg des Irrationalismus von Schelling zu Hitler*, Berlin: Aufbau-Verlag 1955

Machiavelli, N. (2019), *Der Fürst* [1513], Rudolph, E. (ed), Hamburg: Felix Meiner

Machiavelli, N. (1999), *The Prince*, London: Penguin

MacKinnon, R. (2011), 'China's Networked Authoritarianism', in: 22 *Journal of Democracy*, 32 ff

MacPherson, C.B. (2011), *The Political Theory of Possessive Individualism – Hobbes to Locke*, Oxford: Oxford University Press

Maistre, J. de (1797), *Considérations sur la France,* London: Bâle

Maistre, J. de (1992), *De la souveraineté du peuple: Un anti-contrat social, Étude sur la souveraineté* [1794], Paris: Presses Universitaires de France

Mamdani, M. (1996), *Citizen and Subject: Contemporary Africa and the Legacy of Late Colonialism*, Princeton: Princeton University Press

Mannheim, K. (1943), *Diagnosis of Our Time. Wartime Essays of a Sociologist*, London: Paul, Trench, Trubner & Co

Mansfield, H.C. (1993), *Taming the Prince: The Ambivalence of Modern Executive Power*, Baltimore: Johns Hopkins University Press

Manow, P. (2010), *In the King's Shadow*, Cambridge: Polity Press

Manow, P. (2018), *The Political Economy of Populism*, Cambridge: Polity Press

Marcuse, H. (1936), 'Theoretische Entwürfe über Autorität und Familie. Ideengeschichtlicher Teil', in: Horkheimer, M. *et al*, *Studien über Autorität und Familie*, Paris: zu Klampen, 137 ff

Marcuse, H. (1968), 'The Struggle Against Liberalism in the Totalitarian View of the State', in: *id*, *Negations: Essays in Critical Theory*, Boston: Beacon Press, 3 ff

Marek, K. (2009), *Die Körper des Königs. Effigies, Bildpolitik und Heiligkeit*, Paderborn: Fink Verlag

Marshall, T.H. (1950), *Citizenship and Social Class and Other Essays*, Cambridge: Cambridge University Press

Martin, B. K. (2004), *Under the Loving Care of the Fatherly Leader. North Korea and the Kim Dynasty*, New York: Thomas Dunne Books

Marx, K. (1983), 'The Eighteenth Brumaire of Louis Bonaparte', in: Marx, K. and Engels, F., *Collected Works,* vol. 39, 1852–1855, New York: International Publishers

Marx, K. (1975), 'On the Jewish Question', in: Marx, K. and Engels, F., *Collected Works*, Vol 3, London: Lawrence & Wishart, 146 ff

Mayer, K.R. (2002), *With the Stroke of a Pen: Executive Orders and Presidential Power*, Princeton: Princeton University Press

Mbembe, A. (2003), 'Necropolis', in: 15 *Public Culture*, 11 ff

McIlwain, C.H. (1947), *Constitutionalism: Ancient and Modern*, Ithaca: Cornell University Press

Mehta, H.C. and Mehta, J.B. (1999), *Hun Sen: Strongman of Cambodia*. Singapore: Graham Brash Pte Ltd.

Mérieau, E. (2016), 'Thailand's Deep State, Royal Power, and the Constitutional Court (1997–2015)', in: 46 *Journal of Contemporary Asia*, 445 ff

Mérieau, E. (2019), 'French Authoritarian Constitutionalism and its Legacy', in Alviar and Frankenberg, *Authoritarian Constitutionalism*, 185 ff

Michaels, W. (2005), *No Greater Threat: America since September 11 and the Rise of the National Security State*, New York: Algora Publishing

Moffitt, B. (2016), *The Global Rise of Populism: Performance, Political Style, and Representation*, Stanford: Stanford University Press

Mohsin Hashim, S. (2005), 'Putin's *Etatization* project and limits to democratic reforms in Russia', in: 38 *Communist and Post-Communist Studies*, 25 ff

Mommsen, M. and Nußberger, A. (2007), *Das System Putin. Gelenkte Demokratie und politische Justiz in Rußland*, Munich: C.H. Beck

Mommsen, M. (2007), 'Putins "gelenkte Demokratie": ‚Vertikale der Macht' statt Gewaltenteilung' in: Buhbe, M. and Gorzka, G. (eds) (2007), *Russland heute – Rezentralisierung des Staates unter Putin*, Wiesbaden: VS Springer, 235 ff

Montecinos, V. and Markoff, J. (2009), *Economists in the Americas*, Cheltenham: Edward Elgar Publishing

Morsey, R. (ed) (1976), *Das "Ermächtigungsgesetz" vom 24. März 1933*. Reihe: Historische Texte: Neuzeit, Göttingen: Vandenhoeck & Ruprecht

Mounk, Y. (2018), *Der Zerfall der Demokratie*, Munich: Droemer, 2018

Mudde, C. (2007), 'The Populist Zeitgeist', 39 *Government and Opposition*, 541 ff

Mudde, C. (2007), *Populist Radical Right Parties in Europe*, Cambridge: Cambridge University Press

Müller, J.W. (2014), *On Conceptual History. Rethinking Modern European Intellectual History*, Oxford: Oxford University Press

Müller, J.W. (2014), 'The EU as a Militant Democracy, or: Are There Limits to Constitutional Mutations within EU Member States?', in: 165 *Revista de Estudios Políticos (nueva época)*, 141 ff

Müller, J.W. (2017), *What is Populism?*, London: Penguin

Münkler, H. (1984), *Machiavelli. Die Begründung des politischen Denkens der Neuzeit aus der Krise der Republik Florenz*, Frankfurt am Main: Fischer

Mughan, A. and Gunther, R. (2000), 'The Media in Democratic and Nondemocratic Regimes: A Multilevel Perspective', in: *dies.* (eds), *Democracy and the Media. A Comparative Perspective*, Cambridge: Cambridge University Press, 1 ff

Negretto, G.L. and Rivera, J.A. (2000), 'Liberalism and Emergency Powers in Latin America: Reflections on Carl Schmitt and the Theory of Constitutional Dictatorship', in: 21 *Cardozo Law Review*, 1797 ff

Nesbitt, N. (2008), *Universal Emancipation: The Haitian Revolution and Radical Enlightenment*, Charlottesville: University of Virginia Press
Neumann, F. (2009), *Behemoth. The Structure and Practice of National Socialism 1933–1944*, Lanham: Ivan R. Dee, Inc.
Niembro Ortega, R. (2016), 'Conceptualizing authoritarian constitutionalism', in: 49 *Verfassung und Recht in Übersee*, 339 ff
Newton, S. (2017), *The Constitutional Systems of the Independent Central Asian States. A Contextual Analysis*, Oxford: Bloomsbury
Nisbet, R. (1953), 'Ideology and Terror: A Novel Form of Government', in: 15 *The Review of Politics*, 303 ff
Noyer, A. (1966), *La sûreté de l'État (1789–1965)*, Paris: IGDJ
O'Donnell, G.A. (1979), *Modernization and Bureaucratic Authoritarianism: Studies in South American Politics*, Berkeley: University of California Press
O'Donnell, G.A. (1994), 'Delegative Democracy', 5 *Journal of Democracy*, 55 ff
O'Donnell, G.A. (2007), 'The Perpetual Crisis of Democracy', in: 18 *Journal of Democracy*, 5 ff
Oberndörfer, L. (2012), '*Vom neuen zum autoritären Konstitutionalismus*', 2 *Kurswechsel*, 62 ff
Offe, C. (1996), 'Moderne "Barbarei": Der Naturzustand im Kleinformat', in: Miller, M. and Soeffner, H.G. (eds), *Modernität und Barbarei. Soziologische Zeitdiagnose am Ende des 20. Jahrhunderts*, Frankfurt: Campus, 258 ff
Okoth-Ogendo, H. (1993), 'Constitutions without constitutionalism: an African political paradox', in: Greenberg, D. *et al* (eds), *Constitutionalism and Democracy: Transitions in the Contemporary World*, New York: Oxford University Press, 65 ff
Orwell, G. (2007), *1984*, Berlin: Ullstein
Osterhammel, J. (1995), *Kolonialismus: Geschichte, Formen, Folgen*, Munich: Beck
Page, J. (1983), *Peron. A Biography*, New York: Random House
Paine, T. (1953), *The Rights of Man* [1791–1792], New York: Liberal Arts Press
Paretti, G. (2017), 'Arendt on Power and Violence', in: Baehr, P. and Walsh, P. (eds), *The Anthem Companion to Hannah Arendt*, London: Anthem Press
Pasquino, P. (2004), 'The Law of the Exception: A Typology of Emergency Powers', 2 *International Journal of Constitutional Law*, 210 ff
Pateman, C. (1988), *The Sexual Contract*, Stanford: Stanford University Press
Paxton, R. (2005), *The Anatomy of Fascism*, New York: Vintage
Pech, L. and Scheppele, K.L. (2017), 'Illiberalism Within: Rule of Law Backsliding in the EU', 19 *Cambridge Yearbook of European Legal Studies*, 3 ff
Pereira, Anthony W., *Political (In)Justice: Authoritarianism and the Rule of Law in Brazil, Chile and Argentina*, Pittsburg: University of Pittsburg Press, 2005
Perlmutter, A. (1981), *Modern Authoritarianism: A Comparative Institutional Analysis*, New Haven: Yale University Press
Pichl, M. (2019), 'The Constitution of False Prophecies: The Illiberal Transformation of Hungary', in: Alviar and Frankenberg, *Authoritarian Constitutionalism*, 240 ff
Pildes, R.H. (2003), 'The Inherent Authoritarianism in Democratic Regimes', in: Sajó, A. (ed), *Out of and Into Authoritarian Law*, New York: Kluwer Law International, 125 ff
Plumelle-Uribe, R.A. (2004), *Weiße Barbarei. Vom Kolonialrassismus zur Rassenpolitik der Nazis*, Zürich: Rotpunktverlag
Politkovskaja, A. (2005), *In Putins Russland*, Cologne: DuMont
Popham, P. (2016), *The Lady and the Generals: Aung San Suu Kyi and Burma's Struggle for Freedom*, London: Penguin Books

Prembeh, H.K. (2008), 'Progress and Retreat in Africa: Presidents Untamed', 19 *Journal of Democracy*, 109 ff
Preuß, U.K. (1974), *Legalität und Pluralismus*, Frankfurt am Main: Suhrkamp
Preuß, U.K. (1990), *Revolution, Fortschritt und Verfassung*, Berlin: Wagenbach
Priester, K. (2011), 'Definitionen und Typologie des Populismus', in: 62 *Soziale Welt*, 185 ff
Priester, K. (2012), *Rechter und linker Populismus: Annäherung an ein Chamäleon*, Frankfurt am Main: Campus Verlag
Puschke, J. and Singelnstein, T. (eds) (2018), *Der Staat und die Sicherheitsgesellschaft*, Wiesbaden: Springer VS
Quent, M. (2017), 'Studien und Interventionen zu PEGIDA, AfD und der "Neuen Rechten"', in: *Soziologische Revue*, 525 ff
Rabin-Havt, A. and Media Matters for America (2016), *Lies, Incorporated: The World of Post-Truth Politics*, New York: Anchor
Ramraj, V.V. (ed) (2008), *Emergencies and the Limits of Legality*, Cambridge: Cambridge University Press
Rancière, J. (1977), 'Demokratie und Postdemokratie', in: Badou, A. *et al* (eds), *Politik der Wahrheit*, Vienna: Turia + Kant, 94 ff
Rancière, J. (2009), *Hatred of Democracy*, London: Verso
Rancière, J. (2011), *The Emancipated Spectator*, London: Verso
Raz, J. (2009), *Between Authority and Interpretation. On the Theory of Law and Practical Reason*, Oxford: Oxford University Press
Richter, E. (2006), 'Das Analysemuster der "Postdemokratie"', 19 *Forschungsjournal Neue Soziale Bewegungen*, 4 ff
Roberts, A. *et al* (eds) (2016), *Resistance in the Arab Spring: Triumphs and Disasters*, Oxford: Oxford University Press
Rod, E.G. and Weidmann, N.B. (2015), 'Empowering activists or autocrats? The Internet in authoritarian regimes', in: 52 *Journal of Peace Research*, 338 ff
Rödel, U., Frankenberg, G. and Dubiel, H. (1989), *Die demokratische Frage*, Frankfurt am Main: Suhrkamp
Rossiter, C. (1948), *Constitutional Dictatorship: Crisis Government in Modern Democracies,* Princeton: Princeton University Press
Rudolph, E. (2017), *Wege der Macht. Philosophische Machttheorien von den Griechen bis heute*, Weilerswist: Velbrück
Rutherford, B.K. (2013), *Egypt after Mubarak: Liberalism, Islam, and Democracy in the Arab World*, Princeton: Princeton University Press
Sajó, A. (1999), *Limiting Government: An Introduction to Constitutionalism*, Budapest: Central European University Press
Sajó, A. (ed) (2004), *Militant Democracy*, Utrecht: Eleven International Publishing
Sakwa, R. (2009), *Power and Policy in Putin's Russia*, New York: Routledge
Santer, Eric L. (2011), *The Royal Remains; The King's Two Bodies and the endgame of Sovereignty*, Chicago: Chicago University Press
Sartori, G. (1962), 'Constitutionalism: A Preliminary Discussion', 56 *American Political Science Review*, 853 ff
Sartori, G. *Il Sultanato*, Rome: Laterza, 2009
Scheppele, K.L. (2013), 'The Rule of Law and the Frankenstate: Why Governance Checklists Do Not Work', in: 2 *International Journal of Policy Administration and Institutions*, 559 ff
Scheppele, K.L. (2018), 'Autocratic Legalism', in: 85 *The University of Chicago Law Review*, 545 ff

Schmitt, C. (1996), *The Concept of the Political*, Chicago: University of Chicago Press
Schmitt, C. (2005), *Political Theology. Four Chapters on the Concept of Sovereignty* [1922], Chicago: University of Chicago Press
Schulz, D. (2018), 'Verfassungsbilder: Text und Körper in der Ikonographie des Verfassungsstaates', in: 46 *Leviathan*, 71 ff
Schyga, P. (2015), *Über die Volksgemeinschaft der Deutschen. Begriff und historische Wirklichkeit jenseits historiografischer Gegenwartsmoden*, Baden-Baden: Nomos
Sennett, R. (1977), *The Fall of Public Man*, New York: A. Knopf
Sennett, R. (1982), *Authority*, New York: A. Knopf
Séville, A. (2017), *'There is no Alternative' – Politik zwischen Demokratie und Sachzwang*, Frankfurt/New York: Campus
Skinner, Q. (2009), *Hobbes and Republican Liberty*, Cambridge: Cambridge University Press
Slater, D. (2010), *Ordering Power: Contentious Politics and Authoritarian Leviathans in Southeast Asia*, New York: Cambridge University Press
Smith, M. (1991), *Burma. Insurgency and the Politics of Ethnicity*, Ann Arbor: University of Michigan Press
Snyder, T. (2018), *The Road to Unfreedom*, New York: Random House
Somek, A. (2003), 'Authoritarian Constitutionalism: Austrian Constitutional Doctrine 1933 to 1938 and Its Legacy', in: Joerges, C. and Singh Ghaleigh, N. (eds), *Darker Legacies of Law in Europe: The Shadow of National Socialism and Fascism over Europe and its Legal Traditions*, Oxford: Hart Publishing, 361 ff
Southall, A.W. (1970), 'The Illusion of Tribe', in: Peter Gutkind (ed), *The Passing of Tribal Man*, Leiden: Brill, 28 ff
Stanley, J. (2017), *How Propaganda Works*, Princeton: Princeton University Press
Stanley, J. (2018), *How Fascism Works. The Politics of Us and Them*, New York: Random House.
Stern, P. J. (2011), *The Company-State: Corporate Sovereignty and the Early Modern Foundations of the British Empire in India*, Oxford: Oxford University Press
Stockmann, D. and Gallagher, M.E. (2011), 'Remote Control: How the Media Sustain Authoritarian Rule in China', 44 *Comparative Political Studies*, 436 ff
Spaulding, N. (2019), 'States of Authoritarianism in Liberal Democratic Regimes', in: Alviar and Frankenberg, *Authoritarian Constitutionalism,* 265 ff
Strenge, I. (2013), 'Das Ermächtigungsgesetz vom 24. März 1933', in: 7 *Journal der Juristischen Zeitgeschichte*, 1 ff
Strittmatter, K. (2018), *Die Neuerfindung der Diktatur – Wie China den digitalen Überwachungsstaat aufbaut und uns damit herausfordert*, Munich: Piper
Sultany, N. (2017), *Law and Revolution: Legitimacy and Constitutionalism After the Arab Spring*, Oxford: Oxford University Press
Sultany, N. (2019), 'Arab constitutionalism and the formalism of authoritarian constitutionalism', in Alviar and Frankenberg, *Authoritarian Constutionalism*, 292 ff
Taylor, B.D. (2011), *State Building in Putin's Russia. Policing and Coercion after Communism*, Cambridge: Cambridge University Press
Thio, L.A. (2012), 'Constitutionalism in Illiberal Polities', in: Rosenfeld, M. and Sajó, A. (eds), *Oxford Handbook of Comparative Constitutional Law*, Oxford: Oxford University Press, 134 ff
Thompson, M.R. (2004), 'Pacific Asia After "Asian Values": Authoritarianism, Democracy, and "Good Governance"', in: 25 *Third World Quarterly*, 1079 ff
Tocqueville, A. de (2010), *Le despotisme démocratique*, Paris: L'Herne

Tronconi, F. (ed) (2015), *Beppe Grillo's Five Star Movement. Organisation, Communication and Ideology*, Farnham: Ashgate Publishing

Trouillot, M.R. (1995), *Silencing the Past: Power and the Production of History*, Boston: Beacon Press

Tully, James (1980), *A Discourse on Property, Locke and his Adversaries*, Cambridge: Cambridge University Press

Tully, John A. (2005), *A Short History of Cambodia. From Empire to Survival*, London: Allen & Unwin

Tushnet, M. (2015), 'Authoritarian Constitutionalism', in: 100 *Cornell Law Review*, 391 ff

Uitz, R. (2015), 'Can you tell when an illiberal democracy is in the making?' in: 13 *I.CON*, 279 ff

Valdés, J.G. (1995), *Pinochet's Economics. The Chicago School in Chile*, Cambridge: Cambridge University Press

Vehrkamp, R. and Merkel, W. (2018), *Populismus-Barometer. Populistische Einstellungen bei Wählern und Nichtwählern in Deutschland 2018*, Gütersloh: Bertelsmann-Stiftung

Ventura, L. (2017), 'The "Arab Spring" and Orientalist Stereotypes: The Role of Orientalism in the Narration of the Revolts in the Arab World', in: 19 *Journal of Postcolonial Studies*, 282 ff

Vetter, R. (2017), *Nationalismus im Osten Europas. Was Kaczynski und Orbán mit Le Pen und Wilders verbindet*, Berlin: Ch. Link

Ville, J. de (2008), 'Sovereignty without Sovereignty: Derrida's Declarations of Independence', in: 19 *Law and Critique*, 87 ff

Vismann, C. (2011), *Medien der Rechtsprechung, hrsg. v A. Kemmerer and M. Krajewski*, Frankfurt am Main: S. Fischer

Volkmann, U. (2018), *Rechtsphilosophie*, Munich: Beck

Vorländer, H. (1999), *Die Verfassung. Idee und Geschichte*, München: C.H. Beck 1999

Vorländer, H. (2010), *Demokratie: Geschichte, Formen, Formen, Theorien*, 2nd ed., München: C.H. Beck

Vorländer, H. (2011), 'The Good, the Bad and the Ugly', in: 8 *Totalitarianism and Democracy. An International Journal for the Study of Dictatorship and Liberty*, 187 ff

Vorländer, H. (2013), '*Krise, Kritik und Szenarien: Zur Lage der Demokratie*', in: 23 *Zeitschrift für Politikwissenschaft*, 267 ff

Vorländer, H. *et al* (2016), *Pegida. Entwicklungen, Zusammensetzung und Deutung einer Empörungsbewegung*, Wiesbaden: Springer

Wagrandl, U. (2018), 'Transnational militant democracy', in: 7 *Global Constitutionalism*, 143 ff

Waldmann, P. (2003), *Der Peronismus 1943–1955*, Hamburg: Hoffmann & Campe, 1974

Waldmann, P. (2003) *Terrorismus und Bürgerkrieg. Der Staat in Bedrängnis*, München: Gerling Akademie Verlag

Weber, Max (1978), *Economy and Society*, Berkeley: University of California Press

Wilkinson, M. (2013), 'The Spectre of Authoritarian Liberalism: Reflections on the Constitutional Crisis of the European Union', 14 *German Law Journal*, 527 ff

Wilkinson, M. (2019), 'Authoritarian liberalism and authoritarian constitutionalism', in Alviar Garcia and Frankenberg, *Authoritarian Constitutionalism*, 317 ff

Wirth, H.J. (2011), *Narzissmus und Macht*, 4th ed, Stuttgart: Thieme-Verlag

Weiß, V. (2017), *Der autoritäre Aufbruch. Die Neue Rechte und der Untergang des Abendlandes*, Stuttgart: Klett-Cotta

Wiedemann, G. *et al* (2013), 'Postdemokratie und Neoliberalismus', in: 4 *Zeitschrift für Politische Theorie*, 80 ff

Wildt, M. (2017), *Volk, Volksgemeinschaft, AfD,* Hamburg: Hamburger Edition

Wodak, R., Khosravinik, M. and Mral, B. (2013), *Right-Wing Populism in Europe – Politics and Discourse*, London: Bloomsbury

Wohlin, S. (2017), *Democracy Incorporated: Managed Democracy and the Specter of Inverted Totalitarianism*, Princeton: Princeton University Press

Yassin-Kassab, R. (2016), *Burning Country: Syrians in Revolution and War*, London: Pluto Press

Yazbek, S. (2016), *The Crossing: My Journey to the Shattered Heart of Syria*, London: Ebury Press, 2016

Zakaria, F. (1997), 'The Rise of Illiberal Democracy', in: *Foreign Affairs*, December 1997, 22 ff

Ziemer, G. (2013), *Komplizenschaft – Neue Perspektiven auf Kollektivität*, Bielefeld: transcript Verlag

Zürn, M. (ed) (2018), 'Autoritärer Populismus vs. offene Gesellschaft – eine neue Konfliktlinie?', Heinrich Böll-Foundation, Oktober 2018

Index